W9-BMX-149

Ex Líbris

B212 © APCo

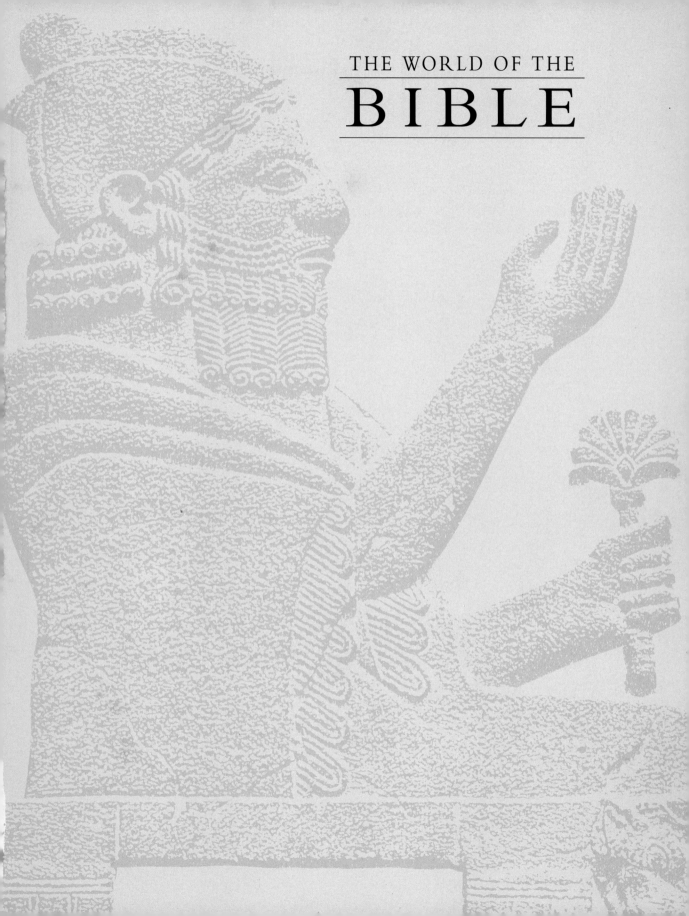

THE WORLD OF THE
BIBLE

ROBERTA L. HARRIS

THE WORLD OF THE

BIBLE

With 294 illustrations, 58 in color

THAMES AND HUDSON

For my parents, Rose and Maurice Harris *and my husband, Jeremy, who have always helped and encouraged me.*

Authors note

I could not have written this book without the support of my husband, Jeremy. My love and thanks go first to him – always. I should also like to acknowledge those friends and colleagues who have read the text of the book, and especially Shimon Gibson, whose advice prevented many errors. Such as are left are all my own. Many friends have allowed me to use their illustrative material, both photographs and drawings, and to them also go my thanks – to Hamam Habib Alwan, Professor Avraham Biran, Peter Bugod, Rupert Chapman, Professor Ehud Netzer, Esther Niv-Krendel, Dino Politis, Professor Avner Raban and Shelley Wachsmann. George Hart and Jonathan Tubb provided useful information. Eliot Braun in Israel gave me much practical advice and last, but not least, those staff at Thames and Hudson who waited so patiently for the book and whose professionalism has been a constant encouragement. They have also made the book a great deal of fun to work on.

Half-title: Bar Rekub of Zinjirli – a detail from his stela, dating to the second half of the 8th century BC, now in the Pergamon Museum, Berlin.
Title page: Fayuum portrait showing a Semitic type, dating to the Ptolemaic period, Egyptian Museum, Cairo.

Any copy of this book issued by the publisher as a paperback is sold subject to the condition that it shall not by way of trade or otherwise be lent, resold, hired out or otherwise circulated without the publisher's prior consent in any form of binding or cover other than that in which it is published and without a similar condition including these words being imposed on a subsequent purchaser.

© 1995 Thames and Hudson Ltd, London

First published in the United States of America in 1995 by Thames and Hudson Inc., 500 Fifth Avenue, New York, New York 10110

Library of Congress Catalog Card Number 94-60285

ISBN 0-500-05073-2

All Rights Reserved. No part of this publication may be reproduced or transmitted in any form or by any means, electronic or mechanical, including photocopy, recording or any other information storage and retrieval system, without prior permission in writing from the publisher.

Printed and bound in Slovenia

CONTENTS

I
THE BIBLE IN CONTEXT

II
IN THE BEGINNING

III
OLD TESTAMENT EMPIRES

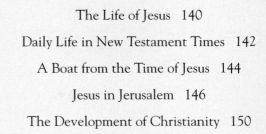

IV
WIDENING HORIZONS

V
THE AGE OF JESUS

VI
THE TURBULENT YEARS

THE BIBLE IN CONTEXT

Unto thy seed will I give this land.
Genesis 12, 7

THE NEAR EAST has always been a region of extraordinary diversity of climate, terrain and cultures. The land of the Bible, tiny in itself and yet in some ways the pivot of the whole vast region, is a microcosm of that diversity. One indication of this is the many names by which the strip of land at the very eastern edge of the Mediterranean is known. To Jews, Christians and Moslems it is the Holy Land; to geographers it is the Levant; to archaeologists, Syro-Palestine; and to modern politicians it comprises the countries of Lebanon and Syria in the north, Israel and Jordan in the south. In ancient times this area was home to both the Israelites and the Canaanites, and, poor though it was, it gave the world two great treasures – the alphabet, and the Bible, which is the origin of and inspiration for three of the world's great religions.

This land has been fought over perhaps more than any other throughout history and possibly even before. In the days of the Bible, as empire succeeded empire, armies marched along the coastal strip, but few of the great kings of Assyria, Babylonia or Egypt thought it worth their while to campaign inland, into the hill country promised to Abraham and his descendants by God. It was never a rich or sophisticated place, and yet it was later conquered, reconquered and conquered again, by Romans, Moslems and Crusaders, to whom every inch of ground was holy. The arrival of European diplomats, missionaries, teachers and doctors in the 19th century marked renewed western interest in the Holy Land, though pilgrims and travellers, some intrepid women among them, had never ceased to visit. Later in the 19th century serious explorers came to map and measure the land scientifically. Then, from all over the world, came the archaeologists. Over the last century archaeology in the Holy Land has developed from a treasure hunt into an exacting and exciting discipline, although, even now, the work has only just begun.

A view of the Judaean Desert from the vicinity of Bethlehem. In the middle distance is Herodium, built by Herod the Great (p. 131). Beyond lies the Dead Sea, with the mountains of Jordan rising steeply on the other side.

GEOGRAPHY AND CLIMATE

Oases such as Jericho or Damascus attracted large numbers of people to settle at them, or to trade or simply to water their animals. Jericho was already a strongly fortified settlement in the late 9th millennium BC (pp. 38–39), when few other places had large populations. In an arid land a reliable water supply is vital and friction between settled farmers and nomadic pastoralists often arose over access (Genesis 21, 25). However, other, more peaceful activities, such as the exchange of news and the arranging of marriages, also took place at oases, wells and springs (Genesis 24, 13–14; 29, 10–11).

O Lord, how manifold are thy works! in wisdom hast thou made them all: the earth is full of thy riches.
Psalms 104, 24

THE AREA KNOWN AS THE NEAR (or Middle) East stretches from the Aegean coast of Asia Minor (that is, Anatolia or Turkey) in the west to the Persian plateau in the southeast, and from the Caucasus mountains and the Taurus/Zagros range in the north and northeast to the very tip of Arabia in the south. Egypt is also included, since that country has always been politically more a part of Asia than of Africa to which it geographically belongs. It is a huge landmass, and yet the areas in which people can live are very restricted. Mountain chains and high plateaux are too cold for human habitation and steppe and sand desert regions are too hot and arid.

People have always congregated in the great river valleys, such as the Tigris and Euphrates in Mesopotamia (this is now inland Syria and Iraq) or the Nile valley in Egypt. They also live along fertile coastal strips, like those of western Turkey, the Levant and southwest Arabia (Yemen), or they settle at oases, such as Damascus, Palmyra, Beersheba or Jericho. Since human beings are endlessly resourceful, at least one of the ancient civilizations of the Near East, the Hittite Empire, arose in the unlikely surroundings of the high steppes of central Anatolia, with its centre at Hattusas (today called Boghazköy). The greatest ancient civilizations of the region, however, arose in the river valleys of Mesopotamia and Egypt and were ultimately dependent on the techniques of irrigation agriculture.

The climate

Summers are hot and dry throughout the whole of the Near East. The coastal areas are a little cooler than the interior but the humidity is consequently greater. At high altitude summers can be pleasant, even a little cool at night, while the deserts daily reach temperatures of over 100 degrees F (38 degrees C). Nights in the desert usually feel chilly by comparison to the days. Winters can be very cold in the mountains or on high plateaux, such as Iran or inland Turkey. Jerusalem, at about 2,400 ft (730 m), may receive snowfall as late as April. Even the deserts of Arabia sometimes

have snow, although it never lasts long. The coasts are not so cold, but are generally more rainy.

Water is easily the most valuable commodity in the region, so rainfall is very important in the places where groundwater resources are scarce. However, the rain is not very predictable from year to year. Wherever it does fall, the ground springs to life and is often thickly carpeted with flowers within days. This means that in the more marginal zones tribal herdsmen must be prepared to migrate frequently. Land which in some years would grow crops for a farmer, in others might only provide scrub grazing for herders. The constant shift in land use has often caused friction between agricultural communities and pastoralists in both ancient and modern times.

The prevailing winds are southwesterly, coming from Africa, and pick up moisture as they cross the Mediterranean. The northern parts of the region have far more rain than the south: about 40 in. (1,000 mm) a year falls in north Lebanon, but only about 5 in. (130 mm) per annum in Gaza. The rain mostly falls on west-facing slopes, while east-facing ones, such as the cliffs above Jericho in the Jordan valley, are in a rain shadow and are consequently arid. Generally, the further east one travels across the region as a whole, the less rain there is.

Rainfall occurs at two seasons. The new year begins in the autumn when the first rains bring fresh life to the parched land after the heat of summer. The gentle 'latter' rains (as they are referred to in the Bible) of late spring arrive in time to help ripen the crops. Winter rains tend to be torrential. For instance, the area around Jerusalem receives about 24 in. (62 cm) of rain per year, roughly the same as, for instance, London. The difference is that whereas in Jerusalem this amount falls on an average of about 50 days and only in winter, in London there can be a steady drizzle all year round.

Such deluges often wash away the surface soil, exposing the bare rock beneath. The problem is worse where the vegetation protecting the soil has been lost through grazing animals (especially goats and sheep) and the felling of trees over the centuries for fuel and building. In the hill country the situation is aggravated by the loss of traditional agricultural terracing. On flat land problems are caused by the use of modern deep-ploughing techniques on soil which is very light and easily blows away if it is not compacted. Today, erosion is a very serious problem for the whole region. Wherever it occurs the water table is lowered and the land rapidly becomes a desert.

The biblical landscape, once fertile and covered with trees, is now, in places, a desolate waste. In Israel, however, a great deal of re-afforestation has been undertaken since the establishment of the new state in 1948. Large areas of pine trees have been created, though in antiquity the hills were blanketed with oak and terebinth. Recently, attempts have been made to recreate the biblical wooded landscape by planting these species, as well as fruit trees, in the Judaean Hills.

The geography of the Levant

The world of the Bible lands centres on the Levant, consisting of Lebanon and Syria in the north, and Israel and Jordan in the south, and, peripherally, the Sinai peninsula. It is a region of extraordinary diversity, both of terrain and climate. Modern Lebanon corresponds to the region called Phoenicia in antiquity, the fertile coastal strip separated from inland Syria by two ranges of mountains and the intervening Bequa'a valley. North of Lebanon the coastal lands of Syria are very productive and support some of the largest Levantine towns of ancient or modern times, such as Antioch, Hama, Aleppo and Homs. Inland Syria is semi-steppe and the only large population centres are at oases such as Damascus or ancient Mari. The southern end of Lebanon is demarcated by a jumble of basalt hills, cutting it off from the hills of upper Galilee. South of Damascus the Golan Heights, the biblical land of Geshur, dominated by the snowy peak of Mt Hermon, overlook the lush plains that lie around the Sea of Galilee.

What's in a name?

The Levant has been known by many names in the course of its history. In the south, the modern state of Israel, occupying much of the land west of the River Jordan, covers most of the territory of the biblical kingdoms of Israel (the northern hill country) and Judah (the southern hills), which was known as Judaea by the Hellenistic era. Most of the hill country is now claimed for a Palestinian Arab state; and Palestine (the word is derived from the Philistines) is perhaps the most enduring name for the whole southern half of the Levant. The coastal strip was not part of the biblical king-

doms but was home to the Canaanites, Philistines and other Sea Peoples.

Several distinct geographical zones run from west to east in the south, the heartland of the Bible. South of Mt Carmel the coastal strip with its sand dunes gives way to the fertile fields of the Sharon valley, with the poorer land of Philistia to the south. East of the latter is the Shephelah, the low southern hills, which produce such good wines. East of the Sharon is the valley of Ayyalon, also very fertile. It rises gently into the Judaean Hills which themselves lead steeply up to Jerusalem. The watershed, at 3,000 ft (915 m), runs along the top of Mt Scopus and the Mt of Olives, just beyond the city. The land then falls away to the east, to the increasingly desert-like conditions of the Judaean Wilderness.

The Jordan valley, which, at around 1,300 ft (395 m) below sea level is the lowest place on the surface of the earth, is an interruption in this terrain. It is bordered on both sides by cliffs which rise steeply to a height of about 3,000 ft (915 m). The valley is part of the great rift system, which runs from eastern Turkey to the East African Rift in Tanzania. Since it is the edge of one of the earth's tectonic plates, it is an area of considerable seismic activity. Transjordan (literally the area beyond the River Jordan) is part of the northern extension of the Arabian steppe. Amman, the capital of the modern kingdom of Jordan, lies on its western edge, on the site of the old Ammonite city, Rabbat Ammon. East of Amman the true desert begins.

Wadis, 'the streams in the dry land' of Psalms 126, 4 are waterless river beds which for most of the year form natural routes for travellers – the 'highways in the desert' of which the prophet spoke (Isaiah 40, 3). Springs just below the surface are marked by lush vegetation, sometimes even a stand of date palms. However, in winter, when rain may be falling many miles distant, torrential floods race down the wadis without warning, sweeping everything away, including the unwary traveller.

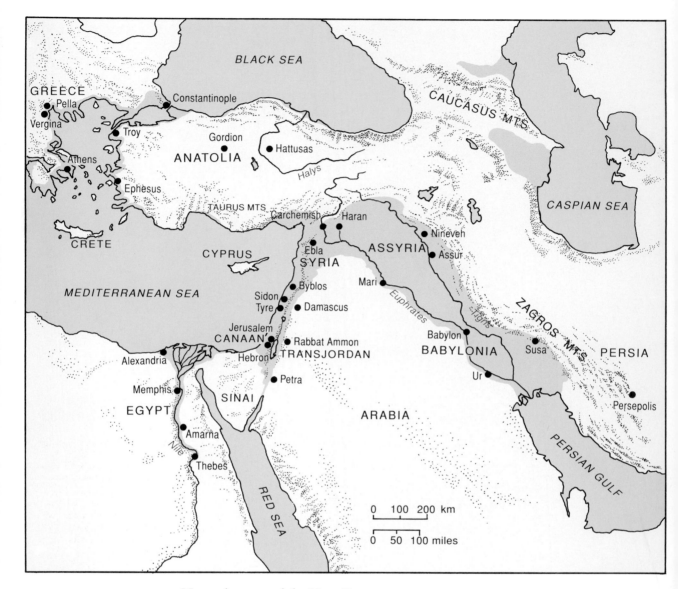

Natural routes of the Near East

The phrase 'the Fertile Crescent' was originally coined to describe the habitable land of the Near East: the area stretching from the Persian Gulf, northwest along the courses of the Tigris and Euphrates, arching west round to the Mediterranean coast and south to Egypt. Although we now know that some people have always lived outside it, the description still fits the area through which most of the great 'trunk roads' passed. In antiquity it was impossible to traverse the waterless deserts of the Arabian steppe. All armies, caravans and nomadic family groups (such as Abraham's) who travelled overland between the Persian Gulf and Egypt had to stay within the boundary of the Fertile Crescent. One of the main caravan cities was Mari, on the Middle Euphrates. From there the caravans made their way to coastal Syria. The oasis of Palmyra became, in late antiquity, an important stopover on this journey. Some routes then led north to Anatolia, others south along the coast. In inland Syria the oasis of Damascus was the most important caravan rendezvous. From here two main routes ran south – the 'Way of the King' (passing east of the Jordan valley into Arabia) and the 'Way of the Sea' (the Roman *Via Maris*). This road crossed the River Jordan north of the Sea of Galilee, past Hazor and across the valley of Esdraelon, and cut through the pass at Megiddo, before following the coast south towards Egypt.

It was the 19th-century scholar Sir Henry Breasted who first coined the expression 'the Fertile Crescent' to describe the swathe of habitable land at the heart of the ancient Near East where some of the earliest civilizations arose. The map (left) shows graphically how this corridor is surrounded by inhospitable areas. All traffic between Egypt in the west and Mesopotamia in the east had to pass through this area. Abraham's family, journeying from Ur in southern Mesopotamia to Mamre (later Hebron) in south Canaan, first had to travel north, to Haran in Syria.

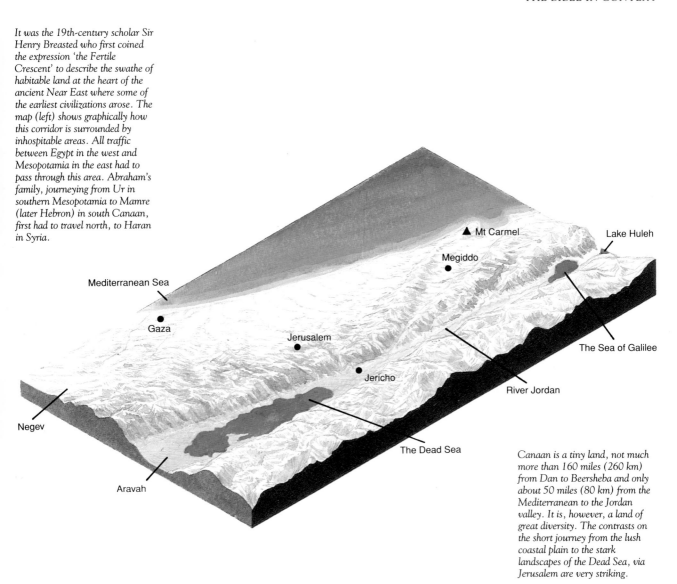

Canaan is a tiny land, not much more than 160 miles (260 km) from Dan to Beersheba and only about 50 miles (80 km) from the Mediterranean to the Jordan valley. It is, however, a land of great diversity. The contrasts on the short journey from the lush coastal plain to the stark landscapes of the Dead Sea, via Jerusalem are very striking.

The strategic nature of the Levant

In essence the Levant is a land bridge between Mesopotamia and Egypt to the north and south, and between Europe and Asia to the west and east, making this area a crossroads of people, trade and ideas. The northern Levant is better favoured in terms of climate and resources – its people learned very early that their cedarwood in particular was much sought after. Most of the trade goods of the Near East were despatched to the Aegean world from the ports of the north of the region. The southern Levant is not as fertile as the north and has few natural resources or good harbours. Its only internationally important trading commodities were olive oil and bitumen. The latter occurs naturally in the Dead Sea area and was used as an adhesive and also in the mummification process in Egypt (*momiya*, hence 'mummy', means bitumen). Foreign influence in the south was much more limited, particularly in the remote and secluded hills, so that their inhabitants were never as wealthy nor as sophisticated.

From ancient times down to the present day the southern Levant has been a buffer zone in international politics. The name of Megiddo, one of its most important cities, has become a byword for the battle which is to take place, according to apocalyptic notions, at the End of Days, between the armies of north and south. Armageddon means 'the hill of Megiddo'.

11

OUTLINE HISTORY OF THE REGION

FLAVIUS JOSEPHUS

Joseph ben Matthias, later known as Flavius Josephus, was born in AD 37 into a priestly family which traced its origins back to the Hasmonaeans. The bust above, dating to the Roman period, has sometimes been thought to be a portrait of him, though there is no strong evidence for the claim.

In later life, with the security of Roman citizenship and a rich estate in Judaea, he became comfortably established in Rome in the old home of his patron, the emperor Vespasian. There he devoted himself to scholarship and became the chief apologist of his people, seeking to defend them against the malicious anti-Semitism that was already prevalent.

Everything we know about the life and career of Josephus comes from his own pen. There is little doubt that he was a man of ability, educated in the best Rabbinic academies of his day, as well as a soldier and an historian. His works include The Jewish War (our main source concerning Herod, as well as the Revolt), and The Antiquities of the Jews, which chronicles the history of his people from the Creation to the eve of the revolt in AD 66. He also wrote Against Apion, a defence of the Jews against anti-Semitic propaganda, and an autobiography. Josephus was much respected by the Church Fathers, such as Eusebius and Jerome, who called him 'the Greek Livy'. He wrote in Greek and Aramaic to reach a wide audience and Latin translations were made in the 4th century AD.

THE WORLD OF THE BIBLE begins with Abraham. He and Sarah stand at the gate of Israel's history as the parents of the nation, entering into the first covenant with the Lord. Although Bible scholars and archaeologists are still engaged in a discussion about the historicity of the man himself (pp. 44–45), the background of the patriarchal world is fixed, in the opinion of many scholars, in the early 2nd millennium BC.

Over 8,000 years separated the era of Abraham and the other patriarchs from the end of the last Ice Age, when the polar ice cap covered most of Europe. During that long period humankind largely ceased to live by hunting and gathering and slowly developed methods of food production. From the 7th millennium BC many groups settled in farming villages wherever climate and soil allowed. Much of the land at that time was covered in forest, the climate was probably milder than today and groundwater resources were more abundant.

Genesis to Exodus

In Mesopotamia and in Egypt urban civilizations evolved in the course of the 4th millennium BC. The reasons behind this are complex, but one stimulus was the development of irrigation agriculture. The social co-operation of large groups of people is necessary for this way of life to succeed; where it does, conditions are in place for advanced cultures to develop. Writing systems were invented in these lands as a means of keeping records in the increasingly complex societies.

The Levant, a fertile corridor between the two opposite poles of Near Eastern civilization, was not as sophisticated as either, although it was open to influence from both. In the north, Syria was much affected by the civilization of Mesopotamia, while the lands to the south were more inclined towards Egypt. Because travel across the waterless desert of the Syrian steppe was impossible in ancient times, all overland journeys between the two great powers had to pass through the Levant corridor and large caravans and powerful armies came and went. In times of stability it was safe for small groups of travellers, such as the patriarchal clans, to make long journeys: the stories of such travels told in Genesis are perfectly feasible.

Egyptian records show that in the first half of the 2nd millennium BC groups of itinerant Semites regularly travelled backwards and forwards across the Sinai desert. Some even managed to gain a strong foothold in the Nile delta in the 18th and 17th centuries BC and became rulers of parts of Egypt at a time of native weakness. A resurgence of Egyptian power came with the princes of Thebes, who became the pharaohs of the 18th Dynasty. The foreign settlers were then no longer welcome and in the middle of the 16th century BC their leaders, known to the Egyptians as the Hyksos, were chased out of the country, mostly back to Canaan. A Semitic peasantry was left behind, some of whom were the ancestors of the Israelites.

About a generation later, the Egyptians under Tuthmosis III (c. 1504–1450 BC) consolidated their hold over Canaan. However, during the Amarna period, Egypt's grip on her Levantine empire weakened, but the pharaohs of the 19th Dynasty, starting with Seti I (c. 1318–1304 BC), again strengthened their grasp on Canaan. Along the desert roads of Sinai, called the Ways of Horus, they established a series of key fortresses, including Gaza in the south of Canaan. Further north they established an important garrison at Beth Shean in the Esdraelon valley, not far from Megiddo.

Ramesses II (c. 1304–1237 BC) is generally considered to be the pharaoh of the Exodus, when the Israelites made their escape from Egypt under the leadership of Moses. Making their way to Canaan took them the whole of the Exodus generation. The first reference to a people called 'Israel' settled in the land of Canaan is found on the Stela of the Year 5 of Merneptah (c. 1236–1223 BC), the successor of Ramesses II. Thus Israel was recognized by this time as a distinct entity, settled in Canaan.

Other newcomers to the land of Canaan

The 13th century saw increasing numbers of would-be settlers, quite alien to the Near East, making their way southwards through the Levant by land and sea. These people are known to us as the 'Sea Peoples', because that is one of their names in Egyptian texts. Before the 13th century BC groups arriving in smaller numbers had been absorbed into Egyptian society, often employed as mercenary soldiers.

Soon, however, the sheer weight of their numbers became too great. Cities, kingdoms, empires collapsed before them and during the 13th century BC the entire fabric of Late Bronze Age civilization in the Levant, Asia Minor, Syria and Egypt was torn apart.

One group of Sea Peoples settled along the coast of the extreme south of the Levant and became familiar to the writers of the Bible as the Philistines. Their characteristic pottery is found widely distributed in southern Canaan in the 11th century BC as they began to expand from the coastal region inland and northwards through the hills of southern Canaan. Here they came into conflict with the Israelites in the first phase of their settlement. Saul could not contain them; but David could, and did, apparently with ease.

David (c. 1004–965 BC), the shepherd boy who became the father of a long line of kings of Judah, also achieved the unification of the 12 tribes of Israel. By taking Jerusalem from the Jebusites and making it his capital he began the long association between his people and the city, establishing a united kingdom of Israel and Judah.

David's united kingdom did not long outlast the reign of his son, Solomon (c. 965–928 BC) who built the Temple in Jerusalem. After Solomon, the kingdom split into two: Israel in the north and Judah in the south. The next centuries were filled with war as the great empires of Assyria and Babylonia strove with Egypt for supremacy. The biblical kingdoms situated between them were often caught up in these struggles and suffered thereby. First Israel succumbed to the Assyrians in 721 BC, and then Judah fell to Nebuchadnezzar of Babylon in 587 BC. The Judaeans, like the people of Israel before them, were sent into exile.

The Judaean exiles in Babylon, however, not only survived the experience but even gained by it. It was in the exilic community that they developed fresh religious philosophies to meet the new challenges to their continued existence as followers of the Lord. Concepts of monotheism and personal responsibility were forged; ideas at the heart of Judaism and, later, Christianity and Islam. When Cyrus, king of the Persians, who succeeded the Babylonians as overlords of the region, allowed the exiles, who now could truly be called Jews, to return home in 538 BC, it was with renewed faith that they built the Second Temple in Jerusalem.

The arrival of Hellenism in the Near East had a great impact on the peoples of the area and was the next threat to the Jews. Alexander's armies brought the Greek language and the Greek way of life to the Near East in the late 4th century BC, and nothing was to be the same again. Among the Jews some were enthusiastic supporters of the new culture, others were vehemently opposed to it. So great was the split within the community in Judaea that when the edict of the Syrian king, Antiochus IV (175–164 BC), forbade the practice of Judaism on pain of torture and death, not all the people rose against him. But many did and eventually, after a long and bloody revolution, an independent Jewish kingdom was established under the Hasmonaean kings.

Within a very short time corruption, political assassinations and disputes over succession in the Hasmonaean kingdom led to the arrival on the scene of Rome, in the shape of Pompey. It was vital that the Romans held the lands of the eastern Mediterranean seaboard against their enemy, Parthia, to the east. Needing a loyal and stable leadership in Judaea they appointed to the throne the most able man they could find. This was not a member of the Hasmonaean family, but Herod, an Idumaean, whose family had been forcibly converted to Judaism less than a century earlier. Herod the Great (37–4 BC) proved a wise choice in many ways. He was a capable ruler, loyal ally and gifted businessman. He was also a murderer of several of his own family as well as many of his subjects and became increasingly feared by his people as his reign progressed. When he died the nation rejoiced, but he left for posterity some of the most extravagant and outstanding buildings of the Roman east.

Jesus and Christianity

Jesus was probably born in the year that Herod the Great died, and his life changed human perception of God and the course of history in the western world. The classic form of Christianity, however, was created after his death, by another Jew, Paul of Tarsus, who began the work of preaching the news of Christ to Gentiles as well as to Jews.

Jewish resentment of their Roman masters exploded in the First and Second Jewish Revolts (AD 66–73 and 132–35). Following the Second Revolt Jews were forbidden entry to Jerusalem. The Emperor Hadrian rebuilt the city as a Roman colony, naming it Aelia Capitolina after his family clan, Aelius. The emperor also gave orders for pagan temples to be built in places hallowed by Christians for their association with Jesus. The centre of the Apostolic church moved to Rome, but in the

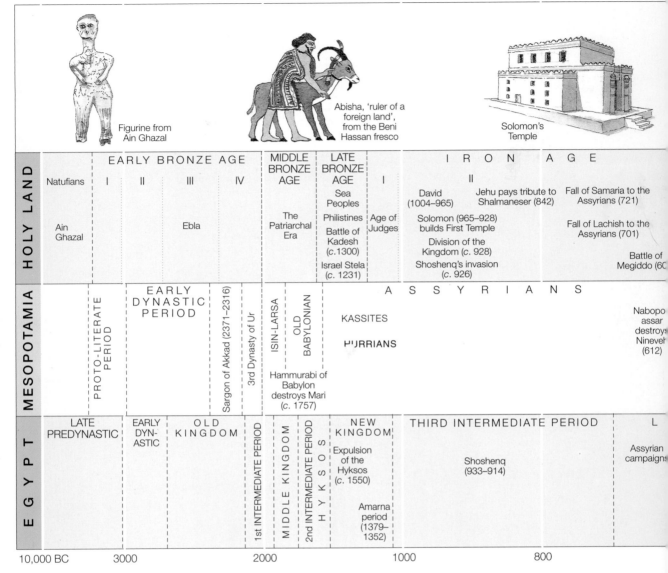

Figurine from
Ain Ghazal

Abisha, 'ruler of a
foreign land',
from the Beni
Hassan fresco

Solomon's
Temple

HOLY LAND	EARLY BRONZE AGE					MIDDLE BRONZE AGE	LATE BRONZE AGE	I	IRON AGE			
	Natufians	I	II	III	IV		Sea Peoples			II		
						The Patriarchal Era	Philistines	Age of Judges	David (1004–965)	Jehu pays tribute to Shalmaneser (842)	Fall of Samaria to the Assyrians (721)	
	Ain Ghazal		Ebla				Battle of Kadesh (c.1300)		Solomon (965–928) builds First Temple		Fall of Lachish to the Assyrians (701)	
							Israel Stela (c. 1231)		Division of the Kingdom (c. 928)			Battle of Megiddo (6C
									Shoshenq's invasion (c. 926)			

MESOPOTAMIA	PROTO-LITERATE PERIOD	EARLY DYNASTIC PERIOD		Sargon of Akkad (2371–2316)	3rd Dynasty of Ur	ISIN-LARSA	OLD BABYLONIAN	KASSITES	ASSYRIANS			Nabopo assar destroy Nineveh (612)
								HURRIANS				
						Hammurabi of Babylon destroys Mari (c. 1757)						

EGYPT	LATE PREDYNASTIC	EARLY DYNASTIC	OLD KINGDOM	1st INTERMEDIATE PERIOD	MIDDLE KINGDOM	2nd INTERMEDIATE PERIOD	HYKSOS	NEW KINGDOM	THIRD INTERMEDIATE PERIOD		L
								Expulsion of the Hyksos (c. 1550)			Assyrian campaigns
									Shoshenq (933–914)		
								Amarna period (1379–1352)			

10,000 BC   3000   2000   1000   800

A simplified timeline of the main
cultures, peoples and events
connected with the Bible lands.

land of Jesus' birth Christianity was all but
eradicated for about three centuries.

Byzantine Christianity

Christianity returned to the Holy Land in the
mid-4th century AD with Queen Helena, the
mother of the emperor Constantine (AD
306–37). She was entrusted with identifying
the holy places connected with Jesus.
Thereafter Christianity flourished in Palestine
until the Islamic conquest of the early 7th century AD. The capital city of the Islamic
Ummayad dynasty was Damascus. At first,
considerable tolerance was shown by the new
rulers of the Levant to both their Jewish and
Christian subjects. The Dome of the Rock was

built in the late 7th century AD, on the Temple
platform, which had probably stood empty
since the Roman destruction of Herod's
Temple in AD 70.

By the end of the 10th century AD the
Fatimids, the Shi'ite rulers of Egypt, had gained
control of the Holy Land. Al-Hakim (AD
996–1021) instituted a reign of terror, during
which he ordered the destruction of the
Church of the Holy Sepulchre in Jerusalem,
which ultimately set in train the events which
led to the Crusades.

At the approach of the millennium excite-
ment mounted in Europe, as Christians foresaw
the end of the present age and the second coming of the Messiah. Pilgrims travelled in ever

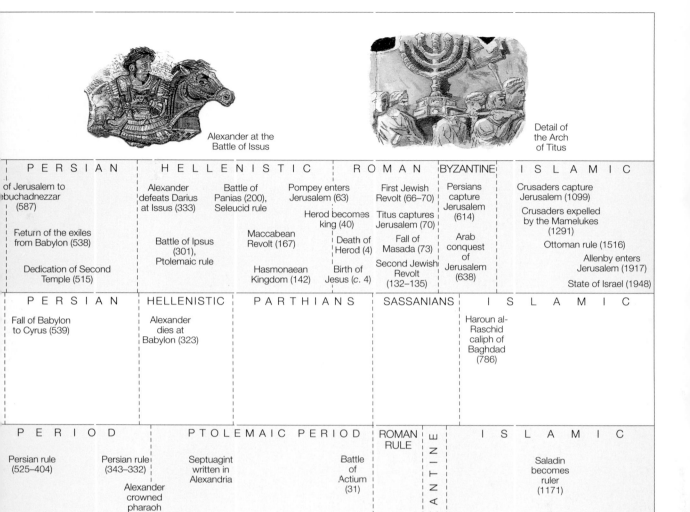

Alexander at the
Battle of Issus

Detail of
the Arch
of Titus

PERSIAN	HELLENISTIC	ROMAN	BYZANTINE	ISLAMIC
of Jerusalem to ebuchadnezzar (587)	Alexander defeats Darius at Issus (333)	Battle of Panias (200), Seleucid rule	Pompey enters Jerusalem (63)	First Jewish Revolt (66–70)	Persians capture Jerusalem (614)	Crusaders capture Jerusalem (1099)
			Herod becomes king (40)	Titus captures Jerusalem (70)		Crusaders expelled by the Mamelukes (1291)
Return of the exiles from Babylon (538)	Battle of Ipsus (301), Ptolemaic rule	Maccabean Revolt (167)	Death of Herod (4)	Fall of Masada (73)	Arab conquest of Jerusalem (638)	Ottoman rule (1516)
		Hasmonaean Kingdom (142)	Birth of Jesus (c. 4)	Second Jewish Revolt (132–135)		Allenby enters Jerusalem (1917)
Dedication of Second Temple (515)						State of Israel (1948)

PERSIAN	HELLENISTIC	PARTHIANS	SASSANIANS	ISLAMIC
Fall of Babylon to Cyrus (539)	Alexander dies at Babylon (323)			Haroun al-Raschid caliph of Baghdad (786)

PERIOD	PTOLEMAIC PERIOD	ROMAN RULE	BYZANTINE	ISLAMIC
Persian rule (525–404)	Persian rule (343–332)	Septuagint written in Alexandria	Battle of Actium (31)		Saladin becomes ruler (1171)
	Alexander crowned pharaoh (332)				

400   200   BC/AD   1000   2000

greater numbers to the Holy Land. The First Crusade began officially on 27 November 1095. In a rabble-rousing speech Pope Urban II, outside the walls of Clermont in France, urged the peoples of Christendom to rescue the holy city of Jerusalem from the Moslem hordes. The Crusaders had a much worse effect on the region than the Moslems whom they supplanted. Because of the Crusaders' inability to recognize their co-religionists, the local Christian communities were in more danger from them than their Moslem overlords. In spite of the magnificent castles which are their lasting glory, by the time the Crusaders set sail from the Holy Land for the last time in 1291 the region was well rid of them.

The Mamelukes, who began as slave recruits in the cavalry of the Egyptian sultan and eventually took over the kingdom, gained control of Palestine in around 1255. Under their rule it became something of a backwater for several centuries, but with the coming of the Ottoman Turks in 1516 the situation improved. The city walls built by the Ottoman sultan Suleiman the Magnificent around Jerusalem are still standing and are very familiar in paintings and photographs today.

The Ottomans remained the rulers of Palestine until the beginning of the 20th century, when Britain was officially entrusted by the League of Nations with the Mandate there following the First World War.

WOMEN TRAVELLERS

Lady Hester Stanhope in local costume.

CAROLINE OF BRUNSWICK
After Helena in the 4th century AD, the next royal lady to travel in the Holy Land arrived soon after the turn of the 19th century. Caroline of Brunswick (1768–1821) had married her first cousin, the Prince of Wales ('Prinny') in 1795. Unfortunately the royal couple took an immediate dislike to each other and they separated formally in 1796, soon after the birth of their daughter, Princess Charlotte. In 1814 Princess Caroline decided to go abroad. With a small retinue she made her way across Europe to Greece and eventually reached the Holy Land. There she visited almost all the holy places. Her itinerary included the Galilee, where she stayed for a short time in Nazareth, the Jordan valley, stopping at Jericho and the Dead Sea, and, finally, Jerusalem. By the time one of her companions published an account of her travels in 1821, the self-styled Queen of England was dead. She died a few days after having been dramatically turned away from the doors of Westminster Abbey during her husband's coronation.

Wady Mousa – at length we have arrived and it is worth all the long way. We descended to the village of Wady Mousa…rode on and soon got into the entrance of the defile that leads to Petra….We went on in ecstasies until suddenly between the narrow opening of the rocks, we saw the most beautiful sight I have ever seen.
Gertrude Bell, Diaries, 29 March 1900

THE HOLY LAND AND THE COUNTRIES around it have attracted visitors from numerous places throughout the ages. Many of them on their return home have published accounts of their travels, complete with maps, illustrations and, from the 19th century on, photographs. Among these visitors there has been a surprising number of women, some of them travelling alone – surprising because the region has been considered generally unsafe for any foreigners, let alone women, for many centuries.

Queen Helena

The first recorded woman traveller was Helena, in the 4th century AD. She was the mother of the Roman emperor, Constantine, who commissioned her to travel to Palestine and identify the holy places associated with the life of Christ. The sites she sought were often revealed to her in dreams, and she founded churches, shrines and monasteries at these spots. Several of her identifications are likely to be historically accurate, including the Church of the Holy Sepulchre in Jerusalem and the Basilica of the Nativity in Bethlehem. If, as some scholars believe, there is a grain of truth in the stories of the Empress finding the True Cross in Jerusalem, together with the nails used in the Crucifixion, then Helena can even be said to be the first archaeologist in the Holy Land.

Egeria

A few decades later, but still in the 4th century AD, a nun whose name is thought to have been Egeria left her quiet convent life somewhere in the western Mediterranean and made her way to the Holy Land. She spent several years on her travels, joining groups of other pilgrims to reach many of the holy places. She stayed for some time in Constantinople and for at least three years, perhaps AD 381–84, in Jerusalem. While based there she made many trips to places of Christian interest, including the

Galilee, where she visited Nazareth, Transjordan, where she made the ascent of Mt Nebo, and Antioch and Edessa in Syria. She also travelled to Egypt, probably twice, and made the difficult journey into Sinai, in order to stand on the mountain where it was believed that Moses received the Ten Commandments. By her day this had already been identified as Santa Katerina in the south of the peninsula.

Egeria wrote down all her experiences for the sisters of her convent at home. Miraculously, a part of her work has survived, in manuscript form, bound in with another work and discovered in a monastery library in Arezzo, Italy, in 1884. It is a great pity that no more than half of her account has survived because it is the best source of information not only for the eastern church of her day, but also for the topography of the Holy Land and other countries she travelled through at this early period. She wrote in haphazard Latin mixed with Greek expressions picked up on her travels. An energetic individual and an indefatigable traveller, Egeria was a pilgrim of strong constitution and an endlessly enquiring mind.

Lady Hester Stanhope

For the next 1,300 years there were apparently no women travellers of note who reached Palestine, until Lady Hester Stanhope (1776–1839). She was a genuine British eccentric: deeply romantic, but at the same time with a pragmatic approach to life which left her with no patience with the female social inhibitions of her class and day. The niece of the English Prime Minister William Pitt, she acted as his housekeeper and hostess until his death in 1806. Although she was then given a royal pension by King George III, she was unable to settle back into the life of a private lady and left England for the Levant in 1810. Once there, she took up residence in a dilapidated castle in a remote village in the Lebanese mountains until her death.

During her time in the Levant she adopted the male costume of the region which, so she said, was preferable to wearing the veil of a woman. She dabbled in the politics of the area and bullied everyone in her vicinity, while keeping open house for all European visitors. From her base she travelled widely and there is, for instance, a picturesque account of her entry into Palmyra. In 1815 she obtained a permit to dig for buried treasure at Ashkelon. Her workmen found a colossal ancient statue, but she had it destroyed, saying that she did not wish to be accused of hunting for curios to 'steal' for the British, as had happened only recently to Lord Elgin in connection with the marbles from the Parthenon in Athens.

Mary Eliza Rogers

In the 19th century many Europeans went to Palestine, then under Ottoman rule. Among them were missionaries, doctors, diplomats, geographers and explorers. Almost all of them had an interest in the biblical heritage of the land and its inhabitants. Many women came with their husbands, brothers or fathers, and one in particular has left an interesting memoir of her stay. Mary Eliza Rogers accompanied her diplomat brother to Palestine in the 1850s. She had access to the harems of the houses her brother visited and wrote detailed studies of the women she encountered. Her insights into the confined lives of the women, who were ignorant of virtually everything beyond the harem walls, make fascinating reading. She travelled widely throughout Palestine with her brother and met not only Arab women, but also those of the Samaritan, Druze and Jewish communities. Often considered by the men she met as an 'honorary man', she was also in some respects a typical Victorian lady, always obedient to the wishes of her brother, whom she obviously adored.

Women travellers in the 20th century

In the 20th century there have been several distinguished women visitors to the Holy Land. Gertrude Bell (1868–1926) fell in love with the Near East during the winter of 1899, which she spent in Jerusalem learning Arabic. Before the First World War she spent many years travelling in the deserts of the Near East, getting to know the people who lived there, and wrote several books about her experiences. She was also a considerable photographer and her pictures of archaeological sites – some of which she excavated – are particularly valuable today as records both of places that have changed considerably and a way of life that has disappeared. In 1923 she was appointed to the British High Commission in Baghdad as Oriental Secretary and was the first Director of Antiquities in Iraq. On her death she left money to found the British School of Archaeology in Iraq.

Rose Macaulay, like Gertrude Bell, was a graduate of Oxford University, where she took a degree in history. She travelled widely in the Levant and some of her novels, such as *The Towers of Trebizond*, have a Near Eastern background. Her most famous travel book, *The Pleasure of Ruins*, was published in 1953 and contains a great deal of perceptive writing on places she visited in the Levant.

No account of women travellers in the Near East would be complete without mentioning Dame Freya Stark, who died in 1993 at the age of 100. One of her many books about her travels, *Alexander's Path*, is a classic of adventure. It recounts her journey through Turkey as, travelling completely alone and for the most part relying on erratic buses, she followed the trail of Alexander the Great across the country. She also learned Arabic and in 1927 journeyed from Venice to Beirut, where she spent a year touring Lebanon and Syria. In 1929 she visited Baghdad and returned to the Near East on numerous occasions after that.

Gertrude Bell outside her tent in Babylon, in 1909. This is a rare photograph of her as she generally preferred to be behind the camera rather than in front of it.

ARCHAEOLOGISTS IN THE HOLY LAND

Lieutenant Charles Warren (right) being presented with a Samaritan book by Yakub es-Shellaby, the Samaritan leader, at the foot of Mt Gerizim. After his work in Palestine, Warren returned to England and became Police Commissioner in London, where he was in charge of the hunt for Jack the Ripper, the murderer who terrorized the city in 1888.

Not for the greed of gold
Not for the hope of fame
Not for a lasting heritage
Not for a far-flung name.
Rather for making history
And for some lore of old
That is our aim and object
Not for the greed of gold!

THIS CAMP SONG of the young and idealistic archaeologists who were 'Petrie's Pups' at Tell Farah on the edge of the Negev desert in Palestine in the 1920s, well illustrates the pioneering spirit of the period. By that time there had been great interest in the Holy Land in Britain and the USA for the best part of a century, inspired in both countries by a strong Christian conviction.

From the early part of the 19th century serious explorers began to arrive in Palestine. One of the most eminent among them was the American historical geographer, Edward Robinson (1794–1863), who succeeded in accurately identifying many biblical sites as he travelled around the country, in 1838 and again in 1852. In the 1850s Dean Arthur Stanley (1815–81) published his best-selling reminiscences of his travels in Palestine. Such

scholarly work laid the basis for the later surveying, mapping and excavation of Palestine.

In 1865 an Englishman, Captain Charles Wilson (1836–1905) of the Royal Engineers, led an Ordnance Survey expedition to Jerusalem in order to make an accurate survey of the city. The success of this venture raised public interest in the Holy Land to new heights in England, and in the same year the Palestine Exploration Fund (p. 20) was established under the patronage of Queen Victoria. Scientific investigations on behalf of the Fund began with the work of Lieutenant Charles Warren (1840–1927) in Jerusalem in 1867, and continued most notably with the Survey of Western Palestine between 1871 and 1877. From July 1872 this work was led by Lieutenant Claude Conder (1848–1910), and its most famous participant was Lieutenant H.H. Kitchener (later Lord Kitchener of Khartoum; 1850–1916). The Survey was the most important contribution made by the British to the archaeology of Palestine in the 19th century. The results were published as a series of 26 sheets of 1-in. maps, covering 6,000 sq. miles. These maps have, until very recently, been the yardstick by which all other maps of the region have been measured and their value for archaeologists and geographers has not diminished over time.

The American Palestine Exploration Society was formed in 1870 and paralleled the work of the British society by conducting a Survey of Eastern Palestine. Unfortunately, the task proved impossible in the face of much local opposition east of the Jordan and the Society was disbanded soon after.

Sir William Flinders Petrie (1852–1943) was the true pioneer of excavation in Palestine with his expedition to Tell el-Hesi in 1890. He was the first to realize that pottery types could be dated according to the layers in a tell. Petrie's greatest love was Egypt, but he returned to Palestine more than 30 years later, by which time he was over 70 years old. Even so, over the next 10 years he conducted several major excavations as well as some smaller ones.

Early 20th-century excavators

In 1920 the British set up the first Department of Antiquities in Palestine, directed by John Garstang (1876–1956), who was then head of the newly founded British School of

Archaeology in Jerusalem. The Palestine Archaeological Museum (now called the Rockefeller) opened in 1939, by which time there were many competent excavators working in Palestine. This was the era of the large, well-funded expeditions set up to excavate the major tells. It was also the period when biblical archaeology was fashionable. Archaeologists and Bible scholars regularly interpreted their findings in the light of biblical history.

This approach did not recommended itself to Kathleen Kenyon (1906–78), the leading British archaeologist of the day (p. 38). She had been trained in field techniques in Britain by the formidable Mortimer Wheeler and she brought his methods to bear on the problems of Palestinian archaeology. She excavated first at Samaria, where she took part in the joint Anglo-American excavations of the 1930s. Her greatest work was undoubtedly at Jericho from 1951 to 1958. The Jericho dig was seminal in the development of excavation techniques in Israel. She also excavated in Jerusalem between 1961 and 1967, principally south of the Temple Mount in the area now known as the City of David.

Britain was not the only country interested in the archaeology of the Holy Land. Individuals and expeditions from all over the world undertook excavations at many sites for over a century. Foremost among these were the Americans, such as the Oriental Institute of Chicago, with an expedition to Megiddo, or W.F. Albright (p. 20) who worked at Tell Beit Mirsim. After the Second World War the pace of exploration increased. American and British archaeologists have retained their high profile, but numerous other nationalities are represented – including Canadian, Dutch, French, German, Japanese and many more.

Israeli archaeologists

Since 1945 a generation of Israeli excavators has grown up with an especially passionate interest in the biblical period and a deep knowledge of the Bible in its original landscape and language. Many chose to specialize in the Iron Age, which was the setting for much of the Old Testament and largely corresponds to the First Temple Period. Yigael Yadin (1917–84) was one of the great figures of Israeli archaeology. Along with others, he was inclined to interpret his findings in line with biblical events, confident that archaeology could throw light on biblical history. Another notable figure is Yohanan Aharoni (1919–76), a historical-geographer and one of the principal archaeologists less bound by the biblical text and thus more objective in their use of archaeological data.

An important development for Israeli archaeology was the reformation of the Israel Department of Antiquities into the independent Israel Antiquities Authority. Many sites are currently being restored so that they can be enjoyed and understood by a wider public and salvage work is undertaken where construction is scheduled. Although there is concern that restoration work may go too far, and that unsuitable methods may be used, there is no doubt that there will be a great benefit in bringing the past within reach of more people.

SIR WILLIAM FLINDERS PETRIE

William Petrie (seen here at Tell Farah South), the British archaeologist, was primarily interested in Egypt. However, the Palestine Exploration Fund, having decided on a programme of field archaeology outside Jerusalem, appointed him to excavate on their behalf in 1890. Petrie chose the site of Tell el-Hesi, in southern Palestine, and spent a six-week season there in 1890. His choice was partly influenced by the fact that a natural section had been cut through the layers of debris on the west side of the tell by the floodwaters of a wadi. Petrie could therefore take samples of pottery and objects from each layer with little effort or disturbance. From these he constructed a relative sequence of pottery for the site, and then extended it to the whole of Palestine. He also compared Egyptian objects from the tell with similar ones he had found in Egypt and whose dates were known. In this way he was able to date the Hesi levels – the method is known as cross-dating – and established a chronology for ancient Palestine. Although his conclusions have since been modified, the method itself is still in universal use.

Petrie spent only one season in Palestine before returning to Egypt. But he did train a whole generation of young archaeologists who subsequently worked in Palestine. Among these was the American, Frederick Bliss, who excavated at Tell el-Hesi from 1891 to 1893 and in Jerusalem between 1894 and 1897.

THE BIBLE AND ARCHAEOLOGY

WILLIAM FOXWELL
ALBRIGHT

Albright (1891–1971) was an extraordinary polymath: an archaeologist, Bible scholar, linguist and historian. The essence of his work was to set the Bible and its history into its context as a part of the cultural environment of the ancient Near East. This was the theme of his most important book, From Stone Age to Christianity, which traced the development of monotheism. As a young man he considered the Bible primarily as a piece of literature, without a basis in historical fact; but his views gradually changed and he became the greatest proponent of its historicity.

His most important experience as a field archaeologist was at Tell Beit Mirsim in southern Palestine, where he dug in the 1930s. He applied the archaeological chronology which he established at that site to the whole country, using the framework of Stone, Bronze and Iron Ages. In his book The Archaeology of Palestine he put forward his conviction that archaeology and the Bible are essentially consistent with each other. His was the most important influence on a whole generation of scholars. Dissenting voices were rarely heard during his lifetime and contrary opinions gained little credence until after his death.

Frontispiece of the Palestine Exploration Quarterly, *showing Warren's shaft and tunnels dug below the Temple Mount in 1870.*

THE NOTION OF BIBLICAL ARCHAEOLOGY is to some extent an outmoded one. It relied on the 19th-century assumption, perpetuated in the middle of the 20th century by W.F. Albright, that archaeological excavations could prove the literal truth of the Bible narrative. No expert in the field of either Bible study or the archaeology of the Near East, especially in the Levant, would deny that archaeology can illuminate the biblical narrative (for instance, the siege of Lachish – pp. 92–95) and even confirm details of the biblical text. Concern arises only if insistence on the absolute historical accuracy of the Bible is such that, even unwittingly, it obscures the objective interpretation of the archaeological evidence.

It is very interesting to compare the 'statements of intent' of the similarly named Palestine Exploration Fund in London and the Palestine Exploration Society in New York, set up within five years of each other (1865 and 1870 respectively). The tasks which they set themselves were comparable, but their ideologies were clearly worlds apart. The objectives of the former were: 'the accurate and systematic investigation of the archaeology, topography,

Palestine Exploration Fund

A SOCIETY FOR THE ACCURATE AND SYSTEMATIC INVESTIGATION OF THE ARCHAEOLOGY, THE TOPOGRAPHY, THE GEOLOGY AND PHYSICAL GEOGRAPHY, THE MANNERS AND CUSTOMS OF THE HOLY LAND, FOR BIBLICAL ILLUSTRATION.

FOUNDED 1865

Patron:
HIS MAJESTY THE KING

President:
HIS GRACE THE ARCHBISHOP OF CANTERBURY

Vice-President:
HIS GRACE THE ARCHBISHOP OF YORK

geology and physical geography, natural history, manners and customs of the Holy Land, for biblical illustration.'

In America the committee of the PES had quite different aims: 'the illustration and defense of the Bible – whatever goes to verify the Bible as real…is a refutation of unbelief. The Committee feels that they have in trust a sacred service for science and for religion.'

Thus, at the outset of archaeological investigations in Palestine, two quite different ideals, which may be defined as the secular and the sacred, were at work.

Albright and after

It has often been said that adherents of biblical archaeology travelled the Holy Land with a Bible in one hand and a spade in the other. Perhaps this is a little exaggerated, but there is a grain of truth in it. Rabbi Nelson Glueck, (1901–71), famous for his pioneering surveys in Jordan and in the Negev, always interpreted archaeological results with respect to the Bible. G.E. Wright (1909–74), the excavator of Shechem and the founding editor of the influential journal *Biblical Archaeologist*, was another enthusiastic supporter of the idea that the Bible and archaeology were always at one.

It was only after the death of Albright in 1971 that dissenting voices gathered strength and facts that did not fit the theories of biblical archaeology began to be re-examined. One of the central problems was that of Jericho and its supposed destruction by the Israelites under Joshua. In accordance with the Bible, Albright advocated a view of the Israelite arrival as a conquest, which took place, he believed, in the 13th century BC. Kenyon's work at Jericho, however, found little trace of a settlement at this period, and none of a destruction. The Bible, it is now realized, cannot be taken as objective history, and most archaeologists today agree with the position of H.J. Franken that their labours are quite separate from those of Bible scholars.

Ironically, it was Franken's own excavations at Tell Deir 'Alla in the Jordan valley that brought to light an inscription mentioning Balaam. The Bible relates how Balaam, at the bidding of Balak, king of Moab, tried to curse the Israelites as they reached the Promised Land but was only able to bless them, at the

Lord's command (Numbers 23–24). Thus the very archaeologist who has had severe doubts about the relevance of archaeology to the Bible is the one who has found this very important reference to an early figure in the Old Testament.

This, perhaps, is the moral of the story, since clearly archaeology can be relevant to the biblical text. The point is that archaeology and Bible study are two separate disciplines which sometimes have a direct bearing on each other. As an archaeological tool the Bible should be treated as rigorously as any other documentary source. Archaeological findings may help the Bible scholar, but ultimately the scriptures are concerned with theology and theological, rather than objective, history.

Current preoccupations and the way ahead

As archaeologists today realize, the biblical period was just one era in the several thousand years of human history and prehistory in the Levant. Many other topics and times are now under investigation. Progress is being made, particularly in regions and periods previously little studied, such as the kingdom of Jordan, or the later Islamic era. Archaeologists are now looking forward to a time when it will be possible for scholars on both sides of the present political divide to become full colleagues in the work of reconstructing the archaeology and ancient history of the whole region – a task which makes the arguments for and against biblical archaeology seem small by comparison.

In recent years there has also been a move away from the preoccupation with the First Temple Period. Both Israeli archaeologists and their foreign colleagues now have a higher degree of interest in questions which do not relate only to the Bible. A completely new approach to the sets of questions which can be addressed by archaeology has emerged. Emphasis now is often placed on the reconstruction of ancient ways of life, frequently by reference to traditional customs of Palestine during the Ottoman period. Other interests include settlement patterns and ancient demography.

James L. Starkey, the excavator of Lachish, pointing to the exact find-spot of the famous Lachish Letters, in the debris of the gatehouse of Level II, destroyed in 587 BC by Nebuchadnezzar.

Archaeology can provide background information about situations known from the Bible. The nature of this information, however, is inherently different from the biblical information – it does not have a message. The Bible presents historical events in the light of a very specific religious interpretation, which archaeological situations do not possess.
H.J. Franken, *Palestine Excavation Quarterly* 1976, pp. 10–11

Biblical theology and Biblical archaeology must go hand in hand if we are to comprehend the Bible's meaning.
G.E. Wright, *Biblical Archaeologist* 1957, p. 17

THE TALE OF A TELL

And Pharaoh commanded the same day the taskmasters of the people and their officers saying, Ye shall no more give the people straw to make bricks as heretofore: let them go and gather straw for themselves.
Exodus 5, 6–7

MANY OF THE MAJOR archaeological sites in the Near East are visible as mounds standing well above the level of the surrounding countryside. Such a site is called a *tell* in Arabic-speaking countries, *tepe* in Iran or *hüyük* in Turkey. Whereas in Europe and America archaeologists are accustomed to start work from the present-day surface and dig down to the past, in the Near East they usually have to climb high above ground level to begin excavating. Tells represent the accumulation of centuries of occupation debris formed mainly from the decay of structures made of mud brick, with some use of stone, usually as foundations. Mud bricks, made of earth mixed with water and

straw and left in the sun to dry, were the basic building blocks in the ancient Near East, and are still used in some places. While simple and easy to make, mud brick decomposes very quickly and the average life of a mud-brick building is only about 30 years, although with good upkeep it may last longer. If a building or settlement was destroyed by fire, the conflagration baked the mud bricks, making the resulting layers of debris almost indestructible.

The characteristic shape of a tell is round or oval, with sloping sides. With each successive period of building the mound grows higher, the sides steeper and the habitable area on top smaller. Foundations for new city walls were almost always dug inside the line of previous defences for stability. To prevent erosion and to deny attackers an easy foothold, the sloping sides of tells were often encased in a thick layer of plaster, bonded into the slope for strength and sometimes laid over a secure foundation of

Tell Beersheba from the air, showing the areas of excavation. The steep sides of the tell were formed by the creation of a plaster glacis, laid over boulders. At least two city walls were exposed in the deep section trench visible on the left, where the excavators 'sliced' through the defences in order to uncover their sequence.

small boulders. This type of defensive system is called a *glacis* and is the main reason for the distinctive shape of tells. At the top stood a defensive wall, strongly built of mud brick on stone footings. The glacis was usually revetted by another wall at its foot. The origin of this system can be traced to Early Bronze Age cities, as confirmed by recent finds at Tell Jarmuth, southwest of Jerusalem.

A second type of fortification was the rampart. Mounds of earth were thrown up against both sides of a rubble core, effectively sandwiching it between them. Sometimes the ramparts were crowned by a defensive wall. Huge expanses were enclosed in this way: the area within the ramparts of the lower city of Hazor is about 200 acres (80 ha) and in Syria some are even larger: those at Qatna enclose about 250 acres (100 ha). Their construction was probably a communal effort — reminiscent of the rebuilding of the walls of Jerusalem after the Babylonian Exile (p. 108).

Building techniques

The rarity of stone and timber made them valuable commodities in the ancient Near East. Stone was, for the most part, limited to foundations and the ornamentation of palaces, as in Mesopotamia, or temples, as in Egypt. In the Levant ashlar masonry, that is, finely-cut, rectangular monumental stone blocks, was mainly reserved for prestigious royal or public buildings. The lower courses of the walls of such buildings might be faced with plain or decorated stone panels called orthostats. By Hellenistic and Roman times, when rulers had huge numbers of slaves at their disposal, massive structures such as fortresses or theatres might be built entirely of stone. Timber long and strong enough to be used for roofing material or general building purposes was expensive. This stimulated the development of the arch and the dome (originally in mud brick, later in stone), which are now such characteristic features of Islamic architecture.

Identifying archaeological sites

One of the most frequent queries put to archaeologists is 'How do you know where to dig?'. The answer has changed over the past decades as the theoretical questions asked by archaeologists themselves and the field techniques at their disposal have become increasingly sophisticated. Up to the Second World War, the great tell sites of the Near East, such as Kuyunjik (ancient Nineveh) in Mesopotamia, or Beth Shean and Megiddo, in Palestine, were

obvious choices for archaeological expeditions for wealthy institutions in the west. At Megiddo the stated aim of the American archaeological team working there in the 1930s was to strip the tell, layer by layer, down to bedrock. The Americans did indeed remove a large part of the tell, discovering much useful information about the early periods which would not otherwise be available. However, a great deal of the site remains for future investigation. Today, excavation is not the only way of investigating sites and archaeologists are aware of the fact that excavating a site also destroys it. Wherever possible, archaeologists dig only when necessary, due to threats to a site or to solve specific problems, and leave much of it untouched for future researchers.

Large-scale excavations are usually expensive and since the 1970s archaeologists have turned their attention to smaller projects, such as sites occupied only for a short period. In such places one or two seasons of work can often throw light on an aspect of particular interest to the excavators.

Regional surveys, aiming to locate all the ancient sites within a specific area, such as a valley, plain or range of hills, are now carried out alongside the more traditional site surveys, which simply examine a single site for datable material. An individual site is considered as a part of its surroundings — not just its general environment, the basis of its economy and so forth, but also its relationship to other sites — for instance, whether it was a farm complex dependent on a nearby hamlet, a specialist settlement such as a potters' village or a city ruling outlying towns.

Landscape archaeology

Since the 1980s landscape archaeology has become very popular. One scholar has described this approach as 'total archaeology' — the examination of a given area in every respect and throughout time, from the earliest days up to and including the present. Although very comprehensive, it is not particularly expensive to undertake and can be carried out with a very small team of investigators. Everything in an area is carefully studied, mapped and dated: field systems; agricultural terracing; isolated installations such as wine or oil presses; animal pens; walls and all other artificial structures. Studies are made of soil types; land-use and industry; cemeteries and burial practices; water sources and transport routes to gain a complete picture of the region. Actual digging is just one of the tools available

Deir el-Balah, excavated by the Israeli archaeologist Trude Dothan, provides an excellent example of digging according to a predetermined grid, often consisting of 5-m squares. Unexcavated walls known as balks both separate the squares and form sections which are carefully photographed and drawn. The history of all the squares can then be correlated to achieve an overview of the whole site.

allels with societies that have been scientifically studied by anthropologists.

Methods of excavation

When excavating a large tell with city walls of different periods, one traditional method is to cut a trench through the defences from top to bottom. The result resembles a cake with a neatly cut parallel-sided slice removed from it. By careful examination of the sides of the trench, the archaeologist can see all the different phases of the city's defensive systems. Objects such as pottery, metalwork and coins help to date the structures.

Trenching can be extended to examine the site as a whole, and at one time this was the accepted method of excavating a tell. Although it may not reveal the complete plan of any single building, this technique does provide a view of the whole history of the site and material relating to each period of its use. Most archaeologists, however, also want to retrieve the architecture and overall plan of the site, as well as a historical sequence, so they then dig in squares according to a predetermined grid. Within each square the walls, floors, pits and any other feature can be examined, before digging deeper. A combination of a trench through the defences to obtain an overall sequence, and a detailed examination of other areas excavated in squares, is now the approach adopted on most large, multi-period sites.

to the landscape archaeologist and excavations can be very limited in extent.

Other techniques new to archaeology have also recently been introduced. Demographic surveys in different parts of Israel have produced estimates of average carrying capacity of the land of 100 people per acre (25 people per dunam). The renewed interest in ethnography (the use of parallels from social anthropology) has also helped in the interpretation of archaeological data, for example in agriculture. In other words, simple but technical descriptions of objects by archaeologists have given way to the interpretation of their function, using par-

Dating methods

Another question archaeologists regularly have to answer is 'how old is this?'. Modern dating techniques, such as radiocarbon (Carbon 14) dating and tree-ring dating (dendrochronology) are now widely used. Samples are sent to laboratories for analysis, but the results are known only after digging has finished for the season. The archaeologist, however, also needs

A standard typological sequence such as this for pottery oil lamps is a useful tool for dating the different levels in an excavation. Here the main shapes in use between the late 3rd millennium BC and the mid-1st millennium AD are shown. The lamp develops from a simple, round, saucer shape in the Early Bronze Age to an increasingly closed shape. The four-spouted lamps of EBIV are very characteristic of the period.

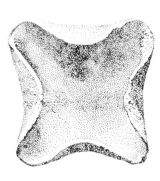

Early Bronze IV

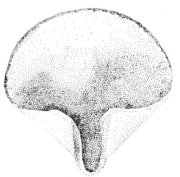

Late Bronze

Hellenistic

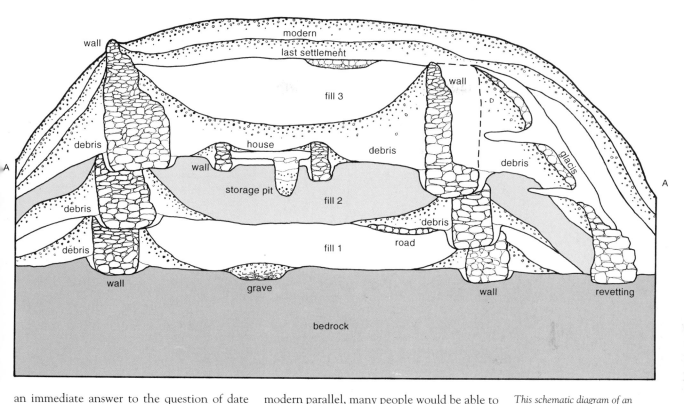

an immediate answer to the question of date while digging is still in progress. Dating finds in the field still relies on stratigraphy and typology, as it has always done.

Stratigraphy is based on the geological principle that superimposed layers form a chronological sequence – so each layer is later than the one below it. In archaeological sites there may be, for example, floors of different periods laid one on top of another, and those finds which can definitely be associated with each floor probably belong to the time it was in use.

Typology is the most useful method for establishing the relative date of finds. To take a

modern parallel, many people would be able to assess the approximate date of a motor car from its appearance. In the same way, oil lamps and bronze axes are good examples of ancient objects for which reliable typological series have been established. Whole pots are very rare finds, except in burial caves, but even fragments can be dated if decoration or handles, rims or bases, characteristic of their period, survive.

Assigning a date in calendar years (an absolute date) to an object in the course of an excavation is more complicated. Flinders Petrie (p. 19) was the pioneer who established the historical framework for Palestine. While digging at Tell el-Hesi he was able to date most levels of the mound by imported Egyptian objects found in them, whose dates he knew from his excavations in Egypt. Everything made locally contained in the same levels as the Egyptian objects could then also be dated, as could similar objects found at other sites. This method is called 'cross-dating', and it relies on a known historical framework, worked out reasonably accurately for the Near East in the 19th century AD. This in turn relies mostly on references in ancient documents to astronomical events, such as eclipses of the sun, whose dates are known to astronomers.

This schematic diagram of an imaginary tell shows how successive walls and the debris of their collapse or destruction build up, forming the mound. The area of building space on its summit decreases as the mound grows higher. Collapsed walls have to be levelled up with a fill to give a reasonably flat surface on which to build new structures. The characteristic steep slopes of the tell were created by the defensive glacis, often laid over boulders and retained by a wall at its foot. 'Horizontal digging' of tells – the stripping of artificial levels – was fashionable between the two world wars. But if this were to be done along the line A–A in this diagram, a mixture of material from several different periods would result, making a correct interpretation of the site almost impossible. It has now been universally recognized that it is essential to dig according to the real levels of each site.

Roman   Byzantine

THE ORIGINS OF THE ALPHABET

GREEK
Official and monumental Greek inscriptions always used capital letters, while the cursive script ('handwriting') was used less formally. The first Greek Bible manuscripts, like the one above, were written in capital letters called 'uncials'. From the 7th century AD manuscripts were written in small cursive letters called minuscules, from which derive the script you are reading in this book today.

HEBREW
The vowels are shown by the addition of dots and dashes above and below the line. The method in use today is that developed by the Massoretes in Palestine in the 1st millennium AD (p. 29). Hebrew was no longer spoken by that time, but it remained the holy language of the Law, read aloud each week in synagogues. It was therefore important to know how to read it properly and thus a vocalization system was needed.

ARABIC
Because the prohibition against the graven image has always been so strong in Islam, the written word has become one of the great inspirations for Moslem artistic creativity. Arabic, like Hebrew, has a vowel system which can be added above or below the words. It also has, to a much greater degree than Hebrew, a system of diacritical marks – these tell the reader how to distinguish between letters that look similar.

> *The Phoenicians who came [to Greece] with Cadmus [Prince of Tyre] introduced into Greece a number of accomplishments of which the most important was writing, an art until then, I think, unknown to the Greeks.*
> Herodotus, *The Histories*, V, 58

LITERACY – READING AND WRITING – is one sign of an advanced society. True writing began in Mesopotamia about 3300 BC and the concept (though not the writing system itself) spread to Egypt very soon thereafter. In both lands the writing method was syllabic, that is, one in which each sign stands for a consonant, often with a vowel sound attached to it, or sometimes a consonant – vowel – consonant. A scribe often needed to learn hundreds of signs before he (or occasionally she) could read and write fluently. Alphabetic writing represents a great advance on Mesopotamian cuneiform or Egyptian hieroglyphic, because on the whole it is far simpler to learn and to use. Wherever syllabic systems were used, literacy tended to be limited to a very few; most rulers were unable to read or write for themselves and always had scribes beside them, even for their personal correspondence. In the places where alphabets were the rule, literacy could and did become widespread. Although scribes were always employed by a majority of the population to read or write letters, many people in the Levant were lettered by the later 1st millennium BC.

The original Canaanite alphabet, from which all Semitic and later European alphabets are derived, had 22 letters. Each sign stands for one single sound rather than a group of sounds. Only consonants are represented. In fact Semitic languages such as Hebrew, Aramaic and Arabic are still generally written without any vowels, although in relatively recent times vowel systems have been added to the script, by the addition of dots and dashes above or below the line of writing.

The notion of alphabetic writing may have arisen twice on the soil of the Levant. The Late Bronze Age scribes of Ugarit wrote in an alphabetic script with new symbols, modelled on the cuneiform principle of wedges stabbed into soft clay, sometime between 1400 and 1200 BC. A small clay tablet discovered at the site bears the 30 letters of their cuneiform alphabet in its correct order, not unlike the order we have today.

Semitic letter names and their English meaning and sound	Proto-Sinaitic, 15th century BC	Proto- or early Canaanite 13th century BC	Phoenician 9th century BC	Classical Greek capitals and letter names
aleph (ox) '				**A** alpha
kaf (hand) k				**K** kappa
maym (water) m				**M** mu
'ayin (eye) '				**O** omicron
ros (head) r				**P** rho
sin (tooth) sh				**Σ** sigma

The tablet was probably a teaching text. Although texts using this script have been found as far afield as northern Canaan, dating to the same period and later, this cuneiform alphabet, along with several like it at Byblos and various other places, eventually came to a dead end.

The early Canaanite alphabet

The real precursor of modern alphabets was already in existence by the time of the Ugaritic version. As far as we know, it had developed out of the hieroglyphic script of Egypt from as early as the 17th century BC. This could have happened in Canaan, or in Sinai, where the Egyptians were mining for turquoise at Serabit el-Khadem, in the western part of the peninsula. Local people, of the same Semitic background as the population of Canaan, worked alongside them. When the Egyptians dedicated a shrine to their goddess, Hathor, the 'locals' were quick to emulate them. They made little figurines of human-headed sphinxes or seated scribes in the Egyptian fashion, and inscribed them with the name of their goddess. When these statuettes were first found at the beginning of the 20th century, the short group of letters was a total mystery. Subsequently Sir Alan Gardiner believed that the signs had been taken from the Egyptian hieroglyphic script and treated as if they were pictures of objects; but the objects had been named by the Semitic miners in their own language. Thus the picture of a house was called in Canaanite 'bayit'. And then, just as an English-speaking child today would say 'H is for House', so the miners said, 'B is for Bayit' – and the alphabet was born. Some scholars call this script Proto-Sinaitic, but others point out that it is also known from short inscriptions in Canaan from this same period (the Middle Bronze Age), and that therefore Early Canaanite is a better name.

The Early Canaanite alphabetic script was so simple that it was used increasingly over the next centuries in a variety of ways: to mark personal possessions such as arrowheads (for easy retrieval from the battlefield); to dedicate offerings in shrines (such as the Lachish ewer; see p. 52); or to keep official records. None of these records have survived, however, since they were written on papyrus or vellum which would have perished in the humid climate of the Levant. Only cuneiform texts inscribed on clay tablets, such as the Amarna Letters – diplomatic correspondence from the time of the Pharaoh Akhenaten (p. 55) – have come down to us.

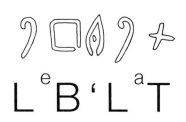

LE BALAAT INSCRIPTION
This inscription, found on several figurines from Sinai, sometimes written left to right and sometimes right to left, was the key to the decipherment of Early Canaanite. The inscription reads 'le Balaat', meaning 'for the goddess', showing that the figurine is a votive gift to 'the Lady', who was the female equivalent of Baal.

The Phoenicians

The earliest known monumental alphabetic inscription carved on stone is on the lid of the sarcophagus of Ahiram, King of Byblos, dating to the 11th century BC. The script had become more regular and had assumed its classical form and from this time on it is usually referred to as Phoenician. Evidence for alphabetic inscriptions before the 1st millennium BC is mostly limited to the southern Levant and it is quite possible that the classic form evolved there; but there is no proof for this at present.

During the 1st millennium BC the Phoenician alphabet spread northwards through Syria and Turkey and westwards to Cyprus. It also travelled with the Phoenicians to their new Punic colonies along the north coast of Africa. However, by the time Carthage and other Punic cities were founded the alphabet had already arrived in the west via the Greeks.

Inscriptions and the Bible

Several inscriptions throw direct light on the narrative of the Old Testament. Among these are the House of David inscription (p. 83), the Balaam text from Tell Deir 'Alla (p. 20–21), the Mesha Stela (p. 28), Hezekiah's inscription from the Siloam Tunnel (p. 91) and the Lachish Letters (pp. 21 and 91). Other textual finds help recreate the atmosphere of the biblical world, for instance the Gezer Calendar (p. 35) and the tomb inscription of Shebna from Siloam, which mentions his concubine. Small inscribed objects include personal seals in a variety of stones, which sometimes bear a design or a device, in addition to the owner's name. If the person held an official position, the title is given in addition to their name. Seals of members of the royal family are also identified as such, for instance that of Jezebel. Other seals belonged to private persons who are otherwise unknown.

The seal of Jezebel – a grey stone seal belonging to the queen whose name is a byword for wickedness. Most of the royal motifs are Egyptian in origin, such as the winged sphinx and the falcon and cobras forming the symbol known as the uraeus. 1 Kings 16, 31 tells us that Jezebel was the daughter of the Phoenician king of Sidon and it is the Phoenician form of her name that appears on her seal.

The Stela of Mesha, King of Moab, recording his victory over an alliance of Israel, Judah and Edom, referred to in 2 Kings 3, 27 (p. 85). The inscription, in the elegant script of the 9th century BC, is in Moabite, a language closely akin to Hebrew and Canaanite.

becomes *beta*) and eventually passed them down to us. Greek belongs to the Indo-European family of languages and the Greeks also added five new letters (*upsilon*, *phi*, *xi*, *psi* and *omega*) at the end of their alphabet for Greek sounds which did not exist in Semitic tongues. To the Greeks also belongs the credit for the invention of the vowel system. With a stroke of genius that seems obvious only in retrospect, they took as vowel signs the Semitic symbols for sounds which had no equivalent in Greek. At first they wrote right to left, in Semitic fashion, or sometimes *boustrophedon*, that is 'as the ox ploughs' – right to left for the first line, then left to right and so on. Eventually the convention was fixed from left to right and the shapes of the letters stabilized into the forms more or less as they are today.

The last element in the transmission of the alphabet into the script you are reading now, took place when the Greeks founded colonies in Italy. The alphabet was taken up by the peoples there, notably the Etruscans, and has come down to us via the Romans, who added a few more letters (C for example) and abandoned some of the Greek ones. In northern Europe in the Middle Ages further refinements were made, including, for instance, the letter W. But ultimately the origin of virtually all the alphabetic systems in use in the world today goes back to the Canaanites of the 2nd millennium BC. The alphabet stands as one of the world's greatest inventions and perhaps the most important inheritance we have from the ancient Near East. Without it we would not have the Bible, nor the rich traditions of Judaism and Christianity, nor the achievements of Classical philosophy and science. The elaborate script of Arabic, the medium for the Koran and the glories of Islamic culture, is also ultimately dependent on the early alphabet of Bronze Age Canaan.

OSTRACA

An ostracon (pl. ostraca) is a pottery sherd which has been written on (p. 97). In the ancient Near East sherds were used as a form of scrap paper, for quick notes, lists, short letters or file copies. It was a form of recycling old material and saved on the cost of using expensive papyrus. It is fortunate for us that this custom was in use, as papyrus deteriorates quickly in damp climates but potsherds are nearly indestructible. Inscribed sherds have been found in many countries and they add enormously to our knowledge.

The alphabet abroad

By the 8th century BC it is clear from the numbers of ostraca (pieces of broken pottery bearing inscriptions) and other marked objects that literacy was on the increase in the Levant. But this was also the time when mercantile contacts with the outside world were developing very fast. It cannot be a coincidence that the mid-8th century BC is precisely the time when alphabetic inscriptions are found for the first time in Greece. The earliest is on a jug from Athens, which seems to have been offered as the prize in a foot race. The Greeks adopted the names of the letters along with their shapes (so, for example, *aleph* becomes *alpha* and *beth*

The earliest known Greek inscription, lightly scratched around the neck of an Athenian jug.

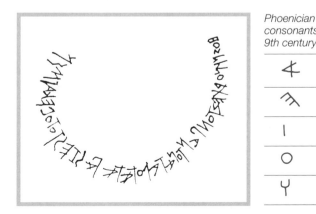

Phoenician consonants 9th century BC	Greek vowels Archaic	Greek vowels Classical
ᚷ	A A	A
∃	∃	E
ǀ	ǀ	I
O	O	O
Ψ	U	Y

Take thee a roll of a book and write therein all the words…
Jeremiah 36, 2

THE BIBLE IS DIVIDED into the Old and New Testaments. Jews consider only the former to be authoritative, and generally refer to it as the Hebrew Bible. Christians believe the New Testament, beginning with the ministry of Jesus in the four gospels (Matthew, Mark, Luke and John), to be more important. To Moslems both sections of the Scriptures are theologically valid and the Bible ranks second only to their holy book, the Koran.

Jews are often called 'the People of the Book', but this simple statement begs the question of what exactly is meant by 'the Book'. The easiest aspect of this issue to resolve is that of the changing physical shape of books. In antiquity the works which make up the Bible were written on rolls of papyrus or leather, and not sewn into the form which we today recognize as a book. The words *sefer* (Hebrew), *biblos* (Greek) and *volumen* (Latin) are always translated into English as 'book', but more properly mean 'a writing scroll'. The format of modern books did not come into general use in the Near East until it was adopted by Christians in the 2nd century AD. True books (called in Latin *codex*, plural *codices*) are more economic than scrolls, because both sides of the sheet can be written on. Thus more material can be contained in a single volume. They are also easier to carry around than a scroll. Jews, however, continue to use parchment Scrolls of the Law (the first five books of the Old Testament), at least for public use in synagogues.

Nobody would dispute that the works contained in the Bible cover a vast span of time from the Creation to the days of Jesus and Paul, nor that they were written by many different authors – historians, scribes, poets, prophets, apostles and even kings. Many authorities would also agree that even within a single biblical text there is evidence that many hands were at work at different times. But it is only within the last few decades that many people have come to understand that standardization of the text of the whole Bible is a relatively recent phenomenon. The realization has come about with the widespread publicity given to the Dead Sea Scrolls (pp. 122–25). If the biblical text had been standard from the beginning, many of the pieces – some long sections, others merely fragments – which were found in the caves of Qumran would duplicate each other, but instead they preserve variant readings. What is more, all of these readings were evidently felt worthy of preservation. Clearly at this time (between the 2nd century BC and the 1st century AD) there was no such thing as a single standard text of the Bible. It was not until after the destruction of the Second Temple by the Romans in AD 70 that the rabbis at Jamnia (Yavneh) began the lengthy task, not completed until nearly a thousand years later, of establishing the 'correct' version of the Hebrew Bible (p. 161).

The Massoretes and the Hebrew Bible

Although the text of the first five books of the Bible, called in Hebrew the Torah, or 'the Law' was never as fluid as the rest of the Hebrew Bible, none of it stabilized completely until the 10th century AD. By this time not only the text, but also its correct pronunciation had become a problem for Jews because Hebrew had fallen out of use as a spoken language sometime after the Second Jewish Revolt (AD 132–35). Jewish scholars called Massoretes (*massorah* means 'tradition') recorded this dying knowledge by inventing systems of vowel signs, accents and even musical notation to guide those who chanted portions of the Torah aloud during synagogue services. The Massoretic additions were not, however, added to the Torah scrolls themselves, which were too holy to be interfered with in any way, but were included in manuscripts intended for private study.

The Bible in Hebrew

The Massoretes were also involved in the creation of a definitive edition of the Hebrew Bible by the addition of a critical apparatus in the margins of the text itself. The most important Hebrew text is that of the Massorete, Aaron ben Asher, who lived in the 10th century AD in Tiberias, on the shores of the Sea of Galilee. Two early manuscripts in ben Asher's tradition are preserved – the Aleppo Codex and the Leningrad Codex. It was Aaron ben Asher's version of the Hebrew Bible which found favour with Maimonides, the great

PAPYRUS AND PARCHMENT
Papyrus paper is made from the long split stems of the plant, called the bulrush in the Bible, which grows plentifully in the Egyptian delta. Thin parallel strips are laid in water with a second layer placed at right angles over them. As the water evaporates pressure is applied and the two layers become glued together, creating a fabric-like material. In late antiquity it was exported to the Mediterranean world from the Phoenician city of Byblos, the Greek name for Gebal. Byblos in Greek originally meant 'papyrus', but came to mean 'book' and eventually the Bible.

Parchment (a word derived from the city of Pergamon in Asia Minor where there was a library in ancient times rivalling that of Alexandria) was originally made from sheep- or calf-skin, prepared by stretching it while wet and then cleaning it with pumice. Far more durable than papyrus, it became the most widespread material in use before rag paper.

ORIGEN'S HEXAPLA

In Caesarea a Church Father and theologian called Origen (c. AD 185–254) produced the Hexapla which arranged six versions of the Old Testament (four of them in Greek) in parallel columns for easy comparison with the Hebrew of the first column. The second column was a transliteration of the Hebrew text into Greek characters.

DIVISIONS OF THE BIBLE

THE HEBREW BIBLE
The Hebrew Bible (or Old Testament) is divided differently by Jews and Christians. It has three major sections: 1 Torah – Genesis, Exodus, Leviticus, Numbers and Deuteronomy – also called 'the Law' (the word means 'instruction'). 2 Neveeim – the Prophets, which further subdivide into a) the Former Prophets (Joshua, Judges, 1 and 2 Samuel, 1 and 2 Kings) and b) the Latter Prophets (Isaiah, Jeremiah, Ezekiel and the 12 Minor Prophets). 3 Ketuvim – the Writings (Chronicles, Ezra, Nehemiah, Job, Psalms, Proverbs, Daniel and the five Megilot (Scrolls) – the Song of Solomon, Ruth, Lamentations, Ecclesiastes and Esther. In Hebrew the Bible is called the Tanach, which is an acronym of the initial letters of the three divisions (with the K pronounced as in 'loch').
THE CHRISTIAN BIBLE
This is divided into 5 parts: 1 The Gospels – Matthew, Mark, Luke and John. 2 Acts of the Apostles. 3 Letters of Paul. 4 Other letters. 5 Revelation.

The Old Testament

Genesis
Exodus
Leviticus
Numbers
Deuteronomy
Joshua
Judges
Ruth
1 Samuel
2 Samuel
1 Kings
2 Kings
1 Chronicles
2 Chronicles
Ezra
Nehemiah
Esther
Job
Psalms
Proverbs
Ecclesiastes
Song of Solomon
Isaiah
Jeremiah
Lamentations
Ezekiel
Daniel
Hosea
Joel
Amos
Obadiah
Jonah
Micah
Nahum
Habakkuk
Zephaniah
Haggai
Zechariah
Malachi

The New Testament

Matthew
Mark
Luke
John
Acts

(Traditionally ascribed to St Paul)
Romans
1 Corinthians
2 Corinthians
Galatians
Ephesians
Philippians
Colossians
1 Thessalonians
2 Thessalonians
1 Timothy
2 Timothy
Titus
Philemon
Hebrews

James
1 Peter
2 Peter
1 John
2 John
3 John
Jude
Revelation

- The Law
- The Former Prophets
- The Writings
- The Latter Prophets
- The Gospels
- Letters
- Acts / Revelation

The New Testament was originally written in Greek, the lingua franca of the Classical world. Nearly 5,500 manuscripts of the New Testament are known, of which about 2,300 are lectionaries – selections used in Christian services – and only 59 contain the complete New Testament. The earliest fragment found so far is this portion of John 18, written on papyrus and dating to between AD 100 and 150 and now in the John Rylands Library in Manchester, Great Britain.

The oldest complete New Testament is the Codex Sinaiticus, found during the 19th century AD in the library of the ancient monastery of Santa Katerina at the foot of Mt Sinai, and now in the British Library. It was written, like its near contemporary, the Codex Vaticanus, on parchment in elegant capital letters called uncials, during the 4th century AD.

Jewish scholar who lived in Spain in the 12th century AD, and which formed the basis of the great Bomberg Bible, printed in Venice in 1524/5. This became the standard text on which most Hebrew bibles have been based ever since.

The Old Testament in translation

Since it now seems that many versions of the same scriptural material were preserved at Qumran (and also in other ancient libraries), they must all have been considered to have equal validity, preserving different traditions and theological points of view.

The difficulty of maintaining textual accuracy is compounded with problems of translation.

All translation inevitably involves interpretation, but many translators of the Bible deliberately went beyond the process of simple translation in order to expound the scriptures in a way appropriate for their own communities. This trend was already apparent in the two Targums (Aramaic) and the Septuagint (Greek), translations made for the Jewish communities of the diaspora in Hellenistic times. Indeed, the Septuagint (p. 113) was originally considered too free by many Jews, although it later came to be venerated almost equally with the Hebrew original. It was quoted extensively in the New Testament and the order of the books in the Septuagint underlies the order of the Christian Old Testament.

The history of the New Testament

For the very earliest Christians the Scriptures still meant the Hebrew Bible, taking from the various versions those readings which best suited their needs. The first truly Christian writings were the letters of Paul to churches around the Eastern Mediterranean. By the middle of the 1st century AD the generation who had witnessed the ministry of Jesus was passing and it was realized that accounts of his life would be needed for the burgeoning Christian communities. Thus oral traditions which had built up about him were gradually collected and written down in Greek, the universal language of the day. Many scholars today think that the gospel according to Mark was the first to be written, and that the accounts in Matthew and Luke depend on it. The gospel of John may be up to a century later in its final form.

The oral and written traditions of the early Christians were as flexible as those of the Jews. Scribal errors and differences of interpretation crept into the texts and, in addition, not all Christian writings were universally accepted among the different communities. The canon of the New Testament was not fixed for the Eastern Church until AD 367 and for the Western Church by the Council of Carthage in AD 397. It took until AD 419 for such works as Hebrews and James to be included in the western canon at the instigation of St Augustine of Hippo. In the west the New Testament now contains 27 works; in some eastern churches the number varies. Among the Copts, for instance, there are 38 canonical books, while for the Nestorians of Syria there are only 22.

Translating the Christian Bible

The work of translating the New Testament from the Greek began very early. By the 2nd century AD there were already versions in at least two languages: Syriac (a Syrian dialect of Aramaic, spoken among remote communities in Lebanon until recently and still used liturgically in the Syrian Orthodox church) and Old Latin. The Latin translations were very fragmentary and frequently became corrupt in the hands of different scribes.

Jerome and the Vulgate

In AD 382 Pope Damasus commissioned Jerome (c. AD 185–254) to produce a text of the Bible in Latin which would be standard throughout the Church. Jerome took up residence in Bethlehem and spent the next two decades on this task, producing the version known as the Vulgate, which is still in use in the west, where

it underlies many translations into modern languages. Before AD 1000 there were versions of the Bible in the vernacular of most countries with Christian communities, such as Coptic, Ethiopian, Gothic and Arabic. In England as early as the 7th century AD various parts of the Bible were translated and in oral use in the liturgy. The written form came a little later, but it was not until John Wycliffe (c. 1329–84) and the Lollards that the complete Bible was translated into English from the Vulgate.

William Tyndale (c. 1494–1536) is often called the Father of the English Bible. Translating from the Greek version of Erasmus (published in 1516 in Holland), Tyndale's New Testament appeared in 1526. It was the first English version to appear in printed form and is the foundation for the King James Version. He only finished work on the first five books of the Old Testament before he was burned at the stake as a heretic, for trying to bring the Bible within reach of ordinary people.

Official sanction was finally given for a translation into English in the reign of James I. A committee of 54 scholars worked for six years before the King James, or Authorized, Version appeared in England in 1611. The invention of printing with movable type brought the Scriptures within reach of more people. The first printed Bible – the Gutenberg Bible – was published in Latin around 1455. In Europe over 100 editions of the Vulgate alone appeared before 1500 and there were numerous vernacular versions too. It is estimated that today the Bible has been translated into about 2,000 different languages in over 300 versions.

No man was so rude a scholar but that he might learn the Gospel according to its simplicity.
John Wycliffe

If God spare my life, ere many years I will cause a boy that driveth the plough shall know more of the scripture than thou dost.
William Tyndale, *when faced with the argument that Christians needed Canon Law (i.e. Church Law) more than God's Law (i.e. the Bible).*

THE TORAH
The Torah (the Scroll of the Law or Five Books of Moses) is the most sacred part of the Jewish scriptures. Orthodox Jews believe that the Torah was dictated by God to Moses on Mt Sinai and is so holy that not one 'jot or tittle' of it may be changed. The scribe (sofer) who writes it must offer special prayers each day before beginning work and uses parchment, ink and reed pens expressly prepared for the purpose. Horizontal lines are lightly inscribed into the parchment and letters are 'hung' from, rather than positioned on them. The individual sheets, each containing several columns of writing, are sewn together with leather thread to make up a complete scroll, which can take up to a year to write.

PLANTS AND ANIMALS OF THE BIBLE

For, lo, the winter is past, the rain is over and gone. The flowers appear on the earth; the time of the singing of birds is come, and the voice of the turtle is heard in our land. The fig tree putteth forth her green figs, and the vines with the tender grape give a good smell.

The Song of Solomon 2, 11–13

Camels were the great beasts of burden in the Bible lands – able to carry heavy loads and well adapted to the desert. However, there is no firm evidence for the domesticated camel before the 1st millennium BC. *The one-humped or Arabian camel is native to the Near East. Here, strange two-humped Bactrian camels are being brought as valuable tribute to the Assyrian king, Shalmaneser. This scene is carved on his Black Obelisk (p. 86).*

For the Lord thy God bringeth thee into a good land, a land of brooks of water, of fountains and depths that spring out of valleys and hills; a land of wheat, and barley, and vines, and fig trees, and pomegranates; a land of oil olive, and honey.

Deuteronomy 8, 7–8

THE LEVANT, THE HEART OF the Bible lands, is a bridge between three continents: Europe, Africa and Asia. In addition to native species of plants and animals, others from all three continents have colonized the Levant, utilizing the great variety of climate, terrain and vegetation which is to be found there.

To the ancient Israelites, Canaan was a land 'flowing with milk and honey' (Exodus 3, 8 and Deuteronomy 26, 15). To the Children of Israel the image this brought to mind was one of forests and rough grazing land, with plentiful pastures for animals and a profusion of wild flowers in winter and spring for the bees. Such a land was suitable for pastoralists, but during all their years of wandering in the wilderness the Israelites dreamed of settling down and becoming farmers once they reached Canaan.

The agricultural harvest taken to the Temple as first-fruits shows that the Israelites did indeed become farmers. Wheat and barley, grapes and figs, olives, pomegranates and dates (probably in fact the source of the honey of the opening quote) were the seven crops which were the main produce in biblical times. Many other crops were grown or gathered of course, but these seven required the most attention. If they failed, famine threatened the people. The crucial time was the period of 50 days between the festivals of Passover and Pentecost (or *Shavuot*), which fall between mid-April and mid-June. The climate of the Levant is so variable from year to year that special prayers for the right combination of rain and warmth were (and are still) offered at this time of the year.

Wind and rain

The north wind brings the rain needed to swell the ripening cereals; but if the temperature rises too early in the season the flowers of the olive trees open too soon and the rain destroys them. The south wind brings warmth and helps to set the fruit of date, grape and pomegranate; but early heat can scorch the ripening wheat and barley. Too much or too little rain or warmth coming at the wrong time brought extreme hardship for the people. Genesis makes clear that the Israelites sometimes had to go to Egypt to buy food: 'for famine was sore in the land of Canaan' (Genesis 47, 4). It has been said that fears about this perilous situation were symbolized, according to Exodus 26, 35, in the Tabernacle in the wilderness. The table for the 12 loaves, one for each of the 12 Tribes of Israel, was placed by the north wall, the quarter of the rain-bearing wind which ripened the wheat; while the seven-branched lamp (*menorah*), which burned pure olive oil, stood at the south, the direction of the warm wind which set the fruit of the olive.

Of hoopoes and hippos

Hoopoes and hippos are two of the more extraordinary creatures of the Bible lands, neither of which were to be eaten according to the rules laid down for the Israelites in Leviticus (11, 9). The hoopoe, with its flamboyant crest, black and white plumage and long beak for grubbing insects out of crevices, is one of the most spectacular birds of the region. The hippopotamus, most scholars agree, is the animal referred to as '*behemot*' in Job 40, 15. It is one of several biblical animals that no longer exist in the region. The Bible texts are also full of more mundane animals, some very familiar, and important, such as sheep, goat, cattle and pig (this last being forbidden food). Among other domestic animals were donkeys, camels and horses, used for traction and as beasts of burden. Chickens were also kept, though they were introduced quite late. Perhaps the earliest mention of them is in the New Testament, as the cock whose crowing marks Peter's betrayal of Jesus.

Sheep (left) were central to the existence of people in biblical times. They provided meat, milk and wool for clothing, as well as being the primary animal offered in sacrifices. Tending the flocks was such an important part of life that the shepherd and his sheep were used as images throughout the Bible to illustrate God's relationship with his people. One of the chief predators of the flocks was the lion (above). Common in Old Testament times, it had become rarer by New Testament days and is now extinct in the region. This lioness and her cub are depicted in a mosaic from a synagogue in Gaza, dating to the early 6th century AD.

The pomegranate (left) ripens towards the end of summer. This exotic-looking fruit has a bright red juicy flesh with numerous seeds, making it a symbol of fertility. It was often used as a decorative motif: for instance, it was embroidered on the hem of the high priest's robe (Exodus 28, 33–4) and ornamented the pillars of Solomon's temple (1 Kings 7, 20).

Many wild animals would have been familiar sights to the inhabitants of the region, such as the wild ass or onager. The ibex, sometimes wrongly translated as 'wild goat', can still be seen today at such places as Ein Gedi, where they delicately browse on the sparse greenery of seemingly sheer cliffs. In the same area there are still conies (the rock hyrax) and leopards, just as there were in biblical days. Other dangerous animals named in the Bible include wolves and lions, and there were scavengers like hyaenas and jackals.

Birds of all kinds abounded and even today huge flocks stream through the Levant corridor on their migrations between Africa and Europe. Some were hunted for food – the best known is the tiny quail which paused in the Israelite camp on its spring migration and was gathered up and eaten with the manna (Exodus 16, 13). Another migrant is the stork, the 'pious bird', which is still a familiar visitor in spring and autumn. Other birds include varieties of eagle, owls, hawks and vultures, as well as doves and partridges, and water birds such as cormorants, pelicans and bitterns. And there was never a lack of the insects that prey on humans, such as fleas and lice, nor of pests like locusts, hornets, scorpions, asps and vipers.

HEARTH AND HOME IN OLD TESTAMENT TIMES

THE YAVNEH YAM
INSCRIPTION
*A message, lightly penned on a
potsherd and dating to the late 7th
century BC, is a complaint by a
reaper to the governor of the small
coastal fortress where it was
found. The reaper says that an
official had confiscated his garment
and demands its immediate return,
in accordance with biblical law
(Exodus 22, 26–27). The reaper
promises then to deliver his grain
'in full', suggesting that he had not
done so previously.*

*The inscription is interesting,
not just for its intrinsic value, but
because it shows that even an
unlettered man could employ a
scribe to write a letter, or, as in this
case, a complaint, on his behalf. It
also demonstrates that an ordinary
peasant was able to find a means
of his redressing wrongs in ancient
Israelite society.*

*She seeketh wool, and flax, and worketh willingly
with her hands. She is like the merchants' ships;
she bringeth her food from afar. She riseth while it
is yet night, and giveth meat to her household, and
a portion to her maidens. She considereth a field,
and buyeth it: with the fruit of her hands she
planteth a vineyard... She perceiveth that her
merchandise is good: her candle goeth out not by
night. She layeth her hands to the spindle, and her
hands hold the distaff.*
Proverbs 31, 13–19

THERE WERE FEW TOWNS of any size in the kingdom in the days of David (10th century BC).
Not many were as large as Jerusalem, which, in
truth, was very small by today's standards.
When large tell sites have been investigated
they usually prove to be royal administrative
and military centres, like Megiddo, Lachish or
Beersheba, in which any ordinary houses were
probably those of the military garrison. Recent
regional surveys have suggested that the majority of the population lived in small settlements
dependent on the nearest large centre for protection and refuge when necessary. The household probably consisted of parents and children with grandparents and other members of
the extended family.

Domestic housing seems to have been of a
reasonably high standard, though it could be
argued that only solidly-built structures would
survive for archaeologists to find. The houses
were built of mud brick on stone foundations
and needed a great deal of maintenance to
keep them weatherproof. A similar building
plan was followed all over the country – often
called the 'four-roomed house', though some
examples had only three rooms at ground-floor
level while others had more than four.

The rôle of women

Women were mostly concerned with the care
of their families and the running of their
homes. Whether a wife, concubine or slave –
and all three might live together under one
roof at this time – a woman's domestic duties
were roughly the same, the only difference
being in her position in the family pecking-

THE FOUR-ROOMED HOUSE

*The typical Israelite house was the
four-roomed house, reconstructed
below and, on the right, rebuilt at
Tell Qasileh. Most domestic
activities took place in the central
courtyard, either at ground level or
on the first floor if the central area
was roofed over. Access to the
upper floor was by a staircase of
wood or stone, with perhaps
another from outside the house, as
in Ahiel's House in Jerusalem.
The rooms were mostly used for
storage, except in bad weather or
for nursing the sick and for women
giving birth. The courtyard and
roof of a house thus formed its
combined kitchen, eating and
living areas and even bedroom, as
is still the case today in many
countries in the Near East. From
the roof of his hilltop palace, David
had a view of Bathsheba, his
future queen, washing herself in
the open air, presumably on the
roof of her house, suitably screened
from the gaze of her neighbours,
but easily visible from above.*

order (Genesis 21, 9–21). Within the family a woman's daily work included fetching water, grinding flour, cooking and looking after children and animals.

Women and girls were also engaged in carding and spinning wool and weaving cloth for family use. The simpler household pots may have been made by women, as in parts of the eastern Mediterranean today, though standardization of pottery types in the First Temple period implies that pots were manufactured in central workshops (Jeremiah 18, 1–2). Women sometimes worked in the fields alongside the men (as in the story of Ruth) and tended the flocks. They also found employment as cooks and bakers in the homes of the wealthy (1 Samuel 8, 13) and acted as midwives, like Shiphrah and Puah in Egypt (Exodus 1, 15).

All women were entirely subject to the men of their family and even though their status was carefully regulated by law, the unfortunate lot of a widow or orphan was proverbial (1 Kings 17, 10–12). Nevertheless, some women had remarkable strength of character. Examples include Miriam, sister of Aaron and Moses, and Deborah, who was both a judge and the leader who goaded Israel into action against Jabin, the Canaanite king of Hazor (Judges 4). Ruth supported her widowed mother-in-law, Naomi, with great fortitude, and became the ancestress of King David and Jesus according to the gospel of Matthew (Matthew 1).

Earning a living

Biblical society was a feudal pyramid, with the king at its peak and the bulk of the population at its base. Between the two estates were the king's officials in key civil and military posts. They were often the king's relatives, as these were the only people he felt he could trust completely. Priests came from families of the priestly tribe of Levi, whose interests were not always the same as the king's. Professional classes, such as traders, metalworkers, doctors, scribes, and weavers and dyers of fine cloth also found their place in society. The majority of the people, however, were peasant farmers, who grew the crops for food and the flax for making garments and hangings, such as those of the Temple. Then, as now, they were also shepherds and goatherds, whose daily routine was that followed by Jacob when he tended the sheep of Laban, his uncle and father-in-law, in Haran (Genesis 30).

Wool from the sheep or goats was spun using a simple weighted spindle, probably in much the same way as this woman does today, near Jericho (far left). One daily domestic task for the women of the biblical household was baking the bread (centre) that was a staple part of the diet. This pottery figurine of a woman kneading dough on a three-legged table is from a Phoenician cemetery at Achziv, as is that of the woman taking her bath (right) in a shallow oval tub, reminiscent of the story of Bathsheba. Both figurines date to around the 8th century BC.

A SCHOOL EXERCISE

The Gezer Calendar, found at Gezer and dated to the late 10th century BC, is scratched into the surface of a soft limestone tablet. The inscription was carved so badly that many scholars think it was a schoolboy's exercise, and this is borne out by the subject matter, which is a mnemonic of the farming year, listed according to the agricultural activity of each season. Several mistakes have been scratched out (for example, the last letter at the left-hand end of the fourth line) and it was scruffily signed with the letters A B I, after which the tablet is now broken. It may have been the name Abijah – and the boy would definitely not have received a good mark for this exercise in penmanship.

II

IN THE BEGINNING

Be fruitful and multiply; a nation and a company of nations
shall be of thee and kings shall come out of your loins…
Genesis 35, 11

AROUND THE 10TH MILLENNIUM BC the people of the Near East began the long technological and cultural journey from gathering and hunting to farming and city-dwelling. By the end of the 4th millennium BC the scene was set for the great urban and literate civilizations of Mesopotamia and Egypt. In the northern Levant (modern Syria and Lebanon) people came into close contact with Mesopotamian culture. In the south (Jordan and Israel), the main stimulus came from the Nile valley.

By around 3000 BC the Amorites of northern Syria had spread out from their homeland and were to be found in cities throughout Mesopotamia. They were a Semitic people (Semites are people who speak Semitic languages). Not all Semitic people lived in cities, however. Many preferred a nomadic life, migrating seasonally with their flocks in search of grazing and water. This is the background of Abraham, traditional forefather of Israel. It should be noted that not all scholars think of him as a historical personage.

In the 17th century BC Semitic tribal groups – some perhaps to be equated with the patriarchal clans of the Bible – gained a foothold in the Egyptian delta, establishing their own Hyksos dynasty. They were expelled by the Egyptians in the 16th century BC at the start of the New Kingdom. For the next 350 years the area of Canaan and Syria came under Egyptian control. This was the great cosmopolitan era of the Late Bronze Age. In the eastern Mediterranean trade flourished, with merchants passing between Egypt, the Levant, Cyprus, Crete and Greece. As part of the Egyptian empire, the level of peace and prosperity had never been higher for the people of Canaan.

A detail from the 'Standard of Ur', dating to around the mid-3rd millennium BC and now in the British Museum, showing a Sumerian with a mixed flock of sheep and goats. The motif of the good shepherd with his flock goes back to the most ancient period of Near Eastern history and also stands for the patriarchs –Abraham, Isaac and Jacob – who, with their extended family clans, were pastoralists rather than farmers.

BEFORE THE BIBLE

There were giants in the earth in those days…
Genesis 6, 4

THE CLIMATE OF THE NEAR EAST around 12,000 years ago was as warm as it is now, but rainfall was higher and forests flourished. Over the following centuries, as the ice of the last glaciation melted, sea level rose worldwide and in the eastern Mediterranean archaeologists have found remains of early villages under the sea, off the coast of Israel. Around this time some groups took the first hesitant steps towards producing their own food and tending herds, rather than relying on hunting and gathering.

The Natufians

The Natufian, dating from the very end of the Old Stone Age (Epipalaeolithic, around 10,500 to 8300 BC), is the best known and most widespread local culture in the Levant at this period. It takes its name from a cave in the Wadi en-Natuf in the Judaean Hills where it was first identified.

In addition to caves, the Natufians were the first people to live in permanent villages, of perhaps up to 150 people. They had simple houses, partly dug into the ground, the sides of the pit held in place by stone boulders. Roofs were made either of skin or thatch. Inside, traces of hearths and storage pits for grain and other commodities have been found. The

Natufians still lived by gathering and hunting and they made seasonal forays from their home settlements into the drier areas to hunt, mostly for gazelle, then a common animal in the region, which was also often represented in art.

The characteristic stone tools of this period are tiny blades called microliths. These were hafted into bone handles to make composite tools used to cut cereal grasses for food, or cane and straw for roofing, mat-making and basket-weaving. Stone pestles and mortars to grind flour from cereal grasses or nuts or acorns are quite common, while at Eynan near the Sea of Galilee, finds include bone fish-hooks, harpoons and net sinkers.

Burials have been found at many Natufian sites, containing bodies buried on their sides in a contracted (tightly crouched), position. The dead were frequently accompanied by jewellery, often of shell, and other grave goods, such as animals carved from stone and bone.

From food gathering to food producing

Much scholarly debate has focused on the shift of emphasis from food gathering to food production and from a mostly nomadic life to a settled existence. This is the point of transition from the Old Stone Age (or Epipalaeolithic in the case of the Natufians) to the New Stone Age (Neolithic), characterized by farming communities. In the Levant the Neolithic is

THE TOWER OF JERICHO

The settlement at the oasis town of Jericho was excavated in the 1950s by the British archaeologist Kathleen Kenyon (right). In the PPNA the site was already large and was surrounded by a defensive system comprising a dry moat and a high stone wall. Behind the wall was a solid tower (left) built of rough stones coated with a layer of mud plaster, still surviving to an impressive height of 27 ft (8.2 m) with a diameter of 28 ft (8.5 m). Inside, a staircase gives access to the top. Since the tower was inside the wall it was probably not built for defence, but it is hard to find another explanation for it. Whatever its purpose, such a monumental structure at this early

period is an astonishing achievement, both architecturally and for the degree of social organization implied in such a large communal public project.

divided into two: the earlier before the invention of pottery (Pre-Pottery Neolithic or PPN) and the latter after it (Pottery Neolithic or PN), dating together to 8300 to 5500 BC.

The Pre-Pottery Neolithic

Several large settlements are known from the first pre-pottery Neolithic period (PPNA), such as Jericho (Tell es-Sultan) in Palestine. With only small variations the culture seems to have been common to the whole region and it was obviously a successful way of life, based on both farming and hunting. While two important cereals, species of barley and wheat, had been domesticated, no animals had yet certainly come under man's control.

Population increased in the following period, PPNB, and large and thriving settlements have been found in various places, such as Tell Abu Hureira on the Middle Euphrates in Syria

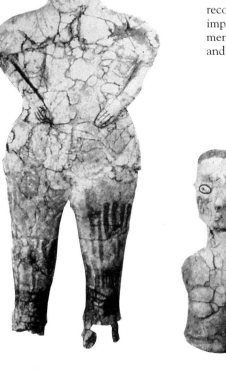

and the site at Ain Ghazal in Jordan. This covers some 30 acres (12 ha), making it the largest known Neolithic site in the Near East.

Houses were now built with straight walls of adobe or mud bricks on stone foundations. Some had floors of lime plaster, a considerable technological advance, though burning the limestone to produce lime consumed a large amount of timber. Crops, such as emmer and einkorn wheat, barley, peas, lentils and flax were grown. Domestic animals including goats and sheep and, later, pigs and cattle were herded, in preference to hunting. People had become skilled in food production and storage and so settlements could grow to some size.

The invention of pottery

By about 6000 BC many sites, at least in the south of the region, had been abandoned. The reasons for this are not clear, but one theory is that primitive agriculture coupled with tree felling brought about intense erosion. In Syria large settlements continued to flourish, both inland, as at Tell Abu Hureira, and on the coast, such as Byblos and Ras Shamra.

Pottery was invented at this time. At first it was handmade and very crude – the clay used contained large amounts of impurities and firing was poor, with vessels almost certainly baked in the low temperatures of the domestic hearth. Although pottery breaks easily it is virtually indestructible. In the archaeological record it replaces flint implements as the most important means of understanding developments and changes, as well as the differences and interrelationships between various groups.

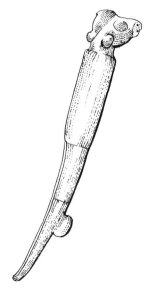

The bone haft of a Natufian knife or sickle, with a representation of a gazelle's head. The delicate carving shows that the Natufians had a developed artistic sense as well as considerable skill. Tiny, sharp bladelets (microliths) of flint were inserted into a groove below the handle and fixed into place with bitumen. When one broke or became blunt, it could easily be replaced.

The site of Ain Ghazal in Jordan has been excavated by a joint American–Jordanian team led by Gary Rollefson and Zeidan Kafafi. Towards the end of the 8th millennium BC Ain Ghazal began as a small settlement of farming hunters. By 6000 BC, however, it had grown, perhaps containing a population of over 2,000.

Among the most interesting finds from the site are the extraordinary statues and busts, measuring between 14 and 35 in. (35 and 90 cm) tall and dating to between around 7000 BC and 6500 BC. Made of lime plaster

modelled on a core of reed and grass, many had painted details in green, red and black. The full figures may represent either men or women and the smaller busts may be of adults also, or possibly children. Over 30 examples have now been found in different caches and they may be evidence of an ancestor cult, like the famous plastered skulls from Jericho, examples of which have also been found at Ain Ghazal. The dead at this time normally had the head removed from the body and buried beneath the floor of a house or in a courtyard.

Some of the remarkable objects from the Nahal Mishmar treasure, which consisted of over 400 pieces made of copper.

Secondary burial may have been the usual way of disposing of the dead in the Chalcolithic. Once the flesh had decomposed the bones were collected up and put in boxes, or ossuaries, some of which were painted to resemble houses.

Early metalworkers

A great technological leap came in the Levant when people first began to exploit copper in the second half of the 5th millennium BC. The Chalcolithic, as this period is known (*chalcos* is Greek for copper), lasted for most of the 4th millennium. Finds of copper objects are quite rare, probably because the metal was highly valued and broken items would have been recycled.

The number of settlements rose, though oddly many were located in marginal areas. Most houses were of the 'broadroom' type, that is a room broader than it was long. This design was one of the most persistent in Canaan for both domestic and sacred architecture, lasting right through the following Early Bronze Age.

There is little evidence for either public planning or works on any scale. A single large building, possibly a shrine, is the most that has been found at any one site. The small temple complex at Ein Gedi, on a cliff high above the oasis, with magnificent views across the Jordan valley, was not attached to any settlement and may have been a religious centre for various tribes and communities throughout the south.

The Cave of the Treasure

Many of the finds of this period display a high technical and artistic sophistication, exemplified by the remarkable copper objects found at Nahal Mishmar in the Cave of the Treasure. Over 400 copper pieces were found, which were apparently ritual in function, including 'crowns' and 'standards', featuring various animals. All may have been made locally, using the lost-wax technique. Ivory for objects in the same hoard possibly came from Africa, via Egypt, or Syria. Such distant trade connections, even if carried on indirectly by intermediaries, are remarkable for the period. Linen and woollen textiles were also preserved in the dry conditions of the cave. The whole assemblage may have been hidden there for safekeeping during some crisis and Professor David Ussishkin has suggested that they in fact originally came from the shrine at Ein Gedi.

Teleilat Ghassul

One characteristic culture of this period is called the Ghassulian, from the village of Teleilat Ghassul east of the River Jordan where it was first found. The site, which covers some

50 acres (24 ha), lies northeast of the Dead Sea in the foothills of the Jordanian Plateau at about 1,000 ft (300 m) above sea level. It flourished from around the late 5th to almost the end of the 4th millennium BC and was frequently rebuilt following earthquakes. Today the environment around the site is almost desert-like, but in the Chalcolithic it would have been much more hospitable. Date palms and olive groves were cultivated, and in addition people grew cereals and pulses. Thus the classic pattern of eastern Mediterranean agriculture was already established. The bones of domestic animals found in Ghassulian settlements show that the inhabitants kept sheep, goats, cattle and pigs, and perhaps some deer as well.

The Beersheba sites

The Beersheba area in this period was well populated – around 63 sites have been found along the valleys of the Nahal Beersheba and the Nahal Besor. In the vicinity of the modern city of Beersheba three sites appear to be separate sections of a single farming settlement, each also specializing in a different industrial activity. For instance, at Bir Matar there is evidence for copper working and at Bir Safadi an ivory workshop was found. A close resemblance exists between the hoard from the Cave of the Treasure and some objects found at the Beersheba sites.

A rather unusual form of architecture was found at these villages. The inhabitants had carved underground caverns and galleries in the soft rock, though it is not certain whether they lived in them or used them for storage.

The end of the Chalcolithic

Most of the sites of the Ghassulian–Beersheba culture seem to have been abandoned suddenly, around 3300 BC. Of these, many, including Teleilat Ghassul itself, were never reoccupied. Different explanations have been put forward for this disaster. Drought may have caused famines and epidemics in the southern marginal zones; or perhaps the Egyptians, at the dawn of the Dynastic period, attacked, forcing the population to flee. It is also possible that immigrants from Syria or Mesopotamia merged with the local people in the north, and formed the Early Bronze Age population there.

The first cities

The Early Bronze Age in the southern Levant spans the millennium roughly between 3300 and 2300 BC. Conventionally it is divided into three main phases, EB I to III, with an additional final phase that differs considerably from all the preceding ones. The earliest phase, EBI

Carved ivory figurines from the Beersheba sites were made to a very high standard, perhaps in the workshop found at Bir Safadi. This male figurine is very worn and measures 13 in. (33 cm) high. The holes around the head were probably to take tufts of hair for a beard.

THE CHALCOLITHIC OF THE GOLAN

Recently a variation on the basic Chalcolithic material culture of southern Canaan has come to light on the Golan Heights, east of the Sea of Galilee. The discovery is largely due to the work of Claire Epstein, who has pursued research in the region over many years. She has located about 24 village sites of the Chalcolithic in the area of the central Golan. Many were quite large, with between 15 and 40 broadroom houses, some of which measured as much as 50 by 20 ft (15 by 6 m). The local basalt rock was used in their construction and for the roughly paved floors. Internal partitions made roofing easier in an area without tall trees.

A unique feature of villages such as Rasm Harbush and Ain el-Harari is that the houses are joined to each other by their short walls and arranged in several parallel rows, with an open space between them, down a hill slope. Doors are generally in the southern,

downhill, long wall, with a step down to the floor of the house. Few houses have courtyards and storage pits are rare, presumably because they are hard to excavate in the basalt. Instead many large pottery storage vessels (pithoi) were found.

Almost every house contained at least one pillar figurine. The one illustrated here is typical, with its beaky nose, beady eyes and lugs instead of ears. Only the small horns on this example are unusual, though by no means unique. Epstein has suggested that the round depression present on the top of each head was used as an offering bowl. The prominent noses, which are such a feature of many Chalcolithic objects throughout Canaan– for instance the ossuary and the ivory figurine also illustrated on this page – may reflect a belief in the nose as the seat of the breath of life, a belief reflected in Genesis 2, 7.

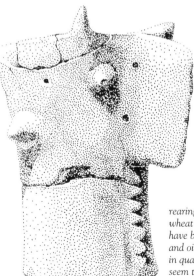

It is not clear whether the villages were occupied year round or only seasonally. The inhabitants practised mixed farming – stock

rearing and raising crops such as wheat and pulses. Olives seem to have been the most common crop, and oil must have been produced in quantity. The villages finally seem to have been abandoned rather than destroyed, because the houses had been emptied of all their portable contents. Possibly a prolonged drought forced the people to move elsewhere.

(c. 3300 to 3050 BC), was, for the most part, still characterized by farming villages. Many of these settlements were founded at new sites rather than at abandoned Chalcolithic ones and several contained houses of oval plan.

Few sites reached any size. One exception was Arad, in the northern Negev – a large settlement built in a bowl created by the slopes of two hills. This location had the advantage of making the most of the rare rainfall, which ran off the slopes to be caught in a large artificial pool at the lowest point of the town. Arad was a fortified settlement and remains of semicircular defensive towers in the line of the walls have been excavated. Jericho also had a strong defensive system at this time. Social organization had thus developed sufficiently for sizeable communal public works to be undertaken.

The growth of cities

It was only in EBII (c. 3050–2700 BC) that urbanism became a significant feature of society in the Canaanite region. This coincides with the emergence of the fully literate urban societies of Sumer, in southern Mesopotamia, and Early Dynastic Egypt. Trade between these powers was growing and many settlements in the Levant were well located to take advantage of the land routes along which trade caravans travelled.

The stimulus for the evolution of cities in the Levant may have come from Egypt, which apart from trade may also have been in contact with the area through colonization or conquest, or alternatively from Mesopotamia, via Syria. Perhaps the impetus was different in the north and south. Sumerian influence was certainly felt in Syria, where the archives of the city of Ebla are beginning to show the extent of that city's commercial links (pp. 46–47).

Megiddo, Beth Shean, Ta'anach and many other settlements developed into urban centres at this time. By modern Near Eastern standards, however, the cities were very small, covering a few acres only. It has been estimated that the total urban area of Canaan in EBII was some 1,500 acres (600 ha), divided between 20 city states, each of which had a hinterland of smaller towns and villages under its control. No one city appears to have been dominant. A standard estimate for the population density of the Bronze Age Levant is 100 persons per acre. This would make the total of urban inhabitants of Canaan in EBII approximately 150,000.

Jordan in the Early Bronze Age is not yet well known, but surface surveys indicate some large cities, for instance Jawa, out in the eastern desert, and Bab edh-Dhra at the southeastern end of the Dead Sea. Neither of these areas could support a large population today and

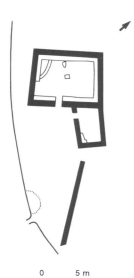

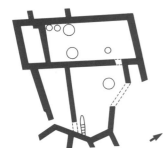

0   5 m
0   16 ft

House plans (above) from Teleilat Ghassul (upper) and Early Bronze Age Arad (lower). The single broadroom unit, with the door in one of the long walls, lasted to the end of the Early Bronze Age for both domestic and cultic buildings.

Aerial view of Arad (right). The Early Bronze Age city is on the left, with its restored defensive wall and semicircular towers. At the lowest (central) point of the site is the reservoir, and, high on the hill, is the Iron Age fortress with its tiny, but important, shrine.

archaeologists believe that they benefited from more rain and a higher water table.

Some cities, both in north and south Canaan, were deserted by the end of EBII. Many different reasons have been advanced for this, including drought, war, epidemics and the failure of trade. Others, however, continued to flourish until the end of EBIII and they presumably absorbed some of the refugees from the abandoned settlements.

The next phase, EBIII (c. 2700–2300 BC), was a troubled time. Many cities were attacked, partly destroyed and rebuilt, some several times. This violence may have been the result of rivalry between the cities rather than outside attack. Perhaps nomadic herders (the forerunners of modern Bedouin) could have been responsible for the some of the destructions; others, as before, may have been due to the Egyptians. One side of the Egyptian Narmer Palette (named after the pharaoh it depicts) shows a vanquished Asiatic lying beside a town with semicircular towers like those of Arad.

Decreasing rainfall and soil erosion brought about by deforestation and primitive agriculture may well have led to disputes between cities over prized agricultural land and good water supplies. Fire finally destroyed EBIII Jericho but not all cities met such a violent end. Archaeologists have found that many others declined gradually and were eventually abandoned without any signs of destruction. At Megiddo, partial occupation of the site continued after the end of EBIII.

The collapse of urbanism

By the end of EBIII urban society in Canaan had entirely collapsed. This dramatic change has sometimes been explained as a result of circumstances elsewhere. Egypt had suffered a temporary decline and the trade that was behind the rise of many Levantine cities must have been disrupted. Another theory suggests that the population of Canaan abandoned the cities and returned to a more nomadic life, perhaps as a result of climate change and soil erosion. Social organization was probably based on the extended family or clan system. Several technological innovations took place at this time – tin was combined with copper to achieve the first true bronze and complex moulds for making metal objects were introduced. For the first time the fast wheel was used in pottery making.

Further north on the Syrian coast, the cities of Ras Shamra and Byblos continued to flourish. Inland, however, the story was different;

cities there suffered the same fate as those further south and the population was sparse. A few villages in eastern Jordan seem to have had permanent or seasonal settlement: at Bab edh-Dhra the urban site shows no signs of decline. In the Judaean Hills remains of hamlets on the hillsides have recently been discovered beneath the agricultural terraces of later ages.

Cemeteries and burials

We have more information about people in death than in life, as the widespread and often large cemeteries are better known than settlements. Unlike the previous and following periods, people were generally buried alone, rather than in family graves. Tombs often took the form of shaft graves, hollowed out of the rock, with a chamber opening from the bottom of the shaft. Most burials are secondary with the bones deposited in disarray – the remains may have been brought to tribal centres for interment long after they had decomposed. Grave goods were few and practical; this was not a wealthy society. Men sometimes had a dagger placed with them, while women were given a few beads. Graves often contain some pottery; one of the commonest vessels is the four-spouted lamp (p. 24), very characteristic of the period. Perhaps the lamps were left burning with the dead to light their way to the next world. Jonathan Tubb of the British Museum has shown that these lamps used fish oil, perhaps more easily available than olive oil, and needed the four wicks to burn properly.

A detail from the Narmer Palette, a ceremonial slate object which depicts victorious scenes from the reign of Narmer, one of the earliest Egyptian pharaohs. Two dead 'Asiatics' (the Egyptian name for the population of the Levant) are shown. Yigael Yadin has theorized that they represent the peoples of the desert and the cultivated lands. The rectangular shape by the left-hand man may be a schematic representation of a city wall with defensive towers like those at Arad; while the 'key-hole' by the figure on the right is perhaps a trap laid out in the desert into which hunters drove game before killing them. Hundreds of such features can be seen from the air in the deserts of Arabia and Jordan, some of them very large.

ABRAHAM THE PATRIARCH

TENSION BETWEEN CAMP
AND CITY

And it came to pass on the third day...that two of the sons of Jacob, Simeon and Levi, Dinah's brethren, took each man his sword, and came upon the city boldly and slew all the males. And they slew Hamor and Shechem his son with the edge of the sword, and took Dinah out of Shechem's house, and went out. The sons of Jacob came upon the slain, and spoiled the city, because they had defiled their sister. They took their sheep, and their oxen, and their asses, and that which was in the city, and that which was in the field.
Genesis 34, 25–28

A family burial cave at Jericho, dating to the Middle Bronze Age. The skeleton of the last person to die lies on the low stone bier, but when the next is buried all the bones will be scattered around the cave. Skulls and bones of the dead can be seen lying in confusion on the floor of the cave, among pottery, grave goods and other debris.

Now the Lord said unto Abram, Get thee out of thy country and from thy kindred and from thy father's house unto a land that I will shew thee...and into the land of Canaan they came.
Genesis 12, 1, 5

ONE OF THE MOST CONTENTIOUS issues in Bible land studies concerns the figure of Abraham (originally Abram), the traditional forefather of Israel. A generation ago scholars such as W.F. Albright and G.E. Wright believed that archaeology would soon be able to prove the historical truth of the Bible (pp. 20–21). Their counterparts today have reacted against this. Many consider that Abraham is the mythic, but not the real, ancestor of Israel.

A few archaeologists and Bible scholars, however, have breathed new life into the ideas of Albright and Wright. They feel that the general agreement between elements of the biblical narrative and archaeological evidence for the Canaanite Middle Bronze Age is too strong to dismiss, making it difficult to accept Abraham simply as a mythical figure. Yet they accept that it is highly unlikely that evidence for Abraham's individual existence will ever be found. He is thus regarded as the ancestor of one element of the various tribes which later joined forces to become the Israelites. Canaan itself is obviously a recognized entity in the biblical account. References to Canaan in the archives at both Ebla (mid-3rd millennium BC)

and Mari (early 2nd millennium BC) show that it was already a known geographical term.

Dating Abraham is another point on which opinions differ. The most radical scholars think he lived at or later than the reign of David (10th century BC). What does seem likely is that the patriarchal narratives of Abraham, Isaac, Jacob and Joseph were preserved orally for centuries before being first written down during the period of David. There must then have been a process of editing which lasted for several centuries until the narratives reached the form in which we now have them. Majority opinion still places Abraham in the Middle Bronze Age – the early 2nd millennium BC.

Archaeology and Abraham

Archaeologists have shown that in the Middle Bronze Age the majority of the Canaanite population once again lived in city-states. Among them, tribal peoples retained a nomadic life, searching for grazing and water for their herds and trading with settled communities.

There are many points of reference between archaeology, historical evidence and the biblical narrative. For instance, excavations in many cemeteries of this period show that it was customary to bury several people in one cave. These may have been members of a single clan who were all buried in the same family tomb, calling to mind the story told in Genesis 23 of Abraham's purchase of the Cave of Machpelah in order to bury his wife Sarah. Abraham was himself buried there, as were many of his descendants. Joseph and his brothers even brought the bones of Jacob, who had died in Egypt, back to the ancestral burial place.

The story of Sinuhe

Texts from Mesopotamia and Egypt have also yielded possible parallels with the way of life described in Genesis. The Middle Bronze Age in Canaan roughly coincides with the rise of the Middle Kingdom in Egypt. A 4,000-year-old text tells how an Egyptian courtier called Sinuhe fled the court of the pharaoh, Sesostris I, and found safety in the tents of a powerful nomadic leader called Ammi-Enshi who seems to have ruled much of inland Syria (an area the Egyptians called Upper Retinu).

Sinuhe married the daughter of the sheikh and was given his own tribal lands to govern. It

A Bedouin household encamped in the desert, such as, perhaps, Abraham and his family would have lived in. This is one of the famous black woollen tents woven on portable looms by the women of the family from the wool of their goats.

was a fertile region, full of cereals, fruit, honey, figs and excellent wine. He owned herds and hunted game. In the years Sinuhe lived with the tribes he played host to many Egyptian travellers, in the best traditions of hospitality witnessed in the patriarchal narratives of Genesis (for instance 18, 1–8). The tale of Sinuhe is reminiscent of the story of Moses in the tents of Jethro (Exodus 2–3), but Sinuhe was eventually pardoned by Sesostris and returned to Egypt, where he wrote his memoirs.

The Semites

Sinuhe calls the man with whom he found refuge an *amu*. The Egyptian word can be translated as 'a Semitic inhabitant of Canaan'. It is language that identifies ethnic affiliation and the Canaanites spoke a Western Semitic language. Many personal names found in the texts in the state archives of Mari (p. 47) and

in Egypt were Semitic, and it is generally agreed that Semites were the dominant element in the population of Syria and Canaan at this time.

It is clear from the documents that the people of the region, both settled and nomadic, were all of the same stock. Many, like Sinuhe's patron, were nomads, wandering throughout the whole Levant. These tribes usually had a home base, perhaps focused on a clan burial site. Such bases could be tent encampments or villages, and were often sited near large towns. Relations between city and camp were potentially explosive and one example of conflict is related in Genesis 34 (sidebar). It is quite likely that the settled population could easily turn to this lifestyle if necessary, as Abraham's family had done. The situation in Middle Bronze Age Canaan is therefore often seen as the background to the story of Abraham's wanderings.

THE LIFE OF ABRAHAM
Abraham was born in Ur in southern Mesopotamia, but at the command of the Lord he and his family became pastoralists and first migrated to Haran, in Syria. After the death of Terah, Abraham's father, they moved south to Canaan, where they settled. Mamre (later Hebron), in the southern Judaean Hills, became their tribal centre, when Abraham negotiated the purchase of the cave of the Machpelah in which to bury his wife, Sarah (Genesis 23, 16–20). The clan periodically returned there to bury their dead and perhaps to trade, exchange news and to barter for brides. The importance of a foreigner acquiring such a site was recognized by both parties to the deal. Abraham came to the court of the town, held as was common at the main gate, and presented himself as a humble supplicant and a stranger in the land. He was offered the hospitality that was due and then negotiations began. By his purchase of the property from Ephron, Abraham was not only able to bury his dead, but had acquired a legal stake in the land itself. The traditional site of the Machpelah is still venerated in the great mosque in the heart of Hebron, the Arabic name of which remembers Abraham – el-Halil, the friend of God.

CITIES OF THE TIME OF ABRAHAM

*And he said, Thy name shall be called no more
Jacob, but Israel.*
Genesis 32, 28

MANY LARGE, POWERFUL cities flourished in the Near East during the late 3rd and 2nd millennia BC. Some of these must have had an influence on developments in Canaan, if only indirectly. Among the best known are Ur, the city from which Abraham traditionally set out for Canaan, then in southern Mesopotamia (now in Iraq), and Ebla and Mari in Syria.

Ebla

In 1975 archaeologists working at a site in northern Syria called Tell Mardikh discovered an archive of clay tablets, jumbled together in a room of the building they had been stored in. Over 15,000 fragments were found, dating to the 23rd century BC. When deciphered it was found that the texts formed the royal archives of the palace of the ancient city of Ebla.

Part of the palace complex was a large audience courtyard. A throne dais was situated under a shady portico on one side, with two archive rooms along an adjacent wall. When the king held court he could call on scribes to bring him any records he needed from the store. The documents were inscribed on soft clay tablets which fitted comfortably in the hand. They were baked hard, and thus preserved, when the palace burned down.

The palace scribes wrote in cuneiform, the script of Mesopotamia, and used two different languages. One was Sumerian, the most ancient of all the languages of Mesopotamia, and the other was the tongue of Ebla itself, often called 'Eblaite'. This is the oldest Western Semitic language so far discovered.

The contents of the tablets cover all manner of subjects, from economic, commercial and legal concerns, to chronicles of the history of Ebla. There are tablets dealing with the activities of the gods of Ebla, who are also known from the tablets found at Ugarit, which date,

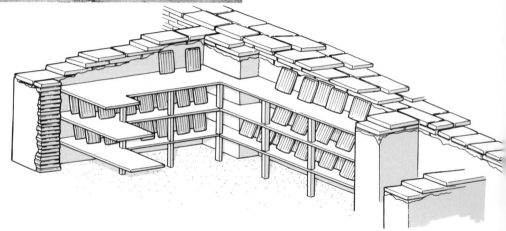

Clay tablets fallen from their shelves in the royal archive at Ebla (above). The destruction of the city by Naram-Sin in the 23rd century BC, later earthquakes and the ravages of time have all contributed to their disarray. Luckily, however, not all the tablets crashed to the floor; some slid gently down, still in the order they were arranged on the wooden shelves – reconstructed right, using the holes preserved in the plaster floor to locate the uprights. The edge of each tablet was marked with its subject and number.

however, to about a thousand years later (p. 52). Collections of hymns, proverbs and rituals as well as other forms of literature were also found among the texts. The Ebla tablets provide a fascinating and remarkable insight into the culture of this sophisticated, literate city-state which flourished between the mid-3rd millennium BC to around 2290/2250 BC when it was destroyed by Naram-Sin of Akkad.

Some spectacular claims were made soon after the decipherment of the contents of the tablets, concerning their relevance to the Bible. For instance, it was maintained that there was a god in Ebla called 'Ya' (the short version of Jehovah) and that one king called Ebrum could be Abraham's ancestor Eber. Following further study many of these assertions have been discounted or modified. While Ebla was not, as was once suggested, in direct contact with the towns of Canaan, it certainly did have trading links with cities to the southeast, including Mari. Interestingly, one personal name in the documents is 'Ishra-il'. It seems that Jacob was not the first man to be called Israel (see opening quote).

Mari

The Amorite city of Mari lies on the middle Euphrates in modern Syria. In the 18th century BC its king, Zimri-Lim, partly rebuilt and enlarged the palace there. Mari had commercial and political ties with the state of Babylon, also Amorite, under its ruler Hammurabi (c. 1792–1750). Late in his reign, Hammurabi began a policy of expansion that eventually led to the destruction of Mari. As at Ebla, the conflagration that razed the city and its palace in about 1757 BC helped to preserve the state archives, housed near the royal audience hall. Again as at Ebla, the texts deal with every conceivable subject. They range from matters of state and international commerce, to the annals of the kingdom and the personal correspondence of its royal family.

Two aspects of the Mari archives are important for the study of the Bible. First, documents relating to the international trade of the city, show that Mari's caravans reached at least as far south as northern Canaan – to Hazor and Laish (later Dan) at the sources of the River Jordan. Second, there are many reports of attacks on outlying towns and villages which were under the protection of detachments of troops from Mari. The attackers were herdsmen, tribal people who were essentially of the same Amorite cultural origin as the citizens of Mari. They were therefore of a similar back-

This rather stern figure is Ishtup Ilum, a governor of the city of Mari before 2000 BC. The statue was found in the sanctuary behind the great throne hall of the palace at Mari and was therefore probably a votive figure. Such statues were placed before the image of a deity as a reminder of the donor's existence, as a faithful worshipper, even when not there in person.

ground to the patriarchal groups (pp.44–45). One tribe is named *b'nai yamin*, remarkably similar to Benjamin, though it in fact may simply mean 'southerners'. Other names are also familiar, such as Ishmael, and this emphasizes that these Semitic tribal herders all ultimately shared the same ethnic roots.

Ur of the Chaldees

The city of Ur in southern Iraq once lay on the River Euphrates, but the course of the river has shifted some 10 miles (16 km) further east since antiquity. As we have seen, the Bible tells how Abraham, with his family, left 'Ur of the Chaldees' on the first part of his journey to Canaan. The Chaldaeans were an Aramaic tribe who only appeared in southern Mesopotamia much later (pp. 96–97). The description must therefore have been a scribal

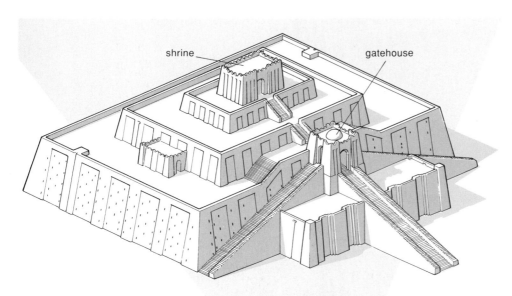

shrine

gatehouse

Ur Nammu's restored ziggurat at Ur still stands, with its staircases, to the second of its original three levels. Woolley's meticulous excavations were able to distinguish the different phases of this spectacular building, but unfortunately few traces were found of the uppermost level or the shrine on the top. However, Woolley felt able to reconstruct them as shown here.

The city of Ur (below) maintained its importance through the centuries and buildings were excavated belonging to various phases. The last Neo-Babylonian ruler, Nabonidus (pp. 104–05), held the city in particular regard and rebuilt the ziggurat and several other structures.

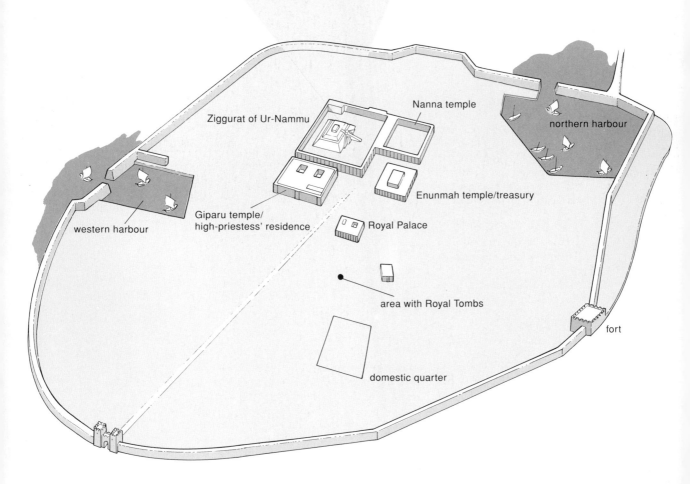

Ziggurat of Ur-Nammu

Nanna temple

northern harbour

western harbour

Giparu temple/
high-priestess' residence

Enunmah temple/treasury

Royal Palace

area with Royal Tombs

fort

domestic quarter

Once thought to represent Abraham's 'ram caught in a thicket' (Genesis 22, 13), this is in fact one of a pair of goat figurines. They may have been supports or stands – the upright can be seen protruding from the animal's back.

gloss to explain the location of Abraham's Ur, written long after the city itself had fallen into ruin.

Ur was one of the earliest and most powerful city-states of Sumer, the southern part of Babylonia. At the very beginning of the 2nd millennium BC, the start of the Middle Bronze Age in Canaan, and the time when Abraham probably set out on his journey, Ur was flourishing and governed other city-states in the region.

Because of its biblical connections, Sir Leonard Woolley (1880–1960) dug at the site as early as 1922. Woolley, along with Flinders Petrie, was one of the first archaeologists working in the Near East to realize the importance of stratigraphy at a site. Of the time he found gold beads from graves in a cemetery at Ur he wrote: 'our object was to get history, not to fill museum cases with miscellaneous curios, and history could not be got unless both we and our men were duly trained.' He thus stopped work on this trench and, despite pleas from his workmen, did not continue excavation there for four years, when he felt sufficiently experienced. When he did return to the spot, in 1926, he uncovered a large cemetery with

'WELL OF COURSE, IT'S THE FLOOD!'

When Woolley came upon a deep flood level in one of the trenches at Ur, he was immediately convinced that it was the remains of Noah's Flood described in the Bible (Genesis 7–8). What Woolley had actually found was a deposit of water-laid muds and silts 8 ft (2.5 m) thick, above and below which was clear evidence for human habitation – traces of walls, floors, pits for fires and rubbish dumps containing fragments of pottery, flint and other man-made objects. Woolley believed in the historicity of the Bible – he had come to Ur hoping to find traces of Abraham. It is not surprising then that he quickly arrived at the conclusion that he had found evidence for the Flood.

Woolley's flood dated in reality to about 4000 BC and in fact did not even affect the entire site. Evidence for flood levels of different dates has been found at many sites in southern Iraq since the 1920s. In their lower courses the Tigris and the Euphrates have extensive flood plains, crossed by numerous tributaries and irrigation canals. Rivers such as these flood easily and the water may stand for a long period on the vast plains.

The biblical Flood may be a reflection of the many local inundations that occurred in the low-lying regions of southern Mesopotamia. Or it may contain the distant memory of one widespread, catastrophic event, passed down the generations. The Epic of Gilgamesh is a 7th-century Assyrian version of an earlier myth, possibly dating to the 2nd millennium BC, which mirrors the

biblical flood very closely. Perhaps both derive from a common tradition. Modern archaeologists and biblical scholars do point out that the story of a flood covering the entire surface of the land is not very appropriate to the hilly terrain of the Levant and so is unlikely to have originated there.

many simple graves as well as the spectacular Royal Tombs of Ur. These were royal burials dating to around 2500 BC, the contents including gold diadems and other jewellery together with many other beautiful objects.

Much more recently, the texts from Ebla have revealed another town called Ur, somewhere in the vicinity of Ebla. Could this Ur, in northern Syria and near the city of Haran, where Abraham's family made a lengthy stay on their journey to Canaan, be the Ur of the patriarchal narratives? The association with Ur of the Chaldees may be another scribal mistake. We simply do not know.

CANAANITES AND HYKSOS

Hazor, northwest of the Sea of Galilee. In the stable Middle Bronze Age there was not sufficient space on the top of the tell for the increased population, and so they built a huge new lower city at its foot as a suburb. Most of the excavated areas visible in the photograph are remains from the time of Solomon and Ahab, when the site was a royal administrative centre rather than a town.

Now when Jacob saw that there was corn in Egypt, Jacob said unto his sons, Why do ye look upon one another? And he said, behold I have heard that there is corn in Egypt: get you down thither, and buy for us from thence; that we may live and not die. And Joseph's ten brethren went down to buy corn in Egypt.
Genesis 42, 1–3

CITIES WERE ONCE AGAIN built in the Middle Bronze Age (*c.* 2000–1550 BC), some of them on top of the abandoned remains of earlier ones. Traditions of urbanism were obviously preserved during the intervening nomadic era, perhaps in the cities of the northern coast, such as Ras Shamra and Byblos. As is apparent from the archaeological record, these cities continued as large-scale and prosperous settlements with no interruption (p. 43).

Although the impressive defences of many Middle Bronze Age cities argue for a degree of strife, the general picture is one of stability. Together with renewed prosperity went a great increase in population. The period was also one of continued technological developments.

The expansion of cities

The first phase of the Middle Bronze Age (*c.* 2000–1750 BC) was a lengthy period when small unfortified villages gradually grew into large cities, especially along the coasts of

Canaan and in the valleys that led inland from them.

By the next period (*c.* 1750–1550 BC) cities were flourishing throughout Syria and Palestine. As they expanded and outgrew their original sites new 'suburbs' were created at the foot of the old tells. At Hazor, in the Galilee area, huge new fortifications were built around 1800 BC to enclose the new Lower Town area. Truly a city, it then covered some 200 acres (80 ha) and may have contained as many as 20,000 inhabitants. It was the most important city of northern Canaan at the time and perhaps held sway over other city-states. The Bible calls it 'the head of all those kingdoms' (Joshua 11, 10). One structure may have been a palace, though its excavator, Yigael Yadin, identified it as a temple. A unique find of this period is the city gate at Tell Dan, the basket arch and barrel-vaulting of which remain intact.

The Execration Texts

Two groups of texts from Egypt tend to corroborate the archaeological information from Canaan. The first texts are written on pottery bowls and date to around 1900 BC; the second are found on figurines made approximately 100 years later. Both sources record curses on the enemies of Egypt in Canaan, hence their name – Execration Texts. The important difference between them is that the earlier texts mention only ten cities by name – Jerusalem is one of them – but there are several instances of regions or tribes with more than one ruler, as might be expected of a partly nomadic society. By contrast, a total of 64 cities, throughout

THE BENI HASSAN FRESCO

The painting from the tomb of Khnumhotep III at Beni Hassan shows a group of Semitic nomads coming to trade in eye-paint in Egypt. They probably also hoped for permission to settle since the whole clan is depicted, complete with baggage, including the lyre one man seems to be playing. The baggage animals are donkeys, rather than camels. There is considerable doubt whether camels were domesticated at this time as no trace of them has been found. Bones of 'equids' (donkeys or

horses – it is difficult to tell them apart from their bones) are found in excavations of sites dating to this period in both Canaan and the Semitic Hyksos sites of the northeastern Nile delta, such as Tell Dhaba, now identified as Avaris, the Hyksos capital.

The clothes the travellers are wearing appear to be made of colourful strips which were woven on the narrow, portable Bedouin-type looms and then stitched together. They could be similar to the 'many-coloured', or perhaps

striped, coat referred to in the story of Joseph. Joseph's family were given permission to settle in the land of Goshen, the northeastern Nile delta, where there was good pasture for their animals. The Pharaoh – unfortunately not named in the Bible – put them in charge of his own flocks and herds (Genesis 47, 6). This was mutually beneficial: herding was not considered a high-status activity in the Nile valley and the nomadic Semites were excellent pastoralists.

Canaan and Jordan, including Hazor, is named in the second group of texts. Each city has only one king, indicating that this was now a region of city-states and reflecting the increase in urbanization in the intervening years.

Canaanite civilization

An independent Canaanite culture flourished in the early 2nd millennium BC, notable for its technical and artistic achievements, including fine metalwork, especially jewellery, and ivory carving. Egyptian elements, among others, were successfully incorporated into a recognizably Canaanite style. In the Late Bronze Age under Egyptian rule this influence became more direct. The Phoenicians (pp. 66–69) were culturally the heirs of these Bronze Age Canaanite craftsmen. It was they who also perfected the alphabetic system of writing possibly first devised by the Canaanites during the 2nd millennium BC (pp. 26–28).

Rulers of Foreign Lands

Another important source of information concerning Canaan at this time is the tomb of a nobleman and provincial governor called Khnumhotep at Beni Hassan in Middle Egypt, dating to the 19th century BC. The walls of the rock-cut tomb are covered with magical paintings illustrating the life of the dead man. One sequence shows a group of 'amu of Shut' being presented to Khnumhotep. Their leader is called 'Abisha, ruler of a foreign land'. The Egyptian hieroglyphs may be rendered as heka hasut – hence the name by which they are known, Hyksos.

The Hyksos leader's name Abisha is of a Semitic type well known in the Bible. The amu constantly mentioned in Egyptian texts from the days of the strong Middle Kingdom and the weak period that followed (the Second

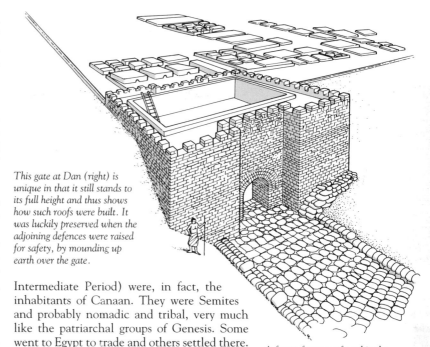

This gate at Dan (right) is unique in that it still stands to its full height and thus shows how such roofs were built. It was luckily preserved when the adjoining defences were raised for safety, by mounding up earth over the gate.

Intermediate Period) were, in fact, the inhabitants of Canaan. They were Semites and probably nomadic and tribal, very much like the patriarchal groups of Genesis. Some went to Egypt to trade and others settled there. This fits in well with the story of Joseph's brothers going to Egypt to buy corn at a time of famine in Egypt.

Excavations have shown that many Canaanites made their home in the eastern delta region, called in the Bible 'the land of Goshen'. During the Second Intermediate Period they exerted control over at least that area of Egypt, and possibly parts of the Nile valley as well. This is the Hyksos period in Egypt, which lasted approximately 200 years, between 1750 and 1550 BC. Their centre was at Avaris (Tell Dhaba) where archaeologists have excavated a palatial structure and found evidence for a material culture that is characteristically Canaanite, as well as remarkable Minoan-style frescoes.

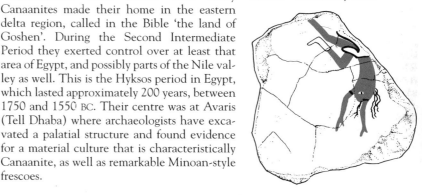

A fresco fragment found in the Hyksos capital of Tell Dhaba. It depicts a scene of bull-leaping and in subject and style is wholly Minoan – the culture of Crete.

THE GODS OF CANAAN

Stela of Baal, from Ugarit, with the god standing above stylized mountains, brandishing a club and a lance.

And the children of Israel did evil in the sight of the Lord, and forgat the Lord their God, and served Baalim and Asherot.

Judges 3, 7

THE BIBLE MAKES IT CLEAR that the Israelites were to have nothing to do with the gods of Canaan. The very emphasis placed on this prohibition seems to suggest that it was not always observed. This is perhaps not surprising. Israel's god was a stern, ethical being, whose relationship with his followers had been set up by covenants (or treaties) with Abraham, their forefather, and Moses, who led them from captivity in Egypt, and was defined by abstract concepts, such as sin and righteousness. For a people unused to intangible, philosophical ideas, the gods of Canaan, who took human form, were much more approachable and far easier to understand. The Bible singles some of them out by name, in particular Baal and Asherah.

Until early in the 20th century little was known about the Canaanite deities apart from references in the Bible. Then, in 1929, texts were discovered at Ugarit (in north Syria, now known as Ras Shamra). These texts were written in characters rather like cuneiform, but used as an alphabetic system (pp. 26–28) and epigraphers soon deciphered them. Although Ugarit was not in Canaan, the gods mentioned in the texts were the same as the Canaanite ones, and their characters and stories were thus revealed for the first time.

The Canaanite pantheon

The high god of the Canaanites was El, the sky god and ultimate creator of the world. His name is the same as one of the names of Israel's God. El was a rather shadowy figure; the most powerful and venerated figure was his son, Baal. Baal was essentially a weather god, who brought the much-needed rain in the autumn. This was when the New Year began, after the arid heat of summer, when the vegetation had died and the land and its people were parched.

Baal was often depicted in the form of a young man with an upraised arm holding a shaft of lightning or a thunderbolt. Alternatively he was represented in the form of a bull. He was usually worshipped outside on *bamot*, which were either high places or open-air altars. Jehovah, the God of Israel, was also worshipped on *bamot*, but this practice was anathema to the prophets, who tried to stamp it out.

The consort of Baal was Asherah, sometimes also called Elat – the feminine form of El. Another version names Baal's spouse as Astarte. Asherah was associated with the sacred tree – the tree of life, nourishing and fertile, rooted deep in the earth. She is often

A fragment from a Late Bronze Age jug found in the Fosse Temple at Lachish (above). The name of the goddess Elat, Baal's consort, appears above the sacred tree.

Two goats or ibexes flank a sacred tree representing the goddess Elat in this painted sherd from Kuntillet 'Ajrud (below), and an inscription mentioning Yahweh and Asherah.

A pillar figurine of the mother goddess (right), smiling benignly. The large numbers and small size of such figurines suggest that they were for domestic use.

depicted as a sacred tree, or with a tree springing from her pubic area. She could also appear as a cow, especially when she becomes confused with her Egyptian counterpart, Hathor. Sometimes, however, she is shown naked and with emphasized genitalia, in a non-Egyptian manner. The Canaanite cults included male and female priest-prostitutes. Intercourse with them was considered an act of worship designed to ensure the fertility of fields, beasts and humankind. These fertility rituals were not incorporated into the ascetic religion of the Israelites, though the fecundity of fields and animals must have been central to their existence. It is understandable then that they sometimes succumbed to the temptations of the gods of Canaan.

'The solitary hill by the water wells'

During the 1980s the small site of Kuntillet 'Ajrud in the northern Sinai desert came to the attention of archaeologists. It is situated on a low hill where three important desert roads meet, and nearby is a rare spring of sweet water. The name means 'the solitary hill by the water wells' and the site must have served as a way-station for travellers over thousands of years. In the 9th to 8th centuries BC it seems that the kings of Israel (then separate from Judah) erected two buildings on the hill, presumably to serve as inns. The better preserved of the two was also a shrine, used by travellers who were devotees of many different gods.

The archaeologists found many pieces of pottery and fragments of wall plaster which have cultic motifs drawn on them or inscrip-

tions, sometimes both. Some mention 'Yahweh of Samaria and his Asherah'. In this context Asherah can only be the consort of the god. We cannot, however, be certain whether this means that some Israelites worshipped Yahweh together with a consort who was called Asherah. This would imply that they were not strict monotheists.

The mother goddess

If Asherah was regarded as the consort of Jehovah by some Israelites in the 8th century BC, her cult was soon suppressed and is not found later. There is certainly evidence for a mother goddess in Canaan at this time, symbolized by the ubiquitous pillar figurines with their large breasts and pleasant smiles. Such figurines may have been among the terafim, or household gods, which Rachel smuggled out of Laban's house (sidebar).

The presence of such goddess figurines, as well as Astarte plaques and indeed all sacred images, male or female, poses a problem for modern scholars. It is often not possible to tell from the contexts they were found in whether they were being used by Israelites, Judaeans or Canaanites. Many fragmentary goddess figurines have been found in Jerusalem, dating to the Iron Age.

It is often difficult to disentangle elements of Canaanite beliefs and cult practices from those of early Israel. For instance, the use of stone monoliths, called matzevot, for various purposes may have been common to both religions and indeed the two sets of beliefs and customs may have overlapped to a surprising degree.

Now Rachel had taken the terafim and put them in the camel's furniture [saddlebags] and sat upon them. And Laban searched all the tent, but found them not. And she said to her father, Let it not displease my lord that I cannot rise up before thee; for the custom of women is upon me. And he searched, but found not the terafim.
Genesis 31, 34–35

A matzevah, or cult pillar, from the Late Bronze Age Stela Temple, lower city of Hazor – the only one of the set of 10 that was carved.

Both these plaques (right) depict the fertility goddess. The ears and wigs of both are reminiscent of the cow-eared Egyptian goddess Hathor. The left-hand terracotta plaque shows the goddess in a very un-Egyptian way – naked and full-face. The gold pendant on the right shows her in a more stylized form, with breasts and pubic triangle – with the sacred tree, the tree of life itself, growing out of it.

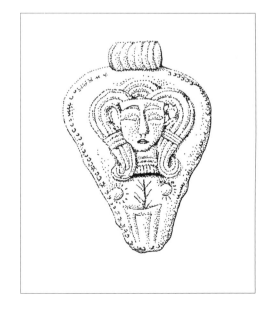

EGYPT'S EMPIRE

And Pharaoh said, Who is the Lord, that I should obey his voice and let Israel go? I know not the Lord, neither will I let Israel go. And they said, The God of the Hebrews hath met with us; let us go, we pray thee, three days' journey into the desert and sacrifice unto the Lord our God.

Exodus 5, 2–3

International trade flourished in the eastern Mediterranean in the Late Bronze Age. The shipwreck discovered off the rocky shore of Anatolia near Ulu Burun provides a glimpse of the prosperity and cosmopolitan interactions of the day. When it sank, the ship was carrying pottery from Greece, Cyprus and the Levant, some of which contained olives, grain, wine and terebinth resin used in making perfume and incense. Ingots of tin from Anatolia and copper from Cyprus were found, as well as bronze tools and weapons, faience and glass objects. Items of precious metals and jewels from Mesopotamia, Egypt, Mycenaean Greece and elsewhere were also included in the cargo.

AROUND 1550 BC, THE PHARAOH Ahmosis (1570–1546 BC) succeeded in expelling the Hyksos from Egypt, marking the end of the Second Intermediate Period. He became the first king of the 18th dynasty, at the beginning of the New Kingdom period. Egyptian records say that the Hyksos were pursued north, into the land of Canaan. This accords well with archaeological evidence, since there are destruction levels at some Canaanite cities at this time, especially in the south. Additionally, an influx of Hurrians, taking refuge from the Hittites, came south and brought a new population element to Canaan. This is reflected by many personal names of Hurrian type found in texts of the Late Bronze Age

The Egyptians consolidated their hold over Canaan during the reign of Tuthmosis III (1504–1450 BC). In about 1490 BC a coalition of 119 rulers from Syria and Canaan came together to face the Egyptians in the valley of Jezreel, but were decisively beaten at the Battle of Megiddo. Tuthmosis proudly recorded the event in the great temple to Amun at Karnak (Thebes), capital of the 18th Dynasty pharaohs. Direct Egyptian rule soon reached as far north as Kadesh on the River Orontes.

Canaan was under the political and cultural domination of Egypt from this point until the end of the Late Bronze Age. The rulers of the once-independent city-states became vassal governors of their own kingdoms, responsible for collecting the tribute and taxation in kind demanded by the Egyptians. However, the Egyptians could not extend their power further to the north because there they came up against the armies of the kingdom of Mitanni.

Peace and prosperity

Under Egyptian control Canaan initially experienced a period of enforced calm. Few cities had new fortifications built during the Late Bronze Age. Archaeologists think that at some sites defences of the Middle Bronze Age continued in use, but were allowed to decay gradually. In other places old city walls may have been torn down. At Lachish, in the hills to the south of Jerusalem, a small temple was constructed in the dry moat of the earlier period.

Peace brought with it prosperity, built on international maritime trade with Egypt, Cyprus and the Aegean. One of the great seaports of the day was Ugarit (Ras Shamra) on the north Syrian coast. This city, the capital of a fertile kingdom, was at the centre of a far-flung trading network, and was a rich and cosmopolitan place. In the palace, archives were found which shed much light on contemporary Canaanite culture and religion (pp. 52–53).

Cypriot pottery was popular in Canaan and many vessels in a range of styles have been discovered. Pottery also came from Mycenaean Greece, some of it made specifically for the Levantine market.

In the other direction the timber of the Levant was much in demand. Grain, olives and livestock, as well as the famous purple dye of the Levant (p. 66) were also exported. Contacts between Canaan and Egypt were frequent and trade goods passed in both direc-

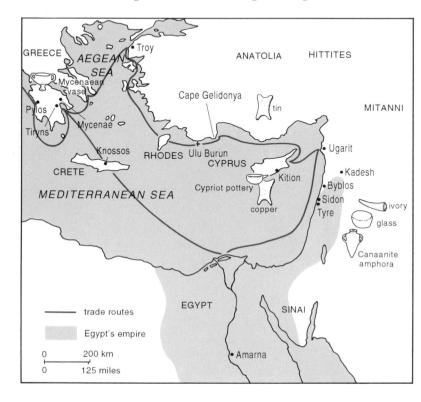

GREECE AEGEAN SEA • Troy ANATOLIA HITTITES
Mycenaean vase
Pylos
Tiryns Mycenae
Knossos RHODES Cape Gelidonya tin MITANNI
CRETE Ulu Burun CYPRUS • Ugarit
MEDITERRANEAN SEA Cypriot pottery Kition • Kadesh
copper • Byblos
• Sidon ivory
Tyre glass
Canaanite amphora
EGYPT SINAI

—— trade routes
▓ Egypt's empire
0   200 km
0   125 miles
• Amarna

Amenophis IV – Akhenaten – shown in the strange, elongated but rather delicate style of his day, known from the modern name of his capital city as the Amarna style.

About 380 letters, or parts of letters, on clay tablets have been found at Tell el-Amarna. They were mostly written in Akkadian, which was the Semitic language of Mesopotamia and used as the international language of diplomacy throughout the Near East at the time. Many of the letters were written by scribes in Canaan. From the mistakes they made in writing Akkadian, it is possible to reconstruct something of their own language, which was Canaanite, a Western Semitic language. Very few texts have been found in southern Canaan itself and so this is very important for an understanding of a language that had much in common with Hebrew.

tions. A noticeable Egyptian influence is detectable in the products of Canaan at this period which were still made to a high standard and considered very desirable.

Two shipwrecks found off the southwestern coast of Anatolia, at Ulu Burun and at Cape Gelidonya, provide a graphic record of the extent and richness of the trading links in the Late Bronze Age. The Ulu Burun wreck contained finished objects and raw materials from many different countries. The merchants were almost certainly Canaanite and they must have been trading their way around the coasts of the eastern Mediterranean when they met with disaster. On board were copper 'ox-hide' shaped ingots, probably from Cyprus, Mycenaean pottery, and Egyptian faience, raw ivory and tin. There were objects of gold, bronze swords and jewellery, amphorae for wine, olives and grain. One pithos was found to hold 18 pieces of Cypriot pottery. Some of the items came from beyond the Mediterranean, such as amber beads, which presumably were from the Baltic.

The Amarna period

The first part of the 14th century BC in Egypt was the era of Amenophis IV, who renamed himself Akhenaten (1379–1362 BC). He built an entirely new capital city at Akhetaten – 'Horizon of the Sun [Aten]', known today as Tell el-Amarna. Akhenaten promoted the cult of the sun god, Aten, above all the other gods of Egypt.

The royal archives at Amarna have yielded a tremendous amount of information about conditions in the Egyptian empire and beyond. One part of the archive consists of international correspondence between Egypt and the rulers of other great powers of the time, including Babylon. The records also contain a series of appeals for help from the vassal states of Canaan. It seems that while Egypt was still recognized as overlord of the area, the administrative system set up by Tuthmosis III had weakened. This gave the individual city-states of Canaan the opportunity to attack each other without serious fear of retribution – it was clearly a troubled time.

This little tented shrine was found at Timnah, in the desert of the Aravah, by Beno Rothenberg, who was investigating ancient copper mining in the area. The open-air sanctuary was founded in the reign of Seti I. The head of Hathor is carved on several pillars, so perhaps the shrine was dedicated to her. It was later used by the Midianite miners, who stayed on after the Egyptians had withdrawn in the mid-12th century BC.

Who were the *habiru*?

One name occurs with some frequency in the Amarna letters – the *habiru*. No single translation of the word seems wholly satisfactory, but perhaps the best is 'outsider'. From the letters it seems the *habiru* were social outcasts of various types – bandits preying on law-abiding people. Some were homeless and dispossessed people who formed disruptive elements on the edge of the community. Occasionally the word is also used of foreign workers or mercenary soldiers in the employ of various Canaanite rulers. Labaya, the king of Shechem, in the northern hill country, had so many *habiru* at his command that he was called their chief by his enemies.

Scholars once thought that the *habiru* were the Hebrews of the Old Testament. The *habiru* turn up much further afield than Canaan, however, for they are mentioned in documents from Anatolia, Mesopotamia and Syria from the early 2nd to the late 1st millennia BC. They cannot therefore be identified exclusively with the Hebrews, but the Israelites might have been called *habiru* by others, as for example by Potiphar's wife when speaking of Joseph. Also an Israelite might refer to himself as an 'outsider' when speaking to a non-Israelite (Genesis 39, 14). This may well be how the word 'Hebrew' (the English translation) came to be applied to the Israelites.

Another group mentioned in the Amarna Letters are the *shashu* – the Bedouin who roamed the deserts in every age. They were not directly related to the Israelites, although some tribes, for instance the Midianites and the Kenites, came into close contact with them.

A large basalt stela erected by Seti I at Beth Shean to commemorate the Egyptian suppression of a revolt in northern Transjordan. During the reign of Seti, Egypt was trying to re-establish control over Canaan after it had weakened during the Amarna period. Beth Shean was a very strategic site, at the southern end of the Esdraelon valley, guarding the crossings of the River Jordan, and became one of the chief garrisons of the Egyptian army. The site had a long history of occupation and a city flourished there in Byzantine times (pp. 166–67).

The 19th Dynasty

Under the kings of the 19th Dynasty Egypt regained its firm grip on Canaan. Pharaoh Seti I (1318–1304 BC) built a strong line of fortresses along the route stretching across the north Sinai desert to southern Canaan. These were to safeguard Egyptian control over the area. The route was known to the Egyptians as the 'Ways of Horus' or the 'Nine Days Road'.

Ramesses II (1304–1237 BC) continued the

process of strengthening Egyptian control over its Asiatic empire and was active in the reorganization of the military administration of Canaan. He created strong garrisons at Beth Shean in the north and Gaza in the south. At Deir el-Balah, Aphek and elsewhere, a particular type of building has been identified as an 'Egyptian Governor's Residency'.

The emergence of a powerful Hittite empire in Anatolia was the main threat to Egypt at this time and may have prompted Ramesses' strengthening of defences in Canaan. Around 1300 BC a battle was fought between Egypt and the Hittites, under Ramesses II and Muwatallis respectively. This was the Battle of Kadesh, on the River Orontes. Each side claimed victory but in reality it was a draw. The subsequent peace treaty defined the limits of the spheres of influence of the two great powers. However, a new menace was soon to make itself felt and would throw the eastern Mediterranean world into confusion (pp. 62–63). In this upheaval familiar Bronze Age civilizations perished and a new Iron Age world arose.

A gold pendant (above) found in the Ulu Burun wreck, off the shores of Anatolia. It shows a naked goddess, holding a gazelle in each hand. It may have been made in Syria.

A monumental statue of the great pharaoh Ramesses II at the temple of Luxor, Thebes in Egypt. Ramesses was a great builder and it may have been at his new cities in the Nile delta that the Israelites toiled under the oppression of forced labour.

EXODUS AND THE WILDERNESS YEARS

And it came to pass, when Pharaoh had let the people go, that God led them not through the way of the land of the Philistines, although that was near; for God said Lest peradventure the people repent when they see war, and they return to Egypt.
Exodus 13, 17–18

The Greek Orthodox monastery of Santa Katerina in the deserts of south Sinai. Here, at the foot of the mountain of the same name, one of several sites traditionally associated with Moses and the receiving of the Ten Commandments, a monastic settlement was first founded by Queen Helena in the 4th century AD. It was rebuilt and much expanded over the centuries, and in the 19th century AD very important manuscripts were found there, including the famous Codex Sinaiticus (p.30).

THE EXODUS FROM EGYPT under the leadership of Moses, the wanderings of the Israelite tribes in the deserts of Sinai and their subsequent entry into Canaan are three episodes of great significance in the biblical story of Israel's development. Given the importance of the revelations by God to Moses on Mt Sinai it is likely that some such events did take place at some time, but not necessarily as recorded in the Bible. In the opinion of many historians and theologians the narratives of the Book of Exodus do indeed deal with historical rather than mythical events. The towering figure of Moses stands in relation to the origins of Judaism as does that of Jesus to Christianity. After intensive archaeological research some facts about parts of the Book of Exodus have emerged. Many Hyksos peasantry stayed on in Egypt under their new masters following the expulsion of their leaders (p. 54). They were not slaves, but more like the serfs of medieval Europe, living in their own villages and cultivating their own fields. They were also subject to the strict restraints which the rulers of Egypt laid on all their subjects, native or foreign.

It was the descendants of these people, as well as other resident foreigners and the peasant population of the eastern delta, who were used as forced labour by the Egyptian pharaohs of the 19th Dynasty. The long reign of Ramesses II is particularly associated with massive building projects, especially the new royal residences or capital cities in the eastern delta. These are known to us from the Bible as Pithom (Per Atum) and Raamses (Pi Ramesse). The Israelites set out from the latter place at the beginning of the Exodus and it has been variously identified; the best candidate is a site called Qantir, near Tell Dhaba.

According to the Book of Exodus, Egyptian oppression led the Israelites to pray for deliverance. At the bidding of God, Moses went to the pharaoh to demand the release of the people, but having failed to gain permission, Moses brought down the ten plagues on the Egyptians, culminating in the death of the first-born. The miraculous crossing of the Red (or Reed) Sea (Exodus 14) cannot be linked archaeologically to the drowning of an Egyptian army, though the escape of some fugitive serfs would be too trivial, or too embarrassing, to be mentioned in the annals of Egypt.

Sinai

Once across the Red Sea and out of Egypt proper, the Hebrew tribes were still in the Egyptian dominated territory of Sinai. Four routes cross Sinai towards Canaan. The northern route would have brought them into conflict with Egyptian forces because the line of fortresses existed there. If refugees did ever take that road, and some in fact may have done, it must have been at a period before Seti I's strongholds were built. It is possible that the Exodus recorded in the Bible is an amalgam of ancestral traditions of many groups who were

later to make up the historical people of Israel.

Two of the other routes across Sinai traverse the centre of the peninsula, while the fourth skirts the south central massif and roughly follows the coastline southwards, passing Santa Katerina. This is the mountain often identified as the Mt Sinai of the Bible, though there are other candidates, including Jebel Musa a little further north. The Egyptians never penetrated the southern part of the Sinai peninsula and so this route seems the most probable. Jewish tradition does not retain a memory of the site of this most important mountain. Apparently it was not a place of pilgrimage in the early days when the religious beliefs of Israel were bound up with Jerusalem, the Temple and Canaan.

Kadesh Barnea

The Israelites spent many years wandering in the wilderness before their entry into the land of Canaan. One site where they remained for a long time and which archaeologists have sought to identify is Kadesh Barnea, now thought to be the oasis of Ein Qudeirat in northeastern Sinai. This would be an ideal place for wanderers in the desert to stay, since it is an area of lush vegetation and bubbling springs in an otherwise barren environment.

Recent intensive archaeological surveys have explored the whole area of the oasis and have found no evidence for structures predating the period of the Israelite monarchy (10th–6th century BC). The Children of Israel may have lived in tents rather than houses, though some of their occupation debris should have come to light.

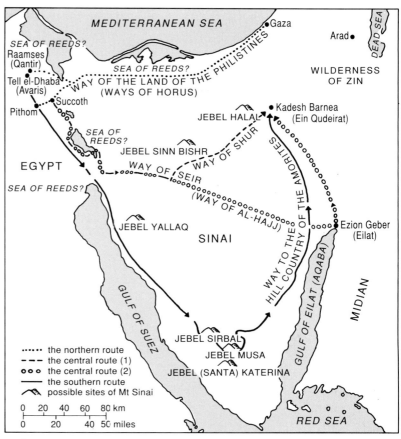

If Ramesses II was the pharaoh of the Exodus, his successor Merneptah was that of the Entry, when, according to the Bible, the Children of Israel were taking possession of the land promised to them by God (pp. 70–71).

Map of Sinai showing the four possible routes by which the Children of Israel could have crossed the peninsula, fleeing from Egypt on their way to the Promised Land.

'ISRAEL'

One piece of historical evidence of crucial importance for dating the presence of Israel in Canaan is the *Stela of Year 5 of Merneptah*. In his 5th year (1231 BC) Merneptah campaigned throughout Canaan and this stela makes large claims about his successes. Among other victories, he asserts that he has wiped the people of Israel (detail below) off the face of the earth. This is the first known mention of the nation of Israel and demonstrates that the Israelites were a distinct entity in Canaan by that time. Despite Merneptah's claims, though, he obviously did not have such a devastating effect on the nation of Israel.

However, a word of caution is necessary: the stela implies that Israel as a nation is present in Canaan at a date around 1231 BC. This does not help in assessing when they first arrived. It may also refer to a group who already lived in the area, rather than a band newly settled there.

III

OLD TESTAMENT EMPIRES

Judah and Israel were many, as the sand which is by the sea in multitude, eating and drinking, and making merry. And Solomon reigned over all kingdoms from the river unto the land of the Philistines, and unto the border of Egypt: they brought presents, and served Solomon all the days of his life.

1 Kings 4, 20–21

THE 14TH CENTURY BC was a time of peace and plenty in the eastern Mediterranean, its prosperity founded largely on international trade. But all this was to change during the 13th century, for the mighty powers of Egypt and Hittite Anatolia began to decline, Mycenaean civilization in Greece crumbled, the flourishing culture of Cyprus foundered and many of the Canaanite city states were destroyed. The political turbulence disrupted the lives of huge numbers of people, many of whom travelled far from their original homes in search of new land to settle.

The collapse of old regimes signalled great changes for the region, since the stage was now set for the growth of new empires. At first only relatively small groups – such as the Philistines – jostled for position. Soon the classic empires of the Bible established themselves, beginning with the Israelites who created a remarkable empire under King David and his son, Solomon. Later the Assyrians were to achieve supremacy, thanks mainly to the military genius of such leaders as Ashurbanipal. But even Assyrian might was to wane eventually, swept away at the end of the 7th century BC by the increasing power of the Babylonians.

Aerial view of the immense tell of Megiddo. Strategically sited in the valley of Esdraelon, it guards a pass through the Carmel range to the coastal plain beyond. It thus controlled two major international highways, which explains why it was occupied from the 4th millennium BC onwards. Solomon fortified Megiddo and made it one of his administrative centres. Many battles were fought in the vicinity of Megiddo and in apocalyptic imagery it is the site of the battle at the end of days. Armageddon means the hill of Megiddo.

THE SEA PEOPLES

... as for the foreign countries, they made a conspiracy in their islands. All at once the lands were on the move, scattered in war. No country could stand before their arms ... Their league was Peleset, Tjeker, Shekelesh, Denyen and Weshesh...
Inscription at Medinet Habu

FROM AROUND THE 14TH CENTURY BC onwards groups of migrants began to arrive in the eastern Mediterranean. These new arrivals are known to us collectively by one of their Egyptian names as 'The Sea Peoples'. They are perhaps best documented in the Harris papyrus in the British Museum, a source of much information on the reign of the pharaoh Ramesses III (1198–1166 BC). The papyrus preserves the names of individual nations or tribes of Sea Peoples who were particularly active against Egypt. Among them were the Sherden, Weshesh, Denyen, Peleset and Tjekker.

Who were these people, depicted by the Egyptians with their strange headgear, long swords and distinctive round shields? They mostly seem to have originated in the general area of the Aegean and southern Anatolia. The Mycenaean civilization in Greece collapsed towards the end of the 13th century and the eastern Mediterranean powers also fell. It was a time of upheaval and crisis. Whatever the precise cause of these disasters, great movements of population followed, generally migrating from north to south. New groups of refugees were constantly being formed and displacing other peoples in their path.

From trickle to torrent

At first the Sea Peoples arrived in small numbers that could easily be absorbed with by their adoptive countries. Ramesses II (1304–1237 BC) encountered and defeated one group, the Sherden, many of whom were then taken as mercenaries into the Egyptian army and who fought for Egypt against the Hittites at the battle of Kadesh, in about 1300 BC. The anthropoid coffins found at the Egyptian garrisons at Deir el-Balah and Beth Shean in Canaan are possible evidence for the presence of Sea Peoples there. The son and successor of Ramesses II, Merneptah (1236–1223 BC), also had to contend with an attack on Egypt by the Sea Peoples in alliance with the Libyans.

From the later 13th century BC the trickle became an uncontrollable torrent, destroying everything in its path and bringing to an end the long and prosperous era of the Late Bronze Age. This was a time of profound change, which saw the old empires, notably Egypt, lose mastery over the region, and the new order of the Iron Age with its biblical kingdoms emerge.

It was at this point that the Hittites of Asia Minor vanished and the city of Ugarit (Ras Shamra) on the Syrian coast was devastated and never rebuilt. All calls for help sent to Egypt went unanswered. In fact Egypt was itself once again in danger and in the eighth year of his reign (c. 1190), Ramesses III fought the Sea Peoples in two battles, one on land and one at sea. A pictorial record of these events, together with an adulatory inscription, is preserved at Ramesses' mortuary temple at Medinet Habu in Western Thebes. The reliefs depict the pharaoh's battles against the invaders in great detail, with various groups being distinguishable by differences in dress and weapons.

The land battle probably took place somewhere in Syria or Phoenicia and the invaders were apparently easily defeated. They are shown on the relief accompanied by their families and all their possessions in the lumbering ox-carts that were carrying them in search of

The naval battle between the Sea Peoples and the Egyptian forces under Ramesses III was depicted in reliefs carved on the walls of the pharaoh's mortuary temple at Medinet Habu. Enemy troops are shown wearing horned helmets and fighting with long swords and round shields, identifying them as Sherden.

The lid of an anthropoid coffin from Beth Shean (above). Some scholars have seen in it a similarity to the feathered helmets of the Philistines in the Medinet Habu reliefs. It is certainly likely that some of the Sea Peoples were employed as mercenaries by the Egyptians to garrison their fortresses in Canaan and such coffins may corroborate this. Their odd appearance has earned them the name 'grotesque'.

Great movements of peoples took place in the eastern Mediterranean in the Late Bronze Age by land and sea (map, right), causing immense disruption.

new homes. The sea battle was fought in the eastern Nile delta, and this too seems to have been a great victory for the pharaoh.

Ramesses' successes may have averted the threat of an invasion of Egypt itself, but we know from both archaeological and biblical sources that Tjekker and Peleset, and perhaps other Sea Peoples, settled along the coast of Canaan, which, in theory, was controlled by Egypt. The Tjekker settled in the area of Dor, south of Mt Carmel, and the Peleset along the southern coastal area. The influence of the Egyptians in the Levant was declining and as they withdrew the Sea Peoples settled with their families in exactly those areas where they had served as soldiers for the pharaohs.

The name that appears in Egyptian hieroglyphs as 'plst' is transliterated with vowels as 'peleset', rendered in Hebrew as 'plishtim' and becomes Philistines in English. The area of the coast they settled, together with its hinterland, is known to us as Philistia.

One more journey, a linguistic one this time, was undertaken by the Peleset. The Greeks began seaborne trade with them in the 8th century BC and they used the name Philistia for

the entire region. Thus, via the Graeco-Roman world, one of the names of the land is still Palestine.

Excavating a naturalistic anthropoid coffin at Deir el-Balah in the Gaza Strip.

THE PHILISTINES

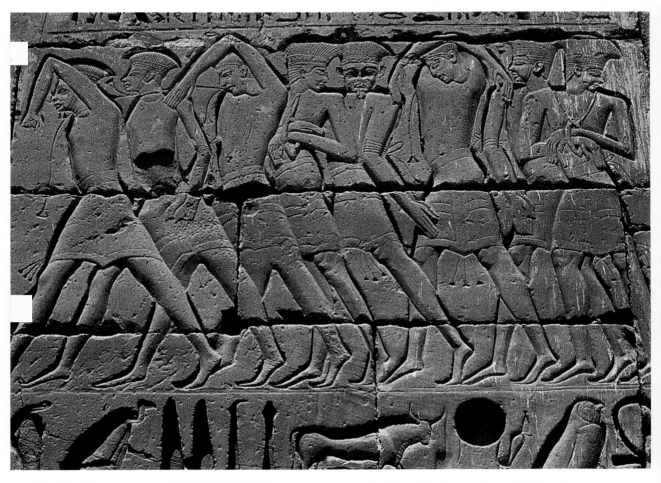

Detail from the reliefs at Ramesses III's temple at Medinet Habu showing enemies captured by the Egyptians. Their feather headdresses identify them as Philistines.

The lords of the Philistines went up against Israel. And when the children of Israel heard it, they were afraid of the Philistines. And the children of Israel said to Samuel, Cease not to cry unto the Lord our God for us, that he will save us out of the hand of the Philistines.
1 Samuel 7, 7–8

THE PHILISTINES ARE THE ONLY group of Sea Peoples to be mentioned by name in the Old Testament, presumably because they were such a thorn in the flesh of the nascent Israelite state. The Bible twice mentions that they came from a place called Capthor (Amos 9, 7 and Jeremiah 47, 4), but its identity is the subject of much debate. Most scholars associate Capthor with either Cyprus or Crete; some evidence certainly suggests that the Philistines had a connection with Crete.

Confrontation with Israel

Once the Philistines had established a foothold in the southern part of the Canaanite coast, they organized themselves into at least five major city-states: Ashdod, Ashkelon and Gaza on the coast, and Gath and Ekron inland. By the 11th century BC the next generation of Philistines had begun to expand their territory eastwards into the low, fertile hills of the Shephelah region and northeastwards into Judaea. Here they came into conflict with Israelite tribes who were themselves expanding westwards from the hill country towards the sea (pp. 70–71).

The Old Testament accounts of these struggles are contained in the books of Judges and 1 Samuel. By the time of Saul, c. 1020 BC, the Philistines had clearly subjugated at least some of the Israelite tribes. The first book of Samuel (1 Samuel 13, 19–22) tells how the Philistines prevented the Israelites from owning weapons and charged exorbitant rates for sharpening even agricultural tools. Some scholars interpret this to mean that the Philistines had a monopoly on ironworking, which allowed them to dominate the Israelites, who only had bronze arms. But no metal is specified. In fact, in the reliefs of Medinet Habu, the Philistines wield great bronze swords; and iron equipment is not generally not found in common use in the eastern Mediterranean until the 10th century BC. What little has been found is mostly jewellery.

Samson and the tribe of Dan

The original territory of the Israelite tribe of Dan on the western edge of Judaea must have borne the brunt of Philistine expansionism. Joshua (19, 46) tells us that the River Yarkon was the boundary between the tribe of Dan and the Philistines, and it is at just this point (now on the northern outskirts of Tel Aviv) that the Philistine town of Tell Qasileh has been excavated. Founded in the second half of the 12th century BC, the town lies on the Yarkon, not far from the Mediterranean; the river would have provided a convenient route to the sea for maritime trade. Tell Qasileh was devastated by fire in the 10th century BC. The scale of the conflagration was so great that archaeologists think it was destroyed by King David during his military operations to control the Philistines.

The social structure of the Israelites in the early days was based on tribal units. These units rarely joined forces, so resistance to the Philistines tended to be organized by tribe. One of the Danite leaders or Judges was Samson, a charismatic hero about whom many stories are told in Judges 13–16 (see box). He managed to hold the Philistines at bay for 20 years, but when he died his tribe could no longer withstand Philistine pressure and fled far to the north, to the sources of the River Jordan. There they captured the Canaanite town of Laish and resettled it under their own tribal name of Dan (pp. 83–84). It is interesting to note that despite all the hostility between the Israelites and the Philistines, social contacts and even marriages took place between the two peoples.

A king in Israel

Philistine power over Israel increased when the Philistines captured the Ark of the Covenant in the second phase of the Battle of Aphek (1 Samuel 4). It was probably in response to the growing Philistine menace that the Israelite people petitioned Samuel for a permanent leader: 'now make us a king to judge us like all the nations' (1 Samuel 8, 5). Samuel, who was the last and the greatest of the Judges, was bitterly opposed to the idea, because it showed that the people rejected God as their king. But he eventually anointed Saul, of the tribe of Benjamin, to be king, 'a man head and shoulders above his fellows' (1 Samuel 9, 2). Saul was never to be successful in overthrowing the Philistines, indeed his house was all but destroyed at the fatal battle of Gilboa, as related in 1 Samuel 31. However, his successor King David seems to have had little trouble in containing them (pp. 72–74).

The Philistines remained an independent entity along the southern part of the coast until at least the late 8th century BC, when Sargon, King of Assyria, devastated Philistia. Sargon's annals mention in particular the revolt of the Philistine town of Ashdod and its swift submission to his army (Isaiah 20, 1). The Assyrians installed local client kings and they used Philistia throughout the 7th century BC as the springboard for their attacks on Egypt. The Philistines do not quite disappear from history until the Babylonian invasions of the early 6th century BC, which swept away both Judah and Philistia.

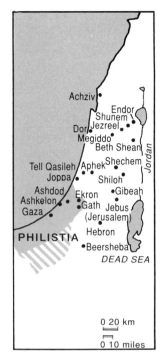

Map showing the area settled by the Philistines and its relationship to the emerging Israelite kingdom.

Philistine art often displays Aegean influence. Found at Ashdod (hence its name, Ashdoda), this female figurine may represent the Mother Goddess in the form of a birthing chair. Some scholars see similarities in her to seated figurines from Mycenae.

SAMSON DEFIES THE PHILISTINES

Samson was born into the tribe of Dan. His impending birth was announced to his mother by an angel, who told her he was to be a Nazirite, that is, dedicated to God all his life. As a symbol of this dedication he was never to drink wine nor to cut his hair, on penalty of losing his God-given strength. This strength and his headstrong nature led him into many adventures and brawls with the Philistines, but he also fell in love with a Philistine girl – Delilah – who cut off his hair while he was asleep. Deprived of his strength, he was at the mercy of the Philistines, who blinded and enslaved him.

At the end of his life the Philistines brought him to their great temple of Dagon. Samson prayed to God to recover his strength just once more. His wish granted, he pushed against the two main supporting pillars of the temple so that the roof caved in, killing him and all his captors.

THE PHOENICIANS AND THEIR NEIGHBOURS

A fine pottery mask of a Phoenician from Achziv, 5 in. (13 cm) high, painted red and black.

This exquisite terracotta figurine was made in a two-part mould and measures just over 9 in. (23 cm) high. It, too, comes from Achziv and dates to the 7th or 6th century BC. Seated on a chair with a stool at her feet, a woman calmly and thoughtfully awaits the birth of her child. This is the finest example of its type found to date, although many other similar ones are known. Such figurines were perhaps intended to ensure, through sympathetic magic, a successful pregnancy and an easy birth.

The Phoenicians, to whom Sidon belongs, live in Syria.
Herodotus, The Histories, 2, 119

So Saul took the kingdom over Israel, and fought against all his enemies on every side, against Moab, and against the children of Ammon, and against Edom…and against the Philistines: and whither soever he turned himself he vexed them.
I Samuel 14, 47

AS EARLY AS THE 9TH OR 8TH centuries BC the name 'Phoenician' was coined by Greek seaborne traders for the people of the northern coast of the Levant, in approximately the area known today as the Lebanon.

Purple folk

The Greek *phoinikoi* can be translated as 'people of the purple dye'. The dye, one of the rarest and most expensive commodities of the ancient world, was derived from two varieties of the murex sea snail, found along the Levantine coast. The colours produced were red purple ('Tyrian purple') and blue purple (violet or hyacinth), respectively called *argaman* and *tchelet* in the Bible. From then on purple has been symbolic of majesty and wealth.

At the time of the Israelite kingdom, Phoenicia consisted of independent city-states, the most important of which were Sidon, Tyre, Gebal (later Byblos) and Arvad. The Phoenicians would not have called themselves by this collective Greek name, but rather considered themselves as citizens of their individual city-states, which is also how the Bible refers to them.

Phoenician civilization can be defined as a new and brilliant phase of Canaanite culture that developed in the cities of the narrow coastal corridor of Syria and northern Lebanon in the 1st millennium BC. The emergence of the Phoenician cities as independent entities after 1200 BC, the onset of the Iron Age, was connected with the great political and social upheavals at this time (pp. 62–63). With the establishment of the new kingdoms, including Israel (pp. 70–71), controlling inland areas, the Phoenicians relied on international trade for their livelihood.

Historically elusive

The best archaeological information about the Phoenicians comes from sites in northern Israel, along the coast from Mt Carmel to Rosh Hanikrah and in the plain of Acre, for instance Tell Keisan and Achziv. At Achziv a large cemetery has been excavated, containing evidence for two kinds of burial practice: inhumation in rock-cut or stone-built chambers and cremation, with ashes placed in pottery vessels. Cremation is uncommon in the Levant before this time, and may be evidence for the arrival of foreigners from the north.

The great Phoenician cities of the Lebanon are still important urban centres today, making extensive excavation difficult. Tyre has produced evidence for pottery styles which reach back into the Early Bronze Age.

The Phoenicians are credited by the Greeks with the invention, or at least the early development, of the alphabet, which was no doubt of great use in their widespread commercial activities. In the virtual absence of surviving Phoenician literature, much of what is known about the Phoenicians comes from the Bible and other literary sources, such as the royal Assyrian archives, Greek writers, especially the Homeric poems, and contemporary inscriptions. A particularly interesting insight into the growing independence of the Phoenician and other cities is given by the Egyptian account of the temple envoy Wenamon of the late 12th century BC. Sent to Byblos to obtain timber, he found himself being treated with less respect than an Egyptian might formerly have expected in this area. While in the Tjekker city of Dor, supposedly under Egyptian control, he was robbed and then chased by the Tjekker in their fleet of ships to Byblos, where he finally managed to obtain his timber.

Great traders

The Phoenicians are especially famous as great seafarers, travelling long distances in pursuit of trade. They established colonies throughout the Mediterranean, from Kition in Cyprus to southern Spain, and, of course, north Africa, where Carthage (founded, according to one tradition, around 813 BC) was their most famous city. The sites chosen by the Phoenicians were usually natural harbours and promontories, which were then transformed into prosperous ports. The most renowned Phoenician trading partnership was that between Hiram of Tyre and Solomon, to Ophir, to obtain gold, gemstones, exotic woods and strange apes (1 Kings 9, 26–28 and 10, 11; 22). Legend has it that the Phoenicians even sailed beyond the Pillars of Hercules (the Straits of Gibraltar) to Britain to trade in Cornish tin.

Brilliant craftsmen

As well as being the foremost traders of the period, the Phoenicians also excelled as craftsmen. Descendants of the Canaanites, they inherited all the technological skills that had produced such excellent craftsmanship under the Egyptian empire. To the south, in Canaan proper, these skills were no longer much in evidence during the Israelite monarchy; perhaps when the Egyptians withdrew from this area they took with them the finest local craftsmen. David and Solomon both turned to Tyrian craftsmen and artists to build the palaces and the Temple of Jerusalem (pp. 80–81).

The fine stone and timber, including pine and cedar, of their native mountains were used to build homes for gods and kings. The Phoenician artists skilfully combined elements of both Egyptian and Canaanite traditions with inspiration of their own, to produce unrivalled wood carvings, ivory furnishings, gold objects, bronzework and other luxury items, such as jewellery, sealstones and terracottas.

Detail of a relief from the palace of Sargon at Khorsabad, showing Phoenician sailors rowing a boat with a prow in the shape of a sea-monster's or horse's head.

A 19th-century AD illustration of Cedars of Lebanon. Cedars are slow-growing, spreading trees of great beauty. It is one of the few native trees of the Levant which grows to a great height and so could be used for roof and wall beams and planking. Its odour is pleasing to humans but repellant to insects and the wood was thus much used in antiquity in palaces and temples, where it gently perfumed the halls and sanctuaries. The interior of Solomon's Temple in Jerusalem was completely lined with cedar, probably ornately carved (1 Kings 6, 15).

CONTEMPORARIES OF THE PHOENICIANS

There were many other small nations in the region where King David established his state in the 10th century BC. At that time, as today, great religious and cultural diversity existed in the Near East, especially in the Levant. The rise of such a small nation as Israel to the status of a great power could only have happened when Mesopotamia and Egypt were at a low ebb. As soon as these lands began to recover, nearly all the tiny kingdoms that had gained ground in the interim were again caught up in the power struggle between the resurgent empires. The Bible names many people in the region. Indeed, the prophets frequently warned the Children of Israel against adopting the cultural and religious practices of their neighbours, showing special intolerance towards the Canaanites, who were the indigenous inhabitants of the land.

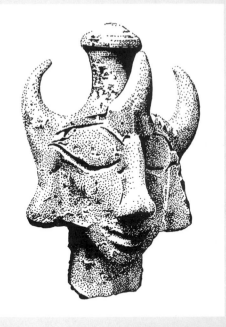

An extraordinary pottery head modelled in the form of a horned goddess (above). This comes from Qitmit, the Edomite cult site, and dates to the 7th or early 6th century BC.

Ammonite limestone sculpture of a bearded male head (left), possibly a god, wearing the Egyptian *atef* crown.

THE ARAMAEANS
To the north, in Syria, lived the Aramaeans, who were one of the Semitic peoples of the area. They, like the Phoenicians and other Canaanites, were organized in small city-states, chief among them Damascus and Zobah. David conquered some and brought others within his sphere of influence, though after his reign there was seldom peace between them and Israel and Judah.

The Aramaeans controlled the main roads to and from Mesopotamia, Anatolia and Egypt. The Aramaic language was widely used throughout the Near East, supplanting Akkadian, the language of Mesopotamia, as the common tongue of the whole region until well into the Roman period.

THE AMMONITES
More closely related to the Israelites were the peoples of Ammon, Moab and Edom in Transjordan. Until recently little was known about them archaeologically. Conquered by David, they partly broke away from his successors. After the Assyrian conquest of Israel in 721 BC, they became vassals of Assyria, though still controlling

both overland trade with Arabia and seaborne commerce on the Red Sea.

The Ammonite capital was at Rabbah (now Amman, the capital of Jordan) 25 miles (40 km) east of the Dead Sea. Some Israelites lived among the Ammonites in the land of Gilead, such as the tribes of Reuben, Gad and half the tribe of Manasseh. David sought refuge among them and Rehoboam, who succeeded his father Solomon, had an Ammonite mother. An inscription from a temple at Tell Deir 'Alla (possibly biblical Succot) tells of a vision of Balaam son of Beor, a prophet (pp. 20–21). The language of the inscription is a dialect of Canaanite, just as Hebrew is, and the script is not dissimilar.

THE MOABITES
Moab, south of Ammon, also had close links with Israel. Ruth, the Moabite girl who twice married Israelites, was the ancestress of

King David. The king sent his parents to safety with King Mizpah of Moab when he fled from Saul (1 Samuel 22, 3–4).

One of the greatest kings of Moab was Mesha. He won his country's independence from Israel after the death of Ahab, around 850 BC; an event recorded on the famous Stela of Mesha (p. 28). Again the language and script differ little from Canaanite or Hebrew of the same period.

THE EDOMITES
In the extreme south of Transjordan lived the Edomites, about whom little is known before the Assyrian conquest. They dominated the southern half of the King's Highway and during the 7th century BC they probably took Tell el-Kheleifeh, at the head of the Gulf of Aqaba, from Judah. They thus controlled sea traffic on the Red Sea and the overland routes to Gaza and to Midian, in Arabia, to the southeast.

In the northern Negev, southeast of Arad, the remains of an isolated cult site stand on a remote hillside. This is Qitmit, almost certainly established by the Edomites around the time of the fall of Judah in 587 BC, as a way-station and travellers' shrine. Their chief god, Qaus, is named in inscriptions on ostraca found there.

The Edomites prospered at the expense of Judah after the Babylonian destruction of Jerusalem (pp. 96–97). Some of them migrated west and established the state of Idumaea in southern Judah, where the population had been greatly depleted by warfare and exile.

In addition to these peoples the Bible mentions many others living among and around the people of Judah. Some, such as the Amalekites and Midianites, were nomadic. All of them exercised influence over the culture of the biblical kingdom.

These were all much sought after and have been found widely outside Phoenicia itself. The products of this artistic tradition are often described as being in the International Phoenician style.

Employing Phoenician craftsmen could prove rather expensive, as Solomon discovered when, in addition to huge annual payments of wheat and olive oil (1 Kings 5, 11), he had to cede 'twenty cities in the land of Galilee' to Hiram, king of Tyre, who was supplying materials and craftsmen. Even then Hiram was apparently not satisfied because he called these cities 'the land of Cabul', a name which seems to mean 'a worn out land' or 'a good-for-nothing country'.

Horvat Rosh Zayit

At a place called Horvat Rosh Zayit on a hillside 8 miles (13 km) inland from Acre, archaeologists have discovered the remains of a massive Phoenician-style fortress with deep storage cellars. This may be the remains of a Tyrian citadel in the land of Cabul (1 Kings 9, 12–13). (There is an Arab village still called

Kabul about a mile away.) Here, on the border between the tribes of Asher and Naphtali, the Phoenicians may have collected taxes in kind from the people of the area. The main entrance to the fort was found blocked, probably as a desperate measure by its defenders when they were beset by the Assyrians in 842 BC. The site was destroyed all the same, for signs of conflagration and destruction can clearly be seen. The expansion of the Assyrians was to have a growing impact on Phoenician cities in the late 9th and 8th centuries BC. For a while local Phoenician rulers were left in place, though paying large amounts of tribute, until the Assyrians seized direct control over the region (pp. 86–87).

HORVAT ROSH ZAYIT
The main building measures some 80 ft (25 m) square and is still standing to a height of about 10 ft (3 m). It is fortified on the west by a wall 6 ft (2 m) wide. The structure has ashlar masonry at its corners and these were precisely laid in a method familiar from other royal buildings of this period. There was a cellar under the southwestern room which held the remnants of storage jars which had contained wheat, wine and olive oil, some still with their original clay stoppers. The fortress was probably destroyed when the army of Shalmaneser III attacked the north in 842 BC.

The main map (below) shows the kingdom of Solomon in relation to its neighbours. The inset shows the the site of Horvat Rosh Zayit and the modern village of Kabul (shown as a square).

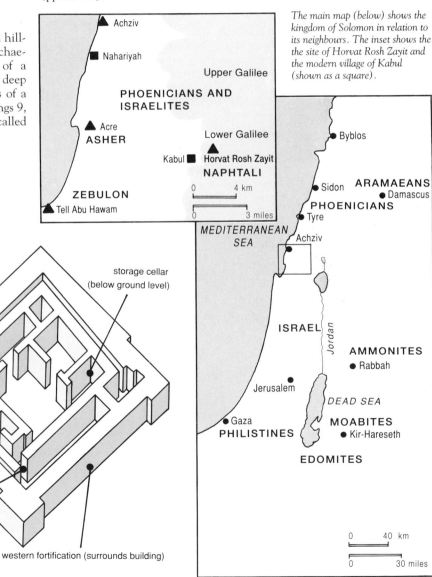

storage cellar (below ground level)

main entrance (blocked)

western fortification (surrounds building)

THE AGE OF THE JUDGES

This delicate and detailed ivory carving (above) of a well-born Canaanite girl conveys something of her modesty and poise. The figurine dates to the Late Bronze Age, but the ivory carving skills needed to produce such an exquisite miniature work of art were not lost during the Early Iron Age, and came to fruition in the famous Phoenician ivories of the 9th and 8th centuries BC.

Now it came to pass in the days when the judges ruled...
Ruth 1, 1

THE BIBLICAL BOOKS OF JOSHUA AND JUDGES contain accounts of the period after the death of Moses when the Israelite tribes were settling in Canaan and the nation of Israel began to emerge. Archaeologically, this corresponds to the early Iron Age, roughly between 1200 and 1000 BC. There is still much debate about the way in which the Israelites settled the area, though recent research has begun to shed some light on this difficult and formative era.

Joshua and Judges tell different versions of the story. Joshua describes a swift and almost total conquest of Canaan by all the people acting together, followed by the allocation of land to the tribes (Joshua 11, 23). Judges, however, tells us the land was allocated first, and only later conquered piecemeal by various tribal groups as their interests dictated (Judges 1, 3).

Archaeological viewpoints

There are several theories about the settlement in Canaan by Israel. A rapid military conquest is perhaps the least probable. Archaeology has established that few of the cities mentioned by Joshua were occupied at this time. Jericho and Ai, two of the most famous, provide good examples of this. Excavation has shown that Jericho was at best a very impoverished village at this period, and may not have been inhabited at all. At Ai, 10 miles (16 km) to the west and some 3,500 ft (1,060 m) higher in the mountains, there had not been a settlement for well over 1000 years. The name Ai means 'mound of ruins', and it could easily have been the editors of the biblical account who first named the Israelites as the destroyers of the city.

Other explanations for the rise of Israel are that the Israelites originated as Canaanite peasants in rebellion against cruel masters, or as refugees from the coastal plains which were troubled by the Sea Peoples, or again as desert nomads settling peaceably among the scattered mountain villages along the spine of the country. There are problems with all these suggestions.

The most likely theory is that the bulk of the Israelites were descendants of patriarchal bands who had remained behind when the other groups went to Egypt, mixed perhaps with native Canaanites whose ancestors had been displaced from their homes, possibly during the 16th century BC when the Egyptians conquered Canaan or during the reorganizations of Ramesses II (pp. 56–57). Perhaps such people are those referred to as *habiru* in texts found at the Egyptian site of Tell el-Amarna and elsewhere, a name which seems to indicate bands of stateless, dispossessed people, who caused trouble to various local rulers around this time. Once thought to be closely identifiable with the Hebrews, it now seems more likely that, while Hebrews were one element among the *habiru*, it was a general name for different homeless peoples.

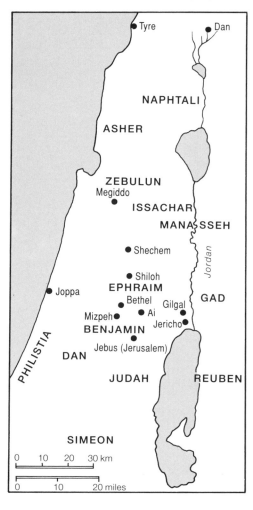

The distribution of the Israelite tribes in Canaan during the Early Iron Age (right).

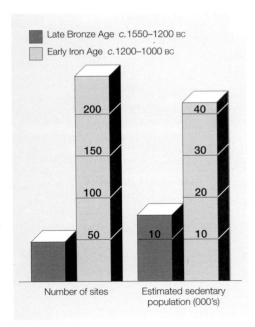

Late Bronze Age c.1550–1200 BC
Early Iron Age c.1200–1000 BC

200	40
150	30
100	20
50	10	10

Number of sites   Estimated sedentary
                   population (000's)

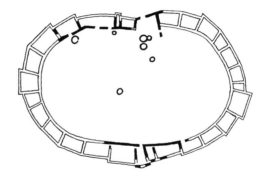

The diagram (left) clearly demonstrates the rise in estimated population and the increase in the number of inhabited sites in Canaan between the Late Bronze Age and the Early Iron Age. The question for the archaeologists is where did all these people come from?

Stratum III at Izbet Sartah (above), a site in the foothills east of Aphek. This phase dates to the Early Iron Age and was probably inhabited by the Israelites. In this period individual houses were often arranged around the periphery of a large central area, reminiscent of nomadic tent encampments.

These *habiru*, then, may have formed the majority of the later Israelites. Their culture and beliefs were little different from other Canaanites, but, remembering their ancestry, they came under the influence of those groups who had journeyed from Egypt via Mt Sinai under the spiritual and practical leadership of Moses and who worshipped Jehovah.

Villages in the hills

By the late 13th century BC these two elements, some of the *habiru* of Canaan and the Israelite tribes who came from Egypt, were drawing together and beginning to settle in the sparsely populated central hill country. The earliest and densest area of settlement was in the area of Ephraim and Manasseh, and also in Gilead across the River Jordan, the home of the tribes of Reuben, Gad and half of Manasseh. In the central hills, where there had been only a handful of settlements up to this time, archaeologists have now discovered remains of over 200 poor villages dating to this period.

From there, settlers moved north to Galilee and south to Judah, which shows no signs of heavy population until the time of King David. All the earliest shrines of Israel are in Ephraim – Gilgal, Bethel, Shiloh, Mizpah and Ramah – and it was not until David established his capital at Jerusalem that Judah became an integral part of the religious life of Israel. It is also interesting to note that the prophet and judge Samuel was from Ephraim, and Saul, the first

king of the united people, was from the tribe of Benjamin, which was bordered by Ephraim to the north and Judah to the south.

In these ephemeral subsistence farming communities a form of domestic architecture evolved which was to develop into the pillared 'four-room house' (p. 34). This became the commonest house-type in Canaan until the 6th century BC.

As the population increased, hilltops were cleared of native woodland (Joshua 17, 15) and terraced for agriculture, with wheat and barley grown on the lower slopes and olive trees and vines wherever possible. One characteristic pot found in these settlements is the collared rim storage jar, a huge amphora most likely for olive oil and wine. The farmers practised dry farming, that is, they relied on groundwater and rainfall with no large-scale use of irrigation, and so they also may have used the jars to store water for domestic use. Remains of rock-cut water storage cisterns have also been found, as have numerous pits which were plastered or lined with stones and used for the storage of large quantities of parched grain.

Dating the emergence of Israel as a separate presence in Canaan is difficult. The individual biblical Judges themselves cannot be historically traced. Towards the end of the 13th century BC the phrase 'the people of Israel' was inscribed on an Egyptian monument of Merneptah (p. 59), indicating that by this time the Israelites were recognized as being one of the peoples of Canaan.

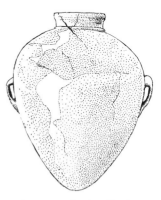

A classic example of a collared rim storage jar of the Early Iron Age. It is mostly found in sites of the central hill country although it is not unknown along the Mediterranean coast and in Transjordan.

DAVID, KING OF ALL ISRAEL

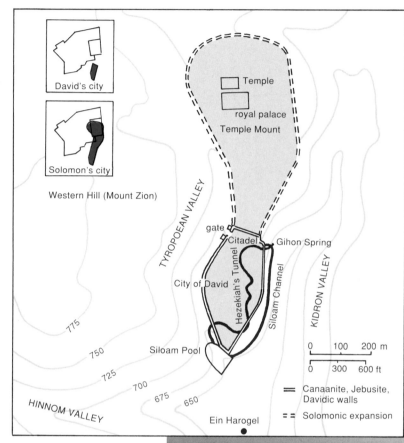

Temple

royal palace
Temple Mount

Western Hill (Mount Zion)

David's city

Solomon's city

TYROPOEAN VALLEY

gate
Citadel
Gihon Spring

City of David

Hezekiah's Tunnel

Siloam Channel

KIDRON VALLEY

Siloam Pool

775
750
725
700
675
650

HINNOM VALLEY

Ein Harogel

0   100   200 m
0   300   600 ft

═══ Canaanite, Jebusite, Davidic walls

══ Solomonic expansion

Then Samuel took the horn of oil, and anointed him in the midst of his brethren: and the Spirit of the Lord came upon David from that day forward.
1 Samuel, 16, 13

SOME OF THE BEST KNOWN BIBLE STORIES centre on King David, yet neither history nor archaeology can substantiate any of them. Scholars generally agree that he lived in the 10th century BC, and remains of structures of this date have been found in Jerusalem, though they may date to Solomon's reign. It is clear, however, that David was a man of enormous charisma. Few people have so gripped and held the imagination for over 3,000 years. Our view of David, the *Mashiach* (or Messiah, literally 'the Anointed One') is coloured by his successes, not least as an expert statesman and propagandist. His official biographies (mostly in 2 Samuel and 1 Chronicles) have an almost uniformly adulatory tone, showing the king as a hero of immense personal integrity and as a man who truly walked with God. Once he had consolidated his hold over his kingdom, he set about a vigorous expansion of his territory. The kingdom reached its greatest extent during his reign. Jerusalem, the city he made his own, is still the centre of three world religions.

Jerusalem, the City of David (above). The plan gives an impression of the natural topography of the city that made it a good choice for a capital in terms of its defensibility and its water supply. The small insets show David's original city and the expansion of it by his son, Solomon.

A view of the Kidron valley with, on the left, the area of the City of David leading up to the Temple Mount in the north, and the Silwan village on the slopes of the Mt of Olives on the right.

Shepherd, soldier and king

David began life as a humble shepherd boy, the eighth and least of the sons of Jesse of the tribe of Judah, who lived in Bethlehem. The story of his youth is told in 1 Samuel 16–31. He was a fighter all his life, first on behalf of Saul and then, driven from Saul's entourage, as a mercenary in the pay of the Philistine king of Gath.

David gathered around him about 400 malcontents (an apt way of translating the word *habiru* – p. 56) and welded them into a highly professional army. After the death of Saul and Jonathan in battle against the Philistines at Mt Gilboa, David began to consolidate his hold on his own tribe of Judah, governing at first from Hebron, while still nominally a Philistine vassal. Following the assassination of Saul's only surviving son, Ish-Bosheth, the northern tribes also declared for David and he looked about him for a suitable place from which to rule over the now-united tribes of Israel. His choice fell on Jerusalem.

The City of David

Before this time Jerusalem was a small Canaanite town called Jebus, owned by the Jebusites, one of the peoples of the hill country. Jerusalem was an excellent choice for David. It lay at the crossroads of important roads running through the hill country both north to south and west to east. It was also virtually on the border between the territory of Judah to the south and the tribes loyal to Saul (nearly all the rest) in the north and was thus neutral territory, claimed by neither side. David laid siege to it and took it with his own trained men, not with a levy of Israelite fighting men, so that the city became his personal holding and is still often called the City of David. He then made Jerusalem the centre of the worship of Jehovah, the God of all Israel, bringing to it the Ark of the Covenant. The Ark was a large but portable chest; it was also the holiest possession of the tribes of Israel, for it contained the Tablets of the Law – the Ten Commandments that Moses had brought down from Mt Sinai (2 Samuel 6). Thus the tiny town acquired a status that it could hardly have aspired to otherwise and one which it still retains to this day.

The topography of Jerusalem

In terms of ancient town planning the siting of ancient Jerusalem was excellent, being virtually impregnable on all sides except the north. Until the Babylonian attacks, no army was able to take it by assault. Low on its eastern flank in the Kidron valley is a perennial supply of water

A 9th-century BC relief from Gozan (Tell Halaf) in northern Syria. It shows a man about to launch a slingshot. This could be a very accurate weapon in warfare – as it was in the hands of the young David when he slew Goliath (1 Samuel 17, 50).

called the Gihon spring. A little further to the south, also in the Kidron valley, is another water source called Ein Harogel. Valuable for irrigating the valley bottom, it was, however, too far from the city to be used as a domestic water supply.

The ancient city was defined by valleys on its western, eastern and southern edges. The western valley is Gehenna or the Hinnom valley (more properly Gai ben Hinnom, or the valley of Hinnom's son) which is deep, hot and airless in the long summer months. This was the location of the Tophet, the altar where pagans made their first-born children 'pass through the fire' to the god Molech (2 Kings 23, 10). No wonder, then, that Gehenna has such a bad reputation, its name often used as a synonym for hell. Gehenna, or the Hinnom valley, first runs north–south from the area of today's Jaffa Gate, and then curves eastwards to meet the Kidron, or eastern valley. This used to be far deeper than today. Over the centuries it has become choked with debris from the city.

Another valley runs north–south though the central area of biblical Jerusalem. Its ancient name is not known, but Josephus, the Jewish historian of the Roman period (p. 12), gave it a Greek name – Tyropoean, or Cheesemakers valley. It is known today either by that name or simply as the Central valley.

Where was David's City?

The exact location of David's city within the larger area of ancient Jerusalem has been the subject of much research for over a century. Many of the early explorers who attempted to find it were obstructed in their searches by the Ottoman authorities.

Recently, excavation has concentrated on the ridge sloping southwards from the Dome of the Rock, bounded on the west by the Central valley and on the east by the Kidron. The late Professor Yigal Shiloh (1938–88), following on the work of Kathleen Kenyon between 1961 and 1967, conducted excavations in the area from 1978 to 1982. Through his excavations, Shiloh has proved conclusively that this was the site of the City of David.

The most important results came from Shiloh's Area G where two huge artificial terraces were found. These may have added as much as 2,150 sq.ft (200 sq.m) of ground to the vulnerable northeastern area of the ridge. They are made up of a series of stone-walled boxes, filled with rubble to form a solid foundation.

Yigal Shiloh's Area G in the City of David, Jerusalem. The stepped stone structure, 44ft (13m) high, reaches up to the summit of the hill, which is probably the site of David's citadel. Because of the press of refugees overcrowding Jerusalem after the fall of Samaria in 721 BC, houses had to be constructed over the stepped stone structure in the late 8th to mid-7th centuries BC. The house seen here is called the 'House of Ahiel' because this name occurs on two potsherds found in it (p. 96).

Using these terraces as a base, David, or perhaps Solomon, constructed a glacis consisting of a stepped stone structure, semicircular in shape and still surviving to 44 ft (13 m) high. Shiloh believed that the Citadel of David, possibly called Zion (2 Samuel 5, 7), was built on top of the hill, utilizing the extended area of the stepped stone structure and looming above the old Jebusite city proper to the south. The citadel was perhaps the house built for David by Hiram, the Phoenician king of Tyre (2 Samuel 5, 11).

Solomon's palace complex was probably north of this citadel, with the Temple to the north again of that. These sections formed a sort of royal acropolis, being relatively inaccessible to the ordinary people of the town. Extensive excavation has not been possible in any of these areas as they are occupied now by private houses, roads and the Haram esh-Sharif or Temple Mount. The eastern line of the city wall of the Jebusite and Davidic city has been found half way down the eastern slope of this ridge, with a gate at a point above the Gihon spring.

Following the reigns of David and Solomon, particularly in the mid- to late 7th centuries BC, perhaps in the reign of Josiah, the stepped stone structure became the foundation for new terraces constructed down the hillside. Houses, some of them belonging to officials, were built on them, because the town had become extremely crowded by that time. Some of the buildings, for example the House of the Bullae, may have been government offices. In fact the town must have been fairly densely occupied from the time of David, since the Jebusites, we are told, stayed on and shared the city with their Israelite conquerors.

A tiny town

The mighty city of David and Solomon was actually no bigger than a small village of today. David's Jerusalem probably covered about 15 acres (6 ha), and even Solomon's extension only reached 37 acres (15 ha). But by the time of King Hezekiah (727–698 BC) the city had grown to about 150 acres (65 ha) and new walls were built (pp. 90–91). This made Jerusalem more than six times larger than any other town in the kingdom. It also had extensive unwalled suburbs, especially to the north. The next largest city at the time, Lachish, covered only about 20 acres (8 ha). Most towns in the ancient Near East were fairly modest in size, except for the great capital cities of empires such as Babylon.

WATER FOR JERUSALEM

The Gihon spring in the Kidron valley was the only reliable water source for Jerusalem in the earliest periods. It is an unfailing siphonic spring, or 'gusher' (perhaps the meaning of its name, Gihon). At irregular intervals it spurts enough water daily to supply about 2,500 people. The water level can be low, however, and so it was necessary to build holding tanks or reservoirs in the Kidron valley.

Three man-made systems were built in the First Temple Period, all depending on the Gihon: Warren's Shaft; the Siloam Channel; and Hezekiah's Tunnel. Dating the first two is difficult: their most recent excavator, Yigal Shiloh, opted for the 10th–9th centuries BC, preferring the late 10th century and the time of Solomon.

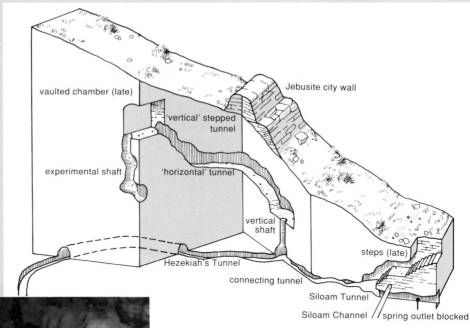

Jerusalem's three water supply systems, all based on the Gihon spring.

Warren's Shaft *was discovered in the last century and named after the man who found it. Only the upper end of the system is man-made – at least in its present form, which dates to the Roman period. The entrance chamber is just south of the citadel area. A tunnel 135 ft (41 m) was cut into the rock, to lead, first by steep steps and then by a nearly horizontal section, to a* *cave and a vertical shaft – both natural features in the limestone. The shaft drops around 40 ft (12.3 m) to the level of the water, which is brought to the bottom of the shaft by a connecting tunnel from the Gihon spring. It was a long, dark walk down both the tunnels to the head of the shaft to draw water. The women of the city must have made the journey*

several times a day, every day. Here and there in the wall can still be seen smoke-blackened niches where oil lamps were placed to light the way.

It used to be thought that Warren's Shaft is the tsinnor mentioned in 2 Samuel (5, 8) in connection with the heroic exploits of Joab and David's conquest of the Jebusite city. The precise meaning of the word is unknown however, and most scholars also feel that the technology of the system is too advanced for the Bronze Age Jebusite city.

The Siloam Channel is about 1,200 ft (365 m) long and ran along the eastern side of the City of David. Partly a slab-covered conduit and partly a rock-cut tunnel, it joined the Gihon waters to reservoirs at the southern end of the city. Some see in it the 'waters of Shiloah that go softly' (Isaiah 8, 6). A system of openings and sluices on its eastern, downhill, side could also channel water for irrigation into the fields and orchards on the floor of the Kidron valley. It was essentially a system for times of peace, since its whole course and the reservoirs

associated with it lay outside the city walls.

Hezekiah's Tunnel was part of that king's enlargement of the city and his improvement of its defences and facilities at the end of the 8th century BC, when it became obvious the Assyrians were going to attack. An inscription was engraved on the wall near the southern end of the tunnel recording how it was cut from both ends by two different teams, who met in the middle (p. 91). There was a natural fissure in the rock through which water already trickled and this allowed the miners to hear each other at work. Otherwise, it seems unlikely that the two tunnels would ever have met up. The tunnel is over 1,600 ft (485 m) long and its average height is just over 6 ft (2 m), although it is much higher at its southern end near the outflow into the new Siloam Pool. This pool was protected by a new city wall built by Hezekiah. From this point the overflow was conducted, via another cutting of the Siloam Channel, to irrigate the Kidron valley. The whole system was hidden from enemy eyes.

KING SOLOMON'S EMPIRE

And when the queen of Sheba had seen all Solomon's wisdom, and the house that he had built, and the meat of his table, and the sitting of his servants, and the attendance of his ministers and their apparel, and his cupbearers, and his ascent by which he went up unto the house of the Lord...she said to the king, It was a true report that I heard in mine own land...

1 Kings 10, 4–6

Map showing the extent of Solomon's empire and economic influence, and how the kingdom expanded progressively under Saul, David and Solomon.

SOLOMON WAS A YOUNGER SON of David. His mother was Bathsheba, whose first husband had been killed on David's orders, to leave her free to remarry the king (2 Samuel 11). Solomon (965–928 BC) was anointed at the

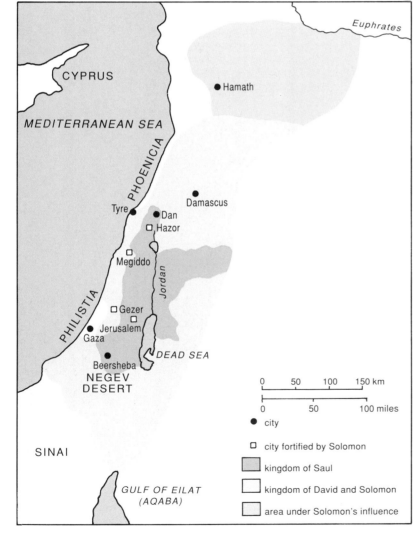

Gihon spring while his father was still alive, and so became co-regent with him in the Egyptian style.

The empire Solomon inherited from his father covered virtually all of Canaan, west and east of the River Jordan, and stretched south through the Negev desert to the port of Ezion Geber at the head of the Gulf of Eilat (Aqaba). Solomon thus gained access to the lucrative seaborne trade of the Red Sea. His father's wars had ensured that the Philistines were no longer a problem, and the Phoenicians, especially Hiram of Tyre, were his allies. He ruled the Aramaean kingdoms of inland southern Syria and his economic influence reached as far as the River Euphrates. In the absence of other great regional powers, Solomon was indeed a force to be reckoned with. He secured his position even further by marrying an Egyptian princess, probably the daughter of Siamun (978–959 BC), one of the last pharaohs of the 21st Dynasty.

From tribal territory to nation state

David, the man of war, had secured the kingdom; Solomon, the man of peace, by engaging in international trade, was able to modernize and develop it. He set up the formal framework of a court and reorganized the state into 12 districts, with a governor and an administrative centre for each. In this way, the traditional tribal system was all but abolished, making Israel more like other nations in the region.

Throughout his reign it seems Solomon was occupied with trading ventures and building projects. A large part of the king's wealth was dedicated to the conspicuous expenditure of an oriental monarch. His palaces and their furnishings, such as his ivory and gold throne flanked by 12 lions (1 Kings 10, 18–20), the Temple with its cedar-wood panels and gold decorations, and his 1,000 wives and concubines (1 Kings 11, 3), would all have been viewed at home and abroad as evidence of his royal rank and his kingdom's high status.

Solomon the builder

Solomon devoted much effort and expense to fortifying the most strategic sites of the realm and to securing the vital trade routes. In these projects he used the skills of Tyrian craftsmen and the labour of a rotating levy of 30,000

A detail of an ivory plaque found at Megiddo, probably dating to the 13th century BC. It is a vivid if idealized portrayal of life in a Near Eastern court, carved in the eclectic style later inherited by the Phoenicians. The king is shown relaxing in a garden, seated on a throne supported by winged sphinxes – the same creatures as the cherubim who guarded the Ark of the Covenant in Solomon's Temple (p. 80). The king's musician plays to him on a harp, as David did before Saul (1 Samuel 16, 23), while an elegantly dressed woman, who is presumably the queen, offers him something. A very similar scene appears on the back of a throne belonging to the Egyptian pharaoh Tutankhamun.

Israelites (1 Kings 5, 13). Apart from Jerusalem, three places are singled out for special mention in the Bible: Hazor, Megiddo and Gezer (1 Kings 9, 15). The third of these, the town of Gezer, had been captured by the pharaoh, Siamun, who then gave it to Solomon as part of his daughter's dowry.

Excavations at these three towns revealed that in Solomon's day they had defensive walls and main gateways built to a standard plan and

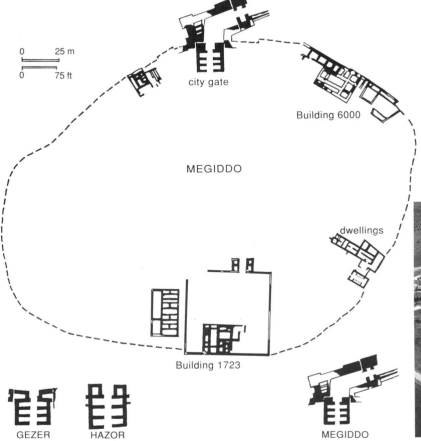

MEGIDDO

Building 6000

dwellings

Building 1723

GEZER   HAZOR   MEGIDDO

Aerial view of Megiddo (below) and a plan of the site (left), showing Solomonic and later buildings. Below left are plans of the standard gateways built by Solomon's army engineers at Gezer, Hazor and Megiddo, three of the most strategically located sites in his kingdom which he singled out for particular attention (1 Kings 9, 15). There is very little evidence at these places for the homes of ordinary people and they may rather have been military garrisons or store cities.

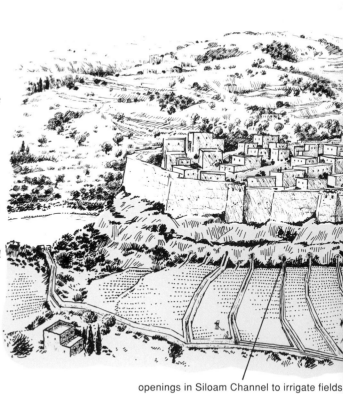

SOLOMONIC JERUSALEM
A reconstruction of Solomon's Jerusalem shows that the township proper is a very small area at the southern end of the hill. Here the inhabitants of the city lived in small, square, flat-roofed houses. North of this is the stepped stone structure which is shown as supporting the citadel. This may be the Millo which, together with the wall of Jerusalem, Solomon built with Israelite labour. This is effectively the dividing point between the rulers and the people of the city. Immediately north of it was probably the royal acropolis. Fine, squared ashlar stone blocks were found here by Shiloh and also previously by Kathleen Kenyon, along with a proto-Aeolic capital, all indicative of royal buildings in the area. Further north again stood Solomon's new Temple closely connected to the royal precinct at the extreme northern end of the city. This was Yigal Shiloh's interpretation of his excavated finds, but not all archaeologists agree with it. It should also be remembered that the stepped stone structure is the only construction that has been found, and its function is not certain.

openings in Siloam Channel to irrigate fields

size, approximately 65 by 55 ft (20 by 17 m). All the gateways have three guard chambers on either side of the entry passage which could be barred by gates when the need arose. They also had projecting guard towers and the defensive walls associated with them are the double-skinned type called casemates. The space between the inner and outer wall could either be divided by short cross walls to make storage rooms or filled with rubble to strengthen the walls if the city was besieged. In some towns, for instance Tell Beersheba in the 8th century BC, these cells were actually elements within the four-room houses.

Solomon's reign saw other developments in royal architecture. At Megiddo, which became one of the administrative centres of his king-

dom, there are remains of large, well-built structures of this date which are often referred to as palaces, though they may be no more than official residences. Building 6000, near the gateway on the northern side of the site, is a monumental building of the *bit hilani* type. This term refers to a regular architectural plan consisting of a broad, pillared portico before an entrance hall which had a staircase on one side, rising to the floor above. The entrance hall, in turn, precedes the main, ceremonial room, perhaps used as a throne room or audience chamber, with other rooms around it. Examples of this arrangement have been found in palaces in northern Syria at this time.

Another building on the south side of Megiddo, 1723, contains similar elements,

This small horned altar comes from the site of Megiddo and dates to the 10th century BC. It was carved from a single block of limestone and was most probably used to offer incense.

A Proto-Aeolic capital carved in stone. Such capitals, often a feature of royal buildings, are also called Proto-Ionic as some scholars see in them the prototype for the Ionic order of Greek architecture.

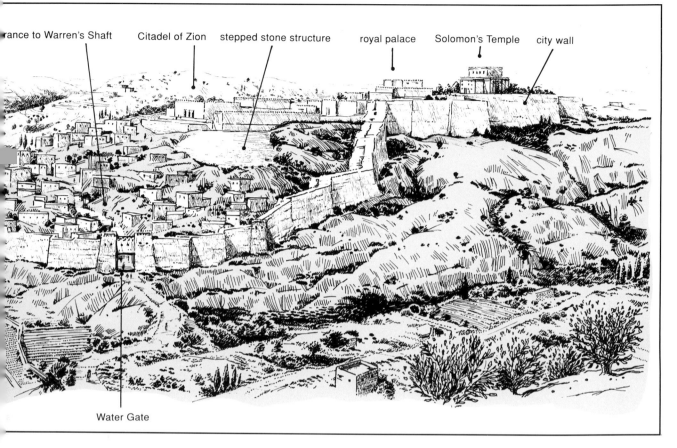

rance to Warren's Shaft   Citadel of Zion   stepped stone structure   royal palace   Solomon's Temple   city wall

Water Gate

though a generally more elaborate design. It stands within its own precinct wall, itself constructed of fine ashlar piers with plastered rubble infill. Examples of so-called Proto-Aeolic capitals were found here, which are usually associated with royal architecture in Israel in the Iron Age. The building measured some 60 by 66 ft (20 by 22 m) and had more than ten rooms and a large courtyard. Remains of a staircase suggest that there was an upper storey too. This may have been the residence of Baana, son of Ahilud, who is mentioned in 1 Kings 4, 12 as Solomon's governor in Megiddo.

On the eastern side of Megiddo was a third important building, which contained a shrine room with pillars. Here was found a fine horned incense altar, possibly similar to altars that would have been used in Solomon's Temple in Jerusalem.

Solomonic Jerusalem

Solomon's construction programme in Jerusalem must have been spectacular. The Queen of Sheba visited the city and was astounded by the splendid buildings, which lived up to the report she had heard (opening quote). Limited by the valleys to the west and east of the city, Solomon created an impressive acropolis area for his Temple and palace complex by expanding to the north, towards, and probably partially including, today's Temple Mount. His buildings may have stood in the area identified by some as the Ophel of Jerusalem (2 Chronicles 27, 3).

There is a detailed description of Solomon's building works in the Bible (1 Kings 7, 1–11), giving an impression at least of his grandiose scheme. There were several buildings, all with different functions, for instance 'the house of the Forest of Lebanon', 'the hall of the throne' and 'the hall of pillars' – which may refer to elements constructed in the *bit hilani* style. Phoenician masons and craftsmen, as well as raw materials, were probably employed on the work, and the decorative details of both the Temple and the palace were in the International Phoenician style. In this context it is worth remembering the cities in 'the land of Cabul' ceded by Solomon to Hiram of Tyre to repay his debts (p. 69).

SOLOMON'S TEMPLE

Behold, I build an house to the name of the Lord my God, to dedicate it to him...
2 Chronicles, 2, 3

THE TEMPLE WAS UNDOUBTEDLY one of the most important buildings in Solomon's royal complex. It was built to hold the supreme national and religious relic of Israel, the Ark, brought down by Moses from Mt Sinai and which had been recaptured from the Philistines by David.

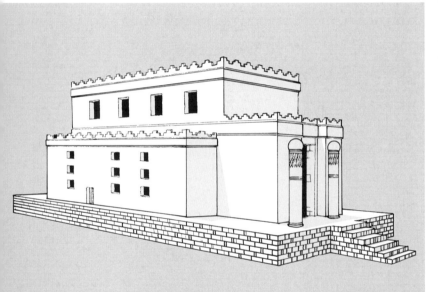

SOLOMON'S TEMPLE

The artist's reconstruction here is based on the description of the temple in 1 Kings 6. It was modest in size – a house for God, not a great cathedral built to shelter the worshippers, though it was probably larger than any other temple at the time. The Holy of Holies was a 30 ft (9 m) cube. The Temple was built of the local Jerusalem limestone, with a roof and beams of cedar. Inside the walls were panelled throughout in cedar. The floor was pine and the doors were olive wood. The inner sanctuary and everything in it was overlaid with gold and ornamented with coloured stone and glass.

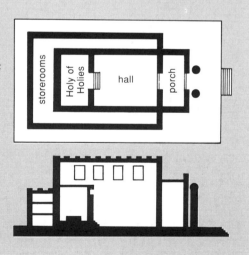

The Ark was the rallying point for all the tribes, and, in its new home, it was firmly under the control of the king.

It is not possible to make a complete reconstruction of the Temple even though it is described in great detail in 1 Kings, 6–7 and 2 Chronicles 3–4. Also in the Bible is the ideal plan of the Temple as remembered by Ezekiel (40–43), who had first-hand knowledge of the original, destroyed by the Babylonians in 587 BC. Excavations are not permitted today on the Temple Mount, the general area where Solomon's Temple stood, because of the sanctity of the place for Moslems and Jews, and also because it is protected under international law. This 'forbidden ground' is the precinct of the Haram esh-Sharif ('The Noble Sanctuary'), whose massive pavement, where the famous gold dome of the Dome of the Rock now stands, was built by Roman engineers for Herod the Great (pp. 134–35). Remains of Herod's Temple may well still exist, and it is even possible that some signs of the foundations of Solomon's Temple may also be buried very deep.

As described in the Bible, Solomon's Temple was built of 'undressed stone' on a podium of ashlar masonry. It was rectangular in shape, and according to the Bible measured 60 by 20 cubits (approximately 100 by 33 ft or 30 by 10 m) and stood 30 cubits high (about 50 ft or 15 m), so it would have been easily visible above the city. The Temple had a tripartite structure consisting of a porch (*ulam*), main hall or sanctuary (*hekhal*) and the Holy of Holies (*devir*); the whole was considered as the House of God (*bayit*), that is His dwelling place among His people. The Holy of Holies, which housed the Ark, may have been a separate room leading on from the main hall, perhaps via a short flight of stairs, or it may have been contained within it, if, as has been suggested, the *devir* was a prefabricated cedarwood room or 'cabinet'.

Two freestanding pillars named Yachin and Boaz stood at the entrance to the Temple; the names probably meaning '(God) established (the House) with might'. These great columns with their copper decorated capitals were cast for the Temple by a man called Hiram whose father had been a Tyrian metalworker (1 Kings 7, 14). With the exception of the porch, the Temple was surrounded by a three-storeyed

annexe, which probably contained objects dedicated to the Lord. It also served as the national treasury.

Canaanite temples

The biblical description of the Temple fits into the tradition of religious architecture in Canaan as known from other sites. Archaeologists working in the 1930s at Tell Tayanat, in northern Syria, found a small royal shrine in close proximity to a palace in *bit hilani* style. This shrine, although smaller than Solomon's and slightly later, being 9th century BC, complements the account of the Temple well. It is rectangular and tripartite and at its entrance still stood one of originally two, huge pillar bases carved in the shape of double lions. Here the pillars may possibly have supported a lintel. Earlier stages of this type of temple building can be found at Ebla and Hazor. Temple H at Hazor, dating to the Late Bronze Age, also contained two column bases, this time with no apparent structural function. A model of a shrine in pottery from Tell Farah North also supports the theory that the Temple's pillars were freestanding.

Decoration and equipment

Wood was used throughout the Temple – cedar and pine covered the walls and pine the floors, with wild olive used for the doors. Apart from the doors this woodwork was ornamentally carved. Everything was overlaid with gold. The decorative motifs are well known from the so-called International Phoenician Style. For instance, the cherubim with wings outstretched over the Ark may have been similar to the winged and apron-wearing sphinxes seen on ivory carvings of the 9th and 8th centuries .

Parallels can be found also for the furnishings and cultic equipment of the Temple. The great horned altar described in Ezekiel 43, 13–17 is comparable to both the huge altar made of limestone blocks, possibly of the 9th century BC, from Tell Beersheba and small incense burners from many ancient sites, such as Megiddo (p. 78).

The God of Israel

Between the 10th and 8th centuries BC Jerusalem was only the principal seat of Jehovah. Shrines were also located elsewhere in the kingdom, but whether these were dedicated to the worship of the God of Israel or to other deities is not completely clear. There is a 'cult room' at Lachish, a 'cult corner' at Megiddo and a 'cultic installation' at Ta'anach. Most famous of all is the sanctuary within the border fortress at Arad in the northern Negev desert (p. 88). Enigmatic inscriptions from a shrine of the 8th century BC in a fortress and way-station at the site known today as Kuntillet 'Ajrud (pp.52–53) mention Baal and El as well as Jehovah. They include the phrase 'Jehovah and his Asherah' on a large storage jar. Some scholars have identified Asherah as the consort of Jehovah, worshipped perhaps in Israel rather than Judah. The theology of the Israelites was heavily influenced, as the Bible itself indicates, by that of the Canaanites and is unlikely to have been absolutely monotheistic until the Babylonian Exile. Solomon built shrines for the gods of his many foreign wives and towards the end of his reign he himself worshipped with them (1 Kings 11, 4).

A sphinx or winged cherub carved in ivory, from Arslan Tash, Syria (left). The cherubim, whose outstretched wings covered the Ark in Solomon's Temple, may have looked similar.

The sacrificial horned altar (above) was reconstructed from fragments found reused in the walls of a storehouse at Tell Beersheba. It may date as early as the 9th century BC. There must have been a shrine to Jehovah at the site, just as there was at Arad (pp. 88–89); the altars at both places were probably torn down during the reforms of Hezekiah.

CUBITS
In the Old Testament period there were two types of cubit. The short cubit measured some 18 in. (45 cm) long, while the Royal cubit was about 20 in. (53 cm) long. It is likely that the royal cubit was used in the construction of the Temple and palaces of Solomon.

THE KINGDOM OF ISRAEL

THE AUTHORIZED
VERSION OF HISTORY
*While the final version of the
history of this period (mainly in the
Books of Kings and Chronicles)
did not crystallize immediately, the
early writers and editors at the
Court in Jerusalem used oral and
written sources from both north
and south to construct their
narratives. Their political and
theological bias is towards the
Davidic dynasty. The north is seen
as the rebel and its kings,
Jeroboam, Omri and Ahab – all
competent and successful rulers –
are considered sinful and accursed.*

*For thus saith the Lord, the God of Israel, Behold, I
will rend the kingdom out of the hand of Solomon,
and will give ten tribes to thee.*
1 Kings, 11, 31

FOLLOWING THE DEATH OF SOLOMON in about
928 BC, his nation split into two parts. The
north, which had been Saul's power base,
became Israel. The tribe of Judah, virtually
alone except for the tiny tribe of Benjamin,
formed the southern kingdom of Judah and
stayed loyal to the family of David. Even in
David's time the northern tribes had never
been fully assimilated and they resented the
heavy burdens of tax and forced labour
imposed on them. Jeroboam ben Nebat
attempted rebellion during Solomon's reign,
and, having failed, fled to Egypt. External
forces were also threatening the security and
prosperity of the empire. Edom revolted, while
a new Aramaean dynasty was founded in
Damascus. The trade monopoly in the region
established by Solomon was beginning to break
up and there were many who were keen to
exploit this situation.

*The division of the kingdom in the
reign of Rehoboam, with Israel by
far the larger entity in the north,
and Judah, with only the tribe of
Benjamin still loyal, in the south.*

The division of the kingdom

It was Rehoboam, Solomon's son and successor, who was responsible for the final schism.
He summoned the northern tribes to the
ancient cult centre of Shechem to affirm him
as king by acclaim in the traditional way.
However, led by the former rebel Jeroboam ben
Nebat, who had returned from exile, the tribes
refused to recognize Rehoboam unless he
agreed to remit some of their taxes. Foolishly
the king instead threatened to increase their
burdens, with the result that the tribes seceded
from his kingdom. Rehoboam hurriedly
returned to Jerusalem and was never able to
bring the north back under his control.

Thus began the period of the Divided
Kingdom. During the next two centuries there
was frequent conflict between Israel and Judah,
with each gaining the upper hand at different
times. The southern state of Judah in its remote
hill country was to remain under David's successors for nearly 350 years, until the time of
the Babylonian conquest (pp. 96–97). The far
larger and more exposed northern kingdom of
Israel had a turbulent history. Without a secure
ruling dynasty it was constantly prey to internal coups and external attacks until its eventu-
al destruction by the Assyrians in the late 8th
century BC.

Sheshonq

The Egyptian pharaoh Sheshonq I (935–914
BC), founder of the 22nd Dynasty and the
Shishak of the Bible, was one of those eager to
take of advantage of the weakness of the
Divided Kingdom. Having supported the rebel
Jeroboam when he was in exile in Egypt, this
pharaoh led a campaign into Israel and Judah,
around 926 BC, following Solomon's death.
References are made in the Bible to his invasion of Judah and to Rehoboam's payment of
ransom to save Jerusalem, perhaps using the
Temple treasury to do so. Other evidence
comes from an inscription from Karnak, in
Egypt, which mentions towns in Israel captured by Sheshonq, and a fragment of a stela of
Sheshonq which was found at Megiddo. The
Egyptian pharaoh did not turn his successes
into a lasting occupation, but returned with his
troops to Egypt, presumably having achieved
his goal of plunder and control of lucrative
trade routes.

THE HOUSE OF DAVID INSCRIPTION

In 1993 at Tell Dan on the headwaters of the River Jordan, an expedition led by Professor Avraham Biran discovered an inscription thought to be of the 9th century BC which seems to have profound importance for biblical history.

The official surveyor of the team, Gila Cook, was making a detailed plan of the remains of a gate. She stooped down to check something and saw incised letters on the underside of one of the stones.

The Phoenician script of the inscription is clear and regular and the text appears to refer to 'the King of Israel' and 'the House of David'. Some scholars see in this the earliest mention of the Davidic dynasty found outside the pages of the Bible.

The inscription appears to be part of a stela possibly recording a victory over a King of Israel and a King of Judah. However, there is as yet no consensus on the precise meaning of this fragmentary text nor who exactly is being referred to.

The stela had been intentionally broken and its pieces reused in a new city gate. Two more fragments have recently been found and the search is on for further pieces which could clarify the text.

Translation
1 …
2 … my father went up …
3 … and my father died, he went to [his fate… Is-]
4 rael formerly in my father's land …
5 I [fought against Israel?] and Hadad went in front of me …
6 … my king. And I slew of [them X footmen, Y cha-]
7 riots and two thousand horsemen …
8 the king of Israel. And [I] slew[… the kin-]
9 g of the House of David. And I put …
10 their land …
11 other … [… ru-]
12 led over Is[rael …]
13 siege upon …

From Dan to Bethel

Jeroboam I (928–907 BC), while an astute ruler, was unable to surround his throne with the aura of divine sanction which David had achieved. He did try to unite the concepts of sacred and secular in the way both David and Solomon had done so successfully in Jerusalem and his first major initiative bears witness to this. Fearing that his subjects might renew their allegiance to Rehoboam if they made the pilgrimage to the Temple in Jerusalem, Jeroboam established two national shrines, Dan and Bethel, on the northern and southern borders of Israel. In both he set up golden statues of bulls (recalling the story of Aaron, the High Priest, at Mt Sinai in Exodus 32) and installed non-Levite priests to serve the cult (1 Kings 12, 27–31). It is a debatable point whether the statues were worshipped as gods or whether they were considered as pedestals for Jehovah, whom it was forbidden to represent by a graven image. Gods shown standing or riding on animals were common in the iconography of the ancient Near East.

Jeroboam was unable to establish a permanent dynastic seat, ruling first from Shechem and later from the site of Penuel, Transjordan, perhaps as a temporary refuge during the invasion of Sheshonq. Later still the seat of government moved to Tirzah (Tell Farah North), near Shechem. Finally, under Omri (882–871 BC), the capital was settled at Samaria.

Tell Dan

Tell Dan, at the extreme northern edge of Jeroboam's territory, contains some of the most interesting remains of the Divided Kingdom;

Professor Avraham Biran has been excavating the site over many years. The tell rises above one of the sources of the River Jordan and today it stands in a delightful watery woodland. It was already a great Canaanite city called Laish when it was conquered and renamed by the tribe of Dan during the 11th century BC, after the death of Samson (p. 65).

In the 9th century BC the lower gateway of the city was built on the southern side of the mound. Against the façade of the inner part of the gate was placed a small ashlar platform, flanked by four stone, bowl-like column bases. These may well have held wooden poles to support a canopy over a chair or throne which was occupied by some high official presiding over public meetings there (pp. 44–45). Nearby a

This small ashlar platform, with its accompanying pillar bases, was found by the inner gate of Tell Dan. To the right of it was a low stone bench. Scholars are divided about the use of the platform – was it the place where the kings or governors held court? Or was it for the statue of a city god, with the bench used for votive offerings?

Professor Avraham Biran of the Hebrew Union College, Jerusalem. He has been directing excavations at the important site of Tell Dan since 1966.

cult niche held several standing stones, or *matzevot*. Beyond the piazza in front of the gate archaeologists have recently discovered another (later) gatehouse. A fragment of stone with the House of David inscription (p. 83) was found reused in this area. A third gate was also built in the 8th century BC at the top of the cobbled road leading into the city.

The most important feature in the city throughout this period was the sacred area overlooking the headwaters of the River Jordan. One element of the temple enclosure was a large, well-built podium. This was once interpreted as a *bamah* or 'high-place' but may have supported a temple structure. Close to the podium, in an open courtyard, was a sacrificial horned altar, measuring 16 by 20 ft (5 by 6 m)

and built of stone blocks. The cult complex also included a sunken pool, perhaps used in rituals, and ancillary rooms.

Founded by Jeroboam, the shrine was enlarged by Ahab in the 9th century BC and is the only example of a royal sanctuary so far discovered in the north. Remains of an earlier cult place were also discovered here and the shrine complex must have remained in use and been rebuilt many times, down to the Roman era.

The House of Omri

Israel had four changes of ruling family in the first fifty years of its existence. In about 882 BC, a military commander, Omri, took control after a civil war. Little is known about him, but during his reign he extended his authority over Moab and parts of Syria, which was to cause conflict between Israel and the Aramaeans of Damascus. The official Assyrian histories recognized his stature (unlike the writers of the Bible), for they recorded the rulers of Israel as being of the House of Omri long after the fall of his dynasty.

During his reign and that of his son Ahab (871–852 BC), Israel was more stable. In part this was ensured by dynastic marriages, firstly of Ahab to Jezebel, a Phoenician princess of Sidon. Later Athaliah, daughter of either Omri or Ahab, was married to the king of Judah, Jehoram (846–843 BC), thus bringing the two kingdoms into an alliance. Both queens encouraged the worship of Canaanite gods in their new countries. Athaliah even managed to

The cult precinct at Tell Dan, which was in use for nearly 1,000 years. A monumental platform of the 10th and 9th centuries BC may have been a bamah, or high place. The reconstruction below shows a great altar of sacrifice in front of the steps to the platform.

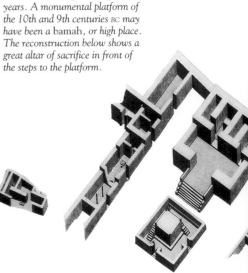

establish a short-lived sanctuary dedicated to Baal within the precincts of the Temple in Jerusalem. The spread of worship of this pagan god throughout both kingdoms provoked the opposition of the prophets Elijah and Elisha to the kings of Israel.

The Hill of Shemer

Omri and Ahab were responsible for much building work in the 9th century BC in Samaria, Hazor and Megiddo. Omri, like David, acquired a hill on which to build his new capital; unlike David, he purchased his site, from a man named Shemer, and the city became Shomron or Samaria (1 Kings 16, 24). It was almost certainly here that Ahab built his 'ivory palace', for many ivory fragments were found in the debris of the buildings.

Hazor and Megiddo were both key fortresses of Israel and royal administrative centres, as they had been under Solomon. At Hazor, Ahab doubled the size of the fortified area and a heavily-protected citadel was created at the western end of the mound. At both sites archaeologists have excavated buildings originally identified as stables, but which were more likely storehouses for the produce collected as taxation and doled out as troop rations or sent to the official storage facilities in Samaria. It may also have been distributed to the populace in times of famine. Such storehouses are now known in many towns of Iron Age Israel and Judah. They were usually built just inside the city gates, beside the public piazzas.

The end of the House of Omri

Ahab was involved in a series of clashes with the Aramaeans of Damascus, and eventually died in battle against them. Earlier the same year, 853 BC, he had joined an alliance of the Aramaeans and others to fight off the common Assyrian threat (p. 86). Ahab was succeeded by his two sons, the first of whom died very soon after his father (2 Kings 1, 17). The younger brother Joram (or Jehoram, 851–842 BC) formed an alliance with the king of Judah, Jehoshaphat (867–846 BC), and the king of Edom, to face a rebellion of the Moabites, who saw the death of Ahab as a chance to recover their freedom from Israel. Mesha, the King of Moab, won the day by sacrificing his son and heir when the battle was going against him (2 Kings 3, 27). The king erected a monument to commemorate his victory, which was found in the last century and is now in the Louvre in Paris (p. 28).

Some years later Joram joined forces with his cousin Ahaziah (843–842 BC), the new king of Judah (Athaliah's son) to fight the Aramaeans of Damascus once more. Joram was badly wounded at the Battle of Ramoth Gilead (842 BC) and was taken to the city of Jezreel, where Ahaziah visited him. Here they were both assassinated by Jehu ben Nimshi, a commander in Joram's army who had already been anointed king by a prophet sent by Elijah. Jezebel died too and Jehu proceeded to eliminate all the royal seed of Israel. He then eradicated the worship of Baal in the country. In Judah, Athaliah seized power, temporarily breaking the line of David. She was herself assassinated in 836 BC. Thus ended Omri's bloodline. A young king, Joash, was crowned in Jerusalem.

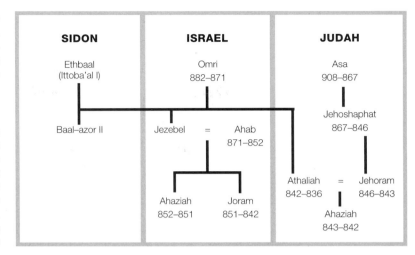

Family trees of the houses of Israel and Judah in the time of the dynasty of Omri and his descendants.

The 'woman at the window' – a motif found in a large number of ivory plaques. One interpretation sees her as a Canaanite priestess, appearing at a balustraded window. Fancifully, she could also be Jezebel, looking down from her palace window at Jezreel at Jehu in his chariot, before her servants threw her down to be trampled by the horses (2 Kings 9, 30–34).

THE MIGHT OF ASSYRIA

Found by A.H. Layard at Nimrud in 1845, the 'Black Obelisk' (below) is 6ft 6 in. (2 m) high and was erected by Shalmaneser to celebrate his victories. Among the scenes of vassals bringing tribute is one of King Jehu of Israel (right), incorrectly called the son of Omri. Assyrian artists are considered very accurate in their depictions of people and so this is probably how Israelites and Canaanites would have looked. Less accurate are the strange images of animals in the lower registers of the obelisk.

The Assyrians amassed large amounts of booty from their campaigns. As well as quantities of raw materials and finished goods in gold, silver, other metals, ivory, exotic woods and cloth exacted as tribute, they captured domestic animals, slaves and craftsmen and gained access to the maritime trade of the Mediterranean.

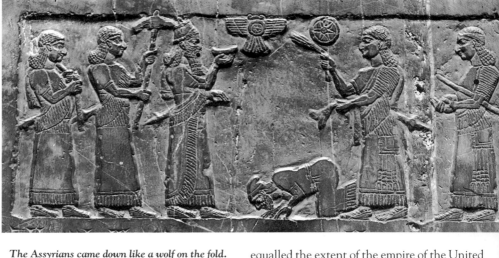

The Assyrians came down like a wolf on the fold. And his cohorts were gleaming with purple and gold.

Byron, *Destruction of Sennacherib*

THE HOUSE OF OMRI fell in 842 BC in Jehu's bloody coup, but in the very year of his accession to the throne of Israel, Jehu was forced to pay tribute to the Assyrian king, Shalmaneser III (858–824 BC). The expansionist threat of the Assyrians had been felt in the area before this: in 853 BC a coalition of 12 kings of the Levant, including Ahab of Israel, had held the army of Shalmaneser III at bay at the Battle of Karqar, on the River Orontes. Shalmaneser returned in 842 BC, and this time was more successful. He besieged Damascus and was able to exact tribute from Sidon, Tyre and Israel. Jehu himself is shown prostrating himself in submission on Shalamaneser's black basalt victory stela. A new Assyrian king, Adad-Nirari III (810–783 BC), resumed campaigns in the region and once more forced Israel, among others, to pay tribute.

The Assyrians, however, were more interested in plunder and tribute from vassal states at this time than lasting territorial gain. They were also troubled by revolts and involved in wars against Urartu in eastern Anatolia. In fact, the earlier part of the 8th century BC marks a time of increased power and prosperity for both Israel and Judah. Jeroboam II of Israel and Uzziah of Judah each regained control over territory and lucrative trade routes, and between them controlled lands that almost equalled the extent of the empire of the United Monarchy.

Uzziah of Judah

During his long reign (769–733 BC) Uzziah, also called Azariah in the Bible, is credited with building up his army and strengthening the defences of Jerusalem by erecting towers. He also fortified other sites in Judah in anticipation of future Assyrian hostilities. A string of forts in the Negev desert dates to this period, and it was almost certainly Uzziah who rebuilt the fortress of Kadesh Barnea.

According to the Bible Uzziah was struck down by leprosy late in life as a punishment for

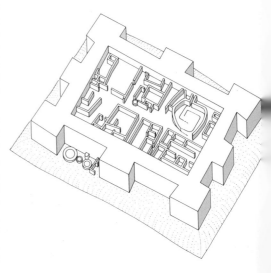

his sins (2 Chronicles 26, 16–23). However, leprosy as it is known today did not exist in the Near East at this time and it must have been another skin disease that afflicted him.

The fall of Israel

The second half of the 8th century BC saw the Assyrians return in force under Tiglath-Pileser III (744–727 BC), the Pul of the Bible. He instituted a new practice of imposing direct rule over troublesome areas by setting up provinces under Assyrian governors. Any rebellion was crushed and punished by mass deportations.

Ahaz, King of Judah (733–727 BC), refused to join an anti-Assyrian coalition led by the Israelite King Pekah (735–733 BC). When threatened with invasion by Pekah and his allies, including Rezin of Damascus, Ahaz called on Tiglath-Pileser for help, even offering him treasure from the Temple. The Assyrian armies conquered city after city in Philistia, Syria and northern Israel, finally capturing Damascus and executing Rezin. Pekah was killed and Tiglath-Pileser installed Hoshea, the last king of Israel, in his place as a tribute-paying vassal. The territories of Damascus were taken under direct rule and a system of provinces was set up.

Hoshea attempted to revolt shortly after the death of Tiglath-Pileser in 727 BC, seeking help from Egypt. This brought the wrath of Assyria, under Shalmaneser V (726–722 BC), down on Israel. Samaria was invested and fell in 722 or 721 BC, after a siege lasting two or three years, in the reign of either Shalmaneser or, more probably, the next king, Sargon (721–705 BC). Samaria seems to have been made the capital of an Assyrian province and eventually it was

Expansion of the Assyrian empire.

refounded as a Hellenistic town, before Herod built his city of Sebaste there.

The aristocratic and wealthy classes of Israel were sent into distant exile in different areas of the Assyrian empire. The Assyrian records of the campaign state that 27,290 were deported, though it is impossible to know whether this is exaggerated. Such exile was not exactly slavery, since family groups were often resettled in village communities as farmers and artisans. Some would have been used as forced labour on building projects.

Israel thus ceased to exist as an independent kingdom and Judah stood alone, beset by the might of the Assyrian empire at its height.

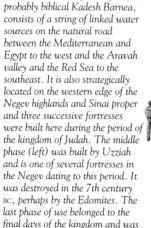

The isolated oasis of Ein Qudeirat, probably biblical Kadesh Barnea, consists of a string of linked water sources on the natural road between the Mediterranean and Egypt to the west and the Aravah valley and the Red Sea to the southeast. It is also strategically located on the western edge of the Negev highlands and Sinai proper and three successive fortresses were built here during the period of the kingdom of Judah. The middle phase (left) was built by Uzziah and is one of several fortresses in the Negev dating to this period. It was destroyed in the 7th century BC, perhaps by the Edomites. The last phase of use belonged to the final days of the kingdom and was destroyed by the Babylonians.

Captives used as forced labour; Sargon's palace, Khorsabad.

LOST TRIBES
It is known that some of the Israelite exiles were sent to Haran beyond the River Euphrates, to settle in an area of ancient Gozan (Tell Halaf on the River Habur in northern Syria) where their descendants were eventually absorbed into the local population. Their disappearance has brought about some of the legends concerning the 'Lost Tribes of Israel'.

Other groups of exiles in the Assyrian empire were imported into Israel. The Bible (2 Kings 17, 24) lists these as coming from Babylon, Cuthah, Avva, Hamath and Sepharvaim. In the course of time they merged with the Israelite peasants left behind, blending their own culture and religion with those they found. Their descendants became the Samaritans (p. 107), who still live as a separate group in the area of modern Nablus, which is ancient Shechem.

JUDAH ALONE

...there was none left but the tribe of Judah only...
2 Kings 17, 18

SMALL THOUGH IT WAS, JUDAH had a relatively peaceful history under successive kings of David's line, from the division of the kingdom to the destruction of Israel by the Assyrians in the late 8th century BC. Thereafter the situation changed abruptly, for Judah was now in the front line of Assyrian attack. Many Judaean towns and villages were destroyed in the Assyrian campaign of 701 BC (pp. 92–95). The earlier 7th century shows signs of revival, but the advent of the Babylonians at the end of the century very soon brought catastrophe and the final downfall of the Judaean kingdom.

The population explosion

One immediate result of the fall of Samaria in 721 BC was an influx of an enormous number of refugees who fled south, swelling the population of Judah. The archaeological evidence for this is clear, since towns and villages were built throughout the realm. The central hills were densely populated and even relatively inhospitable regions such as the northern Negev and the Judaean Desert were heavily settled. The carrying capacity of the land must have been severely taxed. Jerusalem increased in size to some 150 acres (60 ha) and may have held a population of between 10,000 and 20,000 (pp. 90–91). This represents a huge concentration of people at a time when the average Judaean town was between 5 and 8 acres (2 and 3 ha), with perhaps 500 to 1,000 inhabitants.

The new settlements in the outlying regions were vulnerable to encroachments by the Edomites and Bedouin tribes, as well as to Assyrian and Egyptian attack, and the Judaean kings built new fortresses, especially in the northern Negev, to prevent this. It is possible that mercenary soldiers were employed, as East Greek and Cypriot pottery has been found at many sites in the area. Letters written on ostraca to Eliashib, commander of the fort at Arad, mention 'Kittim', who may have been soldiers from Kition in Cyprus.

The fortress and shrine at Arad

High on a desert hilltop northeast of Tell Beersheba, the fortress of Arad dominates the desert. The small shrine found tucked inside it is the only rural sanctuary discovered so far in

Too small to be called a temple, this tiny shrine at Arad served the religious needs of the garrison there. The altar in the courtyard in front of it was undoubtedly for the worship of Jehovah because it was made of undressed stone, in accordance with biblical instructions (Exodus 20, 25): 'And if thou wilt make me an altar of stone, thou wilt not build it of hewn stone, for if thou lift up thy tool upon it, thou hast polluted it.' The altar went out of use some time before the shrine itself was destroyed by the inhabitants of the fort. Many scholars believe the altar was abandoned during the religious reforms of Hezekiah, which only allowed sacrifice at the Temple in Jerusalem (p. 90). The shrine itself disappeared when Josaiah's reforms abolished all places of worship outside Jerusalem.

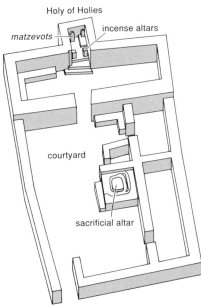

Holy of Holies

matzevots

incense altars

courtyard

sacrificial altar

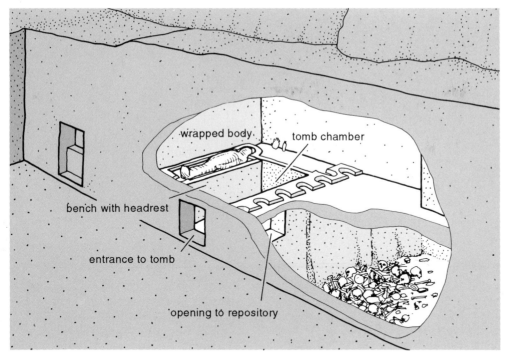

The Ketef Hinnom burial caves west of Jerusalem are typical of the aristocratic tombs of the 7th century BC. Similar ones have been discovered elsewhere around the city and they define its extent at the time, as it was forbidden to all but kings to be buried inside the city walls. The Ketef Hinnom tombs were cut from the limestone hills and their architecture reflects the burial customs of the First Temple era. A central entrance led into a cave with three benches carved from the rock. These had hollows serving as headrests for the dead. Once the bodies had decomposed, the bones were collected and, together with grave goods and small personal items, put in repositories often hollowed out under one of the benches. One repository was found intact in Cave 25. It contained the bones of around 95 individuals and, among other grave goods, two 7th-century silver plaques, inscribed with early versions of the Priestly Blessing.

Judah. It was perhaps established as a border shrine to define the limits of the kingdom, as Dan and Bethel did for Israel (p. 83).

The tiny cult room was flanked by two incense altars, each carved from a single block of smooth stone. Inside were two standing stones (or *matzevot* in Hebrew). Following the discovery of roughly contemporary inscriptions at Kuntillet 'Ajrud which mention 'Yahweh and his Asherah' (p. 53), some scholars have identified the two standing stones at Arad as representing the god and his consort. If this is correct, it explains the vehement repudiation by the prophets of the Canaanite cults which the people found so attractive.

In the eyes of the prophets, not all the kings of Judah in this final period of independence were faithful servants of Jehovah. Hezekiah and Josiah did reform and purify the worship of Jehovah, but others, such as Ahaz and Manasseh, the father and son of Hezekiah respectively, were sinful idolaters who encouraged the cult of Canaanite gods.

Manasseh even went so far as to introduce the rites of Baal and Asherah into the Temple and to 'pass his son through fire' (2 Kings 21, 5–6). This somewhat mysterious phrase is usually taken to indicate child sacrifice, a custom condemned by Old Testament prophets and which seems to have been practised by the Phoenicians.

The tombs of Ketef Hinnom

The worship of Jehovah was, however, strictly observed by some and the earliest fragment of biblical text so far discovered comes from this period of Judah's isolation. In the 7th century BC burial caves were carved in the hills around Jerusalem, including the western slopes of the Hinnom valley. Two tiny, tightly-rolled silver plaques were found in one, with versions of the Priestly Blessing (Numbers 6, 24–26). The tombs must have belonged to wealthy families, possibly of the Priestly class, whose adherence to Jehovah was beyond question.

THE KETEF HINNOM SILVER PLAQUES

The blessing the Priests pronounced over the people was so important by the 7th century BC that it was inscribed on precious metal (and perhaps on less valuable material for the poor) and worn as a talisman or amulet. The use of such charms is mentioned in the Bible, for instance in Isaiah 3, 20, where probably a form of women's jewellery is described, or in Exodus 13, 9 or Deuteronomy 6, 8, where amulets were used for more serious purposes. Many different biblical texts were used on these tefilin, some of which have also been found among the Dead

Sea Scrolls (pp. 122–25). The smaller silver plaque from Ketef Hinnom bears a shortened version of the traditional priestly blessing of Numbers 6, 24–26:

The Lord bless thee, and keep thee; the Lord make his face shine upon thee, and be gracious unto thee; the Lord lift up his countenance upon thee, and give thee peace.

One of the much-folded and creased silver plaques from the repository of Cave 25 at Ketef Hinnom.

HEZEKIAH IN REVOLT

A lamelekh seal impression, one of around 1,200 found on wine jar handles made in 8th-century BC Judah. Two motifs are known (a two-winged sun disc and a four-winged scarab) though all were made with clay from the same source in the Shephelah. Lamelekh means 'belonging to the king' and the word is often combined with the name of one of four Judaean towns. All the seals date to the reign of Hezekiah and must be connected with his preparations to withstand an Assyrian attack.

[Hezekiah] did that which was right in the sight of the Lord, according to all that David his father did. He removed the high places, and brake the images, and cut down the groves...He trusted in the Lord God of Israel.
2 Kings 18, 3–7

HEZEKIAH CAME TO THE THRONE of Judah as co-regent with his father, Ahaz, not long before the Assyrian annihilation of Israel in 721 BC left Judah standing alone. So, when Sennacherib (704–681 BC) ascended the Assyrian throne, Hezekiah decided to exploit the temporary reprieve offered by the change in monarch by forming an anti-Assyrian alliance with Egypt and the petty kingdoms on the coast.

The authors of Kings praised Hezekiah (727–698 BC) for his religious reforms, aimed at consolidating the worship of Jehovah at the Temple in Jerusalem and destroying the cults of other deities which had flourished under Ahaz. He took action against religious centres outside Jerusalem; for instance, at the border shrine of Arad (pp. 88–89) the altar was destroyed. At Tell Beersheba something similar must have happened, as the fine ashlar blocks of the huge stone altar (p. 81) were found built into later structures and have only recently been reconstructed; the shrine it belonged to has completely disappeared.

Jerusalem in Hezekiah's day

After the destruction of Samaria vast numbers of refugees from the areas taken over by the Assyrians flooded south into Judah. Jerusalem had to expand to absorb them and Hezekiah set about refortifying the kingdom as a vital part of his preparations against the inevitable attack by the new Assyrian king, Sennacherib. According to the Bible (2 Chronicles 32, 2–8) Hezekiah repaired the existing wall and built towers.

Two new residential and commercial areas were laid out west of the City of David, across the Tyropoean (Central) valley. These were the Machtesh, in the valley itself, and the Mishneh, on the eastern side of Mt Zion. The whole area must have been fortified during Hezekiah's reign, though no trace has so far been found of the defensive walls.

In the north, in the Jewish Quarter west of the Temple Mount, Professor Nahman Avigad

THE EXPANSION OF JERUSALEM

Two schools of thought exist about the size of Jerusalem in the late 8th century BC. The minimalist view was championed by Dame Kathleen Kenyon who excavated in Jerusalem in the 1960s. Although she never definitively published her interpretation, she was of the opinion that the new part of the city was confined to just a small portion of the Western Hill. In this reconstruction the effort of quarrying Hezekiah's Tunnel would not have brought the waters of the Gihon inside the city walls.

More recently the maximalist theory of Professor Avigad and others has been widely accepted. These scholars include the new water reservoir, the Pool of Siloam fed by Hezekiah's Tunnel, within the city wall where it would be safe from attack. No trace of a wall of this date has been found here,

though research is hampered by a modern road and pipelines.

In the northern part of the city the Broad Wall has been located, as have a tower and wall just to the north of it. This may also have been the line of the First (north) Wall of Jerusalem in Second Temple times, as Josephus describes it. The line of the Western Wall is still unclear.

The area of the city of Hezekiah's time according to the maximalist view would have been up to 150 acres (60 ha), and would have contained somewhere between 10,000 and 20,000 inhabitants.

Plan of Jerusalem in the reign of Hezekiah, showing the maximalist and minimalist theories of its size.

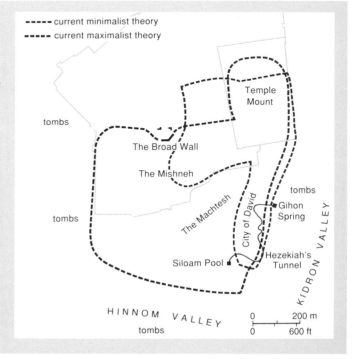

- - - - current minimalist theory
- - - - current maximalist theory

Temple Mount

tombs

The Broad Wall

The Mishneh

The Machtesh

City of David

tombs

Gihon Spring

tombs

KIDRON VALLEY

Siloam Pool

Hezekiah's Tunnel

HINNOM VALLEY

tombs

0   200 m
0   600 ft

has discovered substantial remains of two forti-fication walls of this period. One section, known as the Broad Wall, is 23 ft (7 m) wide and has been traced for a distance of 210 ft (65 m), running in a north–south direction. This is the widest city wall known from the First Temple Period, built to withstand the Assyrian battering rams. In some places the wall was built over the remains of earlier houses, which Isaiah says (22, 10) had been deliberately destroyed to make way for it. North of the Broad Wall Professor Avigad found remains of a tower in another city wall. Hezekiah may have built two fortification walls in this unpro-tected northern part of the city. The Assyrian siege camp was later positioned less than a mile away to the north, to take advantage of the city's most vulnerable point.

The 'Old City'

In the original City of David on the eastern hill overcrowding had also led to changes. The eastern city wall was strengthened and the ter-raced area inside it increased. This was densely built up with flat-roofed houses, producing an effect something like a gigantic staircase from the top of the hill down to the Kidron valley. Space was so scarce that the city expanded beyond the defensive wall in this area as well, since remains of simple houses were found down in the valley to the east of it. These poor homes were abandoned at the approach of Sennacherib's army and were never rebuilt.

Another important part of Hezekiah's prepa-rations for the oncoming war was his reorgani-zation of the city's water supply. Today the tunnel he quarried out beneath David's city still bears his name. A commemorative inscrip-tion tells how the waters of Gihon were brought via this tunnel to the new reservoir sheltering inside the city wall at the south end of the town. In this way the inhabitants of Jerusalem would be ensured a secure and safe water supply in the event of a siege.

The siege of Jerusalem

All Hezekiah's preparations proved their worth when the Assyrian army eventually arrived before Jerusalem. They had marched south along the coastal plain, sacking the cities of Hezekiah's allies. Then swinging north through the Shephelah, they besieged and destroyed Lachish (pp. 92–95). From there Sennacherib despatched part of his army under his chief officers to Jerusalem. But, for reasons that are still uncertain, the city did not suc-cumb on this occasion.

HEZEKIAH'S TUNNEL AND THE SILOAM INSCRIPTION

The impressive feat of cutting a tunnel through rock from both ends and the skill involved in making them meet are described in an inscription found at the south end of Hezekiah's Tunnel, just before its outflow into the new pool. The workmen also made the tunnel floor slope gently down so that there is a drop of about 14 in. (35 cm) from north to south, where it flows into the new pool. 'This is the story of the cutting. While [the stone cutters were swinging their] axes, each towards his fellow, and while there were yet three cubits to be cut, [there was heard] the voice of a man calling to his fellow, for there was a crevice on the right... And on the day of the piercing, the stonecutters struck through each to meet his fellow, axe against axe. Then the water ran from the spring to the Pool for 1200 cubits, and the height of the rock above the heads of the stone cutters was an 100 cubits.'

In fact this is only the lower half of the inscription. A scribe would have chalked the official text on a panel prepared in the tunnel wall for the masons, who were probably illiterate, to carve. Perhaps the arrival of the Assyrian army prevented them finishing the job as the beginning was never carved. Found in 1880 when Palestine was under Ottoman rule, the inscription is now in Istanbul.

SENNACHERIB AND THE SIEGE OF LACHISH

Professor David Ussishkin, Director of the Institute of Archaeology, Tel Aviv University and leader of the excavations at Lachish, 1973–87.

After this did Sennacherib king of Assyria send his servants to Jerusalem, but he himself laid siege against Lachish.
2 Chronicles 32, 9

ON THE REVOLT OF HEZEKIAH and his allies in 701 BC, Sennacherib marched his army swiftly west and launched campaigns not only against the coastal kingdoms but also against the cities of Judah, where he first laid siege to Lachish, which guarded the capital's southern approaches through the hills of Shephelah. Jerusalem, which was besieged later, somehow managed to withstand the Assyrian attack, but Lachish was less fortunate: the Assyrians besieged and captured the city apparently with ease.

The siege of Lachish is a uniquely well-documented episode of biblical history. Not only do we have the Assyrian and biblical accounts (2 Kings 18–19; Isaiah 36–37; 2 Chronicles 32), but we also have the testimony of the archaeologist's trowel, and finally a spectacular pictorial record in the famous series of bas-reliefs discovered in the 19th century by Austen Henry Layard at Sennacherib's palace at Nineveh.

Extensive excavations have taken place at Lachish under the supervision of Professor David Ussishkin. He and his team from the Institute of Archaeology, Tel Aviv University, uncovered evidence of a long history of occupation at the site. They found that during the reign of Hezekiah, Lachish must have been a large, fortified city, bounded by formidable walls and battlements. A huge outer gate complex – facing south at right angles to the defensive wall – controlled access to the palace-fort, shops, houses and all the other buildings within the walls.

The reliefs from Nineveh, now displayed in the British Museum, brilliantly document the Assyrian assault on Lachish, showing the initial march on the city, the breaching of the city walls by battering ram, and the looting and torture that followed the fall of the city. The reliefs were based on the work of Assyrian campaign artists who travelled with the army in much the same way as photographers do today. According to Ussishkin, the Assyrian king and his artists were probably stationed on the hillside adjacent to the southwest corner of the

BATTLE ORDER OF THE ASSYRIAN ARMY

Judging from the Lachish reliefs (pp. 94–95), Sennacherib's army must have been a truly daunting sight. It was organized according to a strict hierarchy and divided into battalions of 1,000 men, companies of 100, squads of 50 and sections of 10.

The army was split into infantry, cavalry and chariotry, the size and relative importance of each component depending on the conditions and the enemy faced. Since the conflict at Lachish took the form of a siege rather than a battle on open terrain, the infantry was of greater importance than the chariotry or cavalry.

The assault on the city was led by battering rams and foot soldiers bearing ladders to scale the walls. Behind them came the archers and spearmen with round shields, two abreast, supported from the back by slingsmen who shot round missiles high over the heads of the

soldiers in front. Auxiliary archers can also be seen in the reliefs (wearing different headgear), who were probably drafted from previously defeated armies.

king = commander-in-chief

field marshal (*tartanu*)

cavalry

chariotry

spearmen

archers

slingsmen

THE WOLF ON THE FOLD: KING SENNACHERIB

Sennacherib ascended the Assyrian throne in 704 BC, following the death on the battlefield of his father, Sargon. Shortly after his accession, in about 703 BC, Sennacherib was forced to lead a campaign against Babylonia, where the one-time king, Merodach-Baladan, had attempted to seize the throne again. Hoping to distract Sennacherib's attention, Merodach-Baladan tried to persuade his friends in Judah to revolt against Assyrian rule. But Sennacherib's first priority was to restore order in Babylonia, which he achieved when Merodach-Baladan fled. Sennacherib then installed a Babylonian noble, Belibni as king of Babylon.

In 701 BC, the Assyrian king advanced into Syria and then marched south, devastating the kingdoms of the coast and attacking many of the towns of Judah, before laying siege to Lachish. Sennacherib was evidently proud of his victory, for soon after, he built his famous monumental palace at his capital Nineveh, covering the walls of one room with reliefs of his triumph at

Lachish. One of these reliefs depicts him on a throne with his feet on a footstool, viewing the aftermath of the siege and receiving the reports of his officers shown climbing the hill towards him. Near the head of the king (which was obliterated by a vengeful hand in later days but restored in this illustration) an inscription describes him 'sitting on his nimedu throne, while the spoil from the city of Lachish passes before him'.

But the Assyrian king failed to capture Jerusalem: his troops were apparently crippled by an epidemic or perhaps diverted once again by problems in Babylon, where Sennacherib squashed a rebellion and appointed his eldest son king.

Sennacherib was dogged for many years by trouble in the kingdom of Elam, near the Persian Gulf. The conflict culminated in a great battle between the Assyrians and the combined forces of the Elamites and Babylonians who had rebelled yet again and assassinated Sennacherib's son. Both sides claimed the victory, both suffered horrific losses; but in 689 BC

Sennacherib seated on his throne receiving reports of the fall of Lachish.

Sennacherib captured Babylon a third time, and razed it to the ground. The new Assyrian crown prince was installed as king.

Sennacherib was to reign in relative peace for another eight years, until he met a bloody end, murdered by his sons in 681 BC.

---

city, from where they would have had an excellent view of the action. The king could thus monitor the progress of the battering rams and siege engines, as they battled their way slowly up the ramp constructed for them by the hapless prisoners of other successful Assyrian sieges.

Between this hill and Lachish itself was a lower saddle, from which a road led up the side of the mound to the outer gate of the city. This saddle was the city's most vulnerable point, since on all other sides it was protected by deep natural wadis (dry river beds). Wisely, the Assyrians chose this particular spot from which to launch their main attack, focusing on the outer gate.

Archaeology confirms the story in the reliefs

Ussishkin's excavations uncovered the remains of the attackers' siege ramp – the only ancient Assyrian siege ramp yet discovered. It reached up the southwest angle of the city mound to the defensive wall, where huge amounts of weapons and debris have been found. The ramp consisted of a steep slope of boulders, of

which the uppers layers were made from stones bound into position by a mortar which is still as hard as concrete.

To Ussishkin's surprise, he also found evidence for a Judaean counter-ramp, erected within the city in haste and probably under fire, to give the defenders the advantage of height and to protect the walls against the onslaught of the battering rams. But the defenders' valiant efforts in hurling torches and missiles on to their attackers proved insufficient. At the point where the Assyrians eventually breached the walls the excavators found literally hundreds of iron and bone arrowheads. They also recovered many ball-shaped slingshots.

The return to Assyria

Sennacherib did not attack Jerusalem in person. From his comfortable base camp at Lachish he sent three of his most senior officers against the capital city. But Jerusalem did not fall, a point on which all the sources and the archaeologists agree. Instead, for reasons unknown to us, the king marched home to Assyria. A combination of the heavy tribute

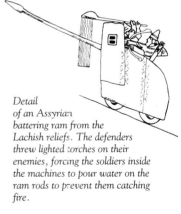

Detail of an Assyrian battering ram from the Lachish reliefs. The defenders threw lighted torches on their enemies, forcing the soldiers inside the machines to pour water on the ram rods to prevent them catching fire.

Lachish as it might have appeared during Hezekiah's reign. The whole town was protected by a massive system of fortifications comprising thick walls and a great gate complex, while at the centre of the royal citadel was a huge palace-fort. The Assyrians built their siege ramp at the vulnerable southwest corner of the mound, at the foot of the gateway.

paid by Hezekiah (perhaps it should be called 'protection money') and the new system of defences around Jerusalem seem to have helped save the day. Assyrian records confirm that indeed Jerusalem did not fall in this campaign.

According to the Bible's version of events, a miracle took place which mysteriously struck down the Assyrian army: 'And it came to pass that night, that the angel of the Lord went out, and smote in the camp of the Assyrians an hundred four score and five thousand; and when they arose early in the morning, behold they were all dead corpses' (2 Kings 19, 35). This was apparently followed by the hurried retreat of the Assyrian army and the murder of Sennacherib at the hands of his sons (2 Kings 19, 37).

There is no direct evidence either for or against these events as related in 2 Kings. We

The Lachish reliefs vividly depict the bloody events of Sennacherib's assault on the city. One detail (left) shows the defenders desperately shooting arrows at their opponents, while exiles leave by the gate below.

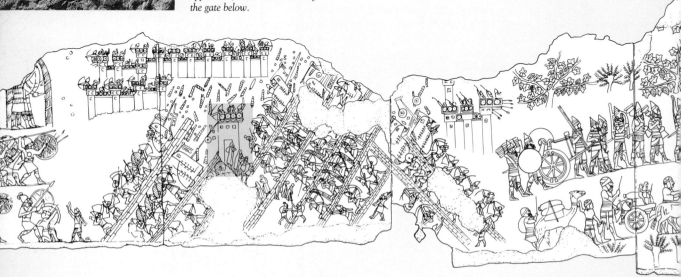

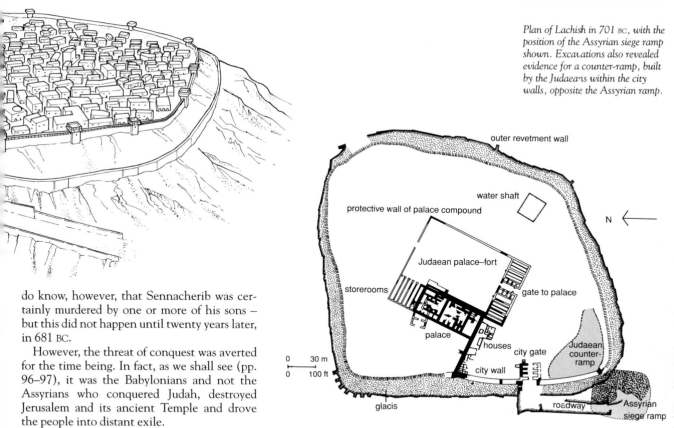

Plan of Lachish in 701 BC, with the position of the Assyrian siege ramp shown. Excavations also revealed evidence for a counter-ramp, built by the Judaeans within the city walls, opposite the Assyrian ramp.

outer revetment wall

water shaft

protective wall of palace compound

Judaean palace–fort

gate to palace

storerooms

palace

houses

city gate

city wall

Judaean counter-ramp

N

0   30 m
0   100 ft

glacis

roadway

Assyrian siege ramp

do know, however, that Sennacherib was certainly murdered by one or more of his sons – but this did not happen until twenty years later, in 681 BC.

However, the threat of conquest was averted for the time being. In fact, as we shall see (pp. 96–97), it was the Babylonians and not the Assyrians who conquered Judah, destroyed Jerusalem and its ancient Temple and drove the people into distant exile.

NEBUCHADNEZZAR DESTROYS JERUSALEM

Thus saith the Lord; Behold, I will give this city into the hand of the king of Babylon, and he shall burn it with fire…Then Jeremiah the prophet spake all these words unto Zedekiah king of Judah in Jerusalem, when the king of Babylon's army fought against Jerusalem, and against all the cities of Judah that were left, against Lachish, and against Azekah, for these defenced cities remained of the cities of Judah.

Jeremiah 34, 2 and 6–7

FROM THE DEATH OF HEZEKIAH to the destruction of Judah by the Babylonians in 587 BC was only a little over a century, but it was a time of enormous change in the Near East. The Assyrians continued to exert power over the region in the reign of Hezekiah's son Manasseh (698–642 BC) and it seems Judah was still paying a heavy tribute. Sennacherib, however, had to deal with rebellions in different parts of the empire and in 689 BC destroyed Babylon.

The city was rebuilt under his son, Esarhaddon (680–669 BC) and at some point, perhaps after joining a rebellion, Manasseh was temporarily exiled there. However, he proved his loyalty and returned to Jerusalem and was even allowed to rebuild its fortifications. It is not certain whether this happened in the time of Esarhaddon or his successor, Ashurbanipal (668–627 BC), the last great Assyrian king. Ashurbanipal, too, faced challenges on different fronts and under his successors the end of the Assyrian empire came quickly. In 626 BC the Chaldaean chieftain Nabopolassar (625–605 BC) captured Babylon, making it his capital city, and declared independence. He made an alliance with the Medes, and in 612 BC the combined armies attacked and destroyed the Assyrian capital Nineveh.

Josiah's reforms

During Manasseh's rule the cult of Baal and other pagan deities was reintroduced. Josiah (639–609 BC), who succeeded Manasseh's son, Amon (641–640 BC) implemented radical religious reforms. These were put into effect after 'the Book of the Law' was found during renovations to the Temple in Jerusalem (2 Kings 22, 8–20). Today, this book is thought to have been either a section of the Book of Deuteronomy or else a forerunner of it. It emphasized in particular that sacrifice to the Lord could only be offered in one central sanctuary. It seems that no one, from the king down, was in any doubt that Jerusalem was meant by this. Thus all other provincial shrines were abolished during Josiah's reign. Arad is probably the best known example (p. 88).

In the 7th century BC, perhaps during the reign of Josiah, there was more building activity in Jerusalem. In the City of David well-built houses that may have doubled as government offices were constructed on new terraces over the stepped stone structure in Area G to make the most of the cramped space near the palace. One of these houses is known as Ahiel's House because of the name mentioned in two inscriptions on sherds found inside it.

The last days of Judah

Josiah was killed in 609 BC in battle at Megiddo against the Egyptian pharaoh Necho II (610–595 BC). The Egyptian king was marching north into Syria to assist the Assyrians against the Medes and Babylonians. Necho was able to place his own choice as king, Jehoiakim (608–598 BC), on the throne of Judah and the country had to pay tribute to the Egyptians. In

An example of the common 'four-room house' plan. Ahiel's House measured 24 by 36 ft (8 by 12 m) and was well-built, with dressed limestone blocks forming its doorways. There were strong pillars to support the roof of the rooms and behind the back room was a service wing of three tiny rooms. One of these was apparently a toilet. Fragments of 37 storage jars were found in another.

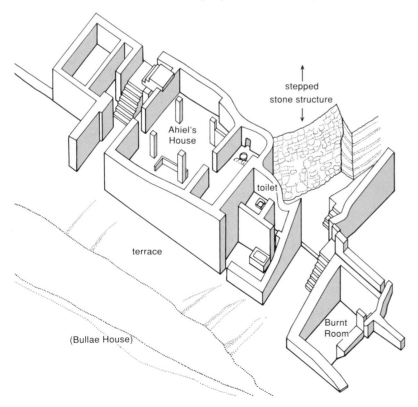

stepped stone structure

Ahiel's House

toilet

terrace

(Bullae House)

Burnt Room

605 BC, the Assyrians and their Egyptian allies were finally defeated at the Battle of Carchemish by the Babylonians under crown-prince Nebuchadnezzar (604–562 BC), the son of Nabopolassar. He then marched south, destroying Ashkelon and seizing Assyrian lands. Judah, under Jehoiakim, now became a vassal of the rising Neo-Babylonian empire.

Jehoiakim rebelled against the Babylonians in 598 BC, but died before Nebuchadnezzar arrived at Jerusalem to take revenge. Jehoiachin, his son, surrendered on 16 March 597 BC – a date recorded in the Babylonian Chronicles.

Nebuchadnezzar deported the 18-year-old Jehoiachin to Babylon as a hostage to ensure the good behaviour of his uncle, Zedekiah, who was then enthroned as the Babylonian client-king. Zedekiah, after a decade of loyalty to the Babylonians, was persuaded to enter into an alliance with Egypt, against the solemn warning of the prophet Jeremiah. The Babylonian response was swift and terrible. The army marched through Judah, destroying everything in its path.

The devastation of Judah

In the very last days of the kingdom, when only the cities of Lachish and Azekah were still standing, Jeremiah prophesied that the capital itself would be destroyed (opening quote). The archaeologist J.L. Starkey working at Lachish found a number of pottery sherds, many of them from the same vessel, in one of the guardrooms of the city gate (p. 21). Yigael Yadin suggested that these are either scribal drafts or file copies of letters that were then written out on papyrus and sent by the garrison to the high command in Jerusalem. One of the letters (number 4) must have been written after Jeremiah made his prophecy. The commander of Lachish writes that he is lighting the signal fires of Lachish in accordance with instructions because 'we cannot see [the bonfires of] Azekah'. The implication is clear: Azekah had already fallen.

The Babylonian army next moved on Jerusalem. After a siege of 18 months, during which the inhabitants suffered severe famine, the city fell in the summer of 587 BC. The Babylonians first looted Jerusalem, destroying the Temple, and then set the city on fire.

Dramatic evidence for these events has been found by archaeologists. In the Burnt Room in the City of David wooden beams and furniture had blazed so fiercely that the mud brick walls, still standing to the height of the second floor,

retain traces of blackening. Some of the ceiling beams were carbonized and one was preserved to a length of nearly 20 ft (6 m). Numerous arrowheads of bronze and iron were found in the area – vivid testimony of the horror of war. The Babylonians undermined the city wall and terraces above the Kidron, with the result that the houses toppled down the hill.

Zedekiah fled the city but was captured and brought before Nebuchadnezzar at Riblah in Syria. He was forced to witness the execution of his sons, was then blinded and taken to Babylon in chains. Many of the important citizens of Jerusalem were sent after their king into exile, though some of the poorest were allowed to remain behind. Whole families must have packed up their belongings on ox-carts, to make the terrible journey of several hundred miles to a strange new land.

Nebuchadnezzar appointed a Judaean aristocrat called Gedaliah to govern on his behalf. Unable to stay in the ruined capital Gedaliah set up headquarters at Mizpah (Tell en-Nasbeh) about 8 miles (13 km) to the north. Jeremiah and some of the army commanders joined him there and together they tried to rebuild their country. Within a short time, however, Gedaliah was assassinated and a renewal of the revolt was declared. Fearing Babylonian reprisals, the survivors decided to flee the country, taking Jeremiah with them, much against his will. They fled south to swell the already considerable numbers of Judaean refugees in Egypt, where there was to be a flourishing Jewish community for many centuries.

This last sad chapter in the history of an independent Judah is related in 2 Kings 24–25 and Jeremiah 40–43. Jeremiah wrote to the Babylonian Exiles, exhorting them to remain faithful to their God while they were in a land of pagan deities.

Lachish letter number 4. In Yigael Yadin's translation, the last sentence of this letter reads: [Please take] note that we are tending the signal fires of Lachish, in accordance with the instructions which my lord has given, for we cannot see Azekah.

Map of the Neo-Babylonian empire.

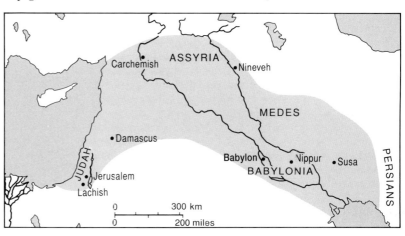

IV

WIDENING
HORIZONS

*Build ye houses and dwell in them; and plant gardens, and eat
the fruit of them; take ye wives and beget sons and daughters;
and take wives for your sons and give your daughters to
husbands, that they may bear sons and daughters; that ye may
be increased there, and not diminished. And seek the peace of
the city whither I have caused you to be carried away captives,
and pray unto the Lord for it: for in the peace thereof ye shall
have peace.*
Jeremiah 29, 5–7

THE BABYLONIAN EXILE ushered in an age when the
Children of Israel, no longer sheltered by the remote
hills of their homeland, were forced to adapt to a world
of ever-widening horizons. Communities of Jews were now to be
found in many regions of the Near East, from Egypt and Syria to
Mesopotamia. In Babylon, scribes and scholars such as Ezekiel
were collecting and writing down texts that laid the foundations
for the future course of Judaism.

The Exile, however, was not to last the 70 years predicted by
Jeremiah, writing to the Jews from Israel. Within 50 years the
Babylonian Empire had fallen to Cyrus the Great, King of the
Medes and Persians, who issued a decree allowing all exiles to
return to their homelands. Some Jews had settled so comfortably
in Babylonia that they preferred to stay. Those who did return
set about rebuilding the Temple and the walls of Jerusalem.

The rule of Persia lasted for about two centuries, until in its
turn it fell victim to the inexorable advance and spectacular
conquests of Alexander the Great. But even his achievements
were later to be superseded by the rise of another great power in
the ancient world – Rome. After Alexander's death and the
division of his empire, Judaea fell under the sway of the
Ptolemies and then the Seleucids, until freed by Judas
Maccabaeus. The independent Jewish kingdom established by
the Hasmonaeans lasted only briefly, until it was absorbed into
the growing Roman empire.

*The cliffs opposite the settlement at Qumran. They are honeycombed with
caves, in some of which the Dead Sea Scrolls came to light.*

THE BABYLONIAN EXILE

ROBERT KOLDEWEY

The German archaeologist Robert Koldewey (1855–1925) began excavating at Babylon in 1899 and continued every year until 1917, when he was forced to abandon work at the approach of British forces. Since then, there have been few further investigations, in part because the water table of the region has risen since ancient times, making work difficult, but also because destruction, ancient and modern, has left little to be excavated. Many of the villages in the area of Babylon today are built out of the baked bricks of the ancient city. There has, however, been considerable restoration work at the site in recent years.

In the 18 years of Koldewey's expedition to Babylon he uncovered many of the city's most impressive monuments, including the Ishtar Gate, the ziggurat – the biblical Tower of Babel – and the Royal Palace. Despite these successes, he felt that he had accomplished only a very little of the work required.

The king [Nebuchadnezzar] spake and said, 'Is not this great Babylon, that I have built for the house of the kingdom by the might of my power and for the honour of my majesty?'
Daniel 4, 30

BABYLON WAS ALREADY AN ANCIENT CITY by the time of Nebuchadnezzar. It had probably been founded, or even then refounded, by Hammurabi in the 18th century BC as the capital of the united lands of Sumer and Akkad. The city stood on the Euphrates at the point where it flowed closest to the Tigris, at a key position for communications by both river and road. For over a thousand years the city had suffered many misfortunes and by the time Nabopolassar, the Chaldaean chief, made it into the capital of his new kingdom (pp. 96–97), it was in a badly dilapidated condition.

Nebuchadnezzar (604–562 BC), and his father Nabopolassar (625–605 BC), spared no expense to rebuild Babylon on the most lavish scale as a witness to their independence from the Assyrians. Even before the destruction of the Assyrian capital, Nineveh, in 612 BC by the Babylonians allied with the Medes, Nabopolassar had begun building operations in his capital city. With its magnificent structures and massive defences, Babylon must have seemed a splendid and sophisticated city to the Judaean exiles, far from their homes and arriving footsore and weary. Two buildings in Babylon in particular, the Tower of Babel and the Hanging Gardens, were famous throughout the ancient world.

The fabled Hanging Gardens were one of the seven wonders of the world, a list drawn up in the 2nd century BC. As recounted by many classical writers, King Nebuchadnezzar so loved his wife, homesick for the mountains of her native Persia, that he built an artificial terraced garden for her in the flat lands of her new home in the Land of the Twin Rivers. The German excavator of Babylon, Robert Koldewey, was mistaken in his original identification of the Hanging Gardens. More recently they have been placed in the palace grounds, to the west of the Ishtar Gate, though there is no definite proof for such a location.

Wide-eyed in Babylon

What would the Judaean exiles have seen as they approached the city of Babylon? Enough is known both from Koldewey's excavations and from ancient authors to have some idea of how the city looked. The best description is undoubtedly that of Herodotus, the Greek traveller and historian, writing in the 5th century BC. His account was once dismissed as being highly exaggerated, but Koldewey's work showed his words to be accurate in many respects. For instance, Koldewey discovered that the triple-wall system of the outer defences measured some 90 ft (27 m) across – this would have allowed for a road with ample room to turn a four-horse chariot as Herodotus had stated.

Nearing the Ishtar Gate, the main north entry to the inner city, visitors would have climbed the gentle slope of the Processional Way, lined by high walls with moulded glazed tile reliefs of the Lions of Ishtar set against a brilliant azure background. The Way was paved with great blocks of white limestone and edged by flagstones of white and red breccia. Behind these walls on either side lay fortresses to defend the city.

The Ishtar Gate itself, with its moulded and coloured tiles of the Bull of Hadad and the mythic dragon monster, the *sirrush* of Marduk, was enough to take a stranger's breath away. But beyond were even more magnificent sights: the Royal Palace, where perhaps the king himself might be glimpsed, and, a little further down the Processional Way the two elements of the shrine of Marduk, the city god.

The Royal Palace

Just inside the Ishtar Gate was the main palace of Nebuchadnezzar. A single gateway guarded its entry. The palace was built in different phases and continued in use for several centuries after the Babylonian era. There were five courtyards, the most important of which measured 195 by 180 ft (60 by 55 m), with the king's throne room on its south side.

The throne room was also very large, some 170 by 55 ft (52 by 17 m) and here the king sat in state on a dais in a central niche, easily visible from the courtyard beyond. He would have been framed by magnificent panels of stylized trees, flowers and lions in brilliant shades of white, yellow, blue and red glazed tiles. Fragments of one panel were taken to the Pergamon Museum and reconstructed there.

The Tower of Babel

The temple to the city's patron god, Marduk, was the double precinct of Etemenanki – the 'House of the Foundation of Heavens and Earth' – and Esagila – the 'House that Raises its Head'. Etemenanki was the famous ziggurat or Tower of Babel described by Herodotus: 'The temple is a square building – with a solid central tower – with a second erected on top of it and then a third and so on up to eight. All eight towers can be climbed by a spiral way running around the outside, and about half way up there are seats for those who make the ascent to rest on. On the summit of the top-most tower stands a great temple.' (Herodotus, *The Histories* 1, 181.)

The ziggurat was built on an enormous scale, about 300 ft (90 m) square and perhaps the same high. Each level (there is debate as to whether there were seven or eight stages) was coloured differently. In Genesis the tower was described as a stairway for mankind to reach up to the heavens. The Babylonians thought of it rather as a stairway for their god Marduk to descend to earth. The name Babylon means 'Gateway of the Gods', but to the Israelites it was 'Confusion', as the Lord confused the languages of the people trying to build the sinful tower (Genesis, 11). All that remains of this great structure are the foundations in a water-logged hole.

From Judaean to Jew

There were three waves of deportations of people from Judah to Babylon, the first in 597 BC when Jehoiachin was taken there, the second in 587 BC when Zedekiah's revolt failed and Jerusalem was destroyed, and the last in 582 BC in the unrest following the assassination of Gedaliah (p. 97). The total number of deportees given in Jeremiah 52, 28–30 is 4,600 people, which seems a rather low figure. They were the leaders of Judaean society, who were removed to prevent further trouble.

In spite of the deportations and the flight of some of the population to Egypt and elsewhere, Judah was not left totally empty and devastated. Although there is no evidence to suggest that outsiders were 'imported' into the country (as had been the case, for instance, in the north after the Assyrian deportations), many ordinary peasant families were left to farm their land and pay their dues to the Babylonians. Such people, however, leave no name behind them. The returning exiles, who considered themselves aristocrats, certainly looked down on them.

RATION TEXT OF KING JEHOIACHIN

One of a group of fragmentary texts found by Robert Koldewey in some underground rooms of Nebuchadnezzar's palace, which he wrongly identified as the foundations of the Hanging Gardens of Babylon. These rooms were small and vaulted, with thick walls, suggesting that they supported a large structure above. However, the presence in them of the texts listing rations of foodstuffs issued to various people indicates that this was a storage facility. The texts date between the 10th and 35th year of Nebuchadnezzar (595 to 570 BC) and four of them contain the name Jehoiachin, King of Judah. In three of the texts his five sons are mentioned, all born by the time Jehoiachin was 23 – he probably had several wives and concubines. His eldest son was Shealtiel, who was the father of Zerubbabel (p. 107).

Jehoiachin, the last king

One group of those sent into exile was settled along the River Chebar in the region of Nippur, approximately 80 miles (130 km) downstream from Babylon. In fact, few of the exiles can have lived in Babylon itself, although most of them probably visited it, especially after Jehoiachin was released from prison in 561 BC. He was elevated to live at the court of Nebuchadnezzar's successor, Amel-Marduk (Evil-Merodach of the Bible). Jehoiachin almost certainly held his own court in Babylon. Official records have been found of rations of foodstuffs issued to him and his retinue. The dynastic hopes of Judah and Israel centred on him and his heirs, and the Babylonians clearly recognized him as the legitimate leader of the Judaean community.

By no means all the Judaean community wanted to return to Jerusalem. They were not enslaved but lived in family groups. Some even prospered and became wealthy. In fact, Jews remained in the area from that time until well into the 20th century. It was here that, from the early 3rd century AD, the great *yeshivot*, or academies, of Nehardea, Sura and Pumpedita emerged, and in them the Babylonian Talmud, which is the basis for much of later Judaism, took shape (p. 161).

The hardliners

There were some Judaeans, however, who felt desperately ill at ease in a pagan land. Faced with the challenge of survival a thousand miles from home they turned to the Lord for help: 'How shall we sing the Lord's song in a strange land?' (Psalm 137, 4).

These were men such as Ezekiel and the prophet known only as Deutero-Isaiah, an

Marduk, the city god of Babylon, with the mythical sirrush *dragon.*

*I am the Lord, and there is
none else, there is no God
beside me.*
Isaiah 45, 5

*In those days they shall say no
more, The fathers have eaten a
sour grape, and the children's
teeth are set on edge. But every
one shall die for his own
iniquity: every man that eateth
the sour grape, his teeth shall
be set on edge.*
Jeremiah 31, 29–30

*I will also give thee for a light
to the Gentiles, that thou
mayest be my salvation unto
the end of the earth.*
Isaiah 49, 6

*He is despised and rejected of
men; a man of sorrows and
acquainted with grief and we
hid as it were our faces from
him; he was despised and we
esteemed him not.*
Isaiah 53, 3

important figure of the Babylonian Exile whose
very name has disappeared with the centuries.
Deutero-Isaiah wrote chapters 40 to 55 of the
Book of Isaiah, which is practically a manifesto
of the ideas being debated at the time. These
men and others like them, all leaders of the
community and educated in the Law, developed a new concept of God. The old ways were
gone: the Lord had not preserved them as a free
people in their own land and their Temple had
been destroyed. Now they needed a new theology if they were to survive in this alien environment and to return to their homeland.

The beginnings of Judaism

Perhaps the greatest of these new ideas was the
emergence of monotheism. The people of
Israel had always believed that they had only
one God, but now, surrounded by 'idols with
feet of clay' (Daniel, 2, 33), they developed the
idea that only one God existed in the whole
universe. Therefore, if Israel had been over-
come by her enemies, it must be part of the
Lord's plan, and redemption (by means of
Cyrus, the Lord's anointed one, said Deutero-
Isaiah) was also a part of that plan. Each man
was now understood to be responsible for his
own actions.

The concept of individual responsibility was
first expressed by Jeremiah and then taken up
by Ezekiel (Ezekiel 18) who could remember
the Temple in Jerusalem before its destruction;
and his memories became dreams in which he
projected his ideal of a Messianic era to come.
There would be a new Temple and an Israel
resurrected from a valley of dry bones (Ezekiel

37). God's plans for Israel meant that they
were, in effect His chosen people. Whether the
'Suffering Servant' texts refer to one Messianic
figure, whom Christians believe to be Jesus, or
the whole nation of Israel, has always been
greatly debated.

Scribes continued the process of writing
down early versions of the first books of the

*Nebuchadnezzar's new Babylon
was created on such a huge scale
that the outer walls have a circuit
of about 5 miles (8 km). The
outer city was perhaps a suburb
area and held few public buildings
except the king's Summer Palace.
The inner city, with its own double
defensive walls, was extended to
the west of the Euphrates only in
the reign of Nebuchadnezzar.
Moats surrounded both the inner
and outer city walls and formed
part of the defensive system.*

Summer Palace
Euphrates
Processional Way
Hanging Gardens?
Ishtar Gate
Palace
Etemenanki ziggurat (Tower of Babel)
bridge
Esagila temple
moat
N
0 250 500 m
0 750 1500 ft

Bible, a task which had been begun before the destruction of the kingdom of Judah. These were edited from a mass of oral traditions and from such court records as they had with them. In this way, foundations were laid for the shape of the earlier part of the Old Testament as it is known today. Through such developments the exilic community was able to retain its own, separate identity and was provided with a way forward. It may indeed be said that the people who went into exile in Babylon as the shattered fragments of the Children of Israel returned to Jerusalem as Jews. Their religion at that time was still primitive, but they now formed a nation proud of its heritage and eager to build upon its past.

A head of a lion from the Processional Way (above).

The chief northern entry into the inner city was the Ishtar Gate (left). This has now been rebuilt, mostly from original material, in the Pergamon Museum in Berlin (Der Vorderasiatisches Museum). The outer façade is nearly 45 ft (14 m) high and may originally have been much higher. The gate was decorated with moulded and glazed figures in yellow and white of the bull of Hadad, the weather god, and the composite beast called the sirrush, *the dragon of Marduk, set against a brilliant azure background. Below ground level were 45 ft (14 m) of foundations which also had moulded, but not glazed, animal figures, belonging to an earlier building phase of Nebuchadnezzar's reign.*

CYRUS, KING OF THE PERSIANS

The tomb of Cyrus at Pasargadae. Despoiled not long after his death and restored by Alexander the Great, to whom Cyrus was a hero, this simple but monumental tomb still speaks of the powerful and civilized Persian king who was once buried in it.

Thus saith the Lord to his anointed, to Cyrus, whose right hand I have holden, to subdue nations before him...
Isaiah 45, 1

CYRUS OF ANSHAN, rightly called 'the Great', was a prince of the Achaemenid tribe of Persia and grandson of Astyages, king of the Medes, whom he was destined to overthrow. The Persians were vassals of the Medes to whom they were closely related. Both were Indo-European tribal peoples, originally nomadic, who had reached Iran from Armenia some time before the 8th century BC. The Persians took their name from one of the areas that they conquered, the province of Parsua (modern Fars) near the Persian Gulf.

Herodotus reports that Astyages dreamed before Cyrus' birth that his grandson would live to supplant him, and so he tried to have the boy killed as soon as he was born. As all good myth-histories could have told him, this attempt was doomed to failure and Cyrus grew to manhood as the supposed son of a shepherd, before taking his real place on history's stage

with the defeat of the Medes at the battle of Ecbatana in 550 BC. Once securely enthroned as king of the Medes and Persians, Cyrus did not have his grandfather Astyages executed but, according to Herodotus, treated him with great consideration, allowing him to stay at his court until his death.

By 546 BC Cyrus had conquered the kingdom of Lydia in Asia Minor, ruled by the fabulously wealthy Croesus, and took the capital city, Sardis. He apparently treated the defeated king with every respect, showing the clemency and tolerance for which he was famed. After this success he turned to the Greek cities of Ionia (western Asia Minor), many of which surrendered voluntarily. These cities became the main source of skilled craftsmen who worked on the monumental Persian centres such as Pasargadae and, later, Persepolis.

The conquest of Babylon

Cyrus then set out to add Babylon to his expanding empire, defeating the Babylonians twice in battles along the Tigris. According to Herodotus, the Persian army, led by a turncoat

THE CYRUS CYLINDER

This baked clay cylinder, displayed in the British Museum, records in Babylonian cuneiform script an account by Cyrus of his conquest of Babylon at the wish of the city's patron god, Marduk. Cyrus tells how he brought relief to the people of Babylon and returned the gods, embodied as statues and held captive by the Babylonian kings, to their homelands throughout Mesopotamia. He restored the temples of the various gods in their native cities and allowed their worshippers *to return home also. It is clear that the gods' captivity was inextricably linked with that of the people. The same would have been true of the Jews.*

Though the cylinder does not refer *to the Jews directly, it is certainly related to the Edict of Return as found in the Aramaic text of Ezra 6, 3–5, which almost certainly preserves a paraphrase of the official Persian memorandum.*

Babylonian named Gobryas, diverted the course of the Euphrates and gained access to the city via the dry river bed. Cyrus entered Babylon in 539 BC and seems to have met with little resistance. Possibly there had been dissatisfaction with Nabonidus, the last Babylonian ruler who, among other things, had allowed the worship of Marduk to decline.

Whether or not the populace saw Cyrus as their liberator and opened their gates to him, he certainly treated them with leniency. He abolished the system of forced labour imposed by Nabonidus and rebuilt their homes. The following year, 538 BC, Cyrus 'took the hand of Marduk' at the New Year Festival. He was thus enthroned as king by permission of Babylon's chief god, thereby legitimizing Persian rule. Babylon became the second capital of the Persian empire, after Susa.

The return of the exiles

Cyrus' humanity and benevolence were extraordinary for his day, though the accounts may well include an element of propaganda. One of the main aims of his policy was certainly to restore exiles living in Mesopotamia to their homelands. To quote his own words: 'As to [the lands] as far away as Ashur and Susa, Agade, Eshnunna… I returned to the sanctuaries which had been in ruins for a long time the statues of the gods who used to live there and I established for them everlasting shrines. I gathered all their former inhabitants and returned their habitations to them.'

This enlightened action had two important effects. First, it won Cyrus popularity and support from all those who had been living in exile, many since the days of the Assyrian empire. Secondly, it also eased the population pressure on the densely-inhabited lands of Babylonia, which were nearly exhausted after more than 3,000 years of irrigation farming.

For the Jews this was, of course, excellent news. The actual edict authorizing their return and the rebuilding of the Temple has never been found, but the text of it is preserved in the Old Testament. 'Thus saith Cyrus, King of Persia, the Lord God of heaven hath given me all the kingdoms of earth; and he hath charged me to build him an house at Jerusalem which is in Judah. Who is there among you of all his people? His God be with him, and let him go up to Jerusalem, which is in Judah, and build the house of the Lord God of Israel…which is in Jerusalem' (Ezra 1, 2–4).

The Persian monarch showed the same respect to the Jewish God as to the Babylonian ones. However, since there had never been a graven image of the god of Jerusalem, Cyrus could only return all the cultic equipment which had been seized by Nebuchadnezzar. He also encouraged the rebuilding of the House of the Lord, even giving financial assistance. As a reward, according to Isaiah (45, 1), the God of Israel recognized Cyrus as His Anointed One and 'took his right hand' – an interesting echo of the Babylonian custom noted above.

The Oxus Treasure is a hoard of various objects apparently discovered by chance in a river in Persia at the end of the 19th century. The pieces – including gold and silver bowls, figurines and jewelry(above) – all date from the classic phase of Achaemenid civilization of the 5th and 4th centuries BC. They demonstrate the elegance and exquisite quality of Persian metalwork at that time. A specifically Persian vision is clear in all the objects, blending forms from earlier phases of Egyptian, Mesopotamian and Greek art.

Darius I enthroned, with Crown Prince Xerxes in attendance. From the so-called Treasury at the ceremonial centre of Persepolis, this magnificent relief probably represents the ceremony at which the king received the annual tribute of the peoples of the empire at the New Year Festival. Note the finely depicted lotus blossom in the king's hand and the incense stands placed on each side of the throne dais.

RETURN TO JUDAH

SUCCOT

The Festival of Succot was originally linked to the harvest, when people would go to their fields and sleep there until the harvest was gathered in, as described in the Book of Ruth. The booths they built then would have been very much like those still put up by Bedouin shepherds to protect themselves from the sun. Orthodox Jews today build their booths – succot – in the open, on balconies, roofs or in gardens and live in them for the week of the festival of Succot. They are flimsy structures which are traditionally only roofed with vegetation, especially laurel, and decorated with fresh fruit and vegetables. In cold countries, only meals are eaten in them, but in hot climates people spend all their waking and sleeping hours there.

This silver coin from the 4th century BC is stamped with a falcon and the three letters YHD, pronounced 'Yehud', the Aramaic name for Judah. It appears in the pre-exilic script, which was no longer in general use. Other coins of the period bear the names of cities, such as Ashdod or Samaria, or even the names of governors who minted them. Many Aramaic ostraca and other documents of the Persian period have now been found throughout the area and it seems that literacy was increasing. Aramaic was the commonly spoken language throughout the whole Persian empire.

In the first year of Cyrus the king, the same Cyrus the king made a decree concerning the house of God at Jerusalem. Let the house be builded, the place where they offered sacrifices, and let the foundations thereof be strongly laid; the height thereof threescore cubits and breadth thereof threescore cubits with three rows of great stones, and a row of new timber: and let the expenses be given out of the king's house. And also let the golden and silver vessels of the house of God, which Nebuchadnezzar took forth out of the temple which is at Jerusalem and brought unto Babylon, be restored...
Ezra 6, 3–5

THOSE WHO ELECTED TO RETURN in 538 BC considered that they alone were 'Israel' and that the people who had stayed behind in what was now the tiny area of Judah were of less than no account. This elitist attitude created enormous tensions between the two groups. The latter must have been required to return the houses and land of the absent owners and to pay an extra levy to help rebuild the Temple, in addition to taxes to their Persian masters.

Rebuilding the Temple

Four leaders are associated with the Return to Judah. The first, Sheshbazzar, Prince of Judah, was made Governor of Judah by Cyrus and entrusted with the 'vessels of the House of the Lord' (Ezra 1, 7), the Temple equipment removed by Nebuchadnezzar. Sheshbazzar, who returned to Judah with some 50,000 others (Ezra 2, 64–65), is credited with laying the foundations of the new Temple, but nothing more is known of him. He may have been one of the sons of Jehoiachin and thus the uncle of the second leader, Zerubbabel, son of Shealtiel and grandson of Jehoiachin. Zerubbabel, whose name means 'seed of Babylon', is also said to have begun the foundations for the new Temple, and then he too vanishes from the scene. Is it possible, as some scholars suggest, that these are two names for the same man? The accounts of this whole period, mainly in the Books of Ezra, Nehemiah, Zechariah and Haggai, are very confusing and make it difficult to reconstruct the story.

We do know that building operations on the new Temple were suspended soon after they began. This may have been due in part to internal tensions and economic difficulties, but mostly to the opposition of Judah's enemies,

especially the Samaritans. They misrepresented the situation to the Persian king, telling him the walls of Jerusalem were being rebuilt and that the Jews were planning to revolt. All work was halted by decree of the king and was not resumed until the reign of Darius I (522–486 BC), when a search was made in the archives at Achmetha (Ecbatana, modern Hamadan) and the decree of Cyrus was confirmed. Building work on the Temple was finally undertaken from 520 to 515 BC, some twenty years after the first foundations had been laid. We even know the exact date of the dedication: 3rd Adar in the 6th year of Darius, which equates with 12 March 515 BC. No remains of this Temple have yet been securely identified.

Ezra and Nehemiah

Not much is known about events in Judah between the dedication of the new Temple in 515 BC and the next phase of the Return, under the two other leaders, Ezra and Nehemiah, who are often mentioned together. There is uncertainty about which of them reached Jerusalem first, or whether, in another interpretation, they were both in the city at the same time, as stated in Nehemiah 8, 9. Their work was in many ways complementary because Ezra was involved exclusively in religious reform, while Nehemiah was a secular governor who set about restoring the defences of Jerusalem.

Ezra, the son of Seraiah, was a priest who could trace his ancestry back to Moses' brother, Aaron, the first High Priest. He was also a professional scribe, trained in Babylon in 'The Law of Moses', that is the Torah. Given permission to return to Jerusalem in 458 BC with more exiles, Ezra's mission was to expound the Torah, initiate religious reforms and regulate practices to strengthen the spiritual morale of the new community.

The Reading of the Law

An important event associated with Ezra in Jerusalem took place during the autumn Succot Festival. This was the 'Reading of the Law' to the assembled people over a period of seven or eight days, as described in Ezra (7–10) and Nehemiah (8). During this reading, Nehemiah and the priests stood by to explain and expound the Law to the people, who were moved to tears to hear it.

THE SAMARITANS

At the time of the Return to Judah Samaria seems to have been a Persian province. The governor was named Sanballat. He and his two sons, Deliah and Shelemiah, are known from contemporary documents found in Samaria and Egypt. At this point the Samaritans clearly felt themselves to be part of Israel and were mortified when their offers of help to rebuild the Temple were rejected (Ezra 4, 2). Sanballat then tried to obstruct the rebuilding of the walls of Jerusalem by Nehemiah. This was the start of enmity and mistrust between the two peoples, which lasted to the time of Jesus, as shown in the story of the Good Samaritan.

In the Old Testament the Samaritans are considered as the product of the intermarriage between the peasantry of northern Israel, left in place by the Assyrians in 721 BC, and new peoples from Syria and beyond, forcibly settled in the area. The Samaritans, however, saw themselves as the pure descendants of the northern tribes of Israel. Today (right) they call themselves 'Bnei Yisrael' and claim that their form of Judaism is far purer and closer to the original religion of Israel than that of the Jews.

The Samaritans are now a very small community, numbering only 530 in 1987. Because they marry only among themselves, they suffer from genetically-related disorders. There are two groups, one in Holon (near Tel Aviv) and the other in Nablus, or Shechem, their traditional home at the foot of their holy mountain, Mt Gerizim (below). This was one of the earliest cult centres of the Children

of Israel and was the site of the Samaritan Temple, rival to the one in Jerusalem. No trace of it has ever been found, though many archaeologists have searched for it.

At Succot the Samaritans build their booths inside their houses. They developed this custom during the Byzantine period to protect themselves against persecution.

It would be fascinating to know exactly what form the text read by Ezra took. Orthodox Jews hold that it must have been the Torah, the five books of the Law, also known as the Pentateuch (p. 30), which they believe was given to Moses on Mt Sinai in its entirety. Others are less certain. It now seems likely to many authorities that the Law of Ezra's day combined almost all the pre-exilic oral and written traditions of the Jews, refined in the intellectual crucible of Babylon but not yet finally formulated as we now know it.

Ezra's work went further than the Reading of the Law. He formalized the old prohibitions about intermarriage, telling the men of Israel to put away foreign wives. He urged the people to observe the Sabbath strictly and also the law which stipulated that in the seventh year the land should lie fallow. Finally he reminded the people that they must pay their dues to maintain the Temple.

Nehemiah

Nehemiah may have arrived in Jerusalem in 445 BC, having applied to Artaxerxes I, the Persian king, for the post of Governor of Judah. He was already Cupbearer to the King, an important position in the state, demonstrating that Jews could reach the highest office at this time. He brought with him official permission to rebuild the city walls that Nebuchadnezzar's engineers had toppled so effectively.

Even though Nehemiah had authorization, the work of rebuilding was put in hand quietly, in order to attract as little hostile attention as possible. His first tour of inspection, three days after his arrival in the city, was carried out at night. The labour force, gathered from the city and surrounding areas and organized according to priestly or family clans to build different sections, worked with their swords by their sides until the rebuilding of the walls was accomplished.

The archaeological picture

In Nehemiah's time the city was rebuilt on a much smaller scale than previously and it was now little more than a village. A clear indication of this is given by the fact that when Ezra read the Law in public, all the people were able to gather 'in the street before the water gate' (Nehemiah 8, 1). Archaeological investigation has shown that on the east side of the City of David the wall was at this time located on the very top of the ridge, rather than being rebuilt half way down the slope where it had previously been, and thus enclosed a smaller area. It seems there was very little, if any, resettlement on the Western Hill until the late 2nd century BC.

The Old Testament picture

The Old Testament contains a great deal about the development of the priesthood and the Temple cult at this period. Much of the material comes from priestly circles, usually called the P source. At least some of this originates before the destruction of the First Temple. Great stress is laid on the holiness of priests and the centrality of the Temple in Jerusalem to all Jews everywhere.

This is why the Jewish community of Elephantinae in Egypt, when they rebuilt their Temple after it was destroyed through the jealousy of some local Egyptian priests, did so without an altar for burnt sacrifice, a right which the Jerusalem priesthood guarded fiercely. This, of course, can also be seen as the development of a theme that had already begun in pre-exilic days.

One major change in religious thought was inevitable with the disappearance of Zerubabbel. He was the last heir of David, and with him the Royal Family of Judah vanished. Over the next centuries there was a gradual development of eschatological theories involving the end of the present order of the world, when the 'Day of Jehovah' would come and the Lord himself would judge the nations who oppressed His people. Apocalyptic literature (the word means 'revelation') foretells what will happen at the End of Days. It is couched in esoteric language so that it could only be understood by the initiated. Events such as Armageddon, the Day of Judgment and the Resurrection of the Dead are outlined in such literature.

Theories about the Messiah also began to emerge at this time. Some groups thought there would be two Messiahs, one temporal and one spiritual. In the texts from Qumran (pp. 122–25) we read of the Messiah of Israel and the Messiah of Aaron. For early Christians these ideas came to fruition in the figure of Jesus.

Jerusalem in the time of Nehemiah. The three small diagrams of the city at the right demonstrate the fluctuation in the size of Jerusalem between the 10th and 5th centuries BC.

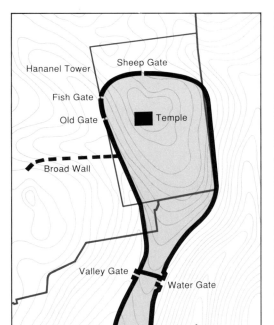

10th century BC

7th century BC

5th century BC

NEHEMIAH'S INSPECTION

So I came to Jerusalem and was there three days. And I arose in the night, I and some few men with me; neither told I any man what my God had put it in my heart to do at Jerusalem: neither was there any beast with me, save the beast that I rode upon. And I went out by the gate of the valley, even before the dragon well, and to the dung port, and viewed the walls of Jerusalem, which were broken down, and the gates thereof were consumed with fire. Then I went on to the gate of the fountain, and to the king's pool: but there was no place for the beast that was under me to pass. Then went I up in the night by the brook, and viewed the wall, and turned back, and entered by the gate of the valley and so returned.
Nehemiah 2, 11–15.

ALEXANDER THE GREAT

And it happened, after that Alexander, son of Philip, the Macedonian…had smitten Darius, king of the Persians and Medes, that he reigned in his stead…and made many wars and won many strongholds, and slew the kings of the earth, and went through to the ends of the earth, and took spoils of many nations, insomuch that the earth was quiet before him…And he gathered a mighty strong host, and ruled over countries and nations and kings, who became tributaries unto him.

1 Maccabees 1, 1–4

PERSIAN RULE IN JUDAH lasted until 333 BC, when Darius III was defeated by Alexander the Great at the Battle of Issus. It is given to few people to change the course of history, but Alexander was undoubtedly one of them. Born in 356 BC, the son of Philip of Macedon and his queen, Olympias, his enormous potential as a leader showed itself while he was still a teenager. He distinguished himself both as a general and as his father's ambassador to the Greek states. He was still only 20 years old when his father was assassinated and he came to the throne of Macedon. He was to die just 13 years later in Babylon, the city of his dreams. By that time he had travelled most of the known world east of Greece, conquered a large part of it and changed the way of life and the patterns of thought of its peoples for ever.

The origins of Alexander's wars lay in the ancient enmity between the Greeks and Persians. Philip of Macedon had been made overlord of all Greece by the Treaty of Corinth in 337 BC when a confederation of Greek states, supported by Philip, swore revenge for the sack of Athens and the Acropolis by the Persians under Xerxes in 480 BC.

On Philip's death his son eagerly inherited this policy and set about preparations for an invasion of the Persian Empire. In 336 BC, the year that Alexander ascended the throne of Macedon, Darius III became King of Persia. Within five years the two men were to meet in battle twice and Darius was to lose his empire and his life.

Alexander in Asia

In 334 BC, within two years of his accession, Alexander was ready to cross the Hellespont and march east. At first, his army, tiny by comparison with the might of the Persian Empire, was not seen as a threat to the established order of the Near East. But Alexander broke the power of the Persian governors, the satraps, of Asia Minor at the Battle of the River Granicus and advanced, virtually unopposed, across Asia Minor. King Darius then assembled his army, together with his entire household, including his mother, wife and children, and marched to the Mediterranean coast near the Bay of Iskenderun (still named after Alexander). He met the Greek army at the River Issus. The Persian army was defeated and forced to flee. Darius abandoned his family to the mercy of Alexander, who treated them with the utmost respect.

Wishing to secure the Mediterranean coast Alexander then marched south, following the coast all the way to Egypt. On his journey he forced the city of Tyre into submission after a seven-month siege. Alexander thought nothing of redesigning the landscape. Since Tyre was an island, Alexander had his troops pile up stone, wood and sand out from the shore until the city could be reached across an artificial causeway. Today Tyre is no longer an island, but a peninsula site.

According to Jewish tradition Alexander was welcomed into Jerusalem by the High Priest, but there is no historical source which mentions Alexander in Judah; indeed it is hard to see why he should have gone to this remote and backward country. Another tradition, on the other hand, states that the Samaritans, who had originally supported him later

This miniature head of Philip II of Macedon, father of Alexander the Great, was found in Philip's tomb at Vergina, northern Greece. It is carved from ivory and is only about just over 1 in. (3 cm) high. Other miniature portraits were found in the same tomb, including one of Alexander as a boy.

Detail of a pebble mosaic floor from Pella, the Macedonian capital, depicting Alexander about to kill a lion.

A fine portrait head of Alexander (left). It is known that Alexander sat for a sculptor while in Athens in 338 BC, aged 18, when he was acting as ambassador for his father.

A gold coin of Alexander (right), struck at Babylon.

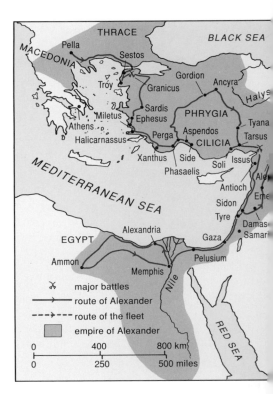

This sturdy tower is one of several that survive at Samaria. Built of large ashlar blocks, it was part of the Hellenistic city walls, which reused some of the old defensive walls of the days of Ahab, visible at the extreme right. The tower and the wall are good embodiments of Hellenistic culture – the fusion of the essentially city-based civilization of Greece and the far more ancient traditions of the Near East.

rebelled. Alexander then razed Samaria before rebuilding it as a military colony.

Reaching Egypt, Alexander visited the Temple of Zeus Ammon at the western oasis of Siwah. It was here that he was hailed by the oracle as the son of the god and allowed himself to be worshipped as divine. This is often cited as evidence of Alexander's megalomania and hubris, but from time immemorial Egypt had treated her kings as gods. The Macedonian conqueror's act was consistent with his policy of allowing old traditions to continue in order to assimilate new subjects into his empire.

Into Persia

From Egypt Alexander marched to Persia to decimate another army led by Darius at the final battle at Gaugamela, in 331 BC. Again Darius fled, this time to be killed, the following year, by his own renegade companions. With Darius' death Alexander had an unassailable claim to the throne of the Persian Empire, which he reinforced by marrying Darius' daughter. Alexander then set off for northern India, in emulation of his hero, Cyrus. It was while he was campaigning there that he married his second wife, the beautiful Bactrian princess, Roxane.

By the year 326 BC, Alexander was still eager to continue eastwards. His army, however, could take no more. Having returned to Kabul from well beyond the Oxus River, they refused to march any further. Reluctantly it seems, Alexander began the journey back to Babylonia. He first marched south to the coast and then sent part of the army back by sea, while he himself marched with the remainder parallel to the fleet along the desolate Makran coast. It proved too much even for his superhuman talents. A large part of the army died in the desert of thirst and hunger. Alexander him-

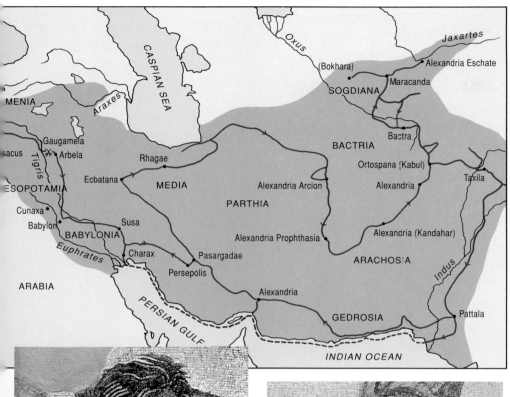

Alexander's empire stretched from Macedonia and Greece in the west as far as Afghanistan and northern India in the east.

Alexander (above) and Darius (right) from a mosaic found at Pompeii depicting the Battle of Issus.

self had recently sustained a slight injury in battle, and he succumbed to this in Babylon, on 13 June, 323 BC.

Given his character and meteoric career, it is not surprising that Alexander has always had his supporters and detractors. On the credit side, he may indeed have wanted to extend the benefits of Greek culture and language – Hellenistic civilization – to all people everywhere, to enhance their lives and unite them in peace. Certainly, wherever he went he founded new cities on the Greek pattern, many of them named after himself – the best known

is Alexandria in Egypt. He also encouraged marriages between his soldiers and women of countries they marched through. These policies had a deep and long-lasting effect on the regions he conquered, including Judah.

Contrary opinion holds that Alexander was a power-crazed dictator who allowed himself to be hailed as a god in Egypt and who let his Persian subjects prostrate themselves before him as they did to their native kings. Whatever the truth about this elusive but compelling genius, Alexander, when he died at the age of 33, certainly deserved the title 'Great'.

THE GORDIAN KNOT

Alexander was a man around whom myths naturally arose. Even today stories about 'Iskander' are still told from Armenia to Afghanistan. The tale of the Gordian knot demonstrates both his impetuous nature and his problem-solving abilities. In a temple in the city of Gordion, capital city of Phrygia, in central Anatolia, lay an ancient chariot, dedicated there by Gordius, the father of Midas, the fabled king. Its harness was secured by an immense and complicated knot and legend had it that whoever untied the knot would rule the world. Inspecting it, Alexander solved the problem instantly – he unsheathed his sword and sliced it through.

IN THE WAKE OF ALEXANDER

A coin of Ptolemy I, one of Alexander's generals and possibly his half-brother.

Plan of the small, walled town of Mareshah (Marisa). Purpose-built on the grid pattern common to Hellenistic sites, it boasted paved streets and a sophisticated drainage system. Separate sectors were for commercial and for administrative, military and religious activities.

So Alexander reigned twelve years and then died. And his servants bare rule every one in his place. And after his death they all put crowns upon themselves; so did their sons after them many years: and evils were multiplied upon the earth.

1 Maccabees 1, 7–9

ALEXANDER'S VISION OF A WORLDWIDE community united by Greek culture and ruled by himself and his heirs passed away with him in 323 BC. He was hardly dead before his generals were disputing the division of his empire. Fierce fighting ensued, but after the Battle of Ipsus in 301 BC three main power blocs emerged. One was in Macedon and Greece. The second was in Syria and Mesopotamia, where Seleucus gained control and founded his capital at Antioch in Syria, on the River Orontes. The third was in Egypt, where Ptolemy was firmly on the throne. He won great prestige in the Hellenistic world by hijacking Alexander's body and bringing it to Egypt, to be buried in state in his capital, Alexandria.

Hellenistic civilization

The Near East, including Judah, was now ruled by Greeks and Greek language and customs were in widespread use. The impact of Hellenism on the region did not start with Alexander, though. Contacts had begun through maritime trade as early as the 8th century BC and had intensified during Persian rule. In the wake of Alexander's conquests, however, Hellenistic influence became much stronger.

New and refounded self-governing cities on the Greek model were springing up everywhere. Examples include Ptolemais (Acre), Neapolis (Shechem), Sebaste (Samaria) and, in Transjordan, Gerasa (Jerash) and Philadelphia (Amman). Foreign settlers, predominantly Greeks and Macedonians, along with local people formed the population of such cities, but these mixed communities did not always live harmoniously together. The tolerant and hedonistic Greek citizens were not easily accepted by their conservative and religious Jewish neighbours.

Mareshah

A good example of a typical Hellenistic town in Judah is Mareshah (its Greek name was Marisa, now Tell Sandahanna). According to Josephus, the site was abandoned in 40 BC after defeat by the Parthians, and so was not covered by later buildings as happened elsewhere. Located in the Shephelah, the fertile hilly country southwest of Jerusalem, it had replaced Lachish as the most important regional centre. The population was made up of people from Sidon, together with locals and Greeks – a good demonstration of the cultural mix of the times.

The upper part of the town, or acropolis, was not very large, covering about 6 acres (2.4 ha). It was well laid out in the typical Hellenistic grid pattern, with a large marketplace surrounded by shops, all securely placed behind a strong defensive wall. Beyond the walls, and all around the slopes of the mound, lay the lower city. What is unusual about Mareshah is that, below the houses, shops, public buildings and streets lay hundreds of caves. Access to them was from the courtyards of the houses or from lanes between the buildings. In the 3rd century BC the caves were used for industrial purposes –

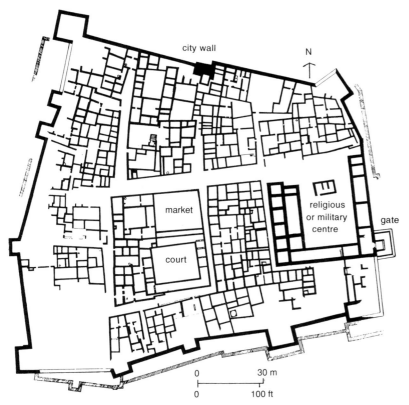

city wall

N

market

court

religious or military centre

gate

0   30 m

0   100 ft

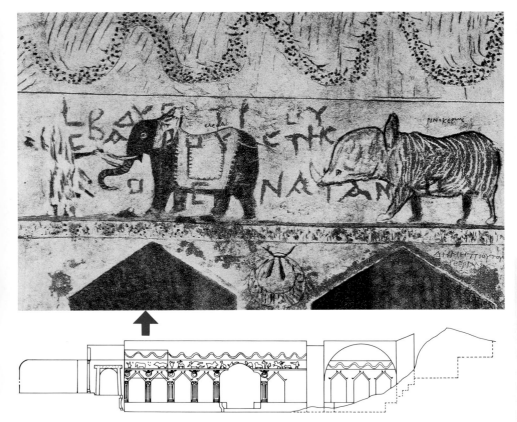

Anitochus III, the Seleucid king of Syria (above).

Detail of a wall painting in a tomb at Mareshah (left), with an elephant and a rhinoceros. Below is a cross-section of the tomb.

THE SEPTUAGINT

The most important ancient translation of the Old Testament into Greek is often called the Septuagint. A legend concerning its origins is contained in the apocryphal Letter of Aristeas, composed in Egypt in the 2nd century BC. According to the Letter, Ptolemy II (285–246 BC) wanted a Greek version of the Jewish Law for his magnificent library at Alexandria. For this purpose he sent for 72 of the best scholars from Jerusalem (six from each of the 12 tribes). The word Septuagint is Greek for 70 (two of the translators were somehow lost) and the scholars produced their translation in just 72 days on the island of Pharos.

The first Greek Old Testament was certainly produced in Egypt, but probably in several stages. There had been Jews in Egypt since the destruction of the First Temple and by the 3rd century BC the Jewish community in Alexandria was one of the most important in the Diaspora (Jews who lived outside Judaea). Greek, rather than Hebrew or Aramaic, was their mother tongue, and they needed a translation of their scriptures from Hebrew into a language they could understand.

Originally condemned by more traditionalist Jews, it soon came to be relied upon by most eminent Jewish writers and thinkers. It was used also by early Christian scholars – it was included in Origen's Hexapla and was certainly known to Jerome when he made his Latin translation (pp. 30–31)

principally the manufacture and storage of olive oil (some twenty oil presses have been found) and the breeding of doves or pigeons. These were kept both for food and for their dung, an excellent fertilizer – about sixty dovecotes (*columbaria*) are known.

At this period very large cemeteries were also situated in caves all around the mound, some with remarkable wall paintings. One frieze depicts exotic animals, including a rhinoceros and a lifelike elephant wearing a decorative cloth on its back. Each extended family or clan had its own burial cave, with body-length niches dug in its walls where the dead were placed. The niche (*loculus* in Latin, or *kokh* in Hebrew) was then sealed. If the niche was needed for another body it could be reopened and the old bones moved to a repository. Often the name of the dead person was crudely painted on the wall by the niche. The names found are Greek or Phoenician, rather than Hebrew or Aramaic.

Ptolemies versus Seleucids

As we have seen, Ptolemy and his successors established themselves in Egypt. At first they also ruled Palestine and parts of Cyprus, while the Seleucids controlled Mesopotamia and Syria. There was constant friction between the two power blocs, however, and once again Palestine became a battlefield.

In 200 BC a battle was fought at Panias (Panion in Greek, later Caesarea Philippi) near the headwaters of the River Jordan. The Ptolemaic army was defeated and the Seleucids annexed Palestine. Initially Seleucid rule was popular, according to Josephus, especially as the king, Antiochus III, eased tax burdens considerably. Unfortunately, he soon came into conflict with Rome and was defeated more than once. By the Treaty of Apamea, signed in 189 BC, he gave up most of Asia Minor and was forced to pay a large annual indemnity to Rome, which meant he had to tax his empire far more heavily. It was from this point that Seleucid popularity began to wane in Judah.

Antiochus was killed in 187 BC, raiding a temple treasury in Elam in order to pay off the Romans. His successor Seleucus IV continued this policy by plotting unsuccessfully to rob the Temple treasury in Jerusalem. Not surprisingly this period saw the rise of Jewish opposition to Seleucid rule and the gradual emergence of a nationalist movement.

REVOLUTION! THE MACCABEES

Antiochus IV, Epiphanes. As his name suggests, he considered himself a personification of Zeus and was portrayed as such on his coins.

Moreover king Antiochus wrote to his whole kingdom, that all should be one people, and everyone should leave his laws: so all the heathen agreed according to the commandment of the king. Yea, many also of the Israelites consented to his religion, and sacrificed unto idols, and profaned the sabbath.

1 Maccabees 1, 41–43

ANTIOCHUS IV, EPIPHANES, came to the Seleucid throne after the assassination of his brother, Seleucus IV, in 175 BC. He needed to unify all the people of his empire against threats from Rome to the west, Parthia to the east and Egypt in the south. One unifying force was his policy of fostering Hellenism, principally through the cult of Olympian Zeus. In Greek fashion he also encouraged his subjects to identify their chief gods with Zeus. On his accession to the throne he had taken the name 'Epiphanes', meaning 'the god appearing', for he considered himself divine and a personification of Zeus. He was virtually penniless as a result of the indemnity paid to Rome from his father's day and so he increased taxation and continued the practice of robbing temples.

None of this endeared Antiochus to his Jewish subjects, who were by now divided in their attitude to Hellenism. Some, especially the young and educated, were eager to adopt Greek culture and integrate it into Jewish society. Others, often men of rank in the community, were uncompromising traditionalists for whom Hellenism was abhorrent.

Matters came to a head in Jerusalem when two men of High Priestly rank tried to outbribe each other in an effort to have Antiochus confer the High Priesthood on them. Huge sums were paid to the king. Onias, the hereditary High Priest, later to be assassinated, was removed by his brother Jason (or Joshua). Jason supported the establishment of a Greek school – gymnasium – within sight of the temple. Here young men, some of them priests, studied Greek culture and took part in sports. Religious men denounced them for wrestling naked in Greek fashion and even worse, for trying to reverse their circumcision by surgery, even though it was the sign of the age-old covenant with the Lord.

Images of naked runners on Greek vases of the 5th century BC and later are good illustrations of aspects of Hellenistic culture that were abhorrent to traditionalist Jews but attractive to some of the young men of Jerusalem:
Whereupon they built a place of exercise at Jerusalem according to the custom of the heathen. And made themselves uncircumcised, and forsook the holy covenant, and joined themselves to the heathen.
1 Maccabees 1, 14–15

The traditional story of Chanukah relates how, when Judah the Maccabee cleansed the Temple of the idols, there was only enough consecrated oil hidden away to light the sacred light for one day. But the Lord caused the oil to stay alight for eight days, exactly the length of time needed to consecrate fresh oil. Each evening at dusk during the eight days of Chanukah (meaning 'dedication') the candles are lit to commemorate the miracle. Children especially love this mid-winter Festival of Light because they are given small presents as each successive candle is lit. On the last evening all eight candles, plus a ninth used to light the others, are ablaze.

The Abomination of Desolation

Jason was himself supplanted as High Priest by Menelaus, a financial official who simply paid Antiochus a larger bribe. Menelaus first assisted the king to plunder the Temple and then, two years later, in 167 BC, stood aside while a Seleucid army, nominally there to suppress an attempt by Jason to recover his position, went on the rampage in Jerusalem, butchering the citizens, raping the women and looting the Temple. The city itself was nearly destroyed.

Following this a Seleucid fortress, called the Akra, was built on the eastern ridge of the city overlooking the Temple Mount, using stone from the city walls. Its precise location is today unknown because it was later destroyed and its remains have so far not been found. The Akra may have been set up as a self-governing *polis* – a Greek city-state – with Jerusalem forming its territory. The Temple became the cult centre of the *polis*, with the worship of Olympian Zeus officially established there and Jehovah being identified with the Greek god. An altar to Zeus was built in the Temple and sacrifices offered on it. This is the 'Abomination of Desolation' referred to in the Book of Daniel. But even this was only the beginning. Antiochus issued decrees forbidding the practice of Jewish religion on pain of torture and death; the Sabbath and the festivals were not to be observed and circumcision was forbidden; copies of the Torah were to be destroyed and Jews were to be forced to offer sacrifices to Zeus and eat the meat of the sacrifice. Pigs were deliberately chosen as the sacrificial animals because they were considered unclean by Jews. Some Jews accepted the reforms. Others called them persecution and refused to submit, dying for their beliefs.

The Maccabean Revolt

At this point, in 167 BC, an elderly priest in Judah called Mattathias was driven by desperation to take action. Hundreds rose to join him. The story is recorded in 1 Maccabees 2, 1–28. Mattathias, a member of the Hashmon family, had left Jerusalem in disgust and returned to his family home in the town of Modein, in the hills east of Lydda. Here, he and his five sons, along with the townspeople, were forced to take part in a sacrifice to Zeus. Mattathias not only refused, but killed both the man who did comply with the order and the king's officer who was enforcing it. The old man and his sons

DANIEL

Although it relies on more ancient sources, the Book of Daniel is essentially a 2nd-century BC composition. It is mainly concerned with nationalist resistance to the Seleucid oppressors, though it superficially relates to the period of the Babylonian Exile. It is also one of the apocalyptic works popular at the time, whose veiled language was understood only by the initiated – references to Nebuchadnezzar really refer to the Seleucid kings.

The tale of the three brave Jewish youths, Shadrach, Meshach and Abednego, refusing to bow down to idols and emerging safe from the lion's den is a call to contemporary Jews to resist the cult of Olympian Zeus. Daniel and his companions rejecting unclean meat and living instead on a vegetarian diet is another element of Jewish defiance against the decrees of Antiochus. The 'prophecies' of the later chapters are more concerned with Alexander the Great and the Seleucid persecutions than with the Persian empire (Daniel 8 and 11).

fled to the hills, where they rallied together all the refugees from the Seleucid persecution and became a centre for the emerging nationalist movement.

Mattathias died in 166 BC, but one of his sons, Judah, or Judas in Greek, became the next leader. He was known as Maccabeus, hence the name of the revolution. The word is usually translated as 'the hammer', although its meaning is not certain. After several years of fighting and guerrilla warfare, Judah was able to lead his troops into Jerusalem. The Seleucid forces still occupied the Akra, but Judah cleansed the Temple of the cult of Zeus and rededicated it. This took place in 164 BC and is remembered in the Jewish festival of Chanukah.

The Hasmonaean kingdom

The fight against the Seleucids was not yet won, however, and all the Hashmon brothers in turn led the struggle. It was the last brother, Simon, who eventually rid the country of the Seleucids; he even ousted them from the Akra in 141 BC. With Simon, we see the rise of an independent Judah for the first time since the Babylonian destruction in the 6th century BC, though the kingdom lasted only 79 years (142–63 BC). Simon's son, John Hyrcanus, expanded its territory considerably and forcibly

Elephants were used by the Seleucids in their fight against the rebels in the Maccabean revolution (1 Maccabees 6, 30–37). Here a Seleucid war elephant with a tower on its back seizes an unfortunate enemy in its trunk.

converted to Judaism many of the people who thus came under his control. Among them were the Idumaeans, descendants of the Edomites of Transjordan, who had migrated west, into southern Judah, when the land was relatively empty following the Babylonian deportations. Herod the Great was a descendant of one of these Idumaean converts.

Alexander Jannaeus, the second son of John Hyrcanus, continued the expansion of the country until it reached the biblical ideal – 'from Dan to Beersheba'. He also encouraged maritime trade through the ports he acquired, Dora (Dor) and Strato's Tower (later to become Caesarea), and gained control of overland routes to Egypt. His reign saw appalling conflict between two powerful but opposing Jewish factions, the Sadducees and the Pharisees (pp. 146–47), which was only partly resolved in the reign of Salome Alexandra, his wife and successor. When she also died, the strife between their two sons, Hyrcanus and Aristobulus, finally brought the Romans directly into the arena. It is ironic that the Hasmonaean dynasty came to power as cham-

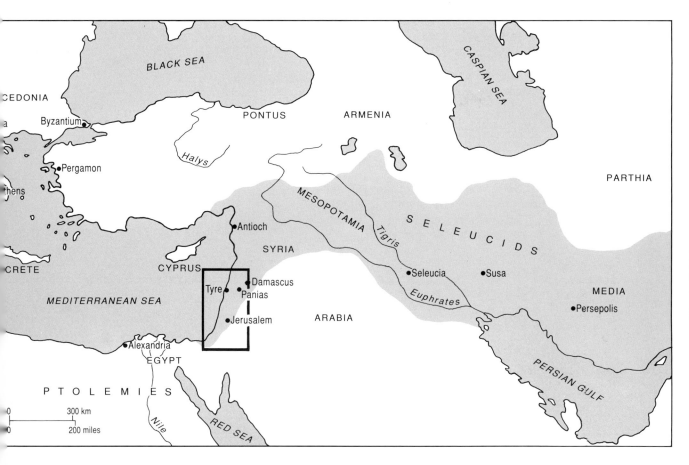

pions of traditional Judaism, and yet, within a short time, they became almost totally Hellenized. In addition, they also took over the High Priesthood, a position to which their lineage did not entitle them. Noteworthy also is that while they were the leaders of a revolt against religious persecution, they then followed a policy of forcible conversion of others.

The Seleucid empire after 189 BC (above). A considerable amount of the territory in the Near East originally conquered by Alexander the Great had regained its independence.

The map above left shows the expansion of the Hasmonaean kingdom.

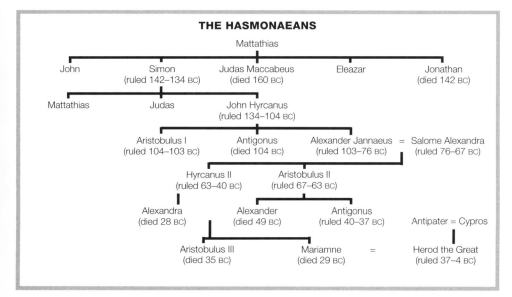

THE HASMONAEANS

Mattathias

| John | Simon (ruled 142–134 BC) | Judas Maccabeus (died 160 BC) | Eleazar | Jonathan (died 142 BC) |

| Mattathias | Judas | John Hyrcanus (ruled 134–104 BC) |

| Aristobulus I (ruled 104–103 BC) | Antigonus (died 104 BC) | Alexander Jannaeus (ruled 103–76 BC) = Salome Alexandra (ruled 76–67 BC) |

Hyrcanus II (ruled 63–40 BC)   Aristobulus II (ruled 67–63 BC)

Alexandra (died 28 BC)   Alexander (died 49 BC)   Antigonus (ruled 40–37 BC)   Antipater = Cypros

Aristobulus III (died 35 BC)   Mariamne (died 29 BC)   =   Herod the Great (ruled 37–4 BC)

117

THE ROMANS IN THE EAST

Gaius Julius Caesar (above). His ambition to rule Rome and his love for Cleopatra brought about the fierce civil wars from which his adopted son, Octavian, emerged the victor. Octavian became the first Roman emperor, under the name of Augustus.

Pompey, the Roman general who first intervened in Palestine, reorganized the area into different provinces (right), mostly at the expense of the Hasmonaean kingdom. The area under direct Jewish rule was thus much reduced.

[The Romans] hold their far-flung empire as the prize of valour, not the gift of fortune.
Josephus, *The Jewish War 3*

ON THE DEATH OF SALOME ALEXANDRA, the Hasmonaean queen, her two sons began protracted wars to gain possession of the kingdom. The older brother was Hyrcanus, the High Priest, but Aristobulus, who was undoubtedly the more able of the two, seized the throne from his brother in 67 BC. Hyrcanus then tried to re-establish himself. He had two advantages: his chief minister was Antipater, an Idumaean and a shrewd politician (and the father of Herod the Great), and he was supported by the Nabataean king, Aretas III (c. 85–62 BC). Eventually both brothers appealed to Rome in the shape of the Roman general, Pompey.

Rome had been engaged in expansion into the eastern Mediterranean for some time. Pompey had been given special powers by the Senate to clear Cilicia, in southeast Turkey, of pirates who were threatening the Roman corn supply. He was later given command in the East, defeating Mithridates of Pontus in 66 BC and annexing Syria in 63 BC. Palestine and Transjordan were of interest to the Romans as a bastion against their enemies in the east – the Parthians, now rulers of Mesopotamia – and it was vital to Rome either to rule this buffer zone directly or to have loyal client kings.

Pompey therefore answered the appeal from Hyrcanus and Aristobulus with great speed. He disposed of the Nabataeans by threatening to invade their territory and set about the pacification of Judaea. He stormed Jerusalem after a siege lasting three months and entered the Holy of Holies in the Temple, which was forbidden to everyone except the High Priest – who himself could only enter on one day a year. However, Pompey showed the utmost respect, telling the priests to resume their duties and sacrifices immediately.

As part of his Eastern Settlement Pompey made Syria into a province and reduced the Hasmonaean kingdom to Judaea, Galilee and part of Idumaea. He made Hyrcanus nominal ruler, as being the more pliant of the brothers, granting him the title Ethnarch – but not king – though Antipater was the real power in the kingdom. Hyrcanus was also confirmed as High Priest. Aristobulus, with his family, was exiled to Rome. Ultimate authority in the area rested with the Roman proconsul of Syria, whose seat was at Antioch, the old Seleucid capital.

The next years were not peaceful ones. Aristobulus and his sons fomented rebellion against Hyrcanus on several occasions, always unsuccessfully. Roman governors were often corrupt and Rome itself was experiencing conflict also, as the growing aspirations of Julius Caesar clashed with republican traditions, championed by Pompey.

The enmity between Pompey and Caesar only ended with the murder of Pompey in 48 BC, when he was struck dead on an Egyptian beach by the order of the Egyptian king, Ptolemy. This ambitious young man had usurped the throne of his older half-sister Cleopatra. The assassination of Pompey gave Julius Caesar the opportunity he had been waiting for. He sailed to Egypt, removed Ptolemy and, falling in love with Cleopatra, set

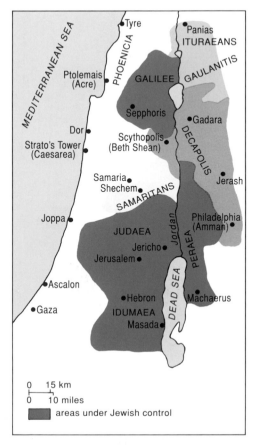

MEDITERRANEAN SEA

Tyre
Panias
ITURAEANS
PHOENICIA
GAULANITIS
Ptolemais (Acre)
GALILEE
Sepphoris
Gadara
Dor
Scythopolis (Beth Shean)
Strato's Tower (Caesarea)
DECAPOLIS
Jerash
Samaria
Shechem
SAMARITANS
Joppa
Philadelphia (Amman)
JUDAEA
Jordan
PERAEA
Jericho
Jerusalem
DEAD SEA
Ascalon
Hebron
Machaerus
Gaza
IDUMAEA
Masada

0   15 km
0   10 miles
■ areas under Jewish control

THE NABATAEANS

The mother of Herod the Great was a Nabataean princess called Cypros. The Nabataeans were a people of northwestern Arabia, whose capital was the famous city of Petra, 'the rose-red city half as old as time'. Their territory sat astride vital overland trade routes from Arabia to Syria, Egypt and the Mediterranean. An important Nabataean export was bitumen from the Dead Sea, which was used in the ancient world as an adhesive.

The Nabataeans rose to prominence in the mid-2nd century BC under Aretas I, the first Nabataean king of whom we have a historical note (2 Maccabees 5, 8). By this time they were earning huge revenues from taxes levied on merchant caravans crossing their territory. Delicate silks from China, pearls and lapis lazuli from Persia, rare frankincense and myrrh from southern Arabia and exotic spices from India all passed through their lands. The loss of the important port of Gaza to the Hasmonaean king, Alexander Jannaeus, in about 100 BC caused a decline in Nabataean fortunes. Some of their cities in the Negev, including Avdat, were abandoned.

Under Aretas III the Nabataeans first came into close contact with Hellenistic culture. They also became involved in the struggle between Hyrcanus and his brother Aristobulus. The intervention of Rome in 63 BC in the form of Pompey led to the withdrawal of the Nabataeans to their home territory in Transjordan, northwest Arabia. By the time of St Paul they had expanded again and governed Damascus. Their cities in the Negev flourished and their empire embraced much of northwest Arabia and Sinai. On the death of Rabel II in AD 106 the Roman emperor Trajan annexed Nabataea and its lucrative trade routes without any apparent opposition. The Nabataean economy entered a new period of prosperity under the Romans and the people, supported by their traditional form of agriculture, remained in place. The Nabataean language, a branch of Aramaic, was in some respects similar to Hebrew, and belonged to the group from which Arabic emerged.

The arid region of the Negev around Avdat was cultivated by the Nabataeans using a system of water conservation which had been in use in the region from much earlier times. Research has shown that the whole area between Avdat, Mampshit and Shivta, about half a million acres, was farmed by irrigation methods. At first, crops were grown by damming small tributary wadis or dry river valleys in localized areas, collecting rainfall on the valley floors and allowing small patches of land to be cultivated.

Much later, a far more complex system of water conservation was developed. The method involved controlling the run-off water from the slopes above the fields by dividing up the whole catchment area with low lines of stones, running obliquely across the slopes. The winter rains, which would otherwise have run straight off as flash floods, were collected and channelled down to the stepped fields. The amount of rain which falls on these slopes is no more than 4 in. (100 mm), but because of the efficient water collection and conservation system, each field in the valley bottom is estimated to have received about 12–20 in. (300–500 mm) of water per year, about the same amount as the hills of Judah. A family of about six people, with their livestock, could live quite comfortably on this amount of water. The farmhouse was usually built near the lowest fields and had its own run-off system. The water was channelled into a deep cistern for domestic use and the animals could also be watered from it. The reconstructed farm at Shivta using these methods today grows excellent crops of fruit, olives, nuts and grapes. Israeli agricultural advisers are also reintroducing this type of low-intensity farming to some drought-stricken areas of Africa.

A view of el-Khasneh, or 'The Treasury' at Petra. This tomb – some think it a temple – dates to the 1st century BC and is the earliest of the rock-cut façades.

Coins of Antony and Cleopatra.

After Caesar's death at the hands of assassins on the Ides (15th) of March 44 BC, and Antipater's by poison in the following year, the stage was set for new players. Following more civil war, Mark Antony and Octavian, Caesar's adopted heir and the future emperor Augustus, emerged as the most powerful figures in Rome. Antipater's son, Herod, was a very able man who inherited his father's political acumen and his strategy of siding with Rome. The Romans, whose overriding concern in the eastern Mediterranean was to have a strong ally, quite literally let him get away with murder on several occasions.

her back on her throne. During his campaigns Caesar had ample cause to thank both Hyrcanus and Antipater for their support. Hyrcanus, as High Priest, instructed the Jews in Egypt to back Caesar, and Antipater led a Jewish detachment in Caesar's army there.

Rewards

A grateful Caesar made Antipater procurator of Judaea and he in turn appointed his sons Phasael and Herod governors, of Jerusalem and Galilee respectively. Caesar also returned to the Jewish state some of the lands lost under Pompey, including the important city of Joppa. Jews throughout the Roman world were granted many privileges at this time. Unusually they were given the right of private assembly, and so they were free to congregate in synagogues. This freedom was especially valuable for St Paul in his missionary work, as he often went first to the synagogue of any city he visited.

The sculpted head of Pompey, the Roman Republican general who gained control of the Levant for Rome in 63 BC. He was married to Julia, the daughter of Julius Caesar, but after her death the increasing hostility between the two men led to Pompey's flight from Rome. He was murdered on setting foot in Egypt by Ptolemy XIII, whom Pompey had removed from the Egyptian throne in favour of his half-sister, Cleopatra.

In 40 BC Herod, backed by Antony and Octavian, was proclaimed king of Judaea by the Roman senate. At that time he was in Rome in exile from his kingdom, having been forced to flee by Antigonus, the son of Aristobulus, who had taken Jerusalem with the support of a Parthian army. But by 37 BC, Herod was firmly and finally set on his throne by the Romans.

Antony was given command in the East, including Egypt, where he too was caught by the charms of Cleopatra – 'the serpent of old Nile'. After more civil strife, Octavian defeated Antony and Cleopatra at the Battle of Actium in 31 BC and became the sole ruler of Rome. Herod, who had supported each party in turn, managed to switch allegiance in time to be on the winning side.

Octavian not only confirmed Herod's position, he also returned to him lands which Antony had bestowed on Cleopatra, whose aim had been to recover all the territories formerly held by the Ptolemies. These included the fertile oasis of Jericho, with its valuable date palms, and the nearby balsam groves at Ein Gedi, both of which provided important revenue for Herod as he began the process of rebuilding his kingdom (pp. 128–31).

The magnificent oval forum at Jerash, in northern Jordan, probably dates to the 2nd century AD. Jerash was one of the independent Hellenistic cities of the loose confederction known as the Decapolis and became very prosperous under Roman rule.

QUMRAN AND THE DEAD SEA SCROLLS

They shall separate from the congregation of the men of falsehood and shall unite, with respect to the Law and possessions, under the sons of Zadok, the priests who keep the Covenant, and of the multitude of the men of the Community who hold fast to the Covenant. Every decision concerning doctrine, property and justice shall be decided by them.
The Rule of the Community V

IN THE TROUBLED SUMMER OF 1947, just before the partition of Palestine, three young Ta'amireh Bedouin were grazing their animals on the northwestern side of the Dead Sea. One of them climbed high among the cliffs in search of a lost goat, and seeing a small opening in the rocks he idly lobbed a stone into it. He heard the clink of pebble on pot rather than the thud of stone on earth that he had been expecting; immediately he thought of buried treasure. Wriggling into the narrow entrance to the cave he was disappointed to see only rows of lidded jars ranged against the wall. Many were broken and fragments lay all about. He left in disgust and went in search of his goat. But he came back the next day with a friend and they had a closer look at the jars. They found some wrapped bundles of what they thought were rags and took them back to their camp, where they unrolled them. In fact, they were skin scrolls with strange writing on them.

In this way the contents of a library hidden in the 1st century AD began to come to light – numerous further documents have been found since then, and more may still await discovery in other caves in the Judaean Desert. It was an astonishing find. Research and debate about the precise nature of the contents of the Dead Sea Scrolls, as well as the identity of the community that wrote them, still continue. The significance of the scrolls lies in the fact that they are written records of a period for which other contemporary documents are very scarce – the next oldest substantial copy of the Hebrew Bible, for instance, dates to the 10th century AD, a thousand years later. The scrolls therefore give a new and direct insight into Judaism and Jewish groups at that time and also reveal something of the historical and social context in which early Christianity developed.

The first seven scrolls found in 1947 went through many vicissitudes before being bought piecemeal for the Hebrew University in Jerusalem. The first three were purchased in the same year by Professor E.L. Sukenik, on the eve of the partition of Palestine by the United Nations. His son, Yigael Yadin, bought the other four in New York some years later. By this time many more scrolls and fragments had been uncovered by the Ta'amireh Bedouin and others, some of which ended up in Jordan and some in Israel. Controversy also surrounds the publication and ownership of the scrolls. At the end of 1993 the scrolls were claimed for the Palestinian nation, on the grounds that they were found on the shores of the Dead Sea, in Palestine.

Books of the Bible

The scrolls can be divided into three main types: books of the Bible; apocryphal works; and sectarian works. There were copies of every book of the Old Testament, with the exception of the Book of Esther, which was probably considered to be a secular fable, or at least non-canonical. The definitive list of biblical books (the Hebrew Canon) had not been established at the time of the Qumran community. This was to be the work of the Council of Jamnia in about AD 100, which also established the standard text of the Bible (p. 160).

In fact, several copies of various books were found – one of the first scrolls brought to light turned out to be the Book of Isaiah. There are now 19 copies of this book, as well as 25 of the Book of Deuteronomy and 30 of the Psalms. The apocryphal works were ones not included in the later Hebrew Canon – such as the Book

A view of the ruins of the settlement at Qumran, identified by some scholars as a 'monastic' community and by others as a fortified farm complex or an aristocratic villa, rather like the one at Masada.

of Enoch, the Book of Jubilees and the Book of Noah.

Sectarian works

In addition to the Old Testament manuscripts and the apocryphal works, there are many others which are of outstanding importance to our understanding of the Qumran community.

One of these is the famous and enigmatic Copper Scroll, so called because it is made of that metal. It is written in a dialect of Hebrew and purports to give a list of the location of treasure hidden all over the country. Some scholars believe that the treasure referred to is that of the Temple in Jerusalem. Another scroll, the Manual of Discipline, forms in effect the Rule of the community – it outlines the

beliefs, ceremonies and regulations of its daily life. The War Scroll is an account of the battle to come at the end of days between the Sons of Light (the Qumran community) and the Sons of Darkness (Rome and Hellenism).

The Temple Scroll, over 28 ft (8 m) long, deals among other things with the rebuilding of the Temple in Jerusalem (even though the Second Temple still existed when the scroll was written). It also sets out the order of worship to be followed there in the days of the Messiah for whom the community was waiting. In fact two Messiahs are mentioned – one of David and one of Aaron (p. 108). The Qumran community would furnish priests for the new Temple, instead of their enemies, the sinful priestly families.

The interior of Cave 4 at Qumran.

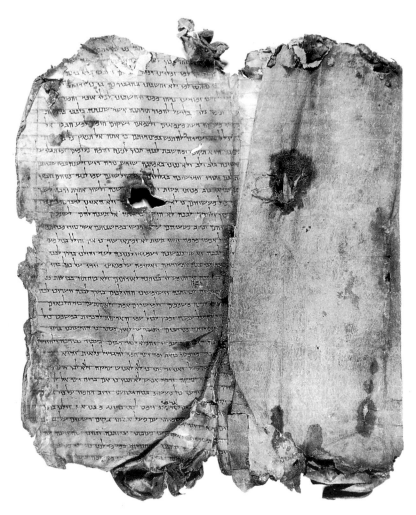

The partially unwrapped Scroll of Thanksgiving, from Qumran. Although the hot, dry climate of the Jordan valley has preserved the parchment very well, considerable damage has been inflicted by insects and vermin. Note how the scribe has 'hung' his letters from the line, rather than position them on it.

The Scrolls and Qumran

It is widely thought that the scrolls may, in some way, be associated with the site known today as Qumran, but long called the 'City of Salt'. As soon as the scrolls came to light archaeologists, under Père Roland de Vaux, a Dominican priest, and G. Lankester Harding, began to excavate the site, which they identified as the headquarters of the Essene sect and the place where the scrolls had been written.

The site lies on a flat-topped plateau, overlooking a deep wadi on the west. Across the wadi, some of the famous scroll caves can easily be seen in the cliffs opposite. Eastwards across the desolate landscape – the area now known to be Qumran's cemetery – lies the Dead Sea.

The scrolls may represent the library of the Qumran community, presumably hidden away for safe keeping at the approach of the Romans at the beginning of the First Jewish Revolt in

AD 66–70 (pp. 156–57). Even the mass of material found at Qumran and elsewhere in the 20th century represents only a fraction of what once existed. From the earliest Christian centuries, through the Byzantine era and into the Arab period there are persistent reports of scrolls turning up all over this region. This has led some scholars to wonder whether the tiny community at Qumran was in fact responsible for writing all this material, and one alternative explanation is that it was just one collection of texts brought from Jerusalem at the time of the Revolt to be hidden in various fastnesses of the Judaean Desert.

The Essenes

Many scholars believe that the men of Qumran were Essenes, a mainly monastic and strictly regulated Jewish sect. They saw themselves as priests but their beliefs and practices differed in fundamental ways from those of the Jerusalem priesthood, even to the extent of having their own religious calendar. The Essenes are described in some detail by Pliny the Elder, the Jewish scholar Philo and by Josephus, but these literary accounts do not agree in every respect with the sectarian writings among the scrolls. This has led some experts to doubt whether the Qumran community was in fact Essene, even though Pliny says that the Essenes lived a little distance from the west shore of the Dead Sea. Others are not convinced that the complex of buildings at Qumran represents the communal headquarters of the sect. Nearly 50 years after the discovery of the first scrolls there is still not a consensus on the identity of the Qumran community, the character of the buildings at the site, the nature of the beliefs of the people who wrote the scrolls, or their relationship, if any, with Christianity. There is even one school of thought that sees the religion of the writers of the scrolls as closer to the fire worship of ancient Persia than to that of the Jewish community of Palestine.

The nature of Qumran

In recent years the very character of the site has come into question. Unfortunately the final excavation report has not yet appeared, and few archaeologists have seen the material from the site or had the chance to interpret the excavated remains for themselves. Père de Vaux and many of the first generation of scholars who investigated the material were Catholic priests and monks and this may have had some influence on them when they identified the ruins as a monastic settlement and

named various rooms 'the scriptorium' and 'the refectory'. This monastic interpretation has since been disputed by other archaeologists who variously see in Qumran a military fortress, an aristocratic villa complex (a sort of small-scale Masada), or simply a fortified farming settlement. The presence nearby of a cemetery with in excess of 1,200 graves, including some of women and children, is rarely discussed, but must have a part to play in identifying the nature of the settlement.

The question of the relationship of the scrolls and the Qumran community to Jesus and the early Christian church is fraught with difficulty. Some see the Messianic nature of the texts as relevant, but there are important differences between the beliefs as set out in the scrolls and the tenets of Christianity. The members of the community certainly do not seem to have been pacifists and they were, perhaps, part of the popular nationalist movement against Roman rule.

The date of Qumran

In order to date the settlement and the scrolls a combination of methods is used. Epigraphists, using the form of the written script of the scrolls, date them to between the mid-3rd century BC and the 1st century AD. Just as there is in the English-speaking world, for example, a difference between the handwriting of the 18th, 19th and 20th centuries, so there were differences through time in the ancient world. Furthermore, scholars can even differentiate between the handwriting of individuals responsible for copying out the texts.

Objects, including lamps and pottery, found both at Qumran and in nearby caves where some of the community lived can be dated to the 1st centuries BC and AD. The site was occupied at different times: the first Second Temple phase, following de Vaux, was some time between 150 and 135 BC and 31 BC, when an earthquake hit the settlement and the consequent fire wiped it out. The final phase began after Herod's death in 4 BC and ended in AD 68 with the Roman destruction during the First Jewish Revolt.

Publication problems

At the Second Biblical Archaeological Conference held in Jerusalem in 1990 it was reported that between 50 and 60 per cent of all the biblical texts among the scrolls had already appeared in print. (This referred only to the more complete biblical texts, leaving aside the problems of the apocryphal and sectarian

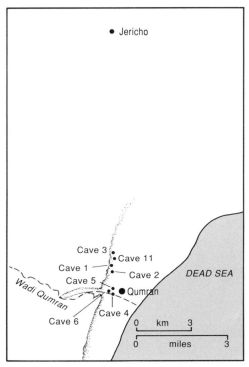

The location of the scroll caves in relation to the settlement at Qumran and the northwest shore of the Dead Sea.

material.) The small, fragmentary biblical texts, each containing only a few words, are more difficult to assess and are taking longer to publish. An international team has now been appointed and progress is being made in the publication and critical discussion of all types of documents. Access to the scrolls before publication has also been made easier. All of this, it is hoped, will help solve some of the mysteries which still surround the scrolls.

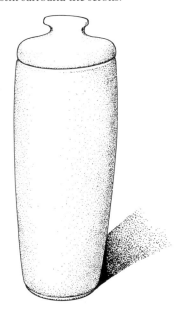

A drawing of one of the scroll jars in which the parchment scrolls were stored in the caves.

V

THE
AGE OF JESUS

And, behold, thou shalt conceive in thy womb, and bring forth a son, and shalt call his name Jesus. He shall be great, and shall be called the Son of the Highest: and the Lord God shall give unto him the throne of his father David: and he shall reign over the house of Jacob for ever; and of his kingdom there shall be no end.

Luke 1, 31–33

JESUS WAS BORN into an era of militant Messianism among the Jews. This was a time when the Last Judgment was daily awaited and a scion of the House of David was expected to return to deliver the tormented nation of Israel. In Judaea there was a constant state of tension and agitation against the might of Rome.

Today it is widely accepted that Jesus was born in 4 BC, the year of the death of Herod the Great. Herod had been an ardent supporter of Rome throughout his life and profited from the association. With his death, the resentment of the non-Hellenized religious and nationalist sections of Jewish society boiled up – but to no avail, since Roman power in the east was absolute. Any possibility of deliverance from Rome was therefore eagerly welcomed by many. Jesus' appeal to the masses lay partly in his supposed militancy against Rome, but he distanced himself from active rebellion: 'Pay Caesar what is due to Caesar' (Matthew 22, 21).

Jesus was certainly an exceptional teacher, possibly of the school of Hillel, the greatest rabbi of the age (the Hebrew word 'rabbi' means 'my teacher'). The life and work of Jesus, together with that of St Paul, changed the course of history. Very few accomplish so much.

The great rock of Masada beside the western shore of the Dead Sea. This aerial view shows the remains of Herod's buildings, particularly his palatial villa on three stepped terraces on the north side (front centre), positioned to take advantage of the afternoon breeze. The Snake Path (left) was the only practical ascent in the days of Herod, but the huge ramp built by the Roman commander Silva, during the siege of AD 73, can be seen on the other side.

HEROD THE GREAT

Herod's bodily strength was as great as the power of his mind.
Josephus, *The Jewish War* 1

HEROD WAS BORN IN ABOUT 73 BC, the son of Antipater and his Nabataean wife, Cypros. Antipater was an immensely able politician and statesman who was made procurator of Judaea by Julius Caesar. Whereupon he in turn appointed Herod governor of Galilee, and Phasael, his other son, governor of Jerusalem.

Shortly after his father's death, Herod was declared king of Judaea by the Roman senate, in 40 BC, though he was not secure on his throne in Jerusalem until 37 BC. His family was of Idumaean origin, a people who had been forcibly converted to Judaism by John Hyrcanus, the Hasmonaean king (pp. 116–17). Many of Herod's subjects therefore considered him an upstart foreigner who had usurped the Hasmonaean throne. To secure his position, Herod married Mariamne, one of the last Hasmonaean princesses, although he was later to have her killed, on suspicion of plotting against him. Perversely, he then mourned her for the rest of his life. Herod's Jewish subjects came to hate him, not only for his allegiance to Rome, but for his exceptionally repressive policies and for the fury which he could unleash even against his own family.

Herod ruled over a large kingdom, which included Judaea and Idumaea in the south, together with Peraea, Jaffa and Galilee further north. Samaria and northern Transjordan were also to come under his control, though many of his territories were added through Roman favours rather than military conquest. He also owned vast private estates, inherited from the Hasmonaeans.

The cornerstone of Herod's policies was his lifelong support of Rome, and because he was a loyal client king and useful to the Romans he flourished. He was happy to pay taxes to them and to compliment them by naming his new cities after them; for instance his great port city was called Caesarea (pp. 136–39), an obvious piece of flattery. An observant Jew while in Jerusalem, undertaking a complete remodelling of the Temple and the Temple Mount, Herod was also a cosmopolitan sophisticate. In the non-Jewish cities of his realm he built pagan temples, even dedicating some to the Roman emperor, Augustus. Building was his passion. Abroad he paid for many elaborate constructions which he donated to cities such as Damascus, Antioch, Sidon and Tyre; he was also responsible for refounding the Olympic Games in Greece.

The master builder

One result of Herod's loyalty to Rome was that he had access to the best Roman technology and the pick of their experts to help him create his cherished architectural projects. He was an immensely wealthy man, both in his own right and through state revenue accruing from his successful economic policies.

Imitating his Roman overlords, Herod became the greatest patron of architecture in the eastern Roman Empire. Apart from his building projects in Jerusalem, the architectural works for which he is best remembered are his complexes at Masada and Jericho, the port of Caesarea and Herodium in the Judaean Desert.

The kingdom of Herod the Great.

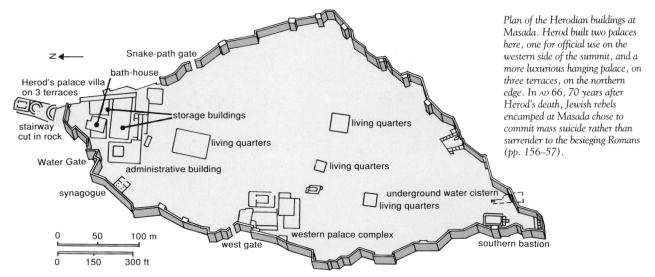

Plan of the Herodian buildings at Masada. Herod built two palaces here, one for official use on the western side of the summit, and a more luxurious hanging palace, on three terraces, on the northern edge. In AD 66, 70 years after Herod's death, Jewish rebels encamped at Masada chose to commit mass suicide rather than surrender to the besieging Romans (pp. 156–57).

Masada

In response to the increasing antipathy of his subjects Herod built a string of mountain fortresses which also served as royal palaces. The flat-topped, boat-shaped rock of Masada was ideally suited to this purpose. The great rock is situated on the western shore of the Dead Sea, rising about 1,300 ft (400 m) above it, and is almost inaccessible from the surrounding terrain. Herod increased its effectiveness by building a double, or casemate, defensive wall around it. There were already some buildings at Masada from about 100 BC, the time of John Hyrcanus, but Herod added a complex of palaces and storehouses for himself and his court. Some were luxurious in the extreme, such as the bath houses and the palace villa, built on three descending terraces at the northern end of the rock to catch the prevailing breeze.

A dependable water supply was vital. Masada is honeycombed with deep cisterns, which were fed by both the infrequent rainfall and an aqueduct leading to the rock from the dammed wadis to the west. One building at Masada has been identified as a synagogue, in part because it is oriented on Jerusalem. If so, it would be one of the earliest known, but it was only certainly used as such during the First Jewish Revolt of AD 66–73 (pp. 156–57).

Most of our knowledge of Masada, and indeed the reign of Herod, comes from the pen of Flavius Josephus (p. 12). He tells us how, in 40 BC, fleeing from the Hasmonaean pretender Antigonus and his Parthian supporters who had captured Jerusalem, Herod went to Rome for help. He left his mother, Cypros, with other women, on Masada, where they held out until

Herod, now created king by the Roman senate, returned to relieve the rock. Masada's impregnability must have impressed him then, and may be the reason he lavished so much care on his building projects there.

The briefest view of Masada makes it easy to imagine the difficulties involved in construction, though Herod had enormous resources of wealth and manpower at his disposal. In 1964

Plastered columns and painted plasterwork of the luxurious room in Roman style on the lowest terrace of Herod's hanging palace.

Herod loved the oasis area of Jericho and built a winter home there early in his reign. In his day, Jericho was a garden city of villas, orchards and vegetable gardens belonging to the aristocratic families of Judaea. In addition to one extensive palace complex and two further palaces, partially reusing the old Hasmonaean buildings, Herod also built a theatre and a racecourse. There were magnificent reception halls, gardens, baths and swimming pools, as well as Jewish ritual baths and industrial facilities, perhaps linked to the production of balsam or persimmon fruit.

Below is the triclinium, or formal dining room, of Herod's third (and largest) palace. It was originally paved with colourful stone slabs laid in patterns, called opus sectile – their imprint is still visible. In the centre there would have been an elaborate mosaic, imported from Rome. The great hall was used to entertain on a truly massive scale.

Yigael Yadin began excavations at the site. With the help of the engineers of the Israel Defence Forces he established a base camp close to the siege ramp by which the Romans captured Masada in AD 73, during the First Jewish Revolt. This was the best access for the archaeologists also, since the ancient and arduous ascent called the Snake Path, on the east side, is very difficult to negotiate. Today's many visitors can make the ascent to the summit by cable car, which completes the journey in a few minutes, and are rewarded with an unparalleled view of the Dead Sea and the surrounding desert.

Herodium

Herodium was perhaps the most spectacular of Herod's projects; it was certainly the most peculiar. The whole site was conceived as a palace, a luxurious royal leisure complex and a fortress. It was also intended to serve as Herod's mausoleum. Recent excavations have unfortunately failed to locate the tomb, which must have been immensely impressive. It may have been completely robbed of its contents, or perhaps it was deliberately destroyed by Herod's enemies after his death.

The site comprises two main parts: a mountain palace/fortress built atop a huge artificial volcano-like cone, which was approached by a long marble staircase; and a further series of buildings at the foot of the hill. The cone-like

shape was created by massing a fill of gravel and sand, some 45–60 ft (14–18 m) thick, against the round outer wall of the building. The king and his family may have been carried up and down on litters; it is hard to imagine Herod climbing the staircase on foot.

Within the protective circular wall of the palace/fortress were all the comforts of a princely Roman villa – a pillared courtyard (peristyle) with a garden, dining hall, living quarters for family, guests and servants, and a bath house with a mosaic floor. It was guarded by an eastward-facing high tower.

The lower compound, covering some 35 acres (14 ha), also contained a royal palace and a water garden, with bath houses and Roman-style pool.

A 'course' lay in front of the lower palace, which may have been used for chariot or horse racing; excavations conducted by the Israeli archaeologist Ehud Netzer, however, have suggested that it was intended for Herod's funeral procession. There were also many other buildings; so many, indeed, that not all have been excavated.

Towards the end of his life Herod was in terrible pain from an unknown illness and tried to alleviate his suffering by bathing in hot springs. He died in his Winter Palace in Jericho in 4 BC, leaving his kingdom materially better off, with many fine buildings and cities. His reign had been relatively stable and prosperous, but he

had been a despotic ruler, ruthless with those he suspected of conspiring against him. While we have no evidence for the 'Massacre of the Innocents', and Josephus does not mention it, 4 BC was certainly a year of turmoil, for the dying Herod had executed a large number of young men who had rejoiced a little too soon at the premature news of his death. Having already killed two of his sons, he crowned a long and infamous rule by having his eldest son, Antipater, put to death.

There are no certain surviving portraits of Herod. Even his coins did not carry a likeness of him, in accordance with the Jewish law. However, the still-impressive remains of his grandiose building projects stand as his memorial and speak to us of the man who built them.

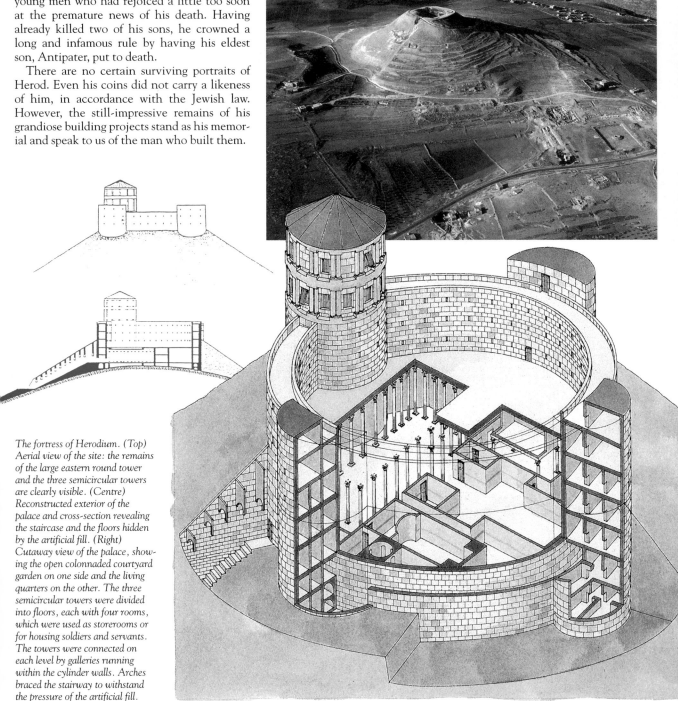

The fortress of Herodium. (Top) Aerial view of the site: the remains of the large eastern round tower and the three semicircular towers are clearly visible. (Centre) Reconstructed exterior of the palace and cross-section revealing the staircase and the floors hidden by the artificial fill. (Right) Cutaway view of the palace, showing the open colonnaded courtyard garden on one side and the living quarters on the other. The three semicircular towers were divided into floors, each with four rooms, which were used as storerooms or for housing soldiers and servants. The towers were connected on each level by galleries running within the cylinder walls. Arches braced the stairway to withstand the pressure of the artificial fill.

HERODIAN JERUSALEM

When Titus entered [Jerusalem] he was astounded by the strength of the city, and especially by the towers which the party chiefs...had abandoned. Observing how solid they were all the way up, how huge each block of stone and how accurately fitted, how great their breadth and how immense their height, he exclaimed aloud 'God has been on our side'.

Josephus, *The Jewish War* 6

LIKE THE EMPEROR AUGUSTUS IN ROME, Herod turned his capital, Jerusalem, into a city of luxury and splendour. His unappreciative subjects were loath to acknowledge this, especially with regard to the resplendent Temple he created. Josephus called it one of the great sights of the world, yet the Rabbinic sources rarely, if ever, acknowledge Herod's part in its construction. In the city itself, Herod's reign saw the extension or founding of fortifications, palaces, an aqueduct, a hippodrome, an amphitheatre and a theatre. He recreated Jerusalem as a Roman city, with all the amenities that could be found in towns throughout the Empire. The villas of the wealthy were also on a grand scale and even the aristocratic tombs of this period are masterpieces of architectural skill. This was the Jerusalem that Jesus would have known.

Herod's buildings

Characteristic Herodian masonry can still be seen throughout Jerusalem, for example in the western city wall which was rebuilt at this time along the line probably first constructed in the

First Temple period, above the Hinnom valley.

At the northern end of this wall Herod built a Citadel with three towers, which he named Hippicus, Phasael and Mariamne, after a friend, his brother and his wife respectively. One still stands to a considerable height and has been rebuilt and reused for centuries.

Herod's palace was south of the Citadel, nestled behind the city wall. It must have been a building of great grandeur, though only traces of the enormous podium on which it was built remain. Close by were the newly rebuilt homes of the wealthy, many of whom were members of the aristocratic priestly families.

Some of these luxurious houses have been excavated and partially restored. They were built in the style of Roman villas of the 1st century AD, well known from Pompeii and Herculaneum in Italy. One has remains of a peristyle court or garden of classic Roman type – unknown at this date in Judaea except in Herod's own palaces. Roman fashions in interior decoration were also popular. However, in keeping with the Jewish prohibition against graven images, the motifs on the frescoed walls avoided representations of humans and animals, and the sophisticated mosaic flooring bore geometric rather than naturalistic patterns. The Jewish beliefs of the owners of these houses are clear in other ways. One fragment of wall plaster has the *menorah* (the ritual seven-branched candlestick) incised on it and all the excavated houses have *mikvehs* (ritual baths) in the basements, alongside ordinary bathrooms.

One of these affluent residences is the House of Katros, so called from the inscription on a stone weight found there: '...son of Katros'. Katros is known to have been the name of one of the priestly families who served in the Temple. From the roof of their house, this family would have been able to see the Temple, shining white and gold across the deep valley which divides Jerusalem into the Upper and Lower cities.

The Temple

The men of these aristocratic families with priestly duties to perform in the Temple had two ways of reaching it from the Upper City. The easier route was along a road carried on a viaduct over the Tyropoean valley half way along the western side of the Temple Mount.

An elegant, reconstructed reception room from one of the aristocratic residences in the Herodian Quarter (p. 142).

The other was by a series of stepped streets and flights of magnificent stairs which gave access to the *stoa* (an arcaded walk) at the southwestern corner of the Temple precinct. There were other approaches to the Temple, especially from the south, the oldest part of the city which had been the original City of David, where most of the pilgrims who came to Jerusalem would have lodged and from where they made their ascent to the Temple Mount.

By Herod's day the old Temple Mount of the time of Ezra and Nehemiah was too small for the large numbers who visited each year. Herod took the decision to enlarge it on a monumental scale, by extending the eastern wall of the precinct north and south above the Kidron valley, and by creating new walls on the other three sides. This extension almost doubled the

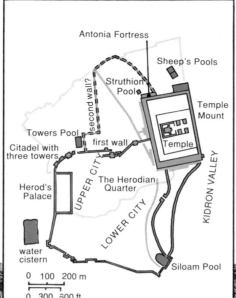

Plan of Herodian Jerusalem (left).

An aerial view of the Dome of the Rock (the Jewish Temple Mount), looking north. The crowded streets of the Old City of Jerusalem press around it on the north and west, except in front of the Western Wall – a holy site for Jews because traditionally it is closest to the Holy of Holies of the Temple, destroyed nearly 2,000 years ago. The Temple Mount excavations lie to the south of the great rectangular enclosure wall built by Herod. The Kidron valley and the Mt of Olives are at the extreme right, while the City of David lies out of sight at the bottom, beyond the road.

area of the Temple platform. To achieve this he had to fill in much of the deep Tyropoean valley and in so doing he virtually remodelled the landscape of Jerusalem.

The Temple enclosure is today known as the Haram esh-Sharif, and the Dome of the Rock and the Aqsa, with their gold and silver domes, still stand on the Herodian platform which originally supported the Temple. This platform was a stunning piece of engineering and the parts that are still visible are very impressive.

The walls encircling the platform measure some 1,000 by 1,600 ft (300 by 485 m) and in places must originally have been 148 ft (45 m) high.

Recently the platform has been investigated by Dan Bahat, who found one foundation block over 40 ft (12 m) long and weighing over 37 tons. According to Josephus, the Temple itself was built in only 18 months, but the entire Temple Mount project took over 60 years to complete, long after Herod's day.

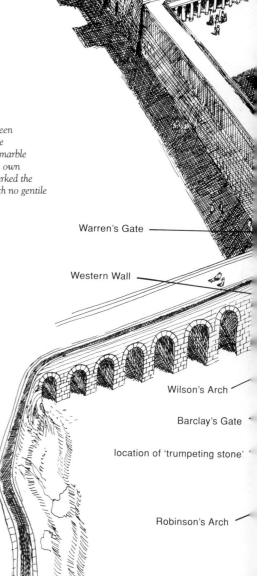

The southwest corner of Herod's Temple Mount can be seen below, as it appears today. In the foreground are the remains of palaces of the early Arab period. Above them, Robinson's Arch (named after the 19th-century explorer who identified it) springs from the Herodian enclosure wall. This arch can also be seen in Peter Bugod's reconstruction of the Temple Mount (right). The arch supported one of the monumental exits from the Mount, leading from the Royal Stoa, where the king entertained important visitors. From the exit a magnificent staircase led down to the Central, or Tyropoean, valley. A road passed under both Robinson's Arch and, a little further north, Wilson's Arch (also named after its discoverer). This second arch carried a viaduct over the deep

central valley to the upper city. The road continued north, past the Antonia Fortress, built by Herod to replace the old Hasmonaean citadel and garrisoned by Roman troops. The section of the road between Wilson's Arch and the Antonia has recently been excavated by Dan Bahat, the acknowledged expert on ancient Jerusalem. It is now possible to walk along this road again, after 2,000 years, in a tunnel far below the present ground level. There were two low-level entries to the Temple Mount on the western side: Warren's Gate and Barclay's Gate. The majority of pilgrims, however, would have entered on the south side, where there are two more gates. There is much debate as to whether the eastern one was double or triple at this time. In Herod's day, the pilgrims emerging

on to the Temple platform would have seen the magnificent Temple building, shining with marble and gold, set within its own precinct wall. This marked the boundary beyond which no gentile could pass.

Antonia Fortress

Warren's Gate

Western Wall

Wilson's Arch

Barclay's Gate

location of 'trumpeting stone'

Robinson's Arch

This mosaic, of which a number of examples are known, shows either the entrance to the Temple itself, or the doors to the Holy of Holies within it, as on the plan (far right). Josephus states that there were curtains before both doors. Some of the cultic equipment is also shown, such as the menorah – the seven-branched candlestick – and the shofar – a ram's horn trumpet.

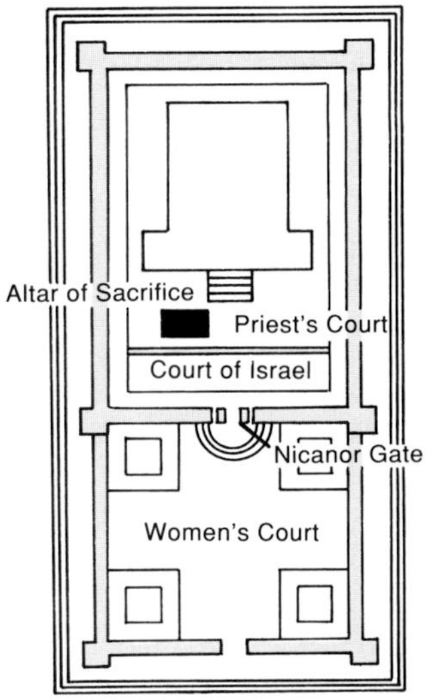

Altar of Sacrifice

Priest's Court

Court of Israel

Nicanor Gate

Women's Court

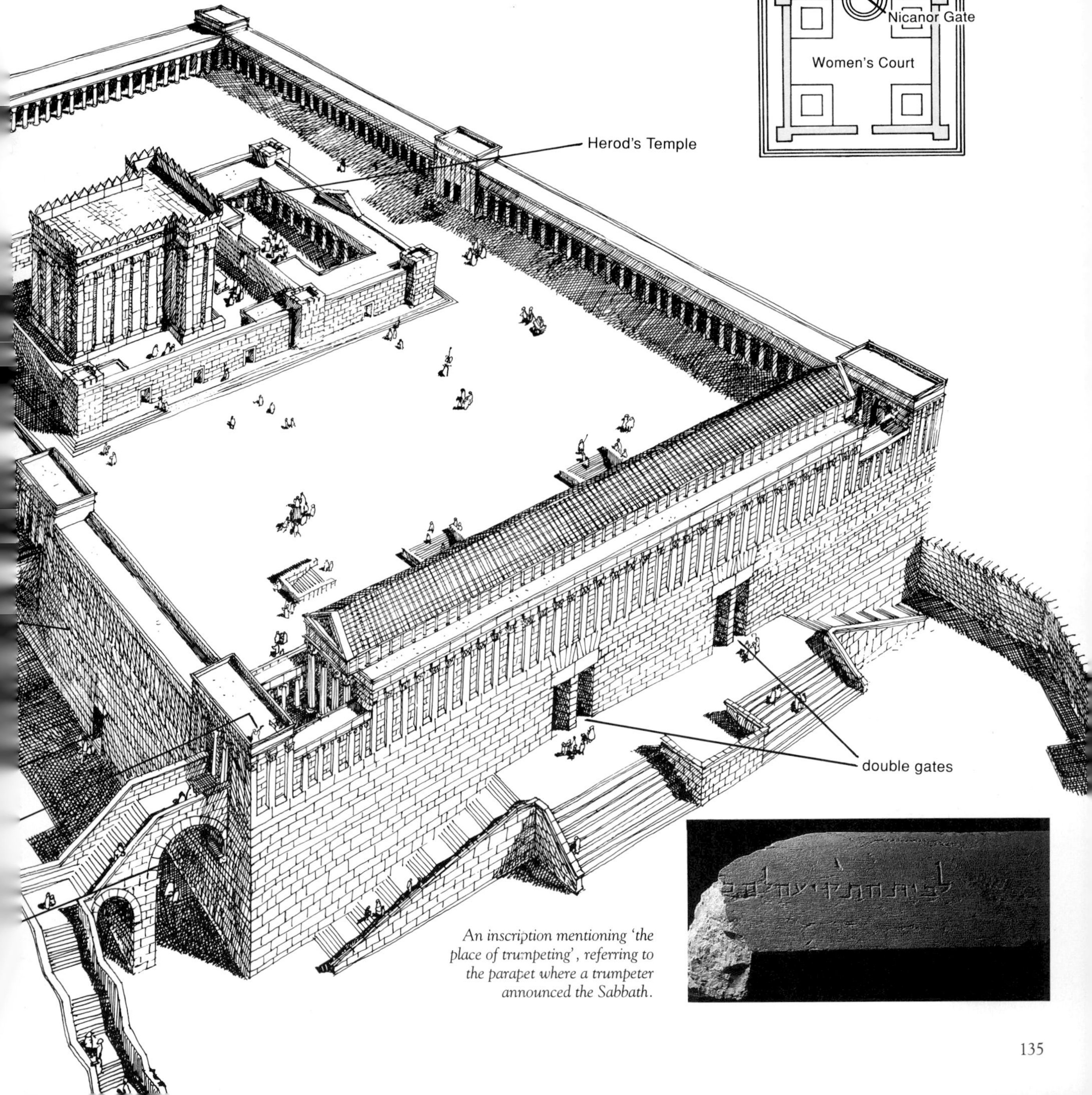

Herod's Temple

double gates

An inscription mentioning 'the place of trumpeting', referring to the parapet where a trumpeter announced the Sabbath.

135

CAESAREA, PORT UNDER WATER

Along the coast Herod discovered a city that was in decay named Strato's Tower, whose location was well suited to receive his generosity. This he rebuilt entirely in marble and ornamented with a most splendid palace.

Josephus, *The Jewish War* 1

BELOW THE WATERS OF THE MEDITERRANEAN off the coast of Israel, archaeologists are discovering the breakwaters, docks and quays of a major ancient port. The structures have sunk beneath the waves and can only be investigated by divers, who, using the techniques of underwater archaeology, are revealing the harbour of Herod's great maritime city of Caesarea.

The divers are members of the Caesarea Ancient Harbour Excavation Project (CAHEP), under the direction of Avner Raban of Haifa University. This is a long-term project and is proceeding alongside land-based archaeologists who are uncovering the buildings of the city of Caesarea.

Strato's Tower

Strato's Tower, as Caesarea was originally known, was a Phoenician port founded by a king of Sidon. It was always modest in size and had changed hands several times before Herod chose it as the site for his port. There were economic motives for the port, as there were no harbour facilities on this strategic stretch of coast between Dor and Jaffa.

Caesarea was perhaps Herod's most ambitious and grandiose project. The entire city, with its port, was built in just 12 years, between 22 and 10 BC. Herod named it Caesarea in honour of his friend and patron Augustus Caesar. The harbour itself he named Sebastos, another

piece of flattery as Augustus in Greek is Sebaste (the name also given by Herod to the city he rebuilt on the site of Samaria). Caesarea was conceived as a great port to rival Alexandria in Egypt, and was built on a scale never seen before in that part of the Mediterranean.

Herod's access to Roman technology and engineering allowed him to construct his new harbour on a coast with extremely dangerous currents and a constant problem of silting. One of the technical advances he was able to make use of was the Roman invention of hydraulic concrete which hardens under water, as described by Vitruvius in his *Ten Books on Architecture* (II, 6, 1), written in 25 BC.

The harbour was protected from currents and storms by two huge breakwaters, lined with warehouses. The breakwaters were constructed in a very ingenious way. Timber frameworks were built on land and were part filled with concrete. They were then towed out into position in the sea and filled with more concrete until they sank. On the sea bed the final concrete was poured in and other material built up on top. We know this because Raban and his team have found not only the remains of the concrete, but also sections of the timber framework, beautifully preserved, showing the high quality of carpentry.

A lighthouse stood at the harbour entrance, at the end of the southern breakwater, its fires tended 24 hours a day. This may be the tower which Josephus tells us was called Drusion, a compliment to Drusus, Augustus' stepson. Josephus also mentions that additional navigational aids were provided by six enormous bronze statues which stood on massive concrete pedestals to mark the position of sandbars north and south of the approach to the harbour. The statues have disappeared but the bases have been found in the positions described by Josephus. The breakwaters enclosed three basins, the innermost of which lapped the esplanade in front of the monumental Temple of Augustus.

Ashore, the city site is so extensive that it has still only been partially explored, but its main outlines are clear. In Herod's time the city covered about 164 acres (66 ha). Beyond the innermost harbour stretched a great urban area, planned by Herod's architects with a grid

Herod built two aqueducts to bring water to Caesarea from Mt Carmel, nearly 13 miles (20 km) away. The high-level aqueduct is itself in fact double, with the western side added by Hadrian in the 2nd century AD. Another aqueduct was built at ground level.

Caesarea's impressive theatre, built originally by Herod to adorn his new city. In use for perhaps five centuries, the building was much modified and repaired over time. It was excavated in the early 1960s by a team of Italian archaeologists. Fully restored, it is used today for concerts and other performances. The famous Pontius Pilate inscription (p. 147) was found in it, reused later as a building block. On the promontory jutting out to sea are the remains of what was probably Herod's palace.

of paved and pillared streets. As in every Roman city of note it had its forum, public baths and theatre (restored and in use again today). Nearby, on a low promontory stood a palatial villa, now badly eroded by the sea. At least one room had a floor of *opus sectile*, very similar to one in Herod's winter palace in Jericho (p. 130). At its centre was a porticoed pool, variously identified as a swimming pool or a fish pond (in Latin a *piscina*), either of which would be appropriate in this setting. This building may have been Herod's palace,

UNDERWATER ARCHAEOLOGY

Underwater archaeology is a relatively new field of study. As a modern discipline it began in the early 1960s with the work of George Bass, now a professor at Texas A&M University, who excavated a shipwreck at Cape Gelidonya, Turkey. This ship was a Phoenician vessel, dating from about 1200 BC. Since then underwater archaeology has made some outstanding discoveries, both of shipwrecks yielding evidence relating to ancient seafaring, and submerged remains of harbour installations and settlements.

As on land the site is surveyed, measured and planned and all features and finds are recorded and mapped in great detail. Small air pipes are used to probe the seabed to discover hidden features, and larger ones, called air lifts, suck up

the overlying layers which can then be sieved to recover any objects. Very heavy objects can be raised to the surface using floats.

Caesarea is undoubtedly the most spectacular site revealed so far by underwater archaeologists along the coast of the Levant, but many other important finds have been made. For instance, Israeli archaeologists have established that until the Early Bronze Age (c.3300 BC) the sea level was between 20 and 33 ft (6 and 10 m) lower than today. Submerged villages have been found, dating from the 9th millennium BC to the beginning of the Early Bronze Age, several hundred yards out from the present shoreline.

It is not just in the Mediterranean that discoveries have been made. In the inland Sea

of Galilee the famous boat from the time of Jesus was recovered, now housed at Kibbutz Ginosar (pp. 144–45). In the Red Sea divers and archaeologists have explored the seas around the Coral Island, just south of Eilat, and have suggested that this is in fact the site of Solomon's port city of Ezion Gezer, rather than Tell el-Kheleifeh at the head of the Gulf of Aqaba, a theory which had to be discarded some decades ago.

While submerged settlements often contain remains of many different periods, shipwrecks represent single events and are effectively time capsules. Finds of wrecks and cargoes, either associated with a ship or jettisoned and lying isolated, give us an excellent idea of the wide range of economic contacts enjoyed in the

Mediterranean from at least the Late Bronze Age (mid-16th century BC) to the Mameluke period (16th century AD) and later.

Underwater archaeologist at work.

CAESAREA, PORT UNDER WATER

The construction of the port of the city of Caesarea, called Sebastos, was a truly staggering undertaking. Herod's engineers had to build a harbour at a site with no natural advantages and with the problems created by a strong current and silting. The larger, southern breakwater varies in width between 195 and 243 ft (60 and 74 m) – Josephus described it as being 200 ft wide. Herod's engineers showed great ingenuity in designing a sluice system to tackle the problem of silting and also built secondary breakwaters to protect the main harbour.

Because of subsidence in the seabed, which may have begun very shortly after Herod's death, the extent and details of the harbour can only be investigated today by divers and underwater archaeologists.

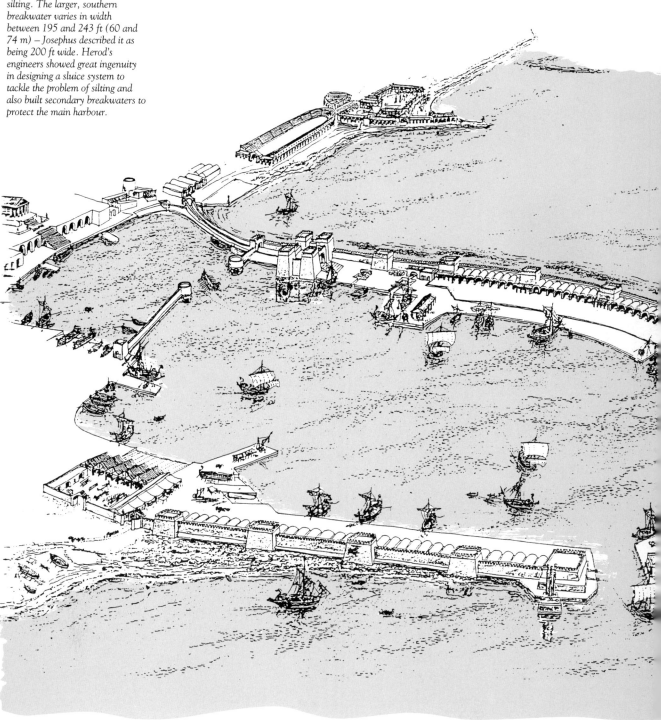

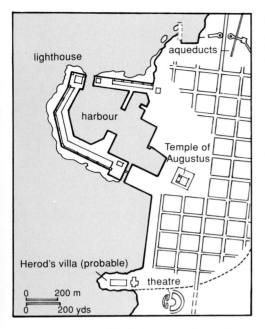

The harbour was only part of
Herod's ambitious project at
Caesarea. This plan gives some
idea of the extent of the city, which
was built on the classical grid
system.

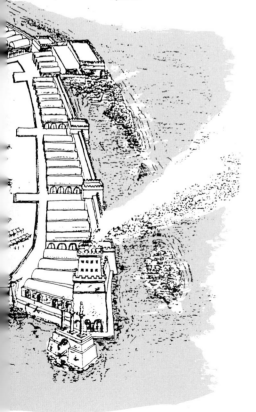

since no other candidate for it has been found.
Josephus has much to say of its splendours.
Caesarea also boasted a hippodrome, apart-
ment blocks and all the other amenities
expected of a Roman city. Water was brought
to the city from Mt Carmel by aqueducts. One
of these is nearly 13 miles (20 km) long, with
its first half tunnelled out of rock and the
remainder carried on arches.

The later history of Caesarea

The Romans deposed Herod's successor and
abolished his kingdom, ruling Judaea thereafter
as a province of Rome. Caesarea became the
seat of the Roman governor or prefect. Pontius
Pilate was certainly a resident, because a dedicatory inscription with his name was found
there (p. 147). St Paul used the port on his missionary travels and was imprisoned in the city
for two years before he set out on his voyage to
Rome (pp. 150–53). It was in Caesarea that
tensions between Jewish and pagan citizens
became so acute as to spark off the First Jewish
Revolt; Vespasian used it as his headquarters to
crush the revolt. The Early Church Fathers
Origen, Pamphilius and Eusebius were all resi-
dents and by the end of the Byzantine period it
had a library to rival that of Alexandria, with
some 30,000 volumes. The city was captured in
turn by Arabs and Crusaders, who built the formidable defences still visible. Caesarea was
finally razed to the ground by the Mameluke
Sultan Baybars in AD 1265.

The breakwaters of Herod's
harbour were built partly of rubble
and stone blocks, one of which
measures 13 by 4 ft (4 by 1.35
m). Stone blocks larger than this
would have caused immense
problems of transport and handling
in boats, and the engineers
overcame this by using hydraulic
concrete, which could be mixed
and poured on site and hardened
under water. Ready-made wooden
frames, the remains of which are
still preserved under the sea, were
towed out and filled with the
concrete.

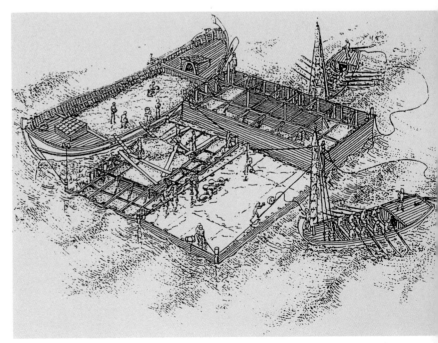

THE LIFE OF JESUS

Map showing the borders of the Roman province created after Herod's death, and sites associated with the life of Jesus.

Think not that I am come to destroy the law, or the prophets: I am not come to destroy but to fulfil.
Matthew 5, 17

JESUS WAS BORN TOWARDS THE END of the reign of Herod the Great, probably about 4 BC. It was a troubled time in Judaea. The cruelty of the dying king, increasing with his suffering, unsettled even further a kingdom which had never taken kindly to the presence of the Romans or to the unpopular 'foreigner' they had appointed to the throne. After Herod's death there were problems over the succession, and his kingdom was divided, with the sanction of Augustus, between three of his sons. Archelaus (4 BC – AD 6) ruled over Judaea and Samaria, Antipas (4 BC – AD 39) over Galilee and Philip (4 BC – AD 34) over the northeastern territories. After a troubled reign Archelaus was removed by Augustus and Judaea was taken under direct Roman rule, administered as a minor province by a prefect or procurator, subordinate to the governor of Syria.

The birth of Jesus

There is no reason to doubt that Jesus was born in Bethlehem. The tradition linking the Church of the Nativity to his birth is an early one: in the 2nd century AD the Emperor Hadrian, finding that Jews and Christians alike were a threat to peace in the area, erected a temple to Venus and Adonis over the site.

Today, there are scholars who believe that Mary and Joseph were natives of Bethlehem and moved to Nazareth during the unrest after the death of Herod. It was Luke who confused matters by associating the Quirinian census of AD 6 with the birth of Jesus. The Greek phrase translated as 'there was no room at the inn' (Luke 2, 7) could equally be 'there was no space in the room'. The less cramped caves behind the house, used for storage and stabling as at Avdat in the Byzantine period, offered the young couple greater comfort and privacy for the birth of their baby than the bustle of a large, extended household. The word 'house' rather than 'stable' is used in Matthew (2, 11).

The biblical Jesus

Apart from the canonical Gospels there are other, very fragmentary stories of the life of Jesus, of which the Gospel of Thomas, found at Nag Hammadi in Upper Egypt, is the best known and may be very early in date. As with the Old Testament authors, the writers of the Gospels relied on traditional sources which may have been little more than oral snippets and tales about Jesus. The main emphasis was

THE CHURCH OF THE NATIVITY, BETHLEHEM

The Church of the Nativity is situated at the centre of Bethlehem. Archaeologists have demonstrated that there was human settlement at this spot since at least the time of David (10th century BC). The caves which lie beneath the church were used from that date onwards.

A church on this site was founded in the 4th century AD by Queen Helena, the mother of the Emperor Constantine (p. 16). The altar was positioned directly over the cave in which it was believed Jesus was born. St Jerome took up residence in Bethlehem and translated the Bible into Latin there – this is the Vulgate version, probably the most important of all Latin translations of the Bible (p. 31). One of the caves below the

church is still called 'St Jerome's Study' and another is thought to be where he was buried.

The Constantinian church was rebuilt on a much larger scale in the reign of the Emperor Justinian (6th century AD) and it is basically this church, much repaired and restored, that the visitor still sees today. The Crusader kings of Palestine held their coronations here. After Christian rule had been replaced by Islamic, the church was still treated with respect, at least until the time of the Ottoman rulers. From the 16th century AD on it was systematically looted and began to deteriorate rapidly. It is said that much of its marble was used to adorn the Haram esh-Sharif (the Dome of the Rock) in Jerusalem.

View of the interior of the Church of the Nativity, looking up the nave towards the altar.

on theological issues rather than historical accuracy. There is no biography or consistent portrait of Jesus – only a series of sketches which bring him into occasional focus.

It is clear, however, that Jesus grew up in the small town of Nazareth, cradled in a bowl of hills above the Sea of Galilee. He was baptized in the River Jordan by his cousin, John the Baptist, in a ceremony which recalls the washing free from sins which Jews underwent in the *mikveh* (p. 143). Jesus then started on his ministry and attracted disciples and a large following of people wherever he taught in public or healed the sick. At the age of about 30, as an observant Jew, he travelled to Jerusalem for the Passover, one of the three religious festivals in the year, when Jews were enjoined to make the pilgrimage to the city. While there he was arrested, tried and put to death (pp. 146–49).

From his teachings preserved in the Gospels, we know that Jesus principally preached the end of the current age and the coming of the Kingdom of God. This vision is part of the Jewish Messianic and apocalyptic movement of his day, also evident in the texts of the Dead Sea Scrolls (pp. 122–25). The 12 apostles were to head the newly ingathered tribes which had been scattered throughout the world. It would take an act of God to assemble them all again in their own land with a Messianic king, descended from the House of David, at their head. The descent of Jesus from David is estab-lished in the genealogical list in Matthew 1. Jesus' claim to be God's Anointed One or Messiah was a very real threat to the estab-lished authorities, both Roman and Jewish. The Jewish community in Judaea was always on the verge of explosion – as seen twice in the 100 years after the death of Jesus. To the Romans the country was an important bulwark against the inroads of eastern barbarians, so civil unrest of any kind could not be tolerated – especially stirred up by someone claiming to be descended from one of the greatest spiritual and political leaders the country had known.

It might perhaps be expected that the Jewish leaders would have welcomed a Messianic king. But Jesus was a challenge to them also. He was a popularist and a liberal thinker at a time when Jewish religious law regimented every aspect of life. His teachings always aimed for the heart and spirit of the law, rather than the mere outward signs of its observance, as in the parable of the Good Samaritan (box).

During his lifetime Jesus preached exclusive-ly to Jews; it was only after his death that his message was spread to Gentiles. He was also a part of the contemporary Jewish movement which anticipated the imminent arrival of the Kingdom of God, following a Day of Judgment. He was therefore received by many with rap-turous acclaim. The Romans brought about his ultimate downfall because his popularity was a threat to their regime.

Christ visualized as the Good Shepherd. A mosaic above the entrance to the mausoleum of Galla Placidia in Ravenna, dating to the 5th century AD. The theme 'Feed my sheep' (John 21, 16) is one of the oldest motifs in the ancient Near East.

THE GOOD SAMARITAN
The parable of the Good Samaritan is an example of the way in which Jesus' attitude to the Jewish law might be interpreted as revolutionary. The man who 'fell among thieves' (Luke 10, 30) was passed by a priest and a levite who ignored his distress. According to Jewish ritual law they could not touch the man lest they themselves became ritually unclean. Relationships between Jews and Samaritans were hardly cordial (pp. 106–07), yet it was a Samaritan who found it in his heart to help the injured Jew. Jesus here emphasizes that the spirit of the Law was observed by a despised foreigner rather than the ritually observant priests.

DAILY LIFE IN NEW TESTAMENT TIMES

This pliable dough, baked on stones over a fire pit, is the original type of unleavened bread (matzah) eaten by Jews at Passover to commemorate the Exodus from Egypt (Exodus 12, 15). Since it was also the bread eaten by Jesus and the apostles at the Last Supper, it is the origin of the communion wafer taken at Mass.

IN THE CENTURIES AROUND the time of Jesus many people in Palestine lived in ancient, huddled townships not unlike the Old City of Jerusalem today. Narrow alleys formed the streets and blank doors led off them into homes which housed large, extended families and their servants. Rooms around interior courtyards served as living and storage space, stabling for animals, washrooms, kitchens and also workshops if the men of the house were craftsmen. Greek and other foreign citizens

lived mostly in newly built cities, such as Herod's Caesarea or Sebaste (founded on the ruins of Israelite Samaria). Like all classical cities they were built on a grid pattern, with regular blocks of buildings divided by straight streets, similar, for instance, to cities in the United States today. Shady porticoes lined the most important streets, such as in Beth Shean (pp. 166–67) and Jerash, providing sheltered access to the shops in summer and winter alike.

Rural communities were far less sophisticated than urban ones, mainly consisting of villages of much simpler, mud-brick dwellings. Exterior courtyards and flat roofs were used for a multitude of purposes, from drying crops to eating, relaxing and even sleeping in the long, hot summer nights. A dry year could bring water shortages and famine; refuse and animal dung littered the streets and hygienic sewage disposal was unknown. Disease and early death were common; many women died during or after childbirth and infant mortality was high. Vermin of all kinds infested people or houses. Jewish law even provided ritual measures for houses attacked by various types of fungal growth.

For most people diet was fairly restricted. Only the rich ate wheat bread; poorer people baked theirs from barley. Jewish dietary law restricted the eating of meat to animals with

FURNITURE AND UTENSILS OF EVERYDAY LIFE

Because pottery could easily become contaminated and would therefore not be kosher, vessels made of stone and glass, which were impermeable and could not become ritually impure, were popular among those who could afford them. In the wealthy houses of Jerusalem archaeologists found many vessels of the soft local limestone which must have been made in workshops in or near the city. Trays, mugs, measuring cups and platters have been found and a type of large water jar, turned on a lathe and set on a pedestal foot. The only pieces of furniture to survive the fire that destroyed Jerusalem in AD 70 were rectangular sidetables of limestone in the dining rooms of Herodian

Quarter houses. Some of the large water jars stood beneath them, one on each side of the table's central support (p. 132). Round stone tops for low sidetables have also been found which were used beside banqueting couches – aristocratic Jerusalemites adopted Roman dining customs. Neither the couches nor the legs of the round tables have survived because they were made of wood or other perishable material, but they can be restored from similar items depicted in Roman wall paintings.

Pottery vessels of all kinds abound in Jerusalem of the Second Temple period. Most are unremarkable domestic vessels, such as the many bowls found at the bottom of the cisterns of

Jerusalem's Herodian Quarter. These had been deliberately pierced and thrown into the cistern. The excavators surmised that because the bowls had perhaps become ritually unclean and so had to be discarded.

Fine imported wares included the Roman polished red ware known as eastern terra sigillata. This variant of the Roman potter's art is thought to have been produced in workshops somewhere on the eastern seaboard of the Mediterranean, perhaps in Syria. Even thinner and more highly burnished is the Italian terra sigillata, also found in some Herodian Quarter houses, where such vessels would have been a very expensive status symbol.

Stoneware

Jerusalem Ware pottery

RITUAL BATHS

Many ritual baths, or mikvehs, were found in the aristocratic houses of the Herodian Quarter of Jerusalem. The majority were cut into the natural rock beneath the houses and lined with waterproof plaster. They had to be deep enough for the bathers to immerse themselves completely and held about 40 seah (198 gallons or 750 litres) of spring or rainwater fed directly into the bath. If this was not possible an adjacent pool was constructed to hold the fresh water – a small amount would render the water in the mikveh ritually pure and a conduit between the two pools allowed the water to mix. Oddly, only one mikveh was found together with a pool in the Herodian Quarter. Other arrangements must have existed to render the water ritually pure.

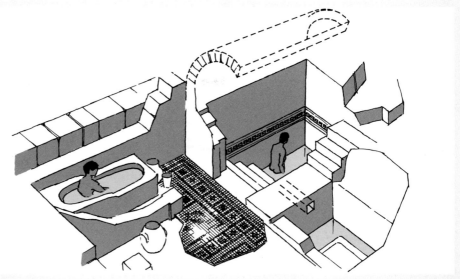

A mikveh or ritual bath.

Most houses in the Herodian Quarter had more than one mikveh, along with luxurious bathrooms for ordinary bathing. Ritual immersion could only be undertaken by people who were already clean. Many things could make a Jew ritually unclean – physical contact with a non-Jew for instance, which was hard to avoid in the crowded cities. Ritual purification was also necessary for women after menstruation and childbirth and indeed it was a common feature of everyday life.

Not everyone, of course, could have a mikveh in their own house and public ones have been found south of the Temple Mount. This was the usual approach for the thousands of pilgrims who would climb the hill towards the Temple from the south, where they lodged in the old City of David. They stopped at the mikvehs to prepare themselves for the final ascent to the sacred precinct. Mikvehs were also built next to synagogues, as at Gamla, Masada and Herodium.

The immersion ritual of Second Temple Judaism became the baptism ceremony of Christianity. John was baptizing people into a new spiritual life in the waters of the Jordan before Jesus came to him to be baptized. Jesus believed that the strict observance of ritual purity, which he called 'the tradition of man', was far less important than observing the commandment of God (Mark 7).

cloven hooves and which chewed the cud – such as cows, sheep and goats but certainly not pigs. They also had to be ritually slaughtered. Only fish with fins and scales were fit to consume (*kosher*). But few people could afford to eat meat or fish on a regular basis, although there is evidence that pigeons were kept as much for food (as is still true today among some Palestinian communities) as for their droppings, which were a precious fertilizer. Fruits such as figs, dates and pomegranates were grown and, of course, olives for oil as well as eating. Vegetables, including several kinds of beans and various types of gourds (squashes), onions, leeks and garlic were plentiful.

Family life

At the time of Jesus a Jewish man was allowed more than one wife, although probably few could afford the additional expense. After a seven-day marriage ceremony (a custom still observed among some orthodox Jews) the wife belonged to her husband's family and was expected to produce as many children as possible. A childless woman was usually divorced by her husband. Divorce was easy for a man, but impossible for a woman. For wives the punishment for adultery was death by stoning (though see John 8, 3–11). A woman could inherit from her family only if there was no male heir, but she could own property and conduct business in her own right. She could not, however, go to law, but had to have an *epitropos*, or representative, in the courts.

Children began their working lives almost as soon as they could walk, with the girls learning to help in the home and the boys gradually mastering the work of their elders in the fields or in trade. Few females had the opportunity to learn to read and write, but, just after the time of Jesus, according to Jewish historical tradition, there were schools in every village for young boys to study Jewish law between the ages of 7 and 13, when they were deemed to become men. Even today the ceremony of coming of age for Jewish boys is set at their 13th birthday and is called *bar mitzvah*. Children reached puberty young, and so marriage could legally take place at 13 for boys and 12 for girls.

A Boat from the Time of Jesus

In 1986 a boat was discovered buried in the mud of the Sea of Galilee, where it had lain for 2,000 years. It was so fragile that it had to be completely encased in polyurethane foam before it could be moved. The boat was winched into its own pool at Kibbutz Ginosar to undergo conservation treatment, which involves pumping a synthetic wax into all its timbers over a period of up to ten years.

And there arose a great storm of wind, and the waves beat into the ship, so that it was now full. And he was in the hinder part of the ship, asleep on a pillow: and they awake him, and say unto him, Master, carest thou not that we perish? And he arose, and rebuked the wind, and said unto the sea, Peace, be still. And the wind ceased, and there was a great calm.
Mark 4, 37–39

IN 1985–86 A SEVERE DROUGHT caused the Sea of Galilee to shrink. Exploring the newly exposed lakebed, two brothers from Kibbutz Ginosar on the shore of the lake noticed the outline of a boat. It was buried so deep in the mud that they began to wonder exactly how old it was, and decided to alert the Underwater Inspection Team of the Department of Antiquities and Museums (now the Israel Antiquities Authority). A preliminary probe assured them it was a very old boat indeed, because it was constructed with mortice and tenon joints – a technique used in the Mediterranean from the 2nd millennium BC to the end of the Roman period.

Archaeology to the rescue

Soon news began to leak out that a wreck from the time of Jesus had been discovered in the Sea of Galilee. Worse, a wild rumour began to make its way round the shores of the lake that the boat contained gold coins. This made it imperative to excavate the boat as quickly as possible, before it was destroyed by treasure hunters. Shelley Wachsmann and Kurt Raveh of the Underwater Inspection Department were put in charge of the project. Wachsmann became responsible for investigating the site and quickly rallied all the help he needed – and more – from the surrounding area. Kibbutz Ginosar loaned the fishing lights their boats used on the lake at night, so that work need not be stopped as darkness descended.

The excavators had to work 24 hours a day because the level of the lake was slowly rising and rain was forecast, threatening to submerge the boat once more. Officials from the Sea of Galilee Authority decided to build a temporary dam seaward of the boat, and pumps were installed to keep the area around the site reasonably dry. But the boat itself had to be kept wet at all times, because its 2,000-year immersion in the soft mud had changed the consistency of the hull's timber to something like soft and spongy cheese. The conservator, Orna Cohen, calculated that 80 per cent of the boat's fabric had changed to water; it would warp and crumble to nothing if it were allowed to dry out. The boat was consequently sprayed constantly with fresh water, which made working conditions very uncomfortable. The boat could support neither its own weight nor that of anyone working inside it, so a moveable frame was constructed overhead with planking placed across it. Thus suspended above the boat, the excavators could carefully remove the mud from inside the vessel.

Preserving the boat

The next important question was how to move the fragile boat without damaging it. After consulting many experts, Orna Cohen decided to try to 'sail' it intact to Kibbutz Ginosar, where it could be worked on more easily. No one had ever attempted to move an ancient wreck in this way. Fibreglass frames were gently laid inside it and the interior filled with quick-setting polyurethane foam. Then tunnels were dug under the width of the boat, extra fibre-glass frames put in position and more polyurethane foam sprayed in. When this was dry the remaining mud was dug out, and the process was repeated. Once the boat had been completely cocooned, water was pumped back into the pit and the dam was dismantled. Then, with Orna aboard it like Cleopatra on her barge, the boat was gently manouevred to the safe haven of Kibbutz Ginosar. Here it became temporarily airborne as a crane winched it into the white tiled tank which had quickly been constructed for it by enthusiastic members of the kibbutz. Brightly coloured fish were added to the pool to help keep destructive bacteria at bay. A small hut/museum has been built over the boat as it lies in its tank.

The conservation programme may take up to a decade, for the water in all the cells of the timber must be gradually replaced with a synthetic wax called polyethylene glycol before the boat can be properly studied and displayed.

Dating the boat

We have several reliable clues as to the boat's age. For example, the way in which the vessel was constructed and two pottery vessels found close beside her suggest a date between the early 1st century BC and the end of the 1st century AD. This has been confirmed by radiocarbon analysis of the timbers at the Weizman Institute of Rehovot, which has yielded a date of 40±80 BC, that is, it was probably built between 120 BC and AD 40.

The boat was very old when it was scrapped. It was probably deliberately sunk in the shallow water of a boatyard (pieces of other vessels were found nearby) and the useful wood of the stem and stern posts, the internal timbers and probably all the topside wood construction, were removed for recycling.

Perhaps inevitably, this boat has come to be associated in the popular press with Jesus. Of course, in Jesus' day there must have been hundreds of boats fishing in the Sea of Galilee, and it is highly unlikely that we have chanced on just the right one. Nevertheless, we can

A reconstruction of the Galilee boat.

assume with near certainty that it was in a boat such as this that Jesus and his disciples travelled and fished. When – battered, bruised and much repaired – it finally came to rest in the mud, it had had a very long lifetime of hard work behind it.

The Sea of Galilee was frequently subject to sudden storms. Jesus calmed just such a storm when he and his disciples were caught in open water in a boat very similar to the one discussed here. The detail below is from an 11th-century AD manuscript and shows Jesus asleep in a boat as a storm is brewing (see opening quotation).

JESUS IN JERUSALEM

And [Joseph of Arimathea] bought fine linen, and took him down, and wrapped him in the linen, and laid him in a sepulchre which was hewn out of a rock, and rolled a stone unto the door of the sepulchre.
Mark 15, 46

IT WAS TO CELEBRATE THE PASSOVER that Jesus and the apostles made the long journey from Galilee. As they did so, they left behind the Jewish kingdom ruled by Antipas (son of Herod the Great) and arrived in a province of the Roman empire. The chief representative of Rome, the Prefect (the title Procurator came later), was Pontius Pilate, who arrived in Judaea in AD 26. He had an unsavoury reputation and seems to have been determined to subdue the people rather than co-operate with them, as previous Roman governors had done. The unlucky official who had to mediate between Jews and Romans was Caiaphas, the High Priest. He was assisted by a council of aristocratic priests, the Sanhedrin, and supported by a large force of armed police. It is not clear whether the High Priest and the Sanhedrin had the power to condemn a man to death at that time.

Herod's Jerusalem (pp. 132–35) rivalled Rome itself in magnificence and many visitors came on business or as pilgrims; thousands of Jews from all over the world visited it during their lifetime. Given the different factions within the Jewish populace, Jerusalem was a difficult city to police, especially during festivals such as Passover. From the Antonia fortress, built by Herod, the Romans kept a particularly watchful eye on the Temple Mount where trouble was most likely to start.

It is not surprising, then, that Jesus was soon noticed by both Roman and Jewish leaders. The Gospels tell us he stayed overnight in Bethany, a village just outside the city on the Jericho road, and was received with rapturous enthusiasm on his entry into Jerusalem. His behaviour in the outer enclosure of the Temple, overturning the stalls of legitimate, if expensive, traders caused considerable disruption. The traders were selling the pilgrims unblemished animals and birds, guaranteed by the religious authorities, to be offered as sacrifice. They were also empowered to exchange ordinary coins for ones without the image of a ruler stamped on them, which were used to pay the Temple tax of half a shekel, which all adult male Jews had to donate annually.

Sadducees and Pharisees

Jesus' disputations on the Temple Mount during the early days of his stay in Jerusalem alienated the two major elements of the Jewish leadership. Firstly there was the Sadducean aristocracy, supposed descendants of Zadok, the High Priest of Solomon's day. They served as priests in the Temple and from their ranks were chosen the Sanhedrin – the religious court. These men were observant Jews who had absorbed the Roman way of life, and were often very wealthy. Many had homes in the luxurious residential quarter of the Upper City.

Secondly, Jesus also upset the Pharisees, whose name may mean 'the Separated Ones'. They insisted on careful observance of every tiny detail of the Torah. Many of them were deeply offended by the teachings of Jesus, more so than the Sadducees, because of his free interpretation of the sacred text. The charge of hypocrisy often levelled against the Pharisees, however, is not correct. Some were ultra-orthodox and might today be called fundamentalists, but there was such a wide range of opinions among them that others would be considered very humane and even liberal. Jesus

Plan of Jerusalem showing the probable sites of events related to the arrest, trial and crucifixion of Jesus. The trial of Jesus probably took place in Herod's palace (1), rather than the Antonia fortress (2) as was once believed. Thus he would not in fact have walked along the Via Dolorosa (3), but would have taken a different route (4). The sites of Golgotha (5) and Jesus' tomb (6) were outside the city walls of the day and are now covered by the Church of the Holy Sepulchre. The Garden of Gethsemane (7) was also outside the city, beyond the Kidron valley. From his arrest here, Jesus was probably first taken to the house of the High Priest, Caiaphas, for questioning, which would have been somewhere in the aristocratic quarter of the city (8).

quotes many Pharisaic sayings. The Pharisees always worked among the people and it is out of Pharisaic Judaism that the traditions of rabbinic Judaism grew.

The arrest of Jesus

Both the Sadducees and the Pharisees wanted Jesus arrested and executed for sedition, but were cautious about acting publicly. After celebrating the Last Supper, Jesus and the apostles left Jerusalem to return to Bethany, stopping to pray in a peaceful garden on the Mt of Olives, just outside the city beyond the Kidron valley. This was the garden of Gethsemane (Gath Shemen), where Jesus was arrested by the Romans with the help of Judas Iscariot.

Today there is still a quiet olive grove in the grounds of the Church of All Nations. The olive trees, though ancient, are not 2,000 years old. Titus, the Roman general and later emperor, who destroyed Jerusalem in AD 70, had most trees in and around the city cut down. New trees probably sprang from the old, however, and the present gardens lie beside the ancient path to the mountain summit and the route to Bethany. Jesus must have been arrested nearby.

Where was Jesus tried?

Jesus was first questioned in the House of Caiaphas, the High Priest, somewhere in the Upper City. The next morning he was handed over to the Romans for trial and sentence. For centuries it was thought that the imprisonment and trial of Jesus took place in the Antonia

Pontius Pilate was Prefect of Judaea at the time of the arrest and crucifixion of Jesus. This inscription mentioning him was found at Caesarea and records the building and dedication of a temple there by Pilate, in honour of the Emperor Tiberius.

fortress at the northwestern corner of the Temple Mount. This was one of the chief Roman positions in the city and an underground tunnel led from it directly into the Temple area. A Roman pavement in the cellar of the Convent of the Sisters of Zion was identified as the pavement (*lithostraton* in Greek or Gabbatha in Aramaic) where Pilate judged Jesus. Spanning the street outside the Convent is an arch known as 'Ecce Homo' ('Behold the man'). Here, it was believed, was the spot where Pilate showed Jesus to the crowd.

ROMAN GOVERNORS OF JUDAEA	
Coponius	AD 6–9
Ambibulus	AD 9–12
Rufus	AD 12–15
Gratus	AD 15–26
PILATE	AD 26–36
Marcellus	AD 36
Marullus (perhaps=Marcellus)	AD 37–41
(King Agrippa I ruled Judea	AD 41–44)
Fadus	AD 44–46
Alexander (nephew of Philo)	AD 46–48
Cumanus	AD 48–52
Felix	AD 52–59
Festus	AD 59–62
Albinus	AD 62–65
Florus	AD 65–66

CRUCIFIXION

For the Romans crucifixion was a common method of execution, usually used for slaves and rebels. Some years ago the bones of a young man who had been crucified were found in a tomb near

Jerusalem. The tomb dated to the time of Christ, but the young man's name was Yochanan (John) rather than Yeshu (Jesus). It is not clear from his bones whether his arms had been nailed or tied to the

horizontal crosspiece. The crosspiece was carried by the victim to the place of execution, where the upright had already been put in place. Sometimes a man's arms were nailed to it, with the nails passing between the bones of the arm at the wrist, not the palm of the hand.

Yochanan's heels, however, had certainly been nailed to the cross since an iron nail was still in place in the heelbone. His lower legs had been broken, as was often the case. This speeded up death since the legs could not then bear the weight of the body. The victim would hang by the arms and die of suffocation as his chest was inexorably squeezed, closing the breathing passage. The cross might have a narrow ledge for the man to

perch on, or one at his feet for support, if his legs had not been broken. This would relieve the pressure on the arms and chest, but would thus prolong death.

Two possible methods of crucifixion and (below) the heelbone, with the nail still embedded, of a crucified man.

The street running below the arch towards the Church of the Holy Sepulchre is traditionally called the Via Dolorosa ('Way of Grief') and the 12 Stations of the Cross are marked for pilgrims. Today, with a better understanding of the topography and chronology of Jerusalem in the 1st century AD, we know that these traditional identifications are mistaken.

Most scholars now believe that Jesus' trial was held in Herod's palace, on the northwestern edge of the city, which by that time was the headquarters of the Roman prefect when he was in Jerusalem. He always came up from his seat in Caesarea to be present in Jerusalem for the festivals, bringing with him a large troop of soldiers in case of trouble.

Where was Jesus crucified?

The prefect's palace lay to the south of the Citadel (now the Jaffa Gate area) and Jesus' real Via Dolorosa lay northwards from the palace to the site of the crucifixion at Golgotha ('the Place of Skulls'). This lay outside the city walls, but close to them, so that the death of a criminal would serve as both an attraction for, and a warning to, the public. The tomb in which Jesus' body was placed was nearby.

The identification of Golgotha and the tomb of Jesus with the traditional locations in the Church of the Holy Sepulchre seems well founded. In Jesus' time the city wall almost certainly ran just south of this area, though its exact line has not been traced in the maze of

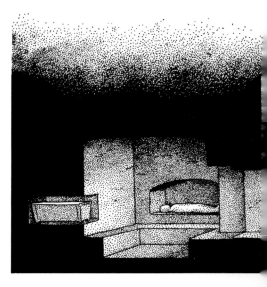

Reconstruction of the type of tomb that was common in Jerusalem in the 1st century AD. The tombs were cut from the rock with two or more rooms. The burial chamber was at the back of the tomb, where the shrouded bodies were laid in full-length niches.

buildings in the Christian Quarter of the Old City. The site where the Church stands today was then a quarry for the limestone Herod used to build his city and it was also a favoured place for cutting tombs. Golgotha itself is a faulty

JEWISH BURIAL CUSTOMS OF THE SECOND TEMPLE PERIOD

Many families had tombs which were used for generations to bury their dead. By the Second Temple period a dead person was wrapped in a shroud and first laid to rest in the tomb. When the flesh had decayed, the bones were carefully gathered up and placed in a stone box, called an ossuary (or bone box). Some were plain, others were ornately carved (below). A tomb found in Jerusalem contained ossuaries with the name Caiaphas carved on them (right). Could these be members of the priestly family which included the High Priest at the time of the crucifixion of Jesus? Some of the wealthiest aristocracy had very elaborate tombs, such as the famous (though misnamed) Tomb of Absalom in the Kidron valley outside Jerusalem. It is one of a number of mausolea of the Second Temple period in the valley, and the area is still a Jewish cemetery. Elsewhere tombs are cut deep into the rock, the entrances of which were sealed with a rolling stone. The best known is the so-called Tomb of the Kings, actually the tomb of Queen Helena of Adiabene. Monuments were sometimes erected over tombs, most commonly a pyramid-type structure such as that of the 'Tomb of Zechariah' in the Kidron valley. Joseph of Arimathea, a wealthy man, had a tomb prepared for himself in a quarry north of the city walls of Jerusalem, and it was here that Jesus' body was hurriedly placed as the Sabbath approached. Normally a body was washed, anointed with various oils and spices and composed for burial before wrapped in shrouds. It was this office that the women were coming to perform the next day, when they discovered that the tomb was empty.

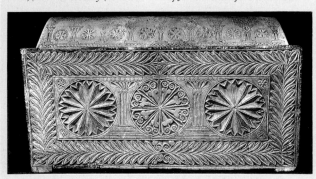

The small entrance led to a central room with niches in the walls for oil lamps. Once the flesh had decayed from the buried bodies, the bones were collected up and put in stone ossuaries, which were either placed in smaller niches or left standing in the tomb.

A large round stone is rolled aside, revealing the low entrance of the rock-cut tomb.

outcrop of rock, unsuitable as building material, and therefore left in place.

The tomb of Jesus

Jesus' body was taken down for burial before the Sabbath, as was customary. He was laid in a rock-cut tomb nearby, hewn in the side of a quarry and sealed by a large rolling stone. This type of tomb was common at the time in the Jerusalem area and was often used as a family mausoleum. Bodies of the dead were laid out on rock-cut benches, sometimes in coffins but often just in shrouds, until they had decomposed. The bones were then gathered up and placed in special stone chests, called ossuaries. These ossuaries were often magnificently decorated with floral or architectural, but never figurative, motifs, because of the prohibition against graven images.

The small entry to these tombs was sealed by large round stones, which rolled in a groove and could be wedged open or shut. Although these stones were well pivoted, they were extremely heavy. The fact that Jesus' body was not in the tomb when it was reopened after the Sabbath was astonishing. Clearly expecting trouble, the Romans had placed a guard over it; it would have been impossible to open such a tomb unnoticed.

An ivory panel dating to c. 400 AD showing the ascension. The tomb is depicted in the form of a grand mausoleum of the time, rather than as it would probably have looked (above).

THE DEVELOPMENT OF CHRISTIANITY

Now they which were scattered abroad upon the persecution that arose about Stephen travelled as far as Phenice and Cyprus, and Antioch, preaching the word to none but unto the Jews only. And some of them were men of Cyprus and Cyrene, which, when they were come to Antioch, spake unto the Grecians, preaching the Lord Jesus.

Acts 11, 19–21

THE EARLY CHURCH IN JERUSALEM was tiny – no more than 120 people (Acts 1, 15) – comprising mostly Jesus' original apostles (except Judas), his mother and a few other women, including Mary Magdalene, and some disciples. Jesus' mantle of leadership had fallen on Peter, who was now indeed the rock on which the group depended. His real name was Simon but his Aramaic nickname was Cephas which means 'rock'. Translated into Greek this becomes Petros or Peter. The apostles continued to preach and to heal the sick, attracting converts among the people of Jerusalem who were all practising Jews. It is usual to call them Judaeo-Christians at this time, for they observed the Jewish law while also being followers of Jesus, whose return they expected daily as the risen Christ or the Messiah for whom all Jews were waiting.

Judaism did not at that time seek to make converts. With one exception, when Peter converted Cornelius the centurion in Caesarea, no member of the original group preached to gentiles, even though they formed a large proportion of the population in Palestine. The position of the Judaeo-Christians was never secure and they were persecuted by other Jews (Acts 2–7). Stephen, who was 'full of grace and power' (Acts 6, 8) was stoned for blasphemy and was the first Christian martyr. The destruction of Jerusalem in AD 70 (pp. 156–57) sealed their fate. When Hadrian founded his city of Aelia Capitolina on the ruins of Jerusalem, in the early 2nd century AD, the church which re-emerged was made up entirely of gentiles.

The conversion of Paul

As a young man studying in Jerusalem, Paul witnessed the stoning of Stephen, sometime around AD 36. He subsequently took part in the persecutions in the city of the people of 'the Way' – the name for Jesus' followers before the word 'Christian' was used (Acts 9, 2). Having asked the High Priest's permission to go to Damascus to seek out more apostates, on the road there he experienced a vision of Jesus that struck him blind. In Damascus his sight was restored by Ananias, a Judaeo-Christian.

There is no zeal like that of a new convert. All the enthusiasm and energy which Paul had previously expended in persecuting Christians was now turned to spreading the teachings of Jesus as widely as possible. Paul, with his forthright style, came into conflict with most of Jesus' original followers as well as with traditional Jews and Roman sympathizers. Most people saw him as a troublemaker and his preaching in the synagogue in Damascus aroused much hostility. The disciples in Jerusalem soon despatched him back to Tarsus for his own (and their) good.

The first Christians

What happened next was totally unforeseen by Jesus' first disciples. After Stephen's death many Judaeo-Christians had fled Jerusalem for Syria and even Cyprus. Antioch in Syria was one of the most important cities in the Roman empire, and it was there that some of them began to preach about Jesus to the Greeks (but not to Jews). News of this so alarmed the people of the Way in Jerusalem that they sent Barnabas to Antioch to investigate.

PAUL

Christianity might have failed had it not been for Paul. He was a Pharasaic Jew, originally named Saul, and was a native of Tarsus in what is now southern Turkey. The city of Tarsus had been granted Roman citizenship and so Paul had all the rights of a Roman citizen. For instance, unlike other subjects of Rome, he could not be imprisoned, tortured or executed without a legally constituted trial. By invoking the law of Provocatio a Roman citizen could demand to be tried by the emperor himself in Rome. Paul did indeed insist on such a trial when he was imprisoned by the Romans at Caesarea and he was despatched to Rome – his final journey.

A man small in size, with meeting eyebrows and a rather large nose, bald-headed, bow-legged, strongly built, full of grace; for at times he looked like a man, and at times he had the face of an angel.

2nd-century AD description of Paul

The head of Diana from a cult statue of the Roman period. There had been an important shrine to Artemis/Diana at Ephesus, on the west coast of Turkey, for many centuries. Her worshippers flocked there to visit the world-famous temple from all over the Mediterranean.

Unexpectedly, he was delighted with the sincerity of the new converts. He then travelled further north to Tarsus, looking for Paul, and brought him back to help with the work in Antioch. The two of them remained there for a year and it was in Antioch that the name Christians was first used, denoting the followers of Christ, meaning 'the Anointed One'.

The notion of Christianity as a religion separate from Judaism seems to have begun in Antioch also. Paul, if not the originator of this idea, certainly accepted it with enthusiasm, and from then on he encouraged Christian belief among Jews and gentiles alike. On his many travels he first preached to the Jewish community in each city he visited, seeking out the synagogue (p. 120). When rejected by the Jews, he took his message to the gentiles, among whom he was more successful. At the Council of Jerusalem in AD 49 it was agreed that gentiles did not have to undergo circumcision or obey the Jewish law in order to be Christians. This was a great relief to those communities who were ready to follow Christ but not to accept the heavy burden of the ritual law as the Judaeo-Christians did. To the ordinary Jewish communities in the cities visited by Paul this decision was anathema. In fact it was not welcomed by all the disciples in Jerusalem either, although Peter, who had converted Cornelius the centurion, and James, the brother of Jesus, seem not to have objected.

Travel in the 1st century AD

Paul now began to spread the word of Christianity far and wide. Travel at this time was relatively easy, as the Romans had set up a comprehensive road system throughout their empire, which was well maintained and properly policed. It was also simple to take passage on almost any ship of the many that plied the Mediterranean. Paul could also keep in touch by letter with the various churches he set up. His correspondence contains a great deal of information about the concerns of his widespread flock. Even more important is the insight gained into Paul's teachings. It should not be forgotten that he had never sat at the feet of Jesus – all his knowledge of Christ came from visions granted directly to him – and he did not always agree with Jesus' first disciples. Preaching to the gentiles was indeed the most difficult idea for those in Jerusalem to accept.

Paul's missionary journeys

Paul's first missionary journey, around AD 47–48, was with Barnabas to Cyprus, a natural choice as it was the latter's home. They also travelled through southern Anatolia (modern Turkey) before returning to Antioch (Acts 13–14). Paul's second journey was far more ambitious (Acts 15, 40–18, 22). This time his companion was Silas, and the trip took them across Anatolia and then by sea to Macedonia. Paul eventually reached Athens (Acts 17).

The theatre at Ephesus in which a hysterical mob rioted against the Christians during Paul's visit, in about AD 55. The silversmiths of the city were fearful that their livelihood, which was based on the pilgrim trade, would be lost as Christianity became increasingly popular and the worship of Diana faded (Acts 19, 23–41).

The routes taken by Paul on his three great missionary journeys, preaching the message of Christianity wherever he went. He established many churches in the communities he visited, and he encouraged and supported them later through his letters. Paul, with his companions, was responsible for the spread of the Christian church over much of the eastern Mediterranean.

His last journey (opposite page) was to Rome, to appeal to the emperor as was his right as a Roman citizen. The journey was very eventful and hazardous. After seeking shelter in the port of Fair Havens on Crete, he was shipwrecked on Malta. Determined to continue, he took

ship again and landed on the Italian mainland near Naples. From there he walked to Rome, where he lived for at least two years, receiving visitors and preaching freely, although officially under house arrest. Then, very suddenly, he disappeared from the stage of history and it is not known what became of him.

THIRD MISSIONARY JOURNEY

SECOND MISSIONARY JOURNEY

FIRST MISSIONARY JOURNEY

The last years of Paul

After much travelling Paul eventually returned to Caesarea. The Jews of Palestine were by this time in an uproar against Felix, a particularly vicious Roman procurator. False prophets abounded, brigands made life intolerable for ordinary people and unrest was everywhere. Nevertheless Paul insisted on going to Jerusalem for the Passover, even though he was *persona non grata* with Jews, Judaeo-Christians and Romans.

It was always Paul's policy to be 'all things to all men, that I might by all means save some' (I Corinthians 9, 22) and it was while he was trying to appease Jews and Christians that he was recognized on the Temple Mount and set on by a mob. He was accused of bringing a gentile into the Temple area and it was only the Roman troops, spotting trouble from their vantage point of the Antonia fortress, who rescued him from certain death (Acts 21, 17–22, 24).

Once he had declared himself to be a Roman citizen he was sent under guard to Felix in Caesarea in AD 58. From there, after two years spent in prison, he appealed to the emperor for a trial in Rome as was his right. He was despatched to Rome by a new Roman governor, Festus, at the beginning of the winter when most shipping had been laid up because of the foul weather. It was therefore a voyage full of incident, ending in a shipwreck off Malta (Acts 27, 41–28, 1). Determined as ever, Paul, together with his companion, possibly Luke (who is credited with writing the Book of Acts), finally reached Italy, landing at Puteoli, near modern Naples.

There he received his greatest rebuff, for the message of Christianity meant little to people educated in the spirit of Greek philosophy. Further south, in Corinth, he was more kindly received (Acts 18, 1–11) and stayed 18 months. Eventually he returned to Palestine after a very successful trip.

Paul could never stay long in one place. Soon he was off again (Acts 18, 21–23, 16), this time to Ephesus on the Aegean coast of Asia Minor. This was the greatest port of the region, a crowded and cosmopolitan city already over a thousand years old. It was fruitful ground for Paul, who spent two years there. Just as he was planning to leave, he became embroiled in a hysterical mob threatening violence against anyone who did not respect Diana, the patron goddess of Ephesus, whose cult attracted huge numbers of pilgrims. Her great temple had stood for centuries on the edge of the city and was one of the seven wonders of the ancient world. Once extricated from the imbroglio Paul sailed for Greece.

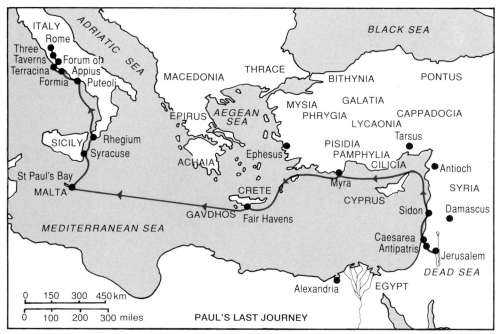

PAUL'S LAST JOURNEY

This painting (below) from the Christian catacomb of Priscilla in Rome shows an early Christian community or church (the word originally referred more to the people than the building) taking part in a communal meal. On either side are baskets of bread, consumed in memory of Christ (Luke 22, 19). The idea of people bound together by a religious belief sharing a meal after a real or symbolic sacrifice is much older than the Last Supper, which this painting superficially resembles. In the Old Testament, Jethro, Moses' father-in-law, offers a sacrifice (Exodus 18, 12) and Aaron and the elders of Israel then come to eat with him 'before God'. The early Christian 'love feast' or agape continued this tradition. It was a collective meal, often on a Sunday. Only the element of taking bread and wine together – Holy Communion or Eucharist (meaning sharing and thanksgiving respectively) – remain.

They walked up the coast to Rome, where they were greeted by a Christian community that already existed in the city. Paul was apparently placed under house arrest by the Romans (Acts 28, 11–16), but was allowed to receive visitors and to preach. It is in Rome, around AD 61–62, two years after his arrival, still preaching to all who came to him and still writing to the faithful communities established by him, that we lose sight of him for the last time. No charges were ever brought against him and we simply do not have any evidence for what happened to him. Tradition has it that he was executed in AD 67. The Basilica of St Paul Without the Wall marks the spot where he is said to be buried.

Peter reached Rome soon after Paul, and it was he not Paul who was destined to be the real head of the church in Rome and therefore throughout the Roman empire. Peter lies buried deep beneath the altar of his great church in the Vatican City where his throne is still occupied by the popes, who are his spiritual descendants.

Roman Catholicism is only one branch of Christianity. Some of the others are at least as old. Paul found well-established communities in southern Italy as well as in Rome. There were non-Pauline groups in Asia Minor and in Egypt, where the Coptic church is one of the oldest in the world. There is no documentation about the origin of these churches as there is for the church of Peter and Paul. What seems

certain, however, is that even at a very early date there was no one set of beliefs nor one single creed for all Christian communities. Even so, Christianity began to spread very fast throughout all the lands around the Mediterranean and beyond. In the early 4th century AD even Rome submitted and Christianity was adopted as the official religion of the Roman empire under Constantine.

VI

THE TURBULENT YEARS

Therefore, son of man, prophesy and say unto Gog, Thus saith the Lord God; in that day when my people of Israel dwelleth safely, shalt thou not know it? And thou shalt come from thy place out of the north parts, thou, and many people with thee, all of them riding upon horses, a great company and a mighty army. And thou shalt come up against my people of Israel, as a cloud to cover the land.

Ezekiel 38, 14–16

JUDAEA IN THE 1ST AND 2ND CENTURIES AD was not a peaceful province of Rome. Enormous tensions between the populace, for the most part observant Jews, and their insensitive or corrupt Roman governors prompted two explosions. Following the First Revolt, which broke out in AD 66, the Temple, and indeed the whole of Jerusalem and much of the rest of the country, was laid waste. The Second Revolt in AD 132 completed the devastation. Traditional Jewish observance was completely disrupted by the cessation of sacrifice in the Temple, although this in fact gave rise to Rabbinic Judaism. Christianity, on the other hand, began to flourish, both inside Judaea and elsewhere. Under Constantine I it became the official religion of the Roman Empire in the early 4th century AD.

Even with the collapse of the Roman Empire the storms had not passed and in the 7th century AD the Arabs swept out of Arabia, bringing with them the new religion of Islam. Over the next centuries various Moslem dynasties governed Palestine. The Crusaders took Jerusalem at the very end of the 11th century AD. By the end of the next century Saladin, the great Ayyubid ruler of Egypt, had clashed with Richard the Lionheart, King of England, on the holy soil of Palestine. Later, Mamelukes and then Ottomans controlled the country, until, in 1918, the British were awarded the Mandate to rule Palestine by the League of Nations in the wake of the First World War. Israeli Independence followed in 1948. The Holy Land has never been a land of peace, but the struggle to achieve it continues.

View from the Mt of Olives westwards towards Jerusalem. The golden dome of the Dome of the Rock and the silver one of the el-Aqsa mosque to the south of it can be seen against the crowded houses of the Old City.

THE TWO JEWISH REVOLTS

Vespasian, the Roman general who put down the First Jewish Revolt of AD 66 and was acclaimed emperor by his own legions in AD 69.

In the end not a man failed to carry out his terrible resolve, but one and all disposed of their entire families, victims of cruel necessity who with their own hands murdered their wives and children and felt it to be the lightest of evils! Unable to endure any longer the horror of what they had done and thinking they would be wronging the dead if they outlived them a moment longer, they quickly made one heap of all they possessed and set it on fire; and when ten of them had been chosen by lot to be the executioners of the rest, every man flung himself down beside his wife and children where they lay, put his arms around them and exposed his throat to those who must perform the painful office. These unflinchingly slaughtered them all, then agreed on the same rule for each other, so that the one who drew the lot should kill the nine and last of all himself.
Josephus, *The Jewish War* 7, 392

The Jews in Caesarea had a synagogue alongside a piece of ground belonging to a Greek citizen. This they had repeatedly tried to acquire, offering many times the real value. Scorning their requests, the Greek further insulted them by beginning to build a factory right up to the dividing line, leaving them a narrow and utterly inadequate passage. The immediate result was that the more hot-headed of the young men jumped in and interfered with the builders.
Josephus *The Jewish War* 1

THE FIRST JEWISH REVOLT was precipitated in AD 66 by a trivial dispute between the Greek and Jewish communities, living uneasily side by side in Caesarea (opening quote). But this was no more than a superficial incident in an explosive chain of events.

Direct Roman administration of Judaea, established in AD 6 following the misrule of Herod's son, Archelaus, had always been resented. This feeling was only exacerbated by the insensitivity and corruption of most of the Roman procurators, few of whom had the welfare of the province at heart. Herod's grandson, Agrippa I, had briefly been installed as ruler of the kingdom, but after his death in AD 44, Judaea reverted once more to direct rule by Rome.

In AD 66 the Roman prefect of Judaea was Gessius Florus, a man whose prime motive in life was to line his own pockets. Unwisely, he was the immediate cause of the insurrection when he tried to rob the Temple treasury, on the pretext that money was required for his programme of public works. The Zealots, a fundamentalist and nationalist group, at once instigated a full-scale uprising in Jerusalem, in spite of all efforts by both the Romans and their moderate allies among the Jews to quell it. Chief among these allies was Herod Agrippa II, king of Chalcis and inland Syria. Great-grandson of Herod the Great, he was an observant Jew and was respected alike by the Romans and the Jewish population.

Cestius Gallus, governor of Syria, led the first attempt to crush the rebellion. He succeeded in entering Jerusalem but the onset of winter meant that his supply lines were weak and he called off the offensive. Jewish rebels ambushed his troops on the homeward journey at Beth Horon, just north of Jerusalem. Their apparently easy victory swept even the peace

party in Jerusalem into a mood of euphoria. The Sanhedrin appointed military commanders to resist the Romans in different districts of the country. Among these was Flavius Josephus, who, according to his own (later) account, was one of the moderates who wished to find an accommodation with the Romans.

The arrival of Vespasian
In spring AD 67 the emperor Nero despatched a middle-aged general called Flavius Vespasianus (Vespasian) to deal with this potentially dangerous threat on the eastern frontier of the empire. Vespasian marched south from Syria, while his eldest son, Titus, came up from Egypt. Together their forces totalled some 60,000 men. Galilee put up little more than a token struggle, except for the heroic resistance of the city of Gamla, in Gaulanitis. By spring of the following year Vespasian was installing his troops around Jerusalem, cutting off the city.

Various Jewish extremist groups in Jerusalem were engaged in vicious internal struggles. Foremost among them were the Zealots, led by John of Giscala and the *Sicarii*, under a Messianic figure called Simon bar Giora. The *Sicarii* were so named for their savage habit of knifing anyone suspected of being a Roman collaborator. These two groups had taken all the strongholds in Jerusalem from the Romans, including the Antonia, the Citadel and Herod's palace, the centre of Roman administration. They had also burned the city's store of grain, stockpiled to withstand siege.

Titus alone
By the middle of AD 69 Nero was dead and Vespasian had been proclaimed emperor. Returning to Rome, with most of Judaea already pacified, he left Titus in charge of the final phase of operations. Titus took up his position with one legion on Mt Scopus, northeast of Jerusalem, preparatory to laying siege to the city. Another legion, the 10th Fretensis, was encamped on the nearby Mt of Olives, while yet another lay to the west. Due to its topography, Jerusalem was only vulnerable from the north, and it was from this direction that Titus launched his attack, concentrating both on the Temple Mount and the Upper City. Famine now gripped the beleaguered capital, but even while the struggle against the

Romans continued, the factional conflicts increased within the walls.

Titus built a huge siege wall around Jerusalem, 8 miles (5 km) long, completely isolating it. A ramp was raised against the north side of the Antonia fortress and enormous battering rams were manoeuvred into place for the attack. Not without difficulty, the Romans succeeded in taking the fortress and then razed it to the ground, in order to extend the ramp on to the Temple Mount itself. After hard hand-to-hand fighting the Temple was taken and set ablaze. Josephus reports that Titus wept to see the destruction. Perhaps; but he also ordered that pagan sacrifice be offered in the midst of its ruins. The legionaries ran riot through the old part of Jerusalem, the City of David, south of the Temple Mount, while preparations were being made to take the Upper City.

Even though the Romans met no further opposition when they did enter the Upper City three weeks later, they engaged in wholesale slaughter, rape and looting. Archaeologists have recently found the bones of people who had taken refuge in water tunnels beneath the streets and had been sealed up there by the Romans. Everywhere in the Herodian Quarter there are traces of intense burning. The House of Katros (p. 132) is also called the Burnt House. In its fire-darkened remains the excavators uncovered a skeletal arm, severed at the elbow – no other bones were found. Few other discoveries could evoke so poignantly the fall of Jerusalem.

Prisoners were either executed or sold off as slaves. Leaders of the Revolt, including John and Simon, were taken back to Rome to be exhibited in Titus' Triumph in AD 71, along with treasures from the Temple, as seen in his arch at the entrance to the Roman Forum.

The aftermath

Once Jerusalem had been captured, other surviving strongholds, including Herodium and Machaerus, soon followed. But Masada, which had been the first Roman garrison to be captured by the Zealots in AD 66, was the last to fall. Zealot soldiers, with their families, managed to hold out under the command of Eliezer ben Yair until the spring of AD 73. The new Roman governor of Judaea, Flavius Silva, commanding the 10th Legion Fretensis, laid siege to it. Establishing his headquarters to the west of Masada, he used Jewish captives and slaves to build a wall all around the rock. The people inside were thus trapped, but it was still no easy matter to capture the fortress.

Silva then constructed a massive siege ramp, nearly 260 ft (80 m) high, up to the defences Herod had constructed around the top of the rock. The Roman legions built a wooden platform and siege tower at the top of the ramp and drew up their fearsome catapults and battering rams. Despite all the defenders could do to prevent it, the Romans took Masada. But when the legionaries marched through the ruined wall the morning after they had breached it, all they found was silence and brightly burning fires.

During the night the Zealots had set the buildings ablaze and then, entering into a suicide pact, had put their families to the sword rather than allow them to fall into the hands of the Romans. After killing their families, the men had drawn lots and ten men were chosen to kill all the others as they lay beside their wives and children. Lots were drawn again and one man killed the other nine and then fell on his own sword. Only two women and a few children escaped death by hiding in caves, and they told the Romans of the dreadful final hours of the fortress of Masada.

The Second Jewish Revolt

Amazingly, only some 60 years after the destruction of the Temple and the tragic fall of Masada the Jews renewed their rebellion against Rome. The Second Jewish Revolt, AD 132–35, was led by Simon bar Kochba, supported by Rabbi Akiva, who was the foremost Jewish spiritual leader of the day. This time the Roman emperor was Hadrian and the revolt was more like guerrilla warfare than a centrally organized insurrection.

The lot of Ben Yair, the Zealot commander of Masada. It is one of eleven lots found at the point where several paths meet on the rock and is a moving reminder of the suicide of the defenders, as recounted by Josephus.

The Roman Senate granted a Triumph – a parade through Rome with the spoils of war – to victorious generals on their return home. A Triumphal Arch of wood and stucco was erected for the day itself, which later was replaced by one of marble and bronze. Only the recipient of the honour could pass through the arch.

Built in AD 81 the Arch of Titus was originally crowned with a chariot and four horses of bronze. One of the panels carved in relief on the inside of the Arch depicts the treasure captured from the Temple in Jerusalem being paraded through the streets of Rome. The seven-branched ritual candlestick (menorah) is clearly visible.

When Rabbi Akiva beheld Bar Kosiba he exclaimed: 'This is the king Messiah!', Rabbi Yohanan ben Torta retorted: 'Akiva, grass will grow in your jawbones and he will still not have come!'
Midrash Rabbah on
Lamentations

There was no equivalent of Josephus to provide us with an overall chronicle of the events of the Second Revolt, and so far less in known about it. The sources we do have are fragmentary and most are not contemporaneous with events. Perhaps the most reliable is Dio Cassius, writing in the 3rd century AD. According to him, the revolt was a reaction to Hadrian's refounding of Jerusalem as a Roman city, named Aelia Capitolina (pp. 162–63), which Jews were forbidden to enter. Hadrian probably also built a temple to Jupiter on the site of the ruined Temple, thus arousing Jewish hostility. This might indeed have been sufficient reason for the revolt, but other sources report that Aelia Capitolina was the result of the revolt, rather than the cause. Hadrian did prohibit circumcision throughout the Empire on pain of death, and this may have been the spark that ignited the war.

Over half a million Jews perished in the fighting, according to Dio Cassius. The Roman troops also suffered very badly, so that, at the end of the war, Hadrian was unable to send the customary message to the Senate: *mihi et legionibus bene* ('all is well with me and the legions').

Son of a Star or Son of a Liar?

The rabbinic sources do, of course, have a lot to say about the revolt, and especially about its leader, Bar Kochba. Much of the information about him, however, is legendary and not always to his credit. For instance, he is reported to have killed an old man when in a rage and it was also said that he cut off a finger from each

of his soldiers to test their bravery. Even his real name is not known for certain. Sometimes he is called Bar Kochba, which means 'Son of a Star', a name with clearly Messianic overtones. Other writers call him Bar Kosiba, which could be translated as 'Son of a Liar' (as in the line below).

אי שמעון ב{נ}וסיבה קי

The caves in the Judaean Desert

In the late 1950s, in the wake of the spectacular discoveries at Qumran (pp. 122–25), archaeologists began looking for other sites in the Judaean Desert, including the wadis to the south of that site. Different teams led by Yigael Yadin and Yohanan Aharoni made important discoveries in Nahal Hever, where two Roman camps had been built on the clifftops above cave openings on each side of the gorge. Some years previously Aharoni had investigated one of these caves and he returned to it in 1961. Because of the large number of human bones found in it, the cave had been called 'The Cave of Horrors'. Looting had left the remains in complete disorder, but they were sorted and found to belong to over 40 men, women and children. It is fairly certain that these are the bones of people who had taken refuge in the cave and were prevented from escaping because of the Romans keeping guard on the clifftop above. They had died of starvation in preference to surrendering to the Romans.

Among the heaps of bones many interesting finds were discovered, including domestic equipment made of pottery, metal and glass. Most exciting were objects of organic material, including ropes, woven baskets and wooden equipment. Such finds are very rare, but because the Judaean Desert is hot and arid they were in an excellent state of preservation, just like the Dead Sea Scrolls. In fact, pieces of parchment and papyri were also found in this cave, mostly tiny fragments of Old Testament texts in either Hebrew or Greek.

The Cave of Letters

Another cave in the cliffs opposite the Cave of Horrors was investigated by Yigael Yadin's team. So much textual material was found in it that it has become known as 'The Cave of Letters'. In this large cave, with successive chambers linked together by narrow passageways, at least 17 people had starved to death rather than be taken by the Romans, watching and waiting above, like cats at a mousehole.

A bronze statue of the Emperor Hadrian. He is depicted wearing a military cloak and a cuirass, or breastplate, on which three pairs of warriors are shown fighting. The statue was found in fragments near Beth Shean and is now one of the most important objects in the Israel Museum.

The largest number of documents found together was the personal archive of a woman called Babata. A total of 35 papyri were neatly wrapped and tied in bundles, all dealing with her various law suits. In a crevice in the rock of the innermost recesses of the cave the archaeologists found a waterskin containing a collection of personal items, clearly belonging to a woman. Among the jewelry, the cosmetic items (including a mirror) and several balls of purple wool for a man's ritual prayer shawl (or *talit*), were 15 carefully folded documents, tied into a single package. This bundle turned out to be the most important collection of documents of this period. They were all letters, written by different scribes, at the dictation of Bar Kochba himself to the leaders of the revolt in the oasis town of Ein Gedi, a little to the north on the shore of the Dead Sea.

The letters are in a mixture of Hebrew, Aramaic and Greek. It is the Greek letters which, because that script is written with vowels, give us a clear indication that Bar Kochba's name was in fact pronounced Bar Kosiba. Another group of six letters bundled up together had been written at Ein Gedi and concern the administration of land there. They are especially illuminating because they are dated in the first, second and third years of 'Simeon

Bar Kosiba, Prince of Israel'. The rebel leader, considered a criminal by the Romans, was obviously accepted by his followers as the legitimate ruler of an independent state in Judaea. His title may also imply that he had Messianic status.

The siege of Bethar

As with the First Jewish Revolt, the Second had little chance of success. The country was firmly held and administered by the Romans. A recently discovered inscription implies that the Roman military presence was doubled sometime before the revolt. Kochba and his soldiers made their last stand at Bethar, about 8 miles (11 km) southwest of Jerusalem.

The citadel of Bethar lies on top of a steep hill, isolated by ravines on all sides except the south and defended by a wall with a semicircular tower. No matter how hard the rebels fought, however, they were no match for the Romans. The besiegers built a wall (*circumvallatio*) around Bethar, much like earlier ones at Jerusalem and Masada. Fighting must have been fierce, and here too death was preferred to surrender. It is known that Bar Kochba died in this final struggle. Not for another 2,000 years would the Jews again have serious aspirations to be an independent people in this land.

A view of Nahal Hever, where the Jewish rebels hid in caves from the Romans during the Second Revolt.

THE DEVELOPMENT OF JUDAISM

A wall painting from the 3rd-century AD synagogue at Dura-Europos in Syria. It illustrates the return of the Ark of the Covenant to the Israelites after its power had destroyed the statue of Dagon in his own temple at Ashdod (1 Samuel 5). The Israelites are shown wearing Roman dress.

BY THE TIME OF THE destruction of the Temple in AD 70 there were Jewish communities as far afield as Italy in the west and India in the east. As Paul had discovered on his travels, there were also many in the eastern Mediterranean. In the 2nd century AD Jews migrated even further, and had settled in most coastal regions of the western Mediterranean, such as Spain and North Africa. Jewish catacombs in Rome contain inscriptions that are evidence of a vigorous community of at least 11 separate congregations.

Judaism in the 2nd century AD was in one of its rare proselytising phases, and was vying with Christianity for converts. The natural focus of all Jewish communities everywhere was the synagogue. One famous example is that at Dura-Europos on the Euphrates, now in Syria, dating to the 3rd century AD, where extensive frescoes were found.

Rabbinic Judaism

Rabbinic Judaism developed from the work and teachings of the Pharisees (pp. 146–47). It was their belief that the religious law comprised not simply the written Torah (as the Sadducees did), but also the oral law – a body of interpretations and rulings on the Torah, handed down by teachers and sages stretching as far back as Ezra (pp. 106–07). Later rabbinic Judaism maintained that the oral law was given

to Moses on Mt Sinai and then 'forgotten' by divine decree. Rabbis in each generation have to assist in the task of rediscovering that law and applying it to their own day.

Problems of integration

Perhaps surprisingly, the destruction of the Temple can be seen as a healthy development for the survival of Judaism. No longer linked to the annual cycle of pilgrimage and rituals in the distant city of Jerusalem, Jews were now free to perform the observances of their religion wherever they lived. Synagogue services or prayer meetings in private houses might be led by any competent man. There is still debate over the status of rabbis within diaspora communities before the 3rd century AD or even later. Rabbis did eventually become the spiritual leaders of their congregations, responsible for interpreting the law and guiding their flock in all religious and community matters.

Inevitably rabbis also came to be the representatives of their people to the non-Jewish world. The absolute monotheism of Judaism, strict observance of the Sabbath and careful dietary laws prevented Jews from integrating comfortably into the Christian and pagan cultures among which they lived. Tension between communities increased and in some places there was virulent anti-Semitism. The Jews themselves were often intolerant of other religions and felt restless in the wake of the destruction of the Temple, conditions which frequently led to trouble. For instance, as early as AD 115, in the reign of Trajan, rebellions of Jews in Egypt, Cyrenaica (on the coast of modern Libya) and Cyprus, led to bloody massacres which effectively wiped out entire Jewish communities. On the whole, however, over the next centuries Judaism was able to renew itself and to flourish as never before.

The Academy at Yavneh (Jamnia)

An outstanding rabbi called Yochanan ben Zakkai initiated changes in Jewish observances necessary for the survival of the religion. Tradition has it that he escaped from Jerusalem during the siege of AD 70 and fled to Yavneh, a small town not far from Jaffa on the coastal plain. There he attracted a number of other learned men and together they began to redefine the practice of Judaism. Forms of service were instituted for use in the home or synagogue which were intended to replace those of the Temple (for instance the *seder* service in the home at Passover) and the Old Testament canon was finally fixed.

Each community of Jews was effectively autonomous, whether in Judaea or elsewhere. Indeed, it is doubtful if the Greek-speaking groups of the diaspora could communicate easily with their co-religionists in Judaea who spoke Aramaic and Hebrew. The authority of Rabbi Yochanan's successor, Gamaliel II, seems to have been widely accepted. He belonged to an illustrious rabbinic family and was regarded as the official leader (or Ethnarch) of the Jewish people by the Romans.

Following the Second Revolt, the centre of Jewish life moved from the ruined areas of Judaea northwards into the Galilee region, where it remained for the next 800 years. One of the most outstanding figures in Judaism belongs to this period. Judah HaNasi (a word meaning 'prince' or 'patriarch') lived in the late 1st to early 2nd centuries AD in Sepphoris. His name is associated with the great work of law codification, the Mishnah, which literally means the 'repetition' of the law, and was the development of the principles underlying the Torah. In later ages, Tiberias on the western shore of the Sea of Galilee became the centre of Jewish learning in Palestine. There, rabbis continued the further refinement of the Mishnah. The work that was to emerge from these centuries is the Talmud, which still forms the basis for the practice of Judaism today. Along with purely legal material, the Talmud contains a great deal else besides. Discussions which led to a particular ruling are often given, and dissident opinions recorded. Popular material such as parables, legends and folklore also have a place.

Babylonian Jewry

Study of the Mishnah was also taking place in the *yeshivot* (academies) of Babylon, where there had been a large and flourishing Jewish community since the days of the First Exile (pp. 100–03). These were Jews who spoke Aramaic and Hebrew and were in frequent contact with the rabbis of Palestine. Indeed, in the aftermath of the disastrous Bar Kochba revolt, many rabbis left Palestine for Babylon. In these *yeshivot* a form of the Talmud evolved which is considered more authoritative than the Palestinian version. Palestinian Jewry went into a slow decline after the Bar Kochba revolt and in the centuries of Christian rule.

Conversely, the Babylonian community had grown stronger and was deemed to have greater standing than that in the homeland.

Later history

By the Middle Ages the aspiration of Jewish people everywhere was to return to Zion. This was a spiritual concept rather than a practical ambition and was bound up with the idea of a Messianic kingdom which would release them from the tyranny of foreigners. Jews drew strength from their close community life. In Europe this was enforced by the ghettoes. Elsewhere, under Islamic rule, life was not always so hard.

The Golden Age of Spain (approximately between AD 900 and 1200) was a time when Jews achieved the highest positions in the land, became international merchants and could take up any profession they chose. Another important Jewish figure lived at this time: Moses Maimonides, who was a physician and scholar. In other Moslem lands, as *dhimmi*, the name given to non-Moslems under Islamic rule, Jewish life was strictly regulated but rarely intolerable.

The Age of Enlightenment came late to Jewry. It first took hold among communities in eastern Europe in the 18th century. This was the Jewish Renaissance movement, which led to greater secularization and participation in the general culture of Europe. Only in the late 19th century did the dream of returning to Palestine to recreate their own independent state begin to take shape.

Jonah beneath the gourd (above), which grew in the space of one night to shelter him and withered the next (Jonah 4). The entire drawing is made up of the words of the narrative in this 13th-century AD Hebrew manuscript.

The graceful Moorish arches of the Ibn Shoshan synagogue (left), now known as Sta Maria la Blanca in Toledo, Spain. Originally founded in 1203, it was rebuilt after a fire in 1250 and in later centuries was put to a variety of uses.

AELIA CAPITOLINA: HADRIAN'S JERUSALEM

At Jerusalem [Hadrian] founded a new city in place of the one that had been razed to the ground, naming it Aelia Capitolina...
Dio Cassius, *Roman History*, LXIX 12

WHETHER THE CAUSE or result of the Second Jewish Revolt, Hadrian's new city was built on the ruins of Jerusalem. It was called Aelia Capitolina as a compliment to the emperor, whose family name was Aelius, and in honour of Capitoline Jupiter, whose new shrine rose on the Temple Mount. Jews were forbidden to enter the city except on one day a year, the 9th Av, the traditional date of the destruction of both the First and Second Temples. Even the name of Judaea vanished and the province was combined with Syria to create the new entity of Syria-Palestina.

In recent decades archaeological work in and around the Old Town of Jerusalem has revealed many remains of Aelia Capitolina. It is now known, for instance, that the southwestern part of the city (beyond the Citadel area, where at least one of Herod's three great towers was still standing), was the military camp of the 10th Legion Fretensis. This legion was quartered in Jerusalem from the time of Titus' siege until the 3rd century AD. Remains of the civilian area of the city, in the northern sector of the city, are best preserved in the Christian Quarter of today, where the grid pattern characteristic of Roman towns has been partly preserved. Some of the original huge paving slabs are still in position here, as in other parts of Aelia.

The Madaba map

A bird's-eye-view of Hadrian's new city is preserved in the mosaic floor of a 6th-century church at Madaba in Jordan. The most important entrance to Aelia, on the north, now lies beneath the Damascus Gate, which in its present form dates to the Ottoman period. Originally, the Roman gate took the shape of a three-arched triumphal gateway. Since no fortification walls have yet been certainly identified around Aelia, it may well have been a monumental and symbolic entrance, rather than a gate through the city's defences. Remains of this Hadrianic gate were once thought to date to the reign of Agrippa I, because many typical Herodian blocks were reused in its construction. Inside the gate was a piazza, paved with enormous stones which were grooved to prevent horses slipping. A tall column is visible in the middle of the paved area in the Madaba map, which may have been surmounted by a statue of Hadrian. To their surprise, the excavators found no trace of this column, which would have been the first thing visitors to the city would have seen.

Cardo and Decumanus

Two main roads led from the piazza. The western one is the *Cardo*, the most important road in any Roman town. Unusually for Roman cities, Aelia also had a secondary *Cardo*, sloping gently to the southeast and running diagonally away from the main one. The reason for this is immediately apparent to the visitor. Jerusalem's topography of hills and valleys made it necessary to have a main route leading to the Temple Mount, by now the site of the temple to Capitoline Jupiter. Beyond the Temple Mount this second route may have continued down the Central valley, which divided the Temple Mount from the Upper Town on what is now called Mt Zion. In Roman times this would have been part of the military camp.

The main *Cardo* ran through the town directly to the military camp. A covered colonnade lined both sides of the road, so that pedestrians could stroll and shop, protected from the summer heat and the winter rain. Some of the columns of this colonnade have been found reused in the present *soukh* (market) which is built over the line of the Roman *Cardo*.

Crossing the *Cardo* at right angles was the *Decumanus*, as in all Roman towns. In Aelia the *Decumanus* divided the civilian and military sectors of the city. David Street and the Street of the Chain today follow the route of the *Decumanus* eastwards from the Citadel towards the Temple Mount. This may well have been the line of the north wall of Herod's city (the First Wall mentioned by Josephus), although no evidence for it has been found.

The two civic centres

The centre of any Roman town, physically and culturally, was its forum. In Aelia this great open space lay to the south of the two most important public buildings, the Temple of

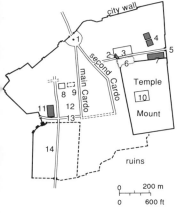

Plan of Hadrian's city, Aelia Capitolina, which he built in the 2nd century AD to replace Jerusalem. The line of the main Cardo runs from the principal gate in the north wall (1), past the Temple of Venus (8) and the basilica (9), where public business was conducted, and ends just south of the city's main forum (12) at the Decumanus (13), which marked the northern boundary of the Roman military camp (14). The city had a second forum (3) north of the site of the old Antonia fortress (6). A road led past here to the eastern gate of the city (5). The Temple of Jupiter (10) had probably been built over the site of the Jewish temple, destroyed by Titus. Various pools (2, 4, 7, 11) supplied the city with water.

Detail of Jerusalem from the magnificent mosaic floor in a church at Madaba, Jordan, which depicts the Holy Land. The main northern gate (1 on the map opposite) is shown at the extreme left, since in accordance with the convention of the day, the map is oriented with the east at the top. The gate gives access to a piazza with a tall column at its centre (reconstructed below; the left-hand tower still stands to its full height). From the piazza the Cardo bisects the city, with a portico on either side. Another road led to the old Temple Mount. The Church of the Holy Sepulchre, with its rotunda, is conspicuous, though not all the buildings are so easy to identify.

Venus and the basilica, which was the municipal law court and town hall. The colonnade around the forum sheltered shops, some remains of which have been found. On the east the forum is bounded by the *Cardo*, and on the south by the *Decumanus*, beyond which lay the military camp.

East of the main forum lay a second one, at the northwest corner of the Temple Mount, to the north of the site of the old Antonia fortress, destroyed by Titus when he took the city. It, too, was paved with massive blocks and this pavement has become known as the *lithostraton* – traditionally believed to be the courtyard of the Antonia where Jesus was tried and scourged. The paved area was supported on enormous arches built over the Struthion pool, one of the reservoirs which supplied the Temple Mount.

In this forum stood another triple-arched triumphal gateway, which, like that on the northern side of the town, formed one of the monumental entrances to Aelia, this time to the east. Spanning the 'Via Dolorosa', the central arch of this gateway is known as the 'Ecce Homo' arch. Beside the road, in the Convent of the Sisters of Zion, the northern side of this arch is also still visible.

The pools of Bethesda

East of the second forum, just beyond the triumphal arch and thus outside the town proper, were the pools of Bethesda, where, over a century before the building of Aelia, Jesus had healed the cripple (John 5, 2–9). At this spot the Romans built a temple to Aesculapius, god of medicine, and a healing sanctuary. Remains of this temple lie at the centre of the pools, partially under a Byzantine church dedicated to St Mary. Today the lovely Crusader church of St Anne stands nearby (p. 177).

THE BYZANTINE ERA

In hoc signo vinces
By this sign you shall conquer
Vision of Constantine, before the Milvian Bridge

IN AD 312 AN EVENT OCCURRED that would change the course of world history. Constantine (AD 306–37), the ruler of the western Roman Empire, triumphed over his rival, Maxentius, who governed Italy and the Mediterranean lands. Constantine's victory at the Milvian Bridge, just outside the gates of Rome itself, ushered in the Christian era, for Constantine was greatly influenced by Christian beliefs.

In common with many Christians of his day he was not baptized until a few weeks before his death, believing that thereby he lessened the likelihood of falling into sin again. But throughout his reign he promoted Christian interests and did his best to undo the results of earlier persecutions. His motives were not purely spiritual, however; his interest in the new faith was partly political. At that time Christianity was fast becoming the most popular religion of the Roman Empire, and was therefore the ideal institution through which the emperor could unite all the different peoples under his rule. In AD 325 Constantine convened the first great ecumenical gathering of bishops at the Council of Nicaea (modern Iznik in Turkey) to discuss matters of theology. It was here that the Nicene Creed was instituted as the basic article of Christian faith.

From Byzantium to Constantinople

Even before the end of the Council it seems that Constantine had reached the decision to transform the ancient township of Byzantium (hence the name 'Byzantine') overlooking the Bosphorus on the extreme southerly point of Europe, into a new capital to be named Constantinople in his honour. In AD 326 he left Rome for ever and took up residence in the swiftly rising city, which straddled Europe and Asia. It was destined to become the centre of eastern Christianity for over a thousand years.

Christians and Jews in Palestine

The Holy Land as a concept in the minds of Christians everywhere arose in the reign of Constantine. The later 4th century AD saw the beginning of the great age of pilgrimage to shrines and holy places throughout the Levant and especially to Palestine and Jerusalem, the scenes of Jesus' life, death and resurrection .

Under Byzantine Christian rule Jews were not allowed to return to live in their holy city, which was still officially called Aelia. Because of the venomously anti-Jewish bias of much Christian writing of the era, it has long been assumed that the Jewish community, in Palestine as elsewhere, suffered considerable hardship during this time. Yet, as archaeologists have recently pointed out, it was in the 4th century AD, precisely when Christianity rose to prominence, that some of the most magnificent synagogues were built by the Jews of Palestine. Research on the Golan Heights, east of the Sea of Galilee, has also unearthed evidence of Christian and Jewish communities living peaceably side by side in the same villages.

Byzantine Jerusalem

During the great days of pilgrimage to the Holy Land Jerusalem was transformed from a dusty provincial town into one of the most magnificent cities of the age. But it was a Christian, rather than a Jewish city. One emperor, however, did try to restore the Jews to their ancient

A colossal head of Constantine, said to weigh over 9 tons. It was part of a statue which was seven times life size and is estimated to have been over 50 ft (15 m) high. It may have been made of wood, with marble and bronze additions, and richly decorated.

capital in the mid-4th century AD. Julian the Apostate (AD 361–63), a confirmed pagan, gave permission to the Jews to rebuild their Temple in Jerusalem, probably more from hatred of Christians than from love of Jews. In fact the plan came to nothing as the emperor was killed in battle in AD 363. Legend has it that he died with the words '*vicisti Galilaee*' ('you have won, Galilean') on his lips.

In the next century the Empress Eudocia, wife of Theodosius II (AD 408–50), went to live in Jerusalem. A pious woman, she had started life as a pagan Greek girl called Athenais whom the emperor married for her beauty and intelligence. Out of favour at court, she arrived in Jerusalem in AD 443 and lived there until her death in AD 460. During that time she rebuilt the walls of the city to enclose both the ancient City of David and Mt Zion, and established hospitals, hostels, monasteries and churches. She also allowed Jews much greater freedom to visit the city on religious festivals, but this privilege did not outlast her death. She was buried in the Church of St Stephen, which she had founded, just beyond the north gate of the city.

It was in the reign of Justinian (AD 527–65) and his strong-minded wife Theodora that Byzantine Jerusalem reached its zenith. Reputedly, in AD 524 the emperor returned the *menorah*, removed from the debris of the Temple and taken by Titus to Rome, as depicted on his victory arch (p. 157). Justinian was an active builder throughout his empire, and Procopius, his biographer, gives details of the projects undertaken during his reign in Jerusalem.

Justinian's major new construction was the magnificent Nea Church, dedicated to Mary, the Mother of God, built at the extreme southern edge of the city. Hadrian's *Cardo* was extended to reach it, over the old camp of the Roman garrison and it is easy to imagine the pomp and majesty of the religious processions that must have travelled between the Church of the Holy Sepulchre in the north and the Nea Church in the south.

The arrival of Islam

Unfortunately the splendours of the great churches of Jerusalem, as depicted in the 6th-century AD Madaba map mosaic (p. 163), did not survive for very long. In AD 614 most of the churches of Jerusalem, including the Church of the Holy Sepulchre, were burned down by the Persians who occupied the city until AD 630. A few years later the city was again invaded, this

The Golden Gate on the east side of the Temple Mount, may date to the triumphal return to Jerusalem of the Byzantine emperor, Heraclius, near the end of the short Persian occupation, in AD 629. It was probably closed in the early Arab period and remains officially sealed to this day. Legend has it that this is the gate through which the Messiah will ride into Jerusalem.

time by the Arabs, sweeping out of Arabia, and bringing the religion of Islam with them. Because Jerusalem surrendered peacefully to the newcomers it was not destroyed, but slowly, over the next centuries it became a Moslem, rather than a Christian city, and its Byzantine magnificence was all but forgotten.

A restored section of the main Cardo of Jerusalem. The opposite side was also colonnaded and some parts were lined with shops. This is the street which is shown on the Madaba map (p. 163).

BETH SHEAN, BYZANTINE CITY

A roundel from a mosaic floor of the 6th century AD in Beth Shean depicts Tyche, the goddess of Fortune, holding her horn of plenty and wearing a crenellated headdress which probably represents the city walls. Tyche was often adopted by cities as their patron goddess, in the hope that she would protect them from enemies and shower wealth and blessings upon them.

BETH SHEAN LIES AT the southern end of the Jezreel Valley, just west of a ford across the River Jordan, on the most important west–east route through northern Palestine. This location and the fertile surrounding landscape, fed by several springs and watercourses, explain the huge size of the tell which was inhabited from the Late Neolithic period onward. On the top of the tell one of the latest buildings is a round Byzantine church; by that time the Roman–Byzantine city at its foot was the largest in Palestine.

The city was still called Nysa-Scythopolis – a purely pagan name, given to it at its foundation as a Hellenistic town in the reign of Antiochus IV (175–164 BC). No one knows for certain why the Scythians are commemorated in the name, but Nysa was a Greek nymph, the nurse of Dionysus; he seems to have held a special place in the affections of the pagan population of the city. Internationally famous as a textile centre, one of its chief products was linen. The flax was grown locally, the abundant local

water supplies facilitating the manufacturing process. Jewish and Christian communities seem to have co-existed peaceably in and around the city.

The city plan

Two grand colonnaded avenues, lined with shops, converge from the southwest and the east on a piazza just below the southern slopes of the tell. Yet another street leads into the piazza from the west and where the three roads meet excavations have revealed the remains of an imposing temple approached by a flight of monumental steps. The temple may have been dedicated either to Dionysus, god of wine, or to Tyche, goddess of fortune – both these deities seem to have been in some sense patrons of the city. East of the temple stood several other impressive public buildings and monuments, among them a decorative fountain (a *nymphaeum*) and a basilica for conducting public business. In Roman times a long monumental pool lined with a columned *stoa* (a covered walkway) lay further along the road which ran east to the city gate. A statue of Dionysus was found not far away. It probably stood with others between the columns, their images reflected in the water. By the Byzantine period this pool had been filled in and shops were built over it. Some of the toppled columns of the *stoa* were found beneath their floors.

Halfway along the other colonnaded street leading towards the theatre, a semicircular piazza was discovered dating to the Byzantine period. In this area part of a mosaic floor was found representing the goddess Tyche. Nearby lay the main public baths complex, with its series of cold, warm and hot steam rooms. In typical Roman fashion, the columned courtyard outside the bath house was used as an exercise ground (*palaestra*) by the young men who frequented the place. Part of the bath complex was superseded by the shops which lined the west side of the porticoed street in Byzantine times. A dedicatory inscription found there proclaimed that the street was built and paid for by a 4th-century AD governor of the city named Palladius.

Due to the natural topography of the site the city could not be laid out in the formal grid pattern of Greek and Roman cities, although some attempt was made to keep to the classical plan.

East of Palladius Street is another, parallel one, which runs past the basilica in the direction of the theatre. On this road, just before the theatre, an ornamental gateway (called a *tetrapylon*) was built to span the crossing point with another major street. Some experts believe that this must mark the geographical centre of the city.

The destruction of the city

The city of Beth Shean was probably the most populous and flourishing in Palestine, not only in the Byzantine period but also well into the early Arab period. It was comprehensively destroyed by an earthquake which devastated much of the country on the morning of 18 January, AD 749. Thereafter, although some of the buildings were renewed, the city entered a period of decline and dwindled into little more than a squatter's camp. Eventually it was completely deserted and vegetation grew over the once populous streets. Until the 1980s only the paving stones of a small part of one street and a single column could be seen above the ground. Since then, teams of archaeologists have laboured to restore Beth Shean's civic centre to something of its former glory. They have succeeded so well that visitors now come from all over the world to marvel at its size and splendour.

An aerial view of the recently excavated site of Beth Shean. At the bottom right is the theatre, which seated more than 5,000 people and was originally built in the Roman period. The gymnasium complex, also Roman, is at the left, and between them is the great colonnaded road, Palladius Street, which leads in the direction of the ancient tell. One of the main temples of the city, dedicated to either Dionysus or Tyche, dominated the piazza at the far end of the street.

EARLY CHURCHES

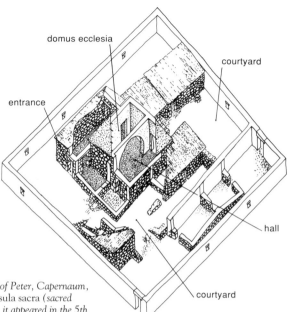

domus ecclesia

courtyard

entrance

hall

courtyard

The House of Peter, Capernaum, set in the insula sacra (sacred quarter), as it appeared in the 5th century AD, surrounded by a new enclosure wall. In the heart of it is the 'venerated hall' of the house of Simon Peter, where Jesus stayed when he was in Capernaum and in which he performed miracles (Mark 1, 29). In the later 1st century AD, it became a domus ecclesia (and marked as such here) for the many pilgrims who came to pray. By the 4th century substantial alterations had to be made to the now ancient fabric. This is the building visited and described by Egeria (p. 16) in the late 4th century AD. She wrote of it: 'The house of the prince of Apostles [Peter] has been changed into a church; the original walls are still standing.'

BEFORE THE BYZANTINE era small Christian and Judaeo-Christian communities in Palestine met for prayer in each others houses, as did many Jews. The house-church – *domus ecclesia* or 'house of assembly' – is exactly the same as the Hebrew *beth kenneset* or Greek *synagogue*. St Peter's House at Capernaum is the most famous example. Originally the word 'church' applied to the group of people, rather than the building. In fact, this is the way the term is used in the Gospels. Christians faced terrible repression in the first three centuries AD, being considered subversive by most of the Roman emperors. They kept a very low profile and suffered many hardships, including persecution and martyrdom. For this reason, even if they had funds, they did not build imposing churches which would only have attracted unwelcome attention.

From the time of the first Christian emperor Constantine, however, conditions changed greatly for Christians, and nowhere more than in the Holy Land itself. Constantine was strongly attracted to Christianity and in AD 326 sent his mother, Queen Helena, to the Holy Land to search for sites connected with the life of Jesus (p. 16). Churches were built at many places thus identified by the queen. After around AD 392 Christianity was adopted as the

official religion of the Byzantine Empire, and churches began to proliferate. In all, about 390 churches of the Byzantine period have been identified in Palestine and pilgrims still visit those established by Constantine and Helena, especially if associated with the birth and death of Jesus: the Church of the Nativity in Bethlehem (p. 140) and the Church of the Holy Sepulchre in Jerusalem (pp. 172–73).

The architecture of early churches

Both these churches are unusual because they combine two distinct types of church plan – circular and basilical. Circular or octagonal churches were often constructed over a particularly sacred site and are called memorial churches, though not all were built to commemorate a specific event. Also known as centred, or centric, churches, they are reminiscent of tombs of Roman emperors, such as that of Augustus in Rome or that belonging to Diocletian in Split (Croatia).

Churches were also built on the basilical plan, just as synagogues were. These large Roman public buildings, with an exterior court – a forum – were very suitable for Jewish or Christian worship, in which the congregation participated, unlike the pagan cults. Normally a Roman basilica had an entrance in one of the long walls, and at one or both of the ends there might be an apse containing a statue of the emperor or a deity. Christian architects adapted this design, usually placing the apse, now holding the altar, at the eastern end, in the direction of the rising sun – symbolic, perhaps, of the resurrection. On entering the church at the end opposite the altar, the eye of the worshipper was drawn along the length of the building to its focal point.

The chancel, or presbytery, as the area around the altar became known, was reserved for the priests, who thus held themselves separate from the people, as in the tradition of the priests of Israel. Sometimes the chancel was raised slightly, especially if relics of a saint or other sacred objects were contained in the crypt beneath. The chancel was often symbolically divided from the rest of the church by a low stone screen. In eastern churches this has now grown to the full height of the building and mass is celebrated behind it, out of sight of the congregation. Hung with icons and paintings of saints and martyrs, it is called the *iconostasis*.

At the western end of the church there was sometimes a vestibule. Called the narthex, this was where people as yet unbaptized would gather during the mass, which they were not allowed to attend. Within the church there might also be a baptistery, sometimes with a font for full immersion, as in Jewish *mikvehs*.

If the apse was 'inscribed', that is set within the walls of the church, it would have two small flanking rooms. Possibly robing rooms for the priests, they were certainly used in the preparation of the bread and wine for the mass. In the middle of the 5th century AD, these were abolished and three apses were built instead – a large central one with a smaller one on each side. Such churches are called triapsidal.

Externally most churches were architecturally restrained, sometimes even severe. No expense was spared in the lavish interiors, however, from the vestments of the priests to the magnificent floors of mosaic or *opus sectile* (large pieces of coloured stone laid in geometric patterns). Perhaps the crowning glory of Byzantine churches are the floor and wall mosaics, such as the Madaba Map mosaic (p.

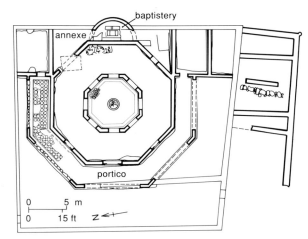

163). In Palestine itself mosaic work was generally somewhat provincial, but it reached its most glorious manifestation in the Byzantine churches of the 7th century AD in Ravenna, Italy, where the craft of mosaics had a continuous tradition back to the Roman era.

Between the end of the Byzantine age in the mid-7th century AD and the Crusader period, very few churches or synagogues were built in Palestine which was under Islamic rule at that time.

The House of Peter, Capernaum, in the later 5th century AD, when an octagonal church was built over the domus ecclesia. *An apse was later added on the east, with a baptismal font. This is a commemorative or ambulatory church.*

The Church of Lot, built in AD 606 and refurbished in May AD 691. We can be precise about the dates as they are written in the mosaic pavements found in the church. It was part of a Byzantine monastic complex around Lot's Cave, at Deir 'Ain 'Abata, near the southeastern end of the Dead Sea in Jordan. A classic basilical form, it has a nave and side aisles. Clerestory windows above the arches of the nave allow light into the interior.

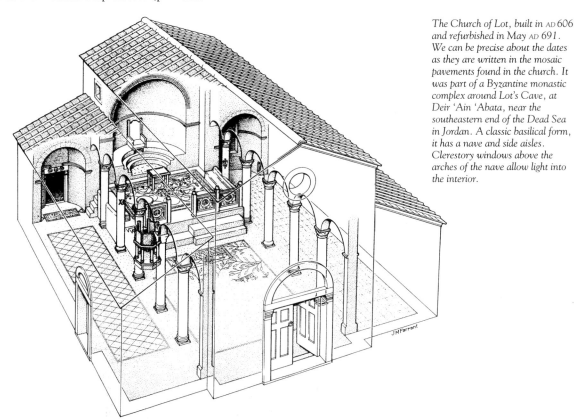

EARLY SYNAGOGUES

Mosaic floors in synagogues often contain details about the local communities. Nearly all had a panel with the name of the donors of the floor, or other parts of the synagogue, and the date of the gift. Some communities observed the prohibition on graven images more seriously than others. At Rehob, for instance, mosaic floors have geometric and vegetational motifs, along with long religious texts, while at nearby Beth Alpha a floor contains a scene of Abraham sacrificing Isaac and a panel (right) representing the front of a shrine, or perhaps the doors of the Temple, flanked by two menorahs – a standard motif repeated in panels in front of the apse or Torah shrine in many synagogues. Between the two panels is a wholly pagan circular zodiac with Helios, the sun god, at its centre. Such zodiacs are known elsewhere; the best preserved is at Hamat Tiberias beside the Sea of Galilee.

May the Lord bless those who come together to maintain synagogues for prayer.
Traditional synagogue prayer.

THE GREEK WORD SYNAGOGUE means 'place of assembly' and synagogues were not simply places for prayer, they were also houses of study (*bet hamidrash*), hostels for visitors and often repositories for the community's wealth. Since a synagogue complex often included a school for children, a ritual bath (*mikveh*) and accommodation for officials, it could cover a large area and in modern terms served many of the functions of a community centre. The Torah was certainly read and studied there, in emulation of Ezra, the first person to read the Law aloud to the people of Jerusalem in the days of their return from the Babylonian Exile.

Development of the synagogue

During the First and Second Temple periods social and civic gatherings took place in open public spaces near city gates – the equivalent of the Greek *agora* or the Roman forum. The destruction of the Second Temple in AD 70 (pp. 156–57) probably marks the point at which meetings for prayer, with reading and exposition of the Torah as their centrepiece, began to be a feature of Jewish life in Palestine.

The notion of a synagogue as a public building, as opposed to a community meeting in people's houses, may have been influenced both by the knowledge that such public buildings were common among Graeco-Roman peoples, and the fact that there were already synagogues in the communities of the Jewish diaspora. The earliest known synagogue building outside the Holy Land itself is on the island of Delos in the Aegean (1st century BC), and ancient authors, including Philo and Josephus, mention synagogues in other places in the 2nd and 1st centuries BC. The Gospels clearly show that in the 1st century AD there were synagogues at the heart of Jewish communities all around the eastern Mediterranean, and presumably there were some in Rome also.

In Palestine, specific buildings for public gatherings were first built by the Jews in the late 2nd or early 1st century BC. Currently the first true synagogues known in Palestine date to the 1st century BC: at Gamla and possibly Masada. The Zealots who held Masada against the Romans during the First Jewish Revolt certainly rebuilt a small structure facing north towards Jerusalem as a synagogue, but the character of its earlier phase is less sure. At Herodium Zealots created a synagogue from the *triclinium* or dining room of the royal villa.

Many prayer gatherings may have been held in people's homes, as was the practice among early Christians. This may be why there is a gap in the archaeological evidence for synagogues in Palestine for nearly 200 years. Between the 4th and 7th centuries AD, in contrast, there seems to have been a resurgence of Jewish wealth and confidence in Palestine, for synagogue buildings appeared everywhere, well constructed and beautifully ornamented. Many were paved with mosaics, in emulation of Roman architectural fashions. In the north of the country, where many Jews had fled from Roman reprisals in the wake of the Second Jewish Revolt, classic synagogues include Capernaum, Chorazin and Qazrin. Examples in the south can be found at Beth Guvrin, Ein Gedi, Jericho and Gaza. Jewish life seems to have flourished under Byzantine rule.

Synagogue architecture

Synagogues were not always built to a standard plan but did have one common feature: all the prayer halls were oriented on Jerusalem. In some the Ark for the Torah scrolls must have been portable, for there is no sign of a permanent emplacement. Masada is an example of an early synagogue where the attention of the congregation was focused on the centre of the room, an indication, perhaps, that it was used for secular as well as religious activities. Later, a fixed and usually ornate shrine was set on a platform or in an elaborately decorated niche in the wall nearest Jerusalem – thus south in Galilean synagogues, north at Eshtemoa in the Hebron hills, roughly east at Gaza, and so on. The congregation prayed facing the niche, and therefore Jerusalem.

One common synagogue plan was based on the standard Roman basilical form. Two or four rows of columns divided the internal space into a nave and side aisles. Above the nave, lines of clerestory windows provided light for the interior. Beth Shean and Gaza are good examples of this type, with apses towards Jerusalem. If no Jewish symbols, such as the *menorah* or emplacement for the Torah shrine, are present

in these synagogues, there is little to distinguish them from churches.

Typical Galilean synagogues have a different plan. Capernaum is the most elaborate example, with an intricately decorated monumental triple entrance in the south wall. Once the congregants had entered, they turned towards the doors to pray, facing Jerusalem. There is rarely a fixed Torah shrine in these synagogues, but at Capernaum low platforms (possibly for a portable Torah shrine) flank the main entrance and two walls were lined with tiers of stone benches, as at Masada. Some synagogues may have had a central platform for the officiants.

A third synagogue plan is known as a 'broadhouse'. There are examples at Eshtemoa and Khirbet Shema in the southern hills. On passing through a door in a short wall of the building, the worshipper turned at a right-angle to face the Torah shrine in one of the long walls.

It was once thought that the Galilean was the earliest type of synagogue plan, followed by the broadhouse and the basilical. However, research indicates that synagogue design, like synagogue decoration, depended on the preferences of the individual community.

The white limestone synagogue at Capernaum, 4th to 5th centuries AD. Here it has two storeys, having an upper gallery probably for use by women, as was usual later. However, this is disputed and it may have been a basilical structure, like the Church of Lot (p. 169). Traces of an earlier building have been found beneath it, dating to the 1st century AD. This may be the synagogue built by the Roman centurion (Luke 7, 5), where Jesus preached and healed the sick (Mark 1, 29).

Four architectural patterns for early synagogues in Palestine (left to right): Masada, phase 2, dating to the later 1st century AD, when the building was unquestionably used as a synagogue; Capernaum, a Galilean synagogue of the 4th to 5th centuries AD; Eshtemoa, a broadhouse synagogue with a large prayer hall, possibly 4th to 5th centuries AD; and Beth Alpha, a basilical synagogue of the 6th century AD. (Not to scale.)

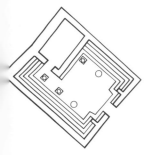

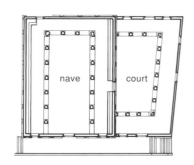

nave

court

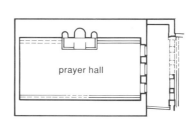

prayer hall

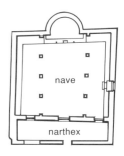

nave

narthex

THE CHURCH OF THE HOLY SEPULCHRE

In the first place she [Queen Helena] founded a church where the life-giving Wood of the all-venerable Cross was found and called it 'Saint Constantine' after her son's name. Similarly she erected holy sanctuaries also at the holy Tomb of the holy Resurrection of our Christ and God and at the Place of a Skull.

from an anonymous *Life of Constantine*

A reconstruction of the Church of the Holy Sepulchre as it might have appeared in the late 4th century AD. The entrance on the old Cardo (left) led to a small, open court, or atrium, in front of the large basilical church, the Martyrium. Beyond the basilica was another open court, the 'Holy Garden', which lay before the Anastasis – the rotunda over the Aedicule containing the tomb of Jesus. At the southeastern corner of the Holy Garden was the rock of Golgotha, shown here enclosed under the smallest dome, though it is uncertain whether the rock was brought within the church in Byzantine times. The modern entrance to the church is now in this vicinity.

ONE OF THE CHURCHES central to the Christian faith is the Church of the Holy Sepulchre, today almost invisible among the buildings of the Old City of Jerusalem. In the opinion of many, though not all, scholars the site is accurately identified as the scene of the crucifixion and burial of Jesus. The church stands outside but close to the city walls of Jesus' day and the sanctity of the area was remembered for around three centuries by the Christians of the city, even though it lay beneath a Roman temple, the first monumental building on the site. On the north side of the forum of Hadrian's Aelia, was the great Temple dedicated either to Capitoline Jupiter or to Aphrodite, the goddess of love – the sources are not precise on this point. In the depths of the present church lie support walls and floors dating not just to the time of the pagan temple, but before that, to the reign of Herod the Great. There are even a few traces of still earlier remains, dating to the days of the First Temple.

In AD 326 the Emperor Constantine entrust-ed his mother, Queen Helena, with a mission to travel to the Holy Land and discover the holy places of the Old and New Testaments (p. 16). Often these were revealed to her in dreams and in this way, according to several semi-legendary accounts, on reaching Jerusalem the Queen discovered beneath Hadrian's temple the tomb of Jesus, the place of his crucifixion and the cross itself, with its nails. The nails and some slivers of the cross she sent to her son in Byzantium. She then set in train a thorough destruction of the Hadrianic shrine and began the erection of an immense sacred complex which would eventually include a great basilical church (the *Martyrium* or 'place of martyrdom'), the scene of the crucifixion (*Calvary* or *Golgotha*, meaning 'the place of the skull' in Latin and Aramaic respectively) and the tomb of Christ (the *Anastasis* or Resurrection). Originally the area had been a quarry where countless generations of Jerusalem's masons had cut their building stone and in which, by the Roman period, wealthy citizens of Jerusalem had their tombs carved in the rock. Within the Church of the Holy Sepulchre today there are still a few traces of niched tombs typical of the Second Temple period (pp. 148–49). Helena gave orders that one of these tombs was to be hewn free of the surrounding stone and enclosed in a shrine (the *Aedicule* or 'small house'). However, there is no

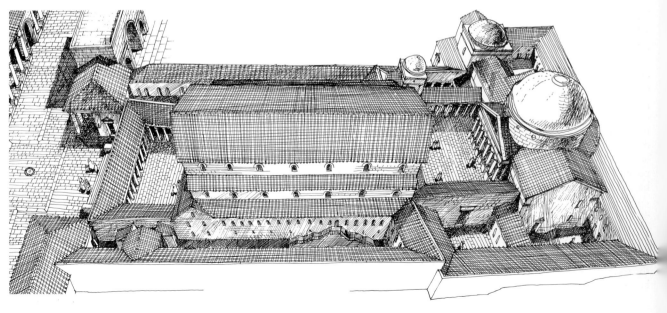

proof that this, rather than any other tomb in the area, was the resting place to which Joseph of Arimathea hurriedly took the body of Jesus at the approach of the Sabbath.

The Basilica of the Martyrium

Helena's entire complex was surrounded by a high precinct wall to guard its sanctity from the bustle of the city beyond. The pillars before the entrance were part of the *Cardo* itself, right at the heart of the city. A flight of steps and three doors in the precinct wall led into an irregular colonnaded atrium. On the far side of the courtyard a second set of triple doors led into the basilica itself, with a central nave and two aisles on each side. It was about 165 ft (50 m) long and 135 ft (41 m) wide, a huge building for its day. In his *Life of Constantine*, published just after the emperor's death in AD 337, Eusebius reported that the ceiling of the basilica was coffered and covered with gold and that the walls were of various coloured marbles, inset with coloured stones. A single apse, the full height of the building, was adorned with 12 columns representing the apostles.

The Holy Garden

Beyond the basilica was another atrium or peristyle court sometimes called 'the Holy Garden' (see John 19, 41). At its southeastern corner, not contained within the church in Byzantine times, was the rock of Golgotha. It was actually a faulty outcrop of the stone, left by the quarrymen because it was unsuitable as building material. The rock, with its natural crack, is still visible today in the Chapel of Adam.

The Anastasis or Rotunda

West of this was the Anastasis, the commemorative church built over the tomb itself. The Aedicule inside, which housed the tomb, was eventually surrounded by a circle or semicircle of lofty columns (one of which, now in two pieces, is still there) and roofed over. When the church was dedicated in AD 335 the Anastasis may not have been completed because of the difficulty of clearing the bedrock away from the area of the tomb. From the accounts of such pilgrims as Egeria, who was in Jerusalem between AD 381 and 384, it is clear that the Anastasis was roofed well before the end of the 4th century AD.

Later history of the church

The complex was badly damaged by fire during the Persian conquest of Jerusalem in AD 614, but restoration work was begun even during

their short period of rule, set in hand by Modestus, the then Patriarch of the city. The Arab conquest of Jerusalem in AD 638 seems hardly to have affected the church, but in AD 1009, under the Fatimid Caliph, al-Hakim, it was vandalized and virtually destroyed. The Constantinian basilica was completely obliterated, and the tomb itself, which until that time had remained a monolithic rock-cut chamber, was hacked to pieces.

In the middle of the 11th century AD the Byzantine emperor, Constantine Monomachus reconstructed the Aedicule and the fabric of the Anastasis, by permission of the later Moslem rulers. The basilica itself was never rebuilt; the plan of that period shows an apse protruding eastwards from the Anastasis into the Holy Garden. In the 12th century AD this apse was converted by the Crusaders into a monumental arch, leading into the Romanesque church which they created by roofing over the area of the Holy Garden.

Today the church substantially retains the plan created in the 11th and 12th centuries AD. The entrance lies at the south, making use of an earlier courtyard.

The Crusader entrance to the Church of the Holy Sepulchre is still used today. Of three original doors, one was closed long ago and the middle one was blocked later.

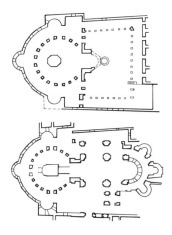

The 11th-century AD Byzantine church (above), with the Holy Garden open; and (below) the 12th-century Crusader church, with the garden roofed over.

THE AGE OF ISLAM

THE HARAM ESH-SHARIF

THE HARAM ESH-SHARIF

In the early Islamic period the old Temple Mount was converted into the Noble Sanctuary or Haram esh-Sharif. The story is told that on the fall of Jerusalem to the Moslems, the Christian Patriarch, Sophronius, would surrender it to no one else but Omar the second caliph (AD 634–44), who entered the city in AD 638. Omar built a large wooden mosque, capable of holding 3,000 people, at the south end of the Temple Mount. This was probably the prototype of the el-Aqsa mosque, much larger then than it is today.

Against the opposition of the Christian community, Omar allowed 70 Jewish families to return to Jerusalem, still officially called Aelia. The Arabic name al-Quds (the Holy City) did not come into use until the 10th century AD. The Jews settled south of the Haram in the area of the old City of David, and during the Umayyad period they served as the caretakers of the great Dome of the Rock (Kubbat al-Saqra). This was built at the end of the 7th century AD by Caliph Abd el-Malik (AD 685–705), to protect the sacred stone, considered to be both the rock of Moriah on which Abraham so nearly sacrificed Isaac (Genesis 22) and the site of the Holy of Holies of both the Jewish Temples. Later Moslem tradition also identifies the rock as the place where Mohammed ascended to heaven on his Night Journey, although an earlier one located it elsewhere on the Haram.

The Dome of the Rock was built by Byzantine craftsmen, and seems to be based architecturally on the Anastasis of the Church of the Holy Sepulchre. It fulfils much the same function – an ambulatory around a sacred site. In this it is unlike any other mosque. The basilical el-Aqsa mosque is much more typical, although neither of these very early mosques have examples of the otherwise ubiquitous minaret from which the Imam (priest) calls the faithful to prayer five times each day.

There is no God but Allah, and Mohammed is His Prophet
The *shahada* or testimony of all Moslems.

THE SPEED WITH WHICH ISLAM, the youngest of the three great monotheistic faiths, spread from its home in Arabia is a startling phenomenon. After the death of Mohammed in AD 632 an unstoppable army of newly converted Moslem tribes swept north and west out of Arabia through the Holy Land and across north Africa, conquering and converting huge numbers of people as they went. Jerusalem fell in AD 638: less than one hundred years later, at the Battle of Poitiers in AD 732, Charles Martel, the grandfather of Charlemagne, finally turned the tide of their advance through Europe. By that time Islam was supreme from north Africa and Spain to the Oxus and from the Caucasus to the Yemen.

Trading caravans took the religion even further, into the steppes of southern Russia and as far east as China. The Arabs were generally tolerant overlords to all their subjects, but particularly towards Jewish and Christian communities, who were accorded a special status. They were called *dhimmi*, and were allowed to organize in *millets* (separate communities) under their own laws. *Dhimmi* were people recognized as sharing a common spiritual heritage with Moslems.

Islamic society, however, was split by religious schism almost from the death of Mohammed. His successors were the Caliphs, whose task was to administer the word of God as revealed to Mohammed. He himself was considered to be the final and greatest prophet of God in the tradition of Abraham, Moses and Jesus. The *Sunni*, or traditionalist, Moslems acknowledged hereditary caliphs who were members of powerful clans, while the *Shi'a* considered that only the descendants of Ali, the cousin and son-in-law of the Prophet, were his legitimate successors.

Within 30 years of Mohammed's death the Ummayad dynasty, originally a Meccan family, had established its capital at Damascus. They were ousted a little over a century later, in AD 750, by the Shi'ite Abbasids. Abandoning Damascus, whose location was now rather peripheral to their interests, the Abbasid caliphs ruled from Baghdad, the new capital, which they founded in AD 762.

The rise of Islamic civilization

As the Moslem faith spread, it came into contact with many ancient cultures and this led to the creation of a new and specifically Islamic culture throughout the lands under Moslem rule. The Arabs themselves, by far the minority in this process, were both the catalyst and the focus of the great flowering of intellectual and artistic activity arising from the fusion of so many different strands. The Islamic nature of the resultant civilization, in all its regional expressions, was supported by the religion itself, by a largely uniform administrative structure and by international trade and the wealth created by it. Scholars from east and west continued the theological and philosophical debates begun in the Classical world. Moslems, Jews and Christians pursued their studies in history, astronomy, geography, literature, medicine, mathematics and many other fields. Technological advances in Islamic areas far outstripped those of contemporary Europe. The Arabic language was the vehicle for the dissemination of this accumulated knowledge. In the field of literature alone, the vigour of Islamic culture is symbolized by the *Tales of 1001 Nights*, compiled in Arabic in Baghdad, during the reign of Haroun al-Raschid (AD 786–809) from the folk stories of Greece, Egypt, India, China and many other countries.

One very Islamic contribution to this burgeoning civilization is the characteristic architecture of mosques, with their domes, minarets and ornate abstract decoration. Islam shares with Judaism the prohibition against representing human or animal figures. The essence of Islamic culture is the creation over several centuries of the great body of Islamic religious or *shariya* law, based on scripture (*Koran*), the sayings of Mohammed (*hadith*) and scholarly debate (*qiya*) in the higher religious schools or *madrasa*.

Fatimids, Seljuks and Mongols

In the 10th century AD the Fatimid dynasty challenged Abbasid supremacy throughout north Africa, from Tunisia to Egypt, which they conquered in AD 969. They also took control of south and west Arabia, no longer the political centre of the Islamic world. The three great Islamic power blocs of the 10th century were the Ummayads, now only masters of

The gilded Dome of the Rock (left) on the Haram esh-Sharif was built by the Caliph Abd el-Malik to enclose the Stone of the Foundation (el-Saqra). Begun in AD 688, it was the first major Islamic sanctuary to be built. In architectural terms it belongs in the Byzantine tradition of round or octagonal churches constructed over holy places. Its ornate but peaceful interior (below) is decorated with mosaics and coloured stone slabs. The inner arcade of columns supports the great dome which is above the Stone of the Foundation.

Spain, the Fatimids in Egypt and Arabia and the Abbasids of Mesopotamia, although a rival Buyid family challenged the latter for power.

The mid-11th century AD saw a new and dangerous presence in the Near East with the rise of the Seljuk Turks, who originated in central Asia. Their capital was first at Isfahan and later Baghdad. Some of the Seljuks overran eastern Turkey and were soon threatening Constantinople, prompting the Byzantine emperor, Alexius I to appeal to the pope for aid (pp. 176–77). Saladin, originally a Kurd from northern Iraq, made himself master of Egypt in 1171 and founded the Ayyubid dynasty. He spent much of his life fighting the Crusaders, but they were never really more than a minor irritant to the wider Moslem world. A more pressing threat came in the early 13th century from the hordes of Mongols, under Genghis Khan, who appeared quite suddenly in the Caucasus mountains. By the middle of the century the Mongol invaders had supplanted the Abbasid caliphs and controlled most of the eastern Islamic countries. They wreaked havoc wherever their armies passed, but such was the powerful influence of Islam that by the 14th century they were converting and beginning to settle down and adopt the culture of their conquered subjects.

The greatest danger posed to the Holy Land by a Moslem ruler had come much earlier, in the 11th century AD. Caliph al-Hakim, one of the Fatimid rulers of Egypt, has been assessed by one scholar as 'a psychopath, ruling by whim and terror'. He murdered his personal servants, his senior officials and his military leaders; he issued and rescinded illogical orders whenever the fancy took him. He also attacked Christian and Jewish communities as he pleased and in AD 1009 he ordered the destruction of the Church of the Holy Sepulchre in Jerusalem. News of this outrage reached Europe and undoubtedly helped to stimulate interest in the idea of freeing the Holy Land from the grip of the infidel – the unbeliever.

CRUSADER PALESTINE

Go to Jerusalem, the centre of the world, the jewel of that holy land which has been made forever sacred by our Saviour … Jerusalem … is now held prisoner by our godless enemies. … Seize back the land taken by pagans. Do not be afraid. Those who die on the journey will have their sins immediately forgiven. I pledge this by the power God has vested in me.

Urban II, preaching the First Crusade

LONG BEFORE THE CRUSADES BEGAN, Christians from the west came in surprisingly large numbers on pilgrimage to the Holy Land. In AD 797 the Emperor Charlemagne even sent a Jewish ambassador to the Caliph Haroun al-Raschid in Baghdad, to negotiate better access for Christian pilgrims to the Holy Places in Palestine. The embassy was a success, and at least one Latin hospice for pilgrims was set up in Jerusalem, with its own church and ancillary services. European pilgrims came in increasing numbers throughout the 9th and 10th centuries AD. The notion of 'liberating' the Holy Land from its Moslem rulers began to take shape only towards the end of this period, and grew in strength probably after AD 1009, when the fanatic Fatimid Caliph al-Hakim destroyed the Church of the Holy Sepulchre in Jerusalem.

Preaching the Crusade

The First Crusade began as the result of an ill-judged request in 1095 from the Byzantine Emperor Alexius I to Pope Urban II for aid against the Seljuk Turks who were at the gates of Constantinople. The pope, broadening the scope of this appeal to include a holy war against all infidels, issued a call to arms to devout Christians everywhere. He first preached the Crusade outside the walls of Clermont in his native France on 27 November 1095, promising forgiveness of sins to all who died in the cause. The first victims were not Moslems, however, but the Jews of eastern Europe, whose communities were devastated as the would-be Crusaders made their way east and south towards Constantinople and the Holy Land.

The entry into Jerusalem

In July 1099 a composite Crusader army entered Jerusalem, having lost nearly two thirds of its manpower in the two years that it had spent crossing Moslem territory. The level of brutality with which they treated the people of Jerusalem was extraordinary and in total contrast to the clemency which had been shown by the Moslem Caliph Omar when he conquered the city in AD 638. Men, women and children were hacked to death by the Crusaders, who did not take the trouble to distinguish between the Moslem, Jewish and Christian citizens of Jerusalem. One Crusader eye-witness account of the aftermath of the battle takes an astonishing delight in the scene of carnage: 'In all the…streets and squares of the city mounds of heads, hands and feet were

KRAK DES CHEVALIERS

Krak stands on a hilly spur with natural protection on all sides except the south, which is therefore where the most impressive defences were built. Because of the strength and solidity of their construction, Krak is still in a remarkably complete state of preservation. The Count of Tripoli sold Krak to the Hospitallers in 1144. Like most Crusader castles belonging to the military Orders it was much more than simply a barracks, arsenal and storage facility. Most of the soldiers were in Holy Orders and the chapel, chapter house and cloister at Krak were built at the heart of the castle, as they were in any monastery.

to be seen. People were walking quite openly over dead men and horses...what an apt punishment!'

In 1100 Baldwin of Boulogne was elected King of Jerusalem (1100–18) by a council of his peers. Further campaigns were undertaken by the Crusaders to expand their holdings – carving estates, principalities and kingdoms out of vast tracts of the Holy Land. Ultimately there were four major Christian kingdoms in 'Outremer' – the regions beyond the sea.

It would be unjust, however, to accuse the majority of Crusaders of mercenary or vicious motives. Many went to fulfil, as they saw it, a religious duty, a kind of military pilgrimage to the land they held sacred. But there were those who profited handsomely out of the Crusades. The First Crusade was undoubtedly the most successful, but over the next two centuries further Crusades reached the Holy Land and joined battle with the Moslems who ruled it.

Crusader castles

Each Crusader warlord originally built his castle to be the seat of his lordship, just as he would have done in Europe. Since they were sited to provide the best military advantage, often on seemingly impregnable mountain tops, they also became increasingly necessary to the defence of the Crusader realm. Literally hundreds were built throughout the Holy Land, often, given the difficulties of terrain, in astonishingly short periods of time. The cost of their upkeep soon became far too expensive for most of the barons, who sold them to the powerful military Orders of the Knights Templar or Hospitaller.

The later history of the Crusades

The Latin kingdom in the Holy Land came under fierce attack from the Moslems. The Franks, as all Crusaders were called by the local population, were never able to establish undisputed control of the Holy Land. Less than a century after their arrival, the Kingdom of Jerusalem was challenged by Saladin, whose empire embraced both Cairo and Damascus. On 4 July, 1187 the 20,000-strong army of Guy, King of Jerusalem, was decimated by Saladin's troops at the Horns of Hattin, overlooking the Sea of Galilee and by 1189 most of the port cities of Palestine were in Saladin's hands. But by then a new wave of Crusaders was on its way from Europe to try to regain the lost territory. The most famous leader of this, the Third Crusade, was Richard Coeur de Lion, King of England. His battles with Saladin have become

The Church of St Anne in Jerusalem is an exquisite Crusader church. Under Saladin it became a Koranic school and has a plaque over the door to that effect.

legendary; both were formidable but extremely chivalrous soldiers and leaders of men.

In 1191 the two concluded a three-year peace treaty, which gave control of the ports back to the Crusaders, thus establishing a Latin Kingdom which was virtually restricted to the coastal strip of Palestine.

Throughout the 13th century further waves of Crusaders battered at the Moslem-held territory of the Holy Land, with varying degrees of success. Jerusalem itself was sometimes in the hands of one protagonist, sometimes the other. Acre had become the Crusader capital and bridgehead into Palestine in 1191. The great Crusader walls of that period still encircle the city today. Caesarea, too, was rebuilt in the first half of the 13th century, by Louis IX, the King of France who became a saint of the Roman Catholic church. The Herodian harbour (pp. 136–39) was partially repaired and brought back into use at this time. It was vital for the Crusaders to have good ports such as Acre and Caesarea through which reinforcements could reach them from Europe.

In the later 13th century the Mamelukes ousted the Ayyubid rulers of Egypt and Syria. For the Crusaders the Ayyubid period had been relatively comfortable by comparison with what was to come. From 1265 the new Mameluke Sultan Baybars (1260–77), a man of great ability and vigour, set about a war of attrition against the Latin kingdom. His fourth successor, al-Ashraf Khalil (1290–93), finally forced the Crusaders to leave the Holy Land in May 1291. These 200 years of Crusader presence in Palestine represent a sorry chapter in the history of the country. Few of the population could have been sad at their departure.

HOSPITALLERS AND TEMPLARS

Chivalry – the ethical code of western Europe in the Middle Ages – has been said to have been brought home by the returning Crusaders who learnt it on their travels in the Islamic east. The establishment of the monastic military orders of knights may well have been influenced by a similar Moslem fighting force. The first Crusader Order was started by Hugh de Payns who formed a patrol of fighting monks to defend pilgrims on the roads around Jerusalem. The monks were assigned headquarters in the el-Aqsa mosque on the Temple Mount in Jerusalem, hence their name – the Knights Templar. The other important Order, the Knights Hospitaller, or Knights of St John, was originally established in the 11th century AD to care for the sick of Jerusalem in the Hospital of St John, but soon became another military Order. The two grew increasingly important in the Crusader kingdoms, and had huge resources of manpower, equipment and provisions at their command. Many of the most formidable Crusader castles were held by these knights, including Belvoir, south of the Sea of Galilee and Krak des Chevaliers in Syria.

MAMELUKES, OTTOMANS AND AFTER

In the land of Israel the Jewish people was born, its spiritual, religious and national identity was formed.
Israel's Declaration of Independence, 1948

Palestine, the land of the three monotheistic faiths, is where the Palestinian Arab people was born, on which it grew, developed and excelled.
Palestine's Declaration of Independence, 1988

WHEN THE CRUSADERS SAILED AWAY from Palestine for the last time in 1291, the people who had vanquished them were not the Ayyubid descendants of Saladin, but a new Egyptian power, the Mamelukes. This dynasty had originated as young slaves, many of them prisoners of war from the steppes of Russia, brought to Egypt to be converted to Islam and trained as soldiers or schooled as administrators. By the middle of the 13th century, with the Ayyubid rulers weakened by the army of Louis IX of France, a Mameluke military junta seized its chance and took control of Egypt. Then, in 1260, the Battle of Ain Jalut in

Palestine gave the Mamelukes victory over the Mongols, and Sultan Baybars (1260–77) began the arduous task of expelling the hated Franks from the country. It was one of his successors, al-Ashraf Khalil who finally occupied Acre in 1291 after a lengthy siege.

The Mamelukes developed an extremely efficient administrative system and a highly sophisticated army. In both spheres they themselves filled all the key positions and so excellent were their schools and *madrasas* that Cairo in the 15th century could lay claim to be the most important centre of Islamic learning and culture in the world.

The Ottoman Turks

Mameluke control of Palestine, however, was overthrown by the Ottomans in the early 16th century AD. Founded by Osman I (1281–1324) in northwest Turkey, the Ottoman state was an expansionist regime in which all the resources of the kingdom were dedicated to the needs of the army. Ottoman power spread further with

The Lion Gate, sometimes called St Stephen's gate, the northeastern entrance into the Old City of Jerusalem. Originally the inner gateway was offset at an angle, like the other gates of the Islamic period, as a defensive measure. During the period of the British Mandate the inner gateway was removed to improve traffic access. The gate takes its name from the lions, or rather panthers, which flank the entrance. Panthers were the heraldic emblem of the Mameluke Sultan Baybars. These particular ones were removed from another building erected by Baybars and inserted into this gate.

each successive reign: south across Turkey and north into the Balkans and beyond. In 1453 the Byzantine capital, Constantinople, at last fell to Sultan Mehmet II (1451–81) and by this achievement – a long-standing Moslem ambition – he became one of the greatest Moslem potentates of his day. The downfall of the Christian imperium in the east was almost complete. A restricted Byzantine kingdom lingered on for only eight more years in Trebizond on the southern shores of the Black Sea, before it, too, fell to the Ottomans.

The 16th century AD saw the reigns of two outstanding Ottoman sultans. The first was Selim I (1512–20), who added Armenia, Syria, Palestine and Egypt to his empire. The second was his son, Suleiman the Magnificent (1520–66), one of the most powerful monarchs of all time. His reign saw Ottoman rule reach from Hungary to Aden and from Algiers to the Crimea. Although he was permanently at odds with the Shi'ite Safavid dynasty of Iran, Suleiman's major military exploits took place in Europe. Suleiman's army overran Hungary and twice besieged Vienna, although both times without success. The King of France, Francis I, was his ally; the Holy Roman Emperor, Charles V, his enemy.

Suleiman was an inspired soldier, a great law-giver and administrator and, like all oriental monarchs, a holy king in the eyes of his people. His royal architect, Sinan, constructed glorious and magnificent buildings for the Sultan throughout his long reign. Among Suleiman's achievements are the walls of Jerusalem which still stand today and it was he who had the Dome of the Rock faced with glorious Iznik tiles in many shades of blue and turquoise. Under Suleiman, the Ottoman system of administration assumed the distinctive form it was to have until the collapse of the empire in the 19th and early 20th centuries.

The 20th century

By the late 19th century the Ottoman Empire had shrunk considerably, for by then it included only Turkey itself, a few of the Aegean islands and parts of the Levant. When the Ottomans allied themselves with the Central Powers in the First World War it signalled the end of their empire. On 11 December, 1917 the British General Allenby rode triumphantly into Jerusalem through the Jaffa Gate and received the formal surrender of the city. The British troops had been aided in their invasion of Palestine by the forces of Hussein, the Sherif of Mecca, under the command of Crown

Prince Faisal (to whom T.E. Lawrence – Lawrence of Arabia – was attached as a military adviser). The Arab nationalists believed that in return for their help, the British would assist them to establish an independent Arab state in Palestine. Initially Faisal even welcomed the Balfour Declaration of 2 November, 1917, which stated that it was the policy of the British government to set up a national homeland for the Jews in Palestine. In fact, a self-determining Arab state in Palestine had been discounted during the war by a secret agreement (the Sykes–Picot) which divided up the lands of the Ottoman Empire among the victorious allies. Palestine, Transjordan and Mesopotamia were allocated to the British. In Palestine tensions gradually grew between the Arab and Jewish populations and guerrilla activity increased year by year. After the Second World War, with few of the Jewish survivors of the Holocaust being allowed into Palestine, the General Assembly of the United Nations voted in November 1947 for the partition of the country into a Jewish and an Arab state. On 14 May, 1948 the State of Israel was declared and the War of Independence immediately broke out between Israelis and Arabs, from which Israel emerged victorious. In April 1950 the Palestinian territory (then usually known as the West Bank) was formally incorporated into the Hashemite kingdom of Jordan, established in 1946 under King Abdallah, Faisal's brother. On 20 July, 1951 the king was assassinated by dissident Arabs on the steps of the el-Aqsa mosque in Jerusalem, and within a few months his teenage grandson, Hussein, had succeeded him on the throne.

The second half of the 20th century has been one of continuing tension in the region. War after war has been fought in and around Israel for possession of the land. A resolution of the conflict was, for a long time, unattainable. Then, in the late 1970s, President Anwar Sadat of Egypt and Prime Minister Menachem Begin of Israel, under the aegis of President Jimmy Carter of the USA, laid the foundations for peace between their two nations. By the early 1990s Chairman Arafat for the Palestinians and Prime Minister Rabin for the Israelis felt themselves able to follow suit. With the renewed rise of Palestinian aspirations to independent statehood and the growth of Israeli empathy for those aspirations, it is possible that these two descendants of Abraham may eventually come to live peaceably side by side in the biblical land which has always belonged to them both.

Suleiman the Magnificent, from an engraving by Melchior Lorch.

KING LISTS

Egypt

(Only selected pharaohs listed)

Early Dynastic period	c. 3000 – 2686 BC
1st Dynasty	c. 3000 – 2800
Narmer	c. 3000
2nd Dynasty	c. 2800 – 2686
Old Kingdom	c. 2686 – 2180
First Intermediate Period	c.2180 – 1991
Middle Kingdom	c. 1991 – 1786
Second Intermediate Period	c. 1786 – 1570
15th Dynasty (Hyksos)	c. 1670 – 1570
New Kingdom	c. 1570 – 1085

18th Dynasty

Ahmosis	1570 – 1546
Amenhotep I	1546 – 1526
Thutmosis I	1525 – 1512
Thutmosis II	1512 – 1504
Hatshepsut	1503 – 1482
Thutmosis III	1504 – 1450
Amenhotep II	1450 – 1425
Thutmosis IV	1425 – 1417
Amenhotep III	1417 – 1379
Amenhotep IV – Akhenaten	1379 – 1362
Smenkhkare	1364 – 1361
Tutankhamun	1361 – 1352
Aya	1352 – 1348
Horemheb	1348 – 1320

19th Dynasty

Ramesses I	1320 – 1318
Seti I	1318 – 1304
Ramesses II	1304 – 1237
Merneptah	1236 – 1223
Seti II	1216 – 1210
Siptah	1210 – 1205
Twosret	1205 – 1200

20th Dynasty

Setnakht	1200 – 1198
Ramesses III	1198 – 1166
Ramesses IV – XI	1166 – 1085

Third Intermediate Period	c. 1085 – 709

21st Dynasty	1085 – 935
22nd Dynasty	935 – 730
Shishak I	935 – 914
Osorkon II	914 – 874
23rd Dynasty	817 – 740
24th Dynasty	730 – 709
Late Period	c.709 – 343
25th Dynasty	750 – 656
26th Dynasty	664 – 525
Psammetichus I	664 – 610
Necho II	610 – 595
Psammetichus II	595 – 589
Psammetichus III	526 – 525
27th Dynasty (Persian)	525 – 404
28th Dynasty	404 – 399
29th Dynasty	399 – 380
30th Dynasty	380 – 343

Assyria

Adad-Nirari I	1307 – 1275 BC
Shalamaneser I	1274 – 1245
Tiglath-Pileser I	1115 – 1077
Ashurnasirpal I	1050 – 1032
Shalmaneser II	1031 – 1020
Tiglath-Pileser II	967 – 935
Adad-Nirari II	911 – 891
Ashurnasirpal II	883 – 859
Shalmaneser III	858 – 824
Adad-Nirari III	810 – 783
Shalmaneser IV	782 – 772
Tiglath-Pileser III	744 – 727
Shalmaneser V	726 – 722
Sargon II	721 – 705
Sennacherib	704 – 681
Esarhaddon	680 – 669
Ashurbanipal	668 – 627

Neo-Babylonian Empire

Nabopolassar	625 – 605 BC
Nebuchadnezzar	604 – 562
Amel-Marduk (Evil-Merodach)	561 – 560
Nergal Sarussur	559 – 556
Nabonidus	555 – 539

Persia (Achaemenids)

Cyrus the Great	559 – 529 BC
Cambyses II	528 – 523
Darius I	522 – 486
Xerxes	485 – 465
Artaxerxes I	464 – 424
Darius II	423 – 405
Artaxerxes II	404 – 359
Artaxerxes III	358 – 338
Arses (Xerxes II)	338 – 335
Darius III	335 – 331

The Kings of Judah and Israel

THE UNITED MONARCHY

Saul	c. 1020 – 1004 BC
David	1004 – 965
Solomon	965 – 928

JUDAH

Rehoboam	928 – 911
Abijam	911 – 908
Asa	908 – 867
Jehoshaphat	867 – 846
Jehoram	846 – 843
Ahaziah	843 – 842
Athaliah	842 – 836
Joash	836 – 798
Amaziah	798 – 769
Uzziah	769 – 733
Jotham	758 – 743
Ahaz	733 – 727
Hezekiah	727 – 698
Manasseh	698 – 642
Amon	641 – 640
Josiah	639 – 609
Jehoahaz	609
Jehoiakim	608 – 598
Jehoiachin	597
Zedekiah	596 – 586

ISRAEL

Jeroboam I	928 – 907
Nadab	907 – 906
Baasha	906 – 883
Elah	883 – 882
Zimri	882
Tibni	882 – 878
Omri	882 – 871
Ahab	871 – 852
Ahaziah	852 – 851
Joram	851 – 842
Jehu	842 – 814
Jehoahaz	814 – 800
Jehoash	800 – 784
Jeroboam II	784 – 748
Zechariah	748/747
Shallum	748/747
Menahem	747 – 737
Pekahiah	737 – 735
Pekah	735 – 733
Hoshea	733 – 724

The Hasmonaeans

Jonathan	152 – 142
Simon	142 – 134
John Hyrcanus	134 – 104
Aristobulus I	104 – 103
Alexander Jannaeus	103 – 76
Salome Alexandra	76 – 67
Aristobulus II	67 – 63
Hyrcanus II	63 – 40
Antigonus	40 – 37

The Seleucids

Seleucus I Nicator	311 – 280 BC
Antiochus I Soter	280 – 261
Antiochus II Theos	261 – 246
Seleucus II Callinicus	246 – 225
Seleucus III Soter	225 – 223
Antiochus the Great	223 – 187
Seleucus IV Philopator	187 – 175
Antiochus IV Epiphanes	175 – 164
Antiochus V Eupator	163 – 162

Dynasty continues in Syria

The Ptolemies

Ptolemy I Soter	304 – 282 BC
Ptolemy II Philadelphus	285 – 246
Ptolemy III Euergetes	246 – 221
Ptolemy IV Philopator	221 – 204
Ptolemy V Epiphanes	204 – 180
Ptolemy VI Philometer	180 – 145
Ptolemy VII Neos Philopator	145 – 144
Ptolemy VIII Euergetes II	145 – 116
Ptolemy IX Soter II	116 – 107, 88 – 81
Ptolemy X Alexander I	107 – 88
Ptolemy XI Alexander II	80
Ptolemy XII Neos Dionysos	80 – 51
Ptolemy XIII	51 – 47
Ptolemy XIV	47 – 44
Cleopatra VII Philopator	51 – 30
Ptolemy XV	44 – 30

Roman Emperors

Augustus	27 BC – AD 14
Tiberius	14 – 37
Gaius (Caligula)	37 – 41
Claudius	41 – 54
Nero	54 – 68
Galba	68 – 69
Otho	69
Vitellius	69
Vespasian	69 – 79
Titus	79 – 81
Domitian	81 – 96
Nerva	96 – 98
Trajan	98 – 117
Hadrian	117 – 138
Division between East and West	283
Diocletian	284 – 305
Constantine the Great	306 – 337

Byzantine Emperors – East

Arcadius	395 – 408
Theodosius II	408 – 450
Marcian	450 – 457
Leo I	457 – 474
Leo II	474
Zeno	474 – 491
Anastasius I	491 – 518
Justin I	518 – 527
Justinian I	527 – 565
Justin II	565 – 578
Tiberius II	578 – 582
Mauricius	582 – 602
Phocas	602 – 610
Heraclius	610 – 641
Constans II	641 – 668
Constantine IV	668 – 685
Justinian II	685 – 695
Leontius	695 – 698
Tiberius III	698 – 705
Justinian III	705 – 711

Islamic Dynasties of Egypt

Umayyads	658 – 750
Abbasids	750 – 868
Tulunids	868 – 905
Ikhshidids	906 – 969
Fatimids	969 – 1171
Ayyubids	1171 – 1250
Mamelukes	1250 – 1517
Ottomans	1517 – 1798

The Crusader Kings and Queens of Jerusalem

Baldwin I	1100 – 1118
Baldwin II	1118 – 1131
Fulk	1131 – 1143
Melisande	1131 – 1152
Baldwin III	1152 – 1163
Amalric	1163 – 1174
Baldwin IV	1174 – 1186
Baldwin V	1185 – 1186
Guy of Lusignan	1186 – 1192
Sybilla	1186 – 1190
Isabella I	1190 – 1205
Aimery of Lusignan	1194 – 1205
John of Brienne	1210 – 1225
Maria	1210 – 1212
Frederick II	1125 – 1243
Yolande	1225 – 1228
Conrad	1243 – 1254
Conradin	1254 – 1268
Hugh III	1269 – 1284
John I	1284 – 1285
Henry II	1286 – 1291
	(fall of Acre)

GAZETTEER

The Bible Lands comprise Lebanon and Syria in the north and Israel and Jordan in the south, together with the desert of the Sinai peninsula, which belongs to Egypt. The two southern states, Israel and Jordan, are the most central to the Bible and they are generally easier for the tourist to visit. The Peace Accord signed between them on 26 October, 1994, means that it has become simpler to plan a trip to include both.

In view of the volatile political situation in the Near East, it is best to contact relevant domestic authorities in the visitor's country of origin to check that trips to the individual countries in the region are advisable at the time. This gazetteer is not designed to be a comprehensive guide to the archaeological sites of the Holy Land, for which the reader is referred to the guide books (see Further Reading). It concentrates on the main sites mentioned in the text of the book and directs the attention of the visitor only to the principal features of each.

There are also museums outside the Holy Land itself that contain important collections that are worth visiting. These include: the British Museum, London; the Pergamon Museum, Berlin; the Louvre, Paris; the Oriental Institute, University of Chicago; and the Metropolitan Museum, New York.

ISRAEL Although there are many archaeological museums in Israel, the most important and comprehensive collections are held in the Israel Museum and the Rockefeller Museum in Jerusalem, and the Eretz Israel Museum, Tel Aviv, where there are also many ethnographical exhibits.

Acre is most interesting for its medieval walled city and port, which lies at the heart of the modern town. The Knights Templar and Hospitaller governed their own city sections and it is the *Hospitaller's Quarter* which is principally worth visiting. Today it appears to be subterranean because of the rise in the street level outside. The buildings are very extensive, but only a part are open to the public, including the 12th-century AD *Refectory* and *fleur de lys* of Louis VII. The *Khan el Umdan* (Inn of the Columns) is the most famous and the best restored of the many khans (part inns and part warehouses). The 18th-century *el-Jazzar Mosque*, partly built over the Crusader halls, is noteworthy for its elegant architecture and a visit to the *museum*, located in an old Turkish bath, is interesting. The *Turkish ramparts* which surround Acre can be climbed to gain a spectacular view of the harbour, the city and its hinterland.

Arad The archaeological site is a little to the west of the modern city and divides into two sections of different periods. The lower part of the site is the *Early Bronze Age town*, whose partially restored fortifications are an outstanding feature. To walk through the streets of Early Bronze Age Arad is an unusual experience. The *Iron Age fortress* is where archaeologists discovered the famous *shrine*, with its large *open air altar*.

Avdat The hill of Avdat or Eboda in the Negev desert overlooks the plain through which trading caravans carried goods from Arabia, via Petra, to the Mediterranean coast. Thus it became a strategic location for the Nabataeans who dominated this trade after the 2nd century BC. After the decline of Nabataean power, Avdat still remained an important centre of Roman population and it is especially interesting for its *Byzantine remains*. On the top of the hill, which was artificially levelled and enlarged, there are several restored *Byzantine churches*, but perhaps the most interesting buildings are the *domestic houses*, which are half built and half quarried into the sides of the hill itself. The artificial *caves* at the rear of the houses were utilized as storerooms, workshops and wine cellars and several have been cleared and can be visited.

Beersheba The tell is probably not the site of the settlement of the patriarchal period as its excavator, Yohanan Aharoni, believed. Nevertheless it is interesting for the restored remains of the 8th-century

BC *garrison town*, with its houses forming a part of the defences and streets which can be walked through today. To the right of the *ancient gate* which still gives access to the town the visitor can see the *storehouses*.

Belvoir is a magnificent Crusader fortress built high above the Jordan valley which it is positioned specifically to guard. The view alone is well worth the climb, which can be done by car on a narrow road. Belvoir is a *concentric castle* with an inner keep and an outer ward.

Beth Guvrin is the region of the southern Shephelah which includes *Tell Mareshah (Marisa)*. There is little to see of the Hellenistic township on the tell, but the whole area is a patchwork of ancient remains from Roman and Byzantine times down to the Crusaders and Mamelukes. Many of the houses in the vicinity of, but not actually on, the tell have large *cellars* dug into the soft limestone to be used as cisterns, for oil presses and as stores. *Family tombs* were also dug out of the hillsides, some of which have lively scenes painted on their walls. There are also several *columbaria*, or underground caverns, which are honeycombed with rows of small, square 'pigeonholes' used for the rearing of doves. Nearby the *Bell Caves* are also worth a visit. They have been recently identified as chalk quarries, originally excavated down and outwards from a small central opening in the roof of each cave.

Beth Shean / Scythopolis The tell dominates the whole area of Beth Shean, but today there is little to be seen on top of it. It is much more interesting to wander the streets of the *Roman/Byzantine city* at its foot. Nearest the car park is the *Roman theatre*, which was built in the 2nd century AD; it has recently been extensively restored and is now used again for modern performances. Beyond it lie the newly excavated *streets, temples, bath houses, shops and public buildings* of the city. There are also *residential areas*, which are less well-known, and a *Roman amphitheatre*, which, it is estimated, could hold an audience of about 6,000 people to watch the gladiatorial and animal contests.

Bethlehem A visit to the *Church of the Nativity* is on the itinerary of every Christian pilgrim to the Holy Land, especially, perhaps, at Christmas. Although the Gospels make no mention of a cave in which Jesus was born, the tradition seems to go back at least to a 2nd-century AD account. Houses in Bethlehem, which is built on a hill, often had caves excavated in the soft rock behind and under them, which could be used as living space, storage or stabling. The caves beneath the church are likely to go back at least to the Roman period and perhaps even earlier. The birthplace of Jesus was discovered by Queen Helena in the early 4th century AD (see p. 16) and the Constantinian basilica was consecrated in AD 339 (see p. 168). The church was rebuilt in the 6th century AD, in the reign of the emperor Justinian, which is the church visited today. There is, however, a *mosaic floor* from the earlier church on view in the nave.

Caesarea Not much of Herod's harbour can be seen from the land today, but his great *aqueduct* on the beach at the extreme northern edge of Caesarea is a magnificent sight. At the other end of the ancient town the *Herodian theatre* has been restored and is again in use. Seawards of the theatre there is a large *wall of the Byzantine period*, and, beyond it on a spit of land jutting out to sea, a *square pool* marks the site of Herod's seaside villa. Just to the north of this are the enormous *walls of the Crusader town*, built in the mid-13th century by Louis IX of France. The *Roman quay*, which originally led to the Temple of Augustus, has recently been discovered in the area of the *Crusader harbour*.

Capernaum The crowded village which was Jesus' home on the Sea of Galilee (Mark 2,1) has only been partly excavated. The two most interesting and monumental buildings are the 4th–5th century AD *synagogue* and the remains of the *octagonal church* built on the site of the traditional House of Peter (p. 168). *Village houses* built of the local basalt densely pack the space between them. There is an *ancient jetty* along the seafront.

Hazor The size of the *tell and lower town* of Hazor reflect its strategic location guarding the vital road from Mesopotamia and inland Syria to Egypt. Because it is agricultural land there is virtually nothing to see of Yigael Yadin's excavation of the lower town, which was a thriving settlement in the Middle and Late Bronze Ages. On the tell the visible remains include the *six-chambered gate* and *casemate wall* of the 10th century BC, built by Solomon and the *storehouse* erected probably by Ahab in the next century. Most interesting of all is the great *water shaft*, also built by him, and the fit visitor is well-advised to climb down the deep shaft and rock-cut tunnel which led to the water level in biblical days. At the narrow western edge of the tell is the *citadel* of the same period, and the additional fortifications which were built to meet the Assyrian threat in the 8th century BC.

Herodium The volcano-shaped mass of Herodium is the artificial top of a natural hill in which Herod the Great built his *royal villa*. It was also reputedly intended as his tomb, but archaeologists have been unable to find any trace of it. There is an extensive area of *palaces, gardens bath houses* and *administrative buildings* at the foot of the hill.

Jericho The oasis city of Jericho is the lowest town on the surface of the earth. Approached from Jerusalem on either the Roman or the modern road it suddenly appears between the almost barren Judaean Hills like a mirage. The area of Jericho contains three ancient sites, all of different periods. **Tell es-Sultan** is biblical, or more properly pre-biblical Jericho, on the western edge of the modern city. In the 1950s Kathleen Kenyon revealed an ancient *tower, wall and dry moat* deep in the heart of the tell, which proved to be over 10,000 years old. **Herodian Jericho**: Herod the Great built a lavish *winter palace complex* at Jericho, utilizing and greatly expanding the Hasmonaean palaces in the area. Today the remains stand in barren desert, but in Herodian times the whole region was a garden city of aristocratic villas, date palms and balsam groves. The wadi which divides the royal palaces is called the *Wadi Kelt*. It is believed to be the 'Valley of the Shadow of Death' of Psalm 23. Above it is the peak on which Herod built the fortress which he named *Cypros* after his mother. **Khirbet al-Mafjar** is popularly called *Hisham's Palace*, and lies a little to the north of modern Jericho. It is a royal pleasure and leisure complex of the Ummayad period, though generally thought to date, not to the reign of Hisham but to the time of his nephew and successor, the dissolute al-Walid. It contained *audience chambers, banqueting halls and bathing pools*. Although the private royal apartments must have been on an upper floor which has now disappeared, some impression of their splendour can be gained from objects from it, including pieces of carved wood and stucco, geometric mosaics and statuary, which are on display in the Rockefeller Museum in Jerusalem.

Jerusalem is an extremely complex city, but can be divided into a number of sections – only the highlights of each can be included here. A great deal of Jerusalem, especially the Old City, is best explored on foot. First time visitors may prefer to take guided walking tours run by several companies, including Archaeological Seminars Inc. (telephone (02) 273 515). **The New City**: *The Garden Tomb*, a short way north of the Old City walls, is one of the supposed sites of the tomb of Jesus. It was mistakenly identified by the British general, Charles Gordon, in 1883 and has been popularized by the Protestant church. *The Model of Herodian Jerusalem* in the grounds of the Holyland Hotel is a scale model, incorporating the latest archaeological data, but still needing some imagination to bring the city of Jesus' day to life. *Herod's Family Tomb*, also known as the *Tomb of Herod's Daughters* is near the King David Hotel. It is a typical example of a 'rolling stone' tomb (p. 148). *The Tomb of the Kings*, north of the Old City, is an interesting complex of rock-cut tombs of the 1st century AD. It is actually the family *Tomb of Queen Helena of Adiabene*, who was a convert to Judaism and lived in Jerusalem for many years. **The Kidron Valley and the Mount of Olives**: *Gethsemane* is the traditional site of the garden in which Jesus prayed. It now lies within the precinct of the Church of All Nations, on the lower slopes of the Mt of Olives. *The Gihon Spring* and the water systems dependent on it – the *Siloam Channel* and *Hezekiah's Tunnel* (pp. 75, 91) – are in the Kidron valley. It is possible to walk through the tunnel to the *Pool of Siloam* (p. 75). Nearby is *Birket el-Hamra*, now a garden but originally the outflow of the Siloam Channel. *The Tomb of Absalom* and *Tomb of Zechariah* are prominent Second Temple tomb monuments

in the Kidron valley. **The City of David**: *Area G* contains the *stepped stone structure* (p. 78) and *Ahiel's House* (p. 96). *Warren's Shaft* (p. 75) – the ancient water system – starts from an entrance nearby. **The Old City**: *The Walls of the Old City* have several access points from which it is interesting to walk the ramparts, viewing the city and its surroundings. Various *gates* should be visited, principally the *Damascus Gate* (p. 162), the *Lion Gate* (p. 178) (also called St Stephen's Gate) and the *Jaffa Gate*, which is the location of the *Citadel*, with remains of many different periods and a *museum* which should not be missed. *The Christian Quarter*, in the northwestern sector, contains the *Church of the Holy Sepulchre* and the *Muristan* (from a Kurdish word meaning 'hospital'), originally the forum of Roman Aelia (p. 162). Later the Knights Hospitaller built a hospital on this spot. *The Moslem Quarter* is the northeast section of the Old City. The Lion Gate leads past the delightful Crusader church of *St Anne's* (p. 176) to the traditional *Via Dolorosa*. It leads under the *Ecce Homo Arch* (p. 162) and past the *Convent of the Sisters of Zion*, in the cellars of which are the *Struthion (Sparrow) Pool* and the *paved forum* of Hadrian's city. *The Jewish Quarter* lies in the southwest, and here the visitor will find the *Broad Wall* of Hezekiah's day (p. 91) and the restored *Cardo* of the Roman/Byzantine city (p. 162). Here also is the *Burnt House* (also called the *House of Katros*) and the *Herodian Quarter* (p. 142), now part of the *Wohl Archaeological Museum*. *The Temple Mount* or *Haram esh-Sharif*, with its famous *Dome of the Rock* (p. 174), is at the southeastern edge of the city. Here stands the monumental *platform* and *wall* of the Second Temple, built by Herod (p. 132). *The Western Wall* and the *tunnel* running north from it give an impression of the sheer size of Herod's undertaking. At the southwestern corner of the Temple Mount is *Robinson's Arch* and the remains of palaces and administrative buildings of the Ummayad period (p. 174). South of the Temple Mount is a maze of remains of different periods, including *Crusader walls*, a restored *Byzantine house* and a *magnificent stairway of Second Temple days*, leading to the blocked entrance of the *Double Gate*, via which pilgrims ascended the Temple Mount.

Lachish is the largest ancient site in the south of Israel. The *Assyrian siege ramp* (pp. 92–95) is still visible high above the *ancient road* at the southwest corner of the tell. The visitor ascends this road to the *gate complex* which gives access to the city. It was in the guardhouse between the outer and inner gates that the famous Lachish Letters came to light (pp. 21, 97). The *inner gate*, of which one side only has been excavated, is of the six chamber type, familiar at Hazor, Megiddo and Gezer. It is later, however, being built in the 9th century BC and is the largest example yet found.

Masada The famous boat-shaped rock on the western shore of the Dead Sea is where Herod the Great built not only a fortress with a large storage facility, but also a palace. After his death it was used as a Roman garrison, but was taken from the Romans in AD 66 by the Zealots at the start of the First Jewish Revolt. The *military camps* and *siege ramp* (White Ramp) built by the Romans in their siege to retake the rock (pp. 156–57) can still be seen. Herod's triple-terraced palace villa or *hanging palace* at the northern edge of the rock can be reached by modern stairways, though some may find the climb arduous. Visitors can now reach the top of the rock by cable car, rather than having to use the ancient *Snake Path*, which was the only access in antiquity. Elsewhere on the top of Masada are *Roman bath houses*, *great water cisterns* (the ruins of the Herodian *aqueduct* which fed them can be seen to the west), an *enormous swimming pool*, another *partially restored palace* and the *tiny synagogue*, oriented towards Jerusalem, which some claim to be the oldest in existence (p. 170).

Megiddo Before ascending the tell by the ancient way which is still in use, it is worth visiting the small *museum* at the entrance. The structures to note during a visit to the tell itself are (a) the *Early Bronze Age sacred area* with a complex of *three temples* and a huge round sacrificial altar or *bamah*; (b) the 10th-century BC *Solomonic gate* with its fine ashlar piers; (c) the areas marked 'stables', which are more likely to be *storehouses*, such as at Hazor and Beersheba, dating to the 9th century BC; and (d) the magnificent *water system* of the same period, with a vertical shaft 590 ft (180 m) deep and an horizontal tunnel 230 ft (70 m) long which leads to the original spring chamber (now dry). The climb down the shaft may be a little difficult for some visitors, but the walk through the water system is immensely evocative. A staircase from the spring chamber gives access to a path which leads the visitor back to the car park and the starting point of the tour.

Nazareth There is little in the town today which can definitely be dated to the time of Jesus. The *modern basilica* (consecrated in the late 1960s) and the traditional site of the *Grotto of the Annunciation* within it are well worth a visit, however. The basilica is on the site of the Crusader church, which itself was built over remains of a Byzantine one. This in turn had been constructed over a building which was perhaps a synagogue or a Judaeo-Christian church. In an area of excavations just beside the main church are remains of houses and storage pits which may date to the 1st century AD.

Qumran It is possible, although not easy, to climb the cliff path to at least one of the *caves* in which the Dead Sea Scrolls were found. The *site* of Qumran is, however, easy to visit and is reached from the road running along the western shore of the Dead Sea. One structure which is easily identifiable is the *watch tower*, from the top of which there is a good view of the whole compound and the surrounding desert terrain. The most striking feature of the settlement is the number of *ritual baths* (or *mikvehs*), some with evidence of *earthquake damage* which, it is believed, led to the temporary desertion of the site in 31 BC. These were fed by an ingenious system of *canals* which runs in from the Wadi Qumran to the west.

Tell Dan (Canaanite Laish) is a great city mound situated on one of the springs of the River Jordan in the north of Israel. The ancient site has three areas of exceptional interest to the visitor. At the southeast corner of the tell is the *Middle Bronze Age gate*, still standing to its full height (p. 50). At the centre of the south side of the tell is the *entrance complex and cobbled street* of the 9th century. It was in this general area that the Tell Dan inscription was found. The *High Place* at the northwest edge of the tell was also first built in the 9th century BC. A *stone precinct wall* enclosed the sacred area, where there are remains as late as the Late Roman era. The great *square stepped platform*, now shaded by trees, must have supported either a temple or an open air altar (p. 82).

Tell Qasileh is in the precinct of the Eretz Israel Museum in Tel Aviv. In the Early Iron Age it was probably a Philistine settlement, as much of their characteristic pottery was found there. There is a unique example of a *Philistine temple* at the site and a series of *four-room houses* of the Israelite period, one of which has been reconstructed (p. 70).

Timna lies in the Aravah valley, 16 miles (26 km) north of Eilat. Open-cast mining for copper in this region goes back to Chalcolithic times, although there is no evidence for it from the time of Solomon, with whom the area is popularly associated. It is worth visiting, however, not only for the extraordinary natural red sandstone columns (called the *Pillars of Solomon*) which have weathered in the rock, but also for the small *Temple of Hathor*, set against one of the cliffs.

JORDAN A visit to the citadel in the capital **Amman** is important for the *museum* where displays include the famous *plastered skulls from Jericho* (p. 38) and the *Copper Scroll* from the Qumran caves. Near the museum are the remains of a decorated *Ummayad palace* and there is also a restored *Roman theatre* of the 2nd century AD at the bottom of the citadel hill.

Iraq el-Amir is a site about 16 miles (26 km) west of Amman. Although there is a large *tell* and part of an ancient *aqueduct* nearby, it is principally noteworthy for the remains of a large and ornate building of the late Hellenistic period, called *Qasr el-Abd* (the Servant's Fortress). Archaeologists have not been able to agree whether it was a temple or a palace, but are certain that it was built in the early 2nd century BC.

Jerash (Gerasa) lies about 20 miles (34 km) north of Amman and was originally one of the Greek cities of the Decapolis (p. 112).

Although the Hellenistic settlement is not well known, Jerash today is an outstanding rebuilt Roman city. It divides into two main sections, separated by the line of the main *cardo* which runs from north to south through it. East of the cardo, the *residential quarter* lies beneath modern houses, but to the west of it are the monumental buildings of the official part of Jerash. Here are *colonnaded streets* and graceful *columned piazzas* (p. 121), passing *theatres, market places, gymnasia* and *temple complexes* with elaborate peristyle courts. Crossing the main *cardo* are two roads (called *decumani*). At the point where the *cardo* and *decumani* cross, there were monumental four-arched gateways, called *tetrapyla. Fourteen churches* of the Byzantine period are also still in existence; most have colourful *mosaics.* The *city wall* is regularly interspersed with a total of 101 *towers*.

Kerak of Moab is one of a line of Crusader castles extending from the Dead Sea to the Gulf of Aqaba. It has a commanding view of its surroundings – its signal fires could be seen as far away as Jerusalem. To distinguish it from Krak des Chevaliers in Syria (see below) it was also called Krak des Moabites or Le Pierre du Desert. It was originally built on the orders of the first Crusader king of Jerusalem, Baldwin I, to be the centre of the Crusader province of Outre Jordan (Beyond the Jordan or Transjordan), but eventually passed by marriage into the hands of Reginald (or Reynauld) de Chatillon, the notorious robber knight who was eventually beheaded by Saladin. There is a famous story about Krak which bears witness to the outstanding chivalry of this great Ayyubid warrior king. He launched a surprise attack on the castle, just as those within were celebrating the marriage of Isabella, the young sister of the leper king, Baldwin IV, to Humfried de Toron, the heir of the castle. A plate of delicacies from the wedding feast was sent out to Saladin, and enquiring which tower the young couple were to lodge in that night, the king forbade his soldiers to attack it. Today the main entry to the castle is blocked, but another gate leads into the outer ward. Much of the structure is ruinous, but with a torch, a tour can be made of the complex system of *tunnels, chambers, stores, dungeons* and *dormitories*, most of which lie beneath the present ground level. The *upper rooms* are open to the sky. There are many deep *wells* and *cisterns*, some of which are unmarked and are a little dangerous. The ruins of the Byzantine *Church of Nazareth* are nearby. It was destroyed by the Mameluke sultan, Baybars. The castle was in use down to the Ottoman era and many objects are on display in the *museum*.

Madaba is in the central part of the country, only 19 miles (30 km) south of Amman. The city is mentioned on the Mesha Stela (p. 28) because it was liberated from the kingdom of Israel after the death of Ahab, by Mesha, the king of Moab in the mid-9th century BC. It was always an important town of Moab, but little is known of it until the Byzantine period, when several important *churches* were built there. The *mosaics* in these churches are worth visiting, especially the famous *Madaba mosaic map* (p. 163), found in 1896, during the construction of a new church on the site of a Byzantine one. It is a map of the Holy Land, unfortunately now in a fragmentary condition. Because this map is oriented on the east, like all ancient maps, it was readable as the worshipper walked up the nave towards the chancel steps.

Mt Nebo is the mountain from which Moses was granted a view of the Promised Land just before his death (Deuteronomy 34, 1–4). Traditionally he is said to be buried in the area. From the *summit* at 2,750 ft (838m) there is a wonderful *view* of the Jordan valley and the Dead Sea, and on a clear day, as far as Jericho and even Jerusalem beyond.

Petra is such a complex site that visitors should provide themselves with a map and a guidebook and can only be briefly described here. It lies in a deep sandstone valley, called the Wadi Musa, the rock of which has been eroded into extraordinary shapes and colours by wind and weather. The famous *Bab es Siq* gorge enters the enclosed city of Petra from the east; it is still the only practicable access for visitors, who may walk or ride donkeys into the city. The inaccessibility has always been a great advantage for the people of Petra with regards to safety. The earliest Hellenistic remains date to the later 3rd century BC, but it is not certain if the inhabitants of those days were the Nabataeans, who made Petra their capital from the late 1st century BC on. Few private houses have been uncovered there; perhaps it was predominantly a monumental royal, religious and administrative centre as well as an aristocratic necropolis. The majority of the population may always have lived outside the gorge. The main points of interest are, of course, the ornate façades of the *rock-cut tombs*. The baroque magnificence of *the Treasury* or *Khasneh* greets the visitor entering Petra from the Siq (p. 119); it probably dates to the 1st century BC. Other majestic examples include the *Palace* and the *Corinthian* tombs and *ed-Deir* and there are many others, more or less eroded or damaged by the hand of man. However, there is much to see in Petra beside the tombs. A walk along the main *cardo*, now with some of its columns re-erected, takes the visitor past the *theatre*. Since it is in the midst of the funerary area of Petra, it may have had a cultic, rather than a dramatic, purpose. Past that are remains of *market places, bath houses* and *gymnasia*. Many of the structures visible today were built in the 2nd century AD or later, after the Roman conquest of Jordan in the reign of the emperor Trajan. A big *triple-arched gate* straddles the *cardo* and gives access to a *sacred temple area*. The main temple here is called the *Qasr el-Bint (the Maiden's Temple)*. Part of its walls have been restored to their full height. Apart from these buildings there are many other places of interest in Petra if the visitor is prepared to climb and scramble over the rocks which surround the central part of the city. Perhaps the most rewarding is the *High Place*, which can be reached on a path near the Siq, but there are many others.

LEBANON At the time of publication there is no up-to-date guide book available on the Lebanon, but one excellent personal account, well worth reading, is Colin Thubron's *Hills of Adonis*, which provides a good introduction to the ancient sites. Although it is again becoming possible to visit the Lebanon, places of interest in the south of the country are not included here. It is hoped that the *Beirut Museum* will open to the public again in 1995.

Amjar is an Ummayad city of the 7th and 8th centuries AD. Many of the *columns* used in its construction are originally of the Byzantine period. Among the ruins are a *bath house, palace* and *tetrapylon* (monumental gateway) at the intersection of the main streets of the city. There are also the remains of over 600 *shops* and many interesting *mosaics* can be seen.

Baalbek is a large classical city. The highlight of any visit is the impressive *Temple of Jupiter*, with its massive columns, on a high platform. Built into the platform are three immense blocks of stone, each weighing over 1,000 tons, called the *Trilithon*. The *Temple of Bacchus* is one of the best preserved in the Roman world and the *Temple of Venus* and the *forum* should also be visited.

Byblos From the well preserved *Crusader castle* there is a good view of the whole site. The area of remains is extensive and includes three *Bronze Age temples*. Look in particular for the site of the *Obelisk Temple*. There is also a Roman Odeon by the sea and a Phoenician necropolis area.

Sidon The *Sea Castle*, originally built in the 13th century AD, reused Roman columns. The *Khan el Franj*, built by Fakhredin II, is a cloistered inn, for merchants and their wares, similar to ones in Acre.

Tripoli The *Citadel* is built on top of the ancient tell. The oldest parts date to the Crusader period. From the Islamic period the *Great Mosque* embodies elements from the Christian cathedral and there is also the lovely 14th-century *Taynal Mosque*.

Tyre Much of the *Roman town* of Tyre is still to be seen. Of great interest is *an aqueduct, a monumental arch* and the *Roman/Byzantine necropolis*. Tyre also had one of the largest *hippodromes* in the Roman world, built in the 2nd century AD to seat about 20,000 people.

SYRIA **Aleppo** has a huge ancient mound, capped by walls of the *citadel* of the 12th–13th centuries AD. **Ain Dhara**, near Aleppo, is a Neo-Hittite (Iron Age) site, where there is a *Temple of Ishtar*.

Amrit (ancient Marathus) on the coast still retains some remains of the Phoenician period. Chief among these is the sanctuary of *el-Ma'abed*, a huge square area cut in the natural rock. It is thought this was flooded with water, leaving the strange pillar-like *Tabernacle*, on its high podium, at its centre. To the south are two areas of *funerary tower tombs*, which probably date to the 5th century BC.

Bosra lies in the Hauran, the region of basalt rock in the extreme south of Syria. Although the city was probably founded in the Hellenistic era, most of the extant remains date to the period after the conquests of the emperor Trajan in AD 106. The most impressive remains are those of the *Roman theatre*.

Damascus, the capital of Syria, is a very ancient oasis city, referred to in the texts of Ebla as well as the Bible. Although there are not many traces of the ancient period, the *Ummayad mosque*, which was the earliest classic mosque ever built, was constructed in the precinct of the Roman Temple of Jupiter and there are remains reaching as far back as the 9th century BC in the area. Visitors to Damascus should also see the *Citadel, the walls of the Old City, the Street Called Straight* of St Paul and the *Tomb of Saladin*. In the new part of the city the *Damascus Museum* contains the rebuilt synagogue from Dura Europos (see below) with its frescoes and the façade of an Ummayad palace from near Palmyra.

Dura Europos, far inland, near the River Euphrates, is a Graeco-Roman city, founded by the Seleucids in the 3rd century BC to dominate routes from Mesopotamia to the coast. It is a vast, sprawling city, not easy for the visitor to comprehend without some help. The remains of the famous *synagogue* which came to light with its Old Testament frescoes of the 3rd century AD (p. 160) in such good condition, are close by the western city wall.

Ebla, or Tell Mardikh, is in northern inland Syria, east of the Aleppo-Damascus road. It is renowned for the *palace* dating to the 3rd millennium BC uncovered there recently, containing important archives. Parts of the palace have now been restored, using a mud plaster of the ancient type to consolidate the mud-brick walls (p. 46).

Kal'at Saman is one of the Roman period Dead Cities of the North, principally famous for the monastery of St Simeon Stylites, born c. 390 AD, who spent 30 years of his life on a 64-ft (19.5-m) high *pillar* there. The stump of this pillar is still to be seen, now surrounded by the remains of an *octagonal ambulatory* within the *Church of St Simeon*.

Krak des Chevaliers It would be impossible to do justice to this most magnificent of all Crusader castles in the space available here. No visit to Syria would be complete without seeing it in detail (p. 176).

Mari The ancient site of Mari stands not far from the Euphrates, near Dura Europos. There are *fortifications* and *temples* visible, but undoubtedly the most impressive remains are those of the *palace of Zimri-Lim*, dating to the 18th century BC. A walk through the extensive remains of this complex building is very rewarding.

Palmyra is an extraordinary Roman city of the 2nd century AD which quite overshadows any other ancient site in the region, except perhaps Petra. The wealth of the oasis city was built on trade. The most famous ruler of Palmyra was Queen Zenobia who was defeated in battle by Aurelian. The *Temple of Bel* and the *Temple of Baal Shamin* are impressive, as are the *Camp of Diocletian* and the *Valley of the Tombs*.

Ras Shamra (Ugarit) is one of the most important Syrian cities of the Late Bronze Age. The acropolis with its two *temples of Baal and Dagan* gives excellent views of the extensive remains of the city. The *palace*, built between the 16th and 13th centuries BC, is in a reasonable state of preservation.

Tartus Now a small fishing port, together with its island neighbour Arwad (ancient Aradus), Tartus was one of the great city states of Phoenicia, like Sidon and Tyre in Lebanon. There is little to see of the most ancient period today, but a walk around the fascinating alleyways of the old neighbourhood brings frequent glimpses of Crusader structures.

Tell Nebi Mend is the site of the great city of Kadesh on the River Orontes. There is little to see except the bulk of the great tell itself, although some of the *Middle Bronze fortifications* are visible in the excavated areas.

FURTHER READING

General
The books in this section are either standard works of reference, or are general books, covering more than one section in the text.

Albright, W.F., *The Archaeology of Palestine*, Penguin, London 1963. Outdated, but interesting from a historical viewpoint.

Albright, W.F., *From Stone Age to Christianity*, Doubleday, New York, 1957 (2nd edn).

Alexander, D. and P., *The Lion Handbook to the Bible*, Lion Publishing, Oxford 1983. A good beginners' guide.

Amiran, R., *Ancient Pottery of the Holy Land*, Masada Press, Jerusalem 1969.

Amitai, J. (ed.), *Biblical Archaeology Today*, Proceedings of the International Congress on Biblical Archaeology, Jerusalem April 1984, Israel Exploration Society, The Israel Academy of Sciences and Humanities and the American Schools of Oriental Research, Jerusalem, 1985.

Avigad, N., *Discovering Jerusalem*, Shikmona Publishing and Israel Exploration Society, Jerusalem 1980.

Ben Arieh, Y., *The Rediscovery of the Holy Land in the 19th Century*, Magnes Press and Israel Exploration Society, Jerusalem 1983.

Ben-Tor, A. (ed.), *The Archaeology of Ancient Israel*, Yale University Press, New Haven and London 1992. This is the standard text for the Israel Open University.

Bienkowski, P. (ed.), *The Art of Jordan*, Alan Sutton Publishing, Stroud 1991. The catalogue of an exhibition at Liverpool.

Biran, A. and Aviram, J., *Biblical Archaeology Today 1990*, Proceedings of the Second International Congress on Biblical Archaeology, Jerusalem June 1990, Israel Exploration Society and the Israel Acadamy of Sciences and Humanities, Jerusalem 1993.

Calvocoressi, P., *Who's Who in the Bible*, Guild Publishing, London 1987.

Dayan, M., *Living with the Bible*, Weidenfeld and Nicolson, London 1978. From the Patriarchs to the United Monarchy.

Finegan, J., *Light from the Ancient Past*, (2 vols), Princeton University Press, 1974. This is a slightly outdated, but reasonable account of life in the Near East from the Neolithic era to Christianity.

Frankfort, H., *The Art and Architecture of the Ancient Orient*, Penguin, London 1970 (4th edn).

Geva, H. (ed.), *Ancient Jerusalem Revealed*, Israel Exploration Society, Jerusalem 1994.

Glueck, N., *Rivers in the Desert*, Farrar, Straus and Cudahy, New York 1959.

Horn, S.H., *Biblical Archaeology: a generation of discovery*, Biblical Archaeology Society, Washington, 1985. An overview, covering the excavation of some important sites.

Kenyon, K.M., *Archaeology in the Holy Land*, Ernst Benn, London 1979.

– *Digging up Jericho*, Ernst Benn, London 1979.

– *Digging Up Jerusalem*, Ernst Benn, London 1974. More recent work has now added to our knowledge, but this is still an important book.

Kempinski, A. and Reich, R. (eds), *The Architecture of Ancient Israel from the Prehistoric to the Persian Period*, Israel Exploration Society, Jerusalem 1992. An architectural history and reference work.

Lloyd, S., *The Art of the Ancient Near East*, Thames and Hudson, London 1963.

Mazar, A., *Archaeology of the Land of the Bible, 10,000-586 BCE*, Doubleday, New York 1990. The best current one volume general introduction to the subject.

Mazar, B., *The Mountain of the Lord; Excavating in Jerusalem*, Doubleday, New York 1975.

Metzger, B.M. and Coogan, M.D. (eds), *The Oxford Companion to the Bible*, Oxford University Press, New York and London 1993.

Millard, A., *Treasures from Bible Times*, Lion Publishing, Tring 1985.

Mitchell, T.C., *The Bible in the British Museum: Interpreting the evidence*, British Museum Publications, London 1988.

Moorey, P.R.S., *Biblical Lands*, Phaidon, Oxford 1975.

– *Excavation in Palestine*, Lutterworth, Cambridge 1981. A very readable account of methodology of archaeology in the Levant.

– *A Century of Biblical Archaeology*, Lutterworth, Cambridge 1991. A history of archaeology and archaeologists in Israel.

Ornan, T., *A Man and his Land. Highlights from the Moshe Dayan Collection*, The Israel Museum, Jerusalem 1986.

Pritchard, J.B., *Ancient Near Eastern Texts relating to the Old Testament*, Princeton University Press, Princeton 1955.

Pritchard, J.B., *The Ancient Near East in Pictures*, Princeton University Press, Princeton 1969.

Rogerson, J. and Davies, P., *The Old Testament World*, Cambridge University Press, Cambridge and New York 1989.

Shanks, H. (ed.), *Ancient Israel: a short history from Abraham to the Roman destruction of the Temple*, Biblical Archaeology Society, Washington D.C., SPCK, London 1989.

Shanks, H. & Mazar, B. (eds), *Recent Archaeology in the Land of Israel*, Biblical Archaeology Society, Washington D.C. and Israel Exploration Society, Jerusalem 1984.

Stern, E. (ed.), *The New Encyclopaedia of Archaeological Excavations in the Holy Land*, Israel Exploration Society & Carta, Jerusalem, 1993. The standard reference work on the sites.

Tal, D., *Stones from the Sky*, (Skyline vol.2), Albatross, Tel Aviv 1994. Wonderful aerial views of the sites.

Thompson, J.A., *Handbook of Life in Bible Times*, Inter-Varsity Press, Leicester 1986.

Tubb, J.N. and Chapman, R.L., *Archaeology and the Bible*, British Museum Publications, London 1990.

Winton-Thomas, D. (ed.), *Archaeology and Old Testament Study*, Oxford University Press, London 1967.

Wiseman, D.J. (ed.), *Peoples of Old Testament Times*, Clarendon Press, Oxford 1973. Covers peoples throughout the ancient Near East.

Yadin, Y., *The Art of Warfare in Biblical Lands*, Weidenfeld and Nicolson, London 1963.

– *Hazor: the rediscovery of a great citadel of the Bible*, Weidenfeld and Nicolson, London 1975. A popular account.

– *Hazor* (Schweich Lecture, 1970), Oxford University Press, London 1972.

– (ed.) *Jerusalem Revealed: archaeology in the Holy City, 1968–1974*, Israel Exploration Society, Jerusalem 1976.

Periodicals
Bulletin of the American School of Oriental Research, **Biblical Archaeologist*, **Biblical Archaeology Review*, **Bulletin of the Anglo-Israel Archaeological Society*, *Israel Exploration Journal*, *Levant*, *Palestine Excavation Quarterly*.
* The most accessible and least technical for the general public.

Atlases
Aharoni, Y., Avi-Yonah, M., Rainey, A.F. and Safrai, Z., *The Macmillan Bible Atlas*, Macmillan, New York 1993.

Bahat, D., *The Illustrated Atlas of Jerusalem*, Simon and Schuster, New York 1990.

Baly, D. and Tushingham, A.D., *Atlas of the Biblical World*, The World Publishing, New York 1971.

Grollenberg, L.H., *Atlas of the Bible*, Nelson, London 1965.

May, H.G. (ed.), *Oxford Bible Atlas*, Oxford University Press, Oxford 1984.

Pritchard, J.B. (ed.), *The Times Atlas of the Bible*, Times Books, London 1987.

Rasmussen, C.G., *NIV Atlas of the Bible*, Zondervan, Michigan 1989.

Rogerson, J. *The New Atlas of the Bible*, Macdonald, London, Facts on File, New York 1985.

Guides
Ball, W., *Syria: a historical and architectural guide*, Scorpion Publishing, London 1994.
Darke, D., *Discovery Guide to Jerusalem and the Holy Land*, Immel Publishing, London 1993.
Gonen, R., *Biblical Holy Places: an illustrated guide*, Macmillan, New York 1987.
Harding, G.L., *The Antiquities of Jordan*, Jordan Distribution Agency and Lutterworth Press, London 1980.
Murphy-O'Connor, J., *The Holy Land: an archaeological guide from earliest times to 1700*, Oxford University Press, Oxford 1992 (3rd edn).
Osborne, C., *An Insight and Guide to Jordan*, Longman, Harlow 1981.
Prag, K., *Blue Guide to Jerusalem*, A. & C. Black, London 1989.

Section I: The Bible in Context
Aharoni, Y., *The Land of the Bible: a historical geography*, Westminster Press, Philadelphia 1979. An excellent work.
Driver, G.R., *Semitic Writing from Pictograph to Alphabet*, Oxford University Press, 1976 (3rd edn).
Healey, J.F. *The Early Alphabet*, British Museum Publications, London, University of Texas Press, Austin 1990. A readable account.
Hepper, N., *Illustrated Encyclopedia of Bible Plants*, Inter Varsity Press, Leicester 1992.
Naveh, J., *Origins of the Alphabet*, Cassell, London 1975.
– *Early History of the Alphabet*, Magnes Press, Jerusalem 1982.
Osband, L. (ed.), *Famous Travellers to the Holy Land*, Prion, London 1989. Short, readable excerpts from diaries, etc.
Readhead, B and Gumley, F., *The Good Book*, Duckworth, London 1987. Transcripts of a radio series about the development and growth of the Bible.
Romer, J., *Testament; the Bible and History*, Michael O'Mara Books, London 1988. A highly readable book to accompany the successful television series.
Walker, W., *All the Plants of the Bible*, Doubleday, New York 1979. Watercolours of biblical plants.
Zohary, M., *Plants of the Bible*, Cambridge University Press, Cambridge 1982.
Wilkinson, J., *Egeria's Travels to the Holy Land*, Ariel, Jerusalem & Aris and Phillips, Warminster 1981 (rev. ed.).

Section II: In the Beginning
Bar-Yosef, O., *A Cave in the Desert: Nahal Hemar*, The Israel Museum, Jerusalem 1985.
Gray, J., *Near Eastern Mythology, Mesopotamia, Syria and Palestine*, Hamlyn, London 1969.
Matthiae, P., *Ebla: an empire rediscovered*, Hodder and Stoughton, London 1977.
Mellaart, J., *The Neolithic of the Near East*, Thames and Hudson, London 1975.
Oates, D. and J., *The Rise of Civilization*, Phaidon, Oxford 1976.
Redman, C.L., *The Rise of Civilization. From early farmers to urban society in the ancient Near East*, W.H. Freeman and Company, San Francisco 1978.
Ringgren, H., *Religions of the Ancient Near East*, SPCK, London 1973. Chapter 3 is on West Semitic – ie. Canaanite – religion.
Rothenberg, B., *God's Wilderness. Discoveries in Sinai*, Thames and Hudson, London 1961.
Rothenberg, B., *Timna: valley of the biblical copper mines*, Thames and Hudson, Londo 1972.
Strommenger, E. and Hirmer, M., *The Art of Mesopotamia*, Thames and Hudson, London 1964.
Woolley, C.L, *Ur of the Chaldees*, revised by P.R.S. Moorey, Herbert, London 1982. The updated edition of Woolley's original account.

Section III: Old Testament Empires
Aharoni, Y., *The Archaeology of the Land of the Bible*, SCM Press, London 1982.
Biran, A., *Biblical Dan*, Israel Exploration Society, Jerusalem 1994.
Dever, W. G., *Recent Archaeological Discoveries and Biblical Research*, University of Washington Press, Seattle and London 1990.
Dothan, T., *The Philistines and their Material Culture*, Israel Exploration Society, Jerusalem 1982.
Dothan, T. and M., *People of the Sea. The search for the Philistines*, Macmillan, New York 1992.
Finkelstein, I., *The Archaeology of the Israelite Settlement*, Israel Exploration Society, Jerusalem 1988. Harden, D., *The Phoenicians*, Penguin, Harmondsworth, 1971.
Heaton, E.W., *Solomon's New Men*, Thames and Hudson, London 1974. A useful historical assessment of Solomon's reign.
Postgate, N., *The First Empires*, Phaidon, Oxford 1977.
Sandars, N.K., *The Sea Peoples. Warriors of the ancient Mediterranean*, Thames and Hudson, London and New York 1985. Still the standard account.
Shanks, H., *The City of David: A guide to biblical Jerusalem*, Biblical Archaeology Society, Washington 1973.
Ussishkin, D., *The Conquest of Lachish by Sennacherib*, Tel Aviv University, Tel Aviv 1982.
Vaux, R. de, *The Early History of Israel*, (2 vols.) Darton, Longman and Todd, London 1978.

Section IV: Widening Horizons
Browning, I.B., *Petra*, Chatto & Windus, London 1989.
Glueck, N., *Deities and Dolphins: the story of the Nabataeans*, Cassell, London 1966.
Green, P., *From Alexander to Actium: the Hellenistic world*, Thames and Hudson, London, University of California Press, San Francisco 1990.
Negev, A., *Nabataean Archaeology Today*, New York University, New York 1986.
Oates, J., *Babylon*, Thames and Hudson, London and New York 1991.
Taylor, J., *Petra*, Aurum, London 1993.
Saggs, H.W., *The Greatness that was Babylon*, Sidgwick and Jackson, London 1962.
Shanks, H. (ed.), *The Dead Sea Scrolls after 40 Years*, Biblical Archaeology Society, Washington D.C. 1992.
Vaux, R. de, *Archaeology and the Dead Sea Scrolls*, (Schweich Lecture 1959), Oxford University Press, London 1973 (rev. edn).
Vermes, G., *The Dead Sea Scrolls: Qumran in perspective*, SCM Press, London 1982.
Vermes, G., *The Dead Sea Scrolls in English*, Penguin, Harmondsworth 1987.
Yadin, Y., *The Message of the Scrolls*, Simon and Schuster, New York 1969.

Section V: The Age of Jesus
Connolly, P., *Living in the Time of Jesus of Nazareth*, Oxford University Press, Oxford 1983. An easy to read introduction with colour illustrations by the author.
Court, J. and K., *The New Testament World*, Cambridge University Press, Cambridge and New York 1990.
Dowley, T. (organizing ed.), *The History of Christianity*, Lion Publishing, Oxford 1990.
Finegan, J,. *The Archaeology of the New Testament. The life of Jesus and the beginning of the early church*, Princeton University Press, New Jersey 1992 (rev. edn). Data on anything that can be associated with Jesus or the Early Church, accompanied by black-and-white photographs: a reference work.
Holum, K.G., Hohlfelder, R.L., Bull, R.J. and Raban, A., *King Herod's Dream. Caesarea on the sea*, W.W. Norton & Company, New York and London 1988.
Levine, L.I. (ed.), *Ancient Synagogues Revealed*, Israel Exploration

Society, Jerusalem 1981.

Millard, A., *Discoveries from the Time of Jesus*, Lion Publishing, Oxford 1990.

Netzer, E., *Herodium, an archaeological guide*, Cana, Jerusalem n.d.

Perowne, S., *The Journeys of St Paul*, Hamlyn, London 1973.

Tsafrir, Y. (ed.), *Ancient Churches Revealed*, Israel Exploration Society, Jerusalem 1993.

Wilkinson, J., *Jerusalem as Jesus Knew It: archaeology as evidence*, Thames and Hudson, London 1978.

Section VI: The Turbulent Years

Ben-Arieh, Y. *Jerusalem in the 19th century* (2 vols), Izhak Ben Zvi Institute, Jerusalem and St Martin's Press, New York 1984.

Billings, M., *The Cross and the Crescent: a history of the Crusades*, BBC Publications, London 1987. Written to accompany a television series on the Crusades.

Eban, A., *Heritage: civilization and the Jews*, Weidenfeld and Nicolson, London 1984.

Gibb, H.A.R., *Islam*, Oxford University Press, Oxford, 1980. Very helpful for the non-Moslem.

Gibson, S. and Taylor, J.E., *Beneath the Church of the Holy Sepulchre, Jerusalem. The archaeology and early history of traditional Golgotha*. Palestine Exploration Fund Monograph, Series Maior 1, London 1994. Report of the most recent archaeological work in the church.

Gumley, F. and Redhead, B., *The Christian Centuries*, BBC Books, London, 1989. Well-written; to accompany a radio series.

Holt, P.M., *The Age of the Crusaders: the Near East from the 11th century*
to 1517, Longman, London and New York 1986.

Kennedy, H., *The Prophet and the Age of the Caliphates: the Islamic Near East from 600 to the 11th century*, Longman, London and New York 1986.

Landau, J.M., *Abdul-Hamid's Palestine*, Andre Deutsch, London 1979. 19th-century photographs of Ottoman Palestine – a vanished world.

Lawrence, T.E., *Crusader Castles*, Michael Haag, 1986.

Lewis, B., *The Jews and Islam*, Routledge and Kegan Paul, London, Melbourne and Henley, 1984. A good introduction to the subject.

Lewis, B. (ed.), *The World of Islam: faith, people, culture*, Thames and Hudson, London and New York 1992.

Norwich, J.J., *Byzantium, the Early Centuries*, Viking, London 1988.

Potok, C. *Wanderings, a History of the Jews*, Fawcett Crest, New York 1978.

Riley-Smith, J. (ed.), *The Atlas of the Crusades*, Times Books, London 1991. An excellent introduction.

Robinson, F., *Atlas of the Islamic World since 1500*, Phaidon, London 1982.

Shanks, H. (ed.), *Christianity and Rabbinic Judaism*, SPCK, London and Biblical Archaeology Society, Washington D.C. 1993.

Talbot Rice, D. *Art of the Byzantine Era*, Thames and Hudson, London 1963, New York 1985.

Yadin, Y., *Bar-Kokhba. The rediscovery of the legendary hero of the Second Jewish Revolt against Rome*, Random House, New York 1971. A popular account.

Yadin, Y., *Masada. Herod's fortress and the Zealots' last stand*, Weidenfeld and Nicolson, London 1966.

ACKNOWLEDGMENTS

Sources of texts and illustrations.
The quotations from the Bible are from the Authorized Version; where variations from this occur, they are direct translations by the author.

Other text sources:
Dead Sea Scrolls: Vermes, G., *The Dead Sea Scrolls in English*, Penguin, Harmonsdworth 1987.
Dio Cassius, *Roman History*, trans. E. Cary, Loeb Classical Library, 1925.
Herodotus, *The Histories*, trans. A. de Selincourt, Penguin, Harmondsworth 1954.
Inscription from Medinet Habu: J.H. Breasted, *Ancient Records of Egypt*, Chicago 1906.
Josephus, *The Jewish War*, trans. G.A. Williams, rev. edn E. May Smallwood, Penguin, Harmondsworth 1981.

Illustration credits
t = top, a = above, b = below, c = centre, l = left, r = right.

The photographs on the following pages are all by Zev Radovan, Jerusalem: 6–7, 22, 23a, 33l, 33r, 33b, 35l, 40a, 42r, 50a, 53bl, 57l, 63b, 72b, 81r, 90a, 91a, 98–99, 106, 107l, 107r, 110b, 115, 122, 123, 126–7, 129, 130, 131, 132, 133b, 134, 135al, 135b, 136, 140, 142a, 142c, 142b, 147a, 147br, 157, 158, 159, 163a.

The drawings on the following pages are by:
George Taylor: 10, 11a, 11b, 14–15, 25a, 34l, 34b, 44, 53br, 63ar, 65a, 66a, 67a, 68l, 68r, 69l, 69r, 70r, 71ar, 71b, 72a, 75a, 76, 77bl, 78–79, 78br, 80, 102–3, 116b, 128, 129a, 133a, 135ar, 139a, 143, 146, 147bl, 147bc, 148–9, 152l, 152c, 152r, 153.
Tracy Wellman: 12, 24–5b, 26a, 26bc, 27a, 27b, 28br, 41b, 42l, 86br 87, 88b, 89a, 89b, 90, 96, 97b, 108, 162.

Annick Petersen: 59a, 82, 92b, 95rc, 102l, 113c, 116a, 117a, 118b, 131b, 140a, 168, 169a, 171b, 173b.
Philip Winton: 46b, 48, 50–51, 51a, 51c, 54, 94–95a, 94–95b, 110–11a, 125a, 125b.

Other credits
Title-page: photo Euphrosyne Doxiadis. 9 Roberta Harris. 16 Fitzwilliam Museum, Cambridge. 17 Gertrude Bell Archive, University of Newcastle upon Tyne. 18, 19, 20, 21 Palestine Exploration Fund, London. 28a Musée du Louvre, Paris. 30 John Rylands Library, Manchester. 31 Roberta Harris. 32 British Museum, London. 34br Roberta Harris. 35ac, r Israel Antiquities Authority. 36–37 Michael Duigan. 38l British School of Archaeology, Jerusalem. 38r Peter G. Dorrell / Jericho Excavation Fund. 39l Kathryn Tubb, Institute of Archaeology. 39r Mellaart, J., *The Neolithic of the Near East*, after Braidwood, R.J. 40b Israel Antiquities Authority. 41a French Archaeological Mission. 43 Egyptian Museum, Cairo. 45 Michael Jenner. 46 Paolo Matthiae. 47 Aleppo Museum, Director General of Antiquities, Northern Syria. 49l, r British Museum, London. 52a Musée du Louvre, Paris. 52br British Museum, London. 53a Richard Lannoy. 55l Egyptian Museum, Cairo; photo Hirmer. 55r British Museum, London. 56a After Beno Rothenberg, *Timna* . 56b Israel Antiquities Authority. 57r Don Frey/INA. 59b Egyptian Museum, Cairo. 60–1 Dubi Tal, Albatross. 62 Marian Cox in Sandars, N. *The Sea Peoples*, after Nelson, H.H., *The Earliest Historical Records of Ramses III, Medinet Habu*. 63al Marian Cox in Sandars, N. *The Sea Peoples*, after Oren, E., *The Northern Cemetery at Beth Shan*, fig.52. 64 Michael Duigan. 65b Marian Cox in Sandars, N. *The Sea Peoples*, after *The Philistines*, ex.cat Jerusalem, 1973. 66b Hillel Burger. 67b From L. de Laborde, *Voyage en Oriente* II, 1839. 70l Oriental Institute, University of Chicago. 71al Geoff Penna. 73 British Museum, London. 74 Roberta Harris. 75b Roberta Harris. 77a Rockefeller Museum, Jerusalem. 77 Yael Braun. 78l Rockefeller Museum, Jerusalem. 81l Michael Duigan.

83a, b, 84a, bl, br Avraham Biran, 85b Michael Duigan. 86a, bl British Museum, London. 87b Musée du Louvre, Paris; photo Hirmer. 88a Roberta Harris. 91b Archaeological Museum, Istanbul. 93a A.H. Layard, *Monuments of Nineveh*. 93b Geoff Penna. 94lc British Museum, London. 98–99 Michael Duigan. 100 John Freeman. 101a Staatliche Museen, Berlin. 101b T. Holland. 103a Michael Duigan. 104 Costa. 105al British Museum, London. 105ar From Culican, W., *Medes and Persians*. 105b Oriental Institute, University of Chicago. 109a Manolis Andronicos. 109b Tombazi, Athens. 110a Michael Duigan. 110c Private collection. 111cl, cr Museo Nazionale, Naples. 112 a British Museum, London. 112b After Blis, F.J. and Macalister, R.A.S., *Excavations in Palestine during the years 1898–1900*. 113ar Musée du Louvre, Paris. 114a British Museum, London. 114b Ancient Art and Architecture Collection. 118a John Ross. 119 K.D. Politis. 120al, r British Museum, London. 120 N.Y. Carlsberg Glyptotek, Copenhagen. 120–1 A.F. Kersting. 124 Shrine of the Book, Jerusalem. 134–5 Peter Bugod. 137a Israel Government Tourist Office. 137b Chris Brandon/Itamar Grinberg. 138–9 Chris Brandon/Avner Raban. 139b Chris Brandon/Avner Raban. 141 Scala. 144 a, b Israel Antiquities Authority. 145a Shelley Wachsmann. 145b Geoff Penna. 148bl British Museum, London. 149a École Biblique. 149b Hirmer. 150 Arian Baptistery, Ravenna. 154l Alinari. 154r Colin Ridler. 153b Pont. Comm. di Arte Sacra. 154–5 Palphot. 156 N.Y. Carlsberg Glyptotek, Copenhagen. 157a Roberta Harris. 158a Roberta Harris. 160 Directorate General of Antiquities, Damascus. 161l Mas. 161r Detail from Masorah, British Museum, London. 163 Peter Bugod. 164 Hirmer. 165a From M. de Vogüé. 165b Esther Niv-Krendel. 166 Peter Bugod. 167 Dubi Tal, Albatross. 169b J.M. Farrant/K.D. Politis. 170 Israel Museum. 171a From Loffreda, *Rediscovering Capernaum* 172 Peter Bugod. 173a, 175a, b, 176, 177, 178 A.F. Kersting. 179 After Melchior Lorch, British Museum, London.

INDEX